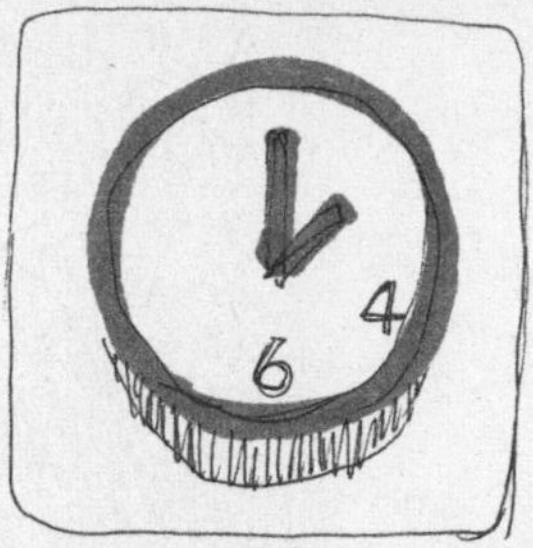

The clock in my living room stopped working, but I didn't get it fixed because I figured I never really use it. Then a month goes by, and it's a big problem.

I didn't think I relied on it, but I actually do.

–Tite Kubo

Bleach is author Tite Kubo's second title. Kubo made his debut with *ZOMBIEPOWDER.*, a four-volume series for *Weekly Shonen Jump*. To date, *Bleach* has been translated into numerous languages and has also inspired an animated TV series that began airing in the U.S. in 2006. Beginning its serialization in 2001, *Bleach* is still a mainstay in the pages of *Weekly Shonen Jump*. In 2005, *Bleach* was awarded the prestigious Shogakukan Manga Award in the *shonen* (boys) category.

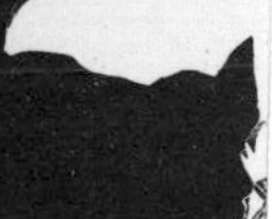

BLEACH
VOL. 64: DEATH IN VISION
SHONEN JUMP Manga Edition

STORY AND ART BY
TITE KUBO

Translation/Joe Yamazaki
Touch-up Art & Lettering/Mark McMurray
Design/Kam Li
Editor/Alexis Kirsch

BLEACH © 2001 by Tite Kubo. All rights reserved. First published
in Japan in 2001 by SHUEISHA Inc., Tokyo. English translation rights
arranged by SHUEISHA Inc.

The stories, characters and incidents mentioned in this publication are
entirely fictional.

Printed in the U.S.A.

Published by VIZ Media, LLC
P.O. Box 77010
San Francisco, CA 94107

10 9 8 7 6 5 4 3 2 1
First printing, July 2015

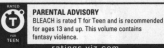

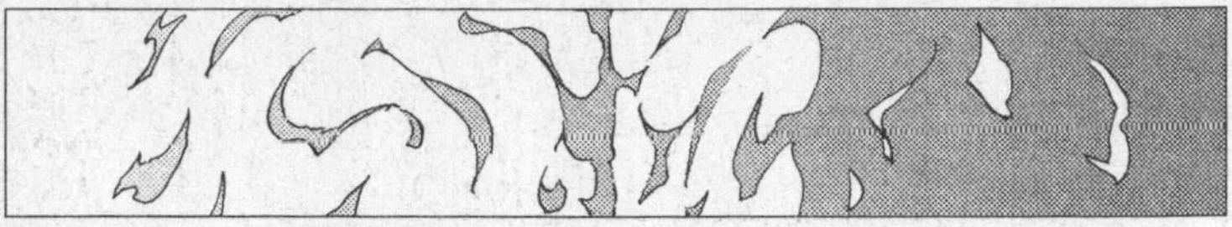

Beauty is nothing being there

BLEACH 64

DEATH IN VISION

Shonen Jump Manga

ALL STARS ★ AND

虎徹勇音
コテツイサネ

ISANE KOTETSU

草鹿やちる
クサジシヤチル

YACHIRU KUSAJISHI

plot

Ichigo Kurosaki meets Soul Reaper Rukia Kuchiki and ends up helping her eradicate Hollows. After developing his powers as a Soul Reaper, Ichigo befriends many humans and Soul Reapers and grows as a person...

Yhwach leads his Quincy army, the Stern Ritters, in an invasion of the Soul Society. The Court Guards stand in their way, but against the mysterious power of the Quincies, even the Soul Reaper captains are in the fight of their lives. As the battle continues, Renji and Rukia return from their training in the royal palace, Reiokyu. Renji then defeats Mask de Masculine while Rukia takes down Äs Nödt, the man who stole her brother's bankai. Meanwhile, Yachiru and Isane watch over the injured. But a new enemy is lurking in the shadows...

BLEACH

GREMMY THOUMEAUX

グレミィ・
トゥミュー

KENPACHI ZARAKI

更木剣八
ザラキケンパチ

STORIES

BLEACH 64

DEATH IN VISION

CONTENTS

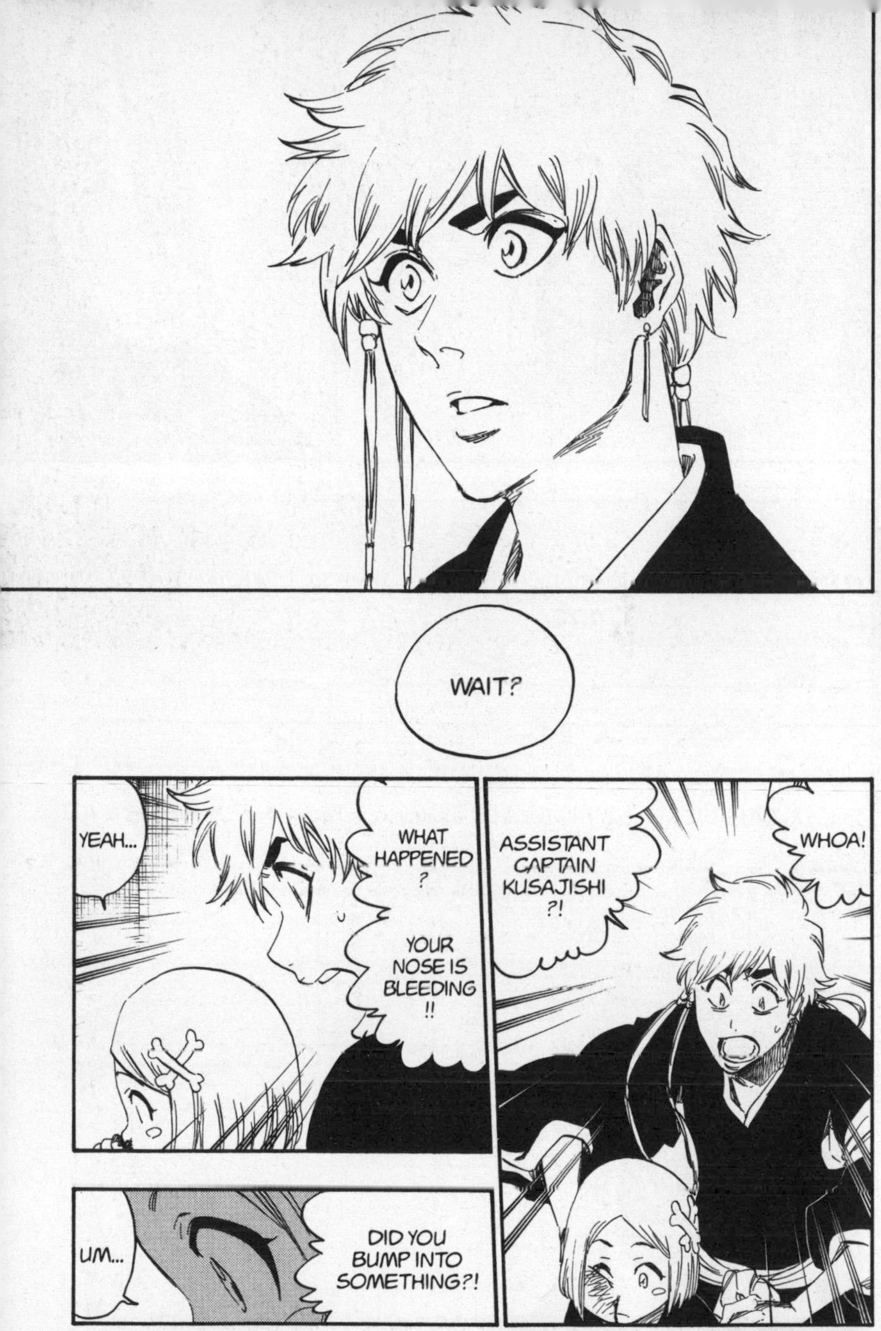
WAIT?
WHOA!
ASSISTANT CAPTAIN KUSAJISHI ?!
WHAT HAPPENED ?
YOUR NOSE IS BLEEDING !!
YEAH...
DID YOU BUMP INTO SOMETHING?!
UM...

571. A DEVILISH PERSPECTIVE

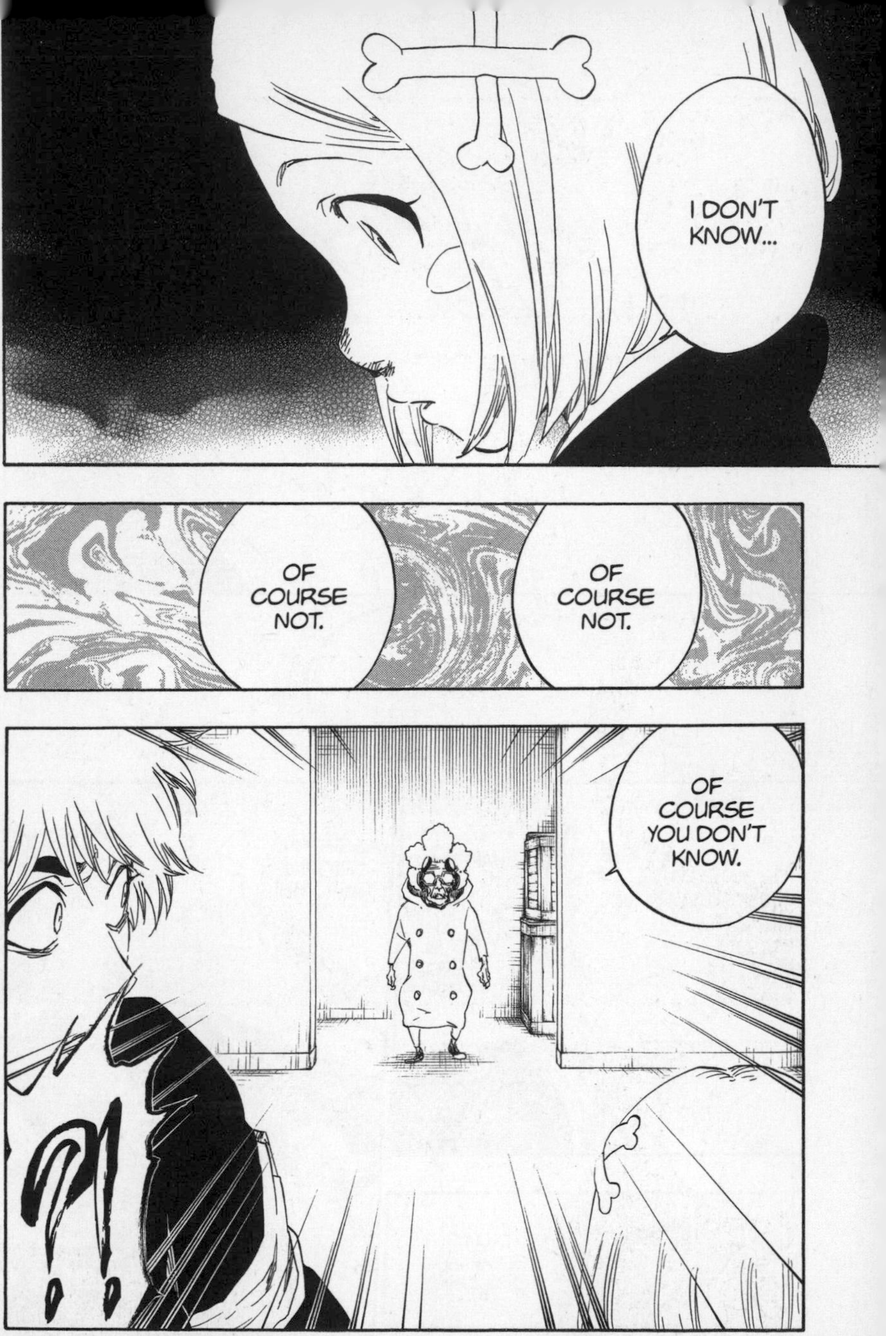
I DON'T KNOW...
OF COURSE NOT.
OF COURSE NOT.
OF COURSE YOU DON'T KNOW.
?!

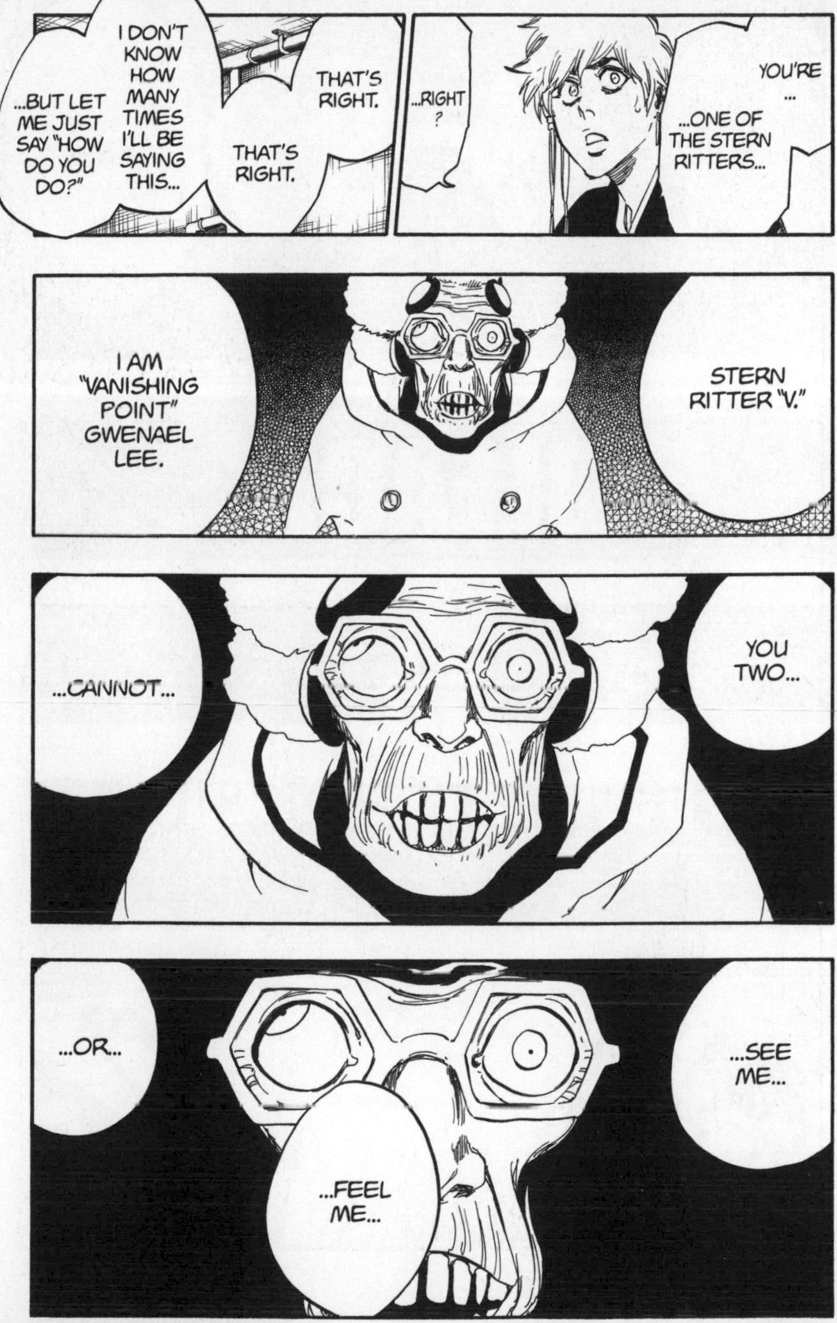
YOU'RE ...
...ONE OF THE STERN RITTERS...
...RIGHT ?
THAT'S RIGHT.
THAT'S RIGHT.
I DON'T KNOW HOW MANY TIMES I'LL BE SAYING THIS...
...BUT LET ME JUST SAY "HOW DO YOU DO?"
STERN RITTER "V."
I AM "VANISHING POINT" GWENAEL LEE.
YOU TWO...
...CANNOT...
...SEE ME...
...OR...
...FEEL ME...

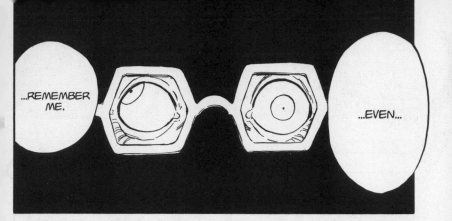

...REMEMBER ME.

...EVEN...

BLEACH

571

a Devilish Perspective

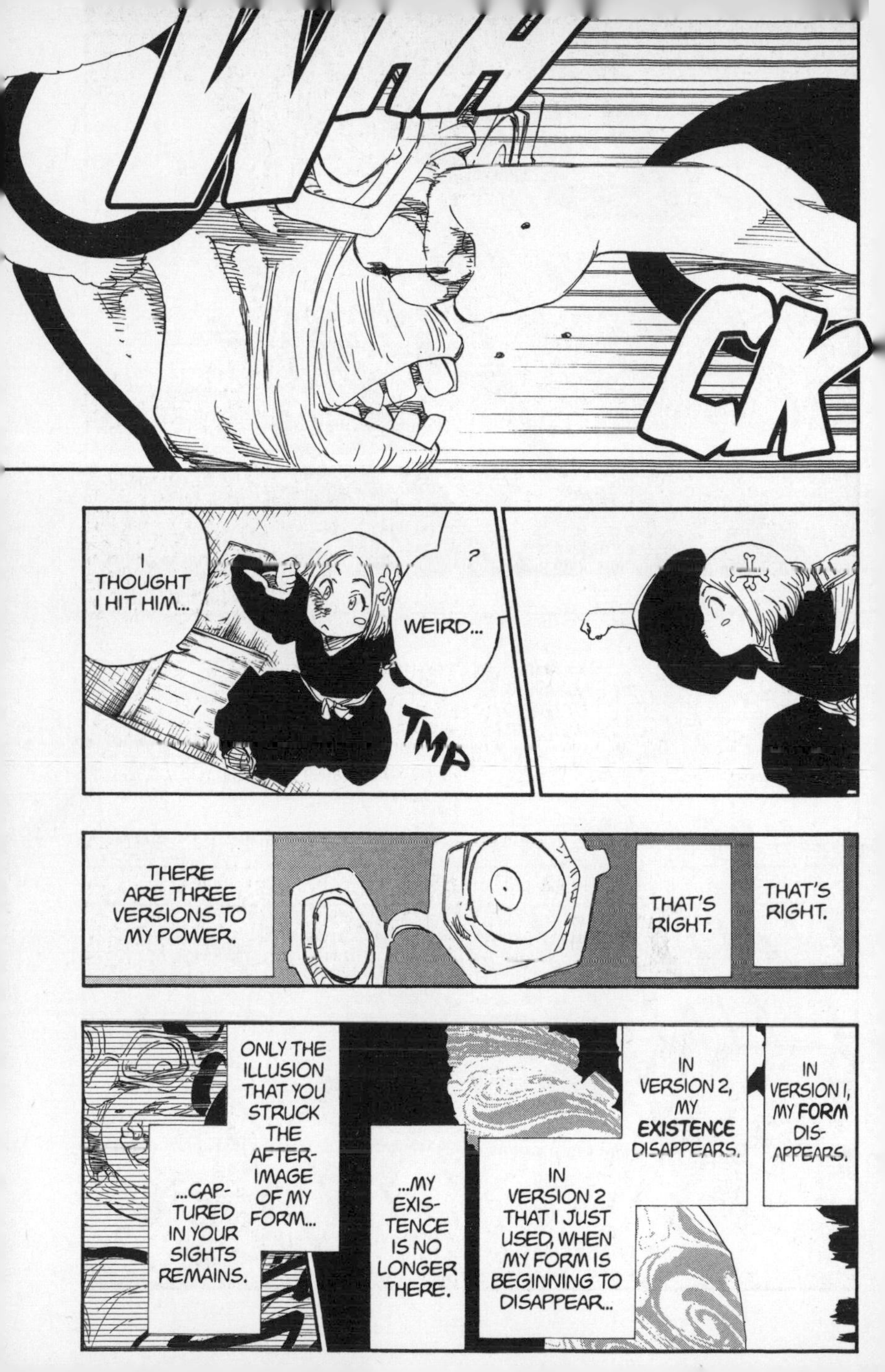
WHA
CK
?
WEIRD...
I THOUGHT I HIT HIM...
TMP
THAT'S RIGHT.
THAT'S RIGHT.
THERE ARE THREE VERSIONS TO MY POWER.
IN VERSION 1, MY **FORM** DISAPPEARS.
IN VERSION 2, MY **EXISTENCE** DISAPPEARS.
IN VERSION 2 THAT I JUST USED, WHEN MY FORM IS BEGINNING TO DISAPPEAR...
...MY EXISTENCE IS NO LONGER THERE.
ONLY THE ILLUSION THAT YOU STRUCK THE AFTERIMAGE OF MY FORM...
...CAPTURED IN YOUR SIGHTS REMAINS.

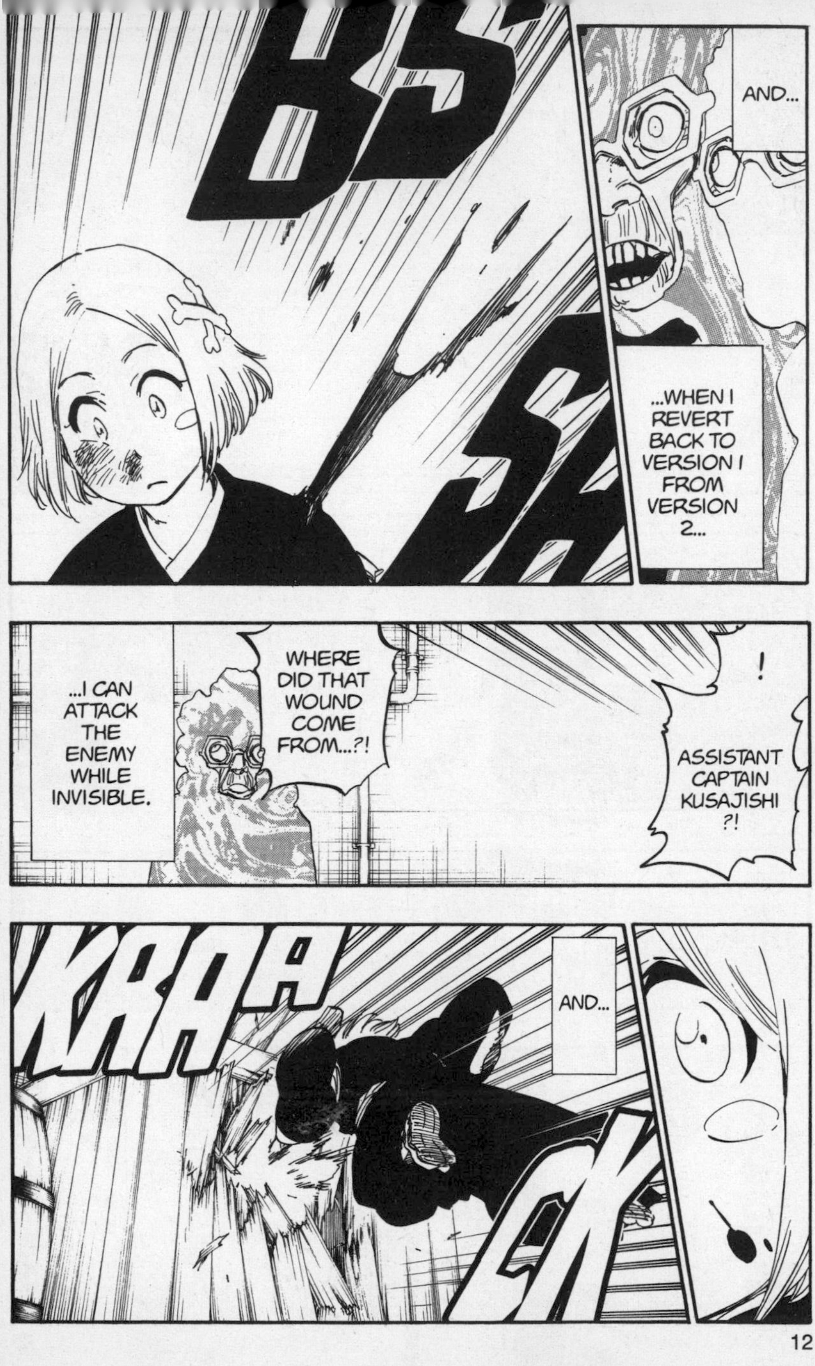
AND...
...WHEN I REVERT BACK TO VERSION 1 FROM VERSION 2...
!
ASSISTANT CAPTAIN KUSAJISHI ?!
WHERE DID THAT WOUND COME FROM...?!
...I CAN ATTACK THE ENEMY WHILE INVISIBLE.
AND...
KRAA
CK

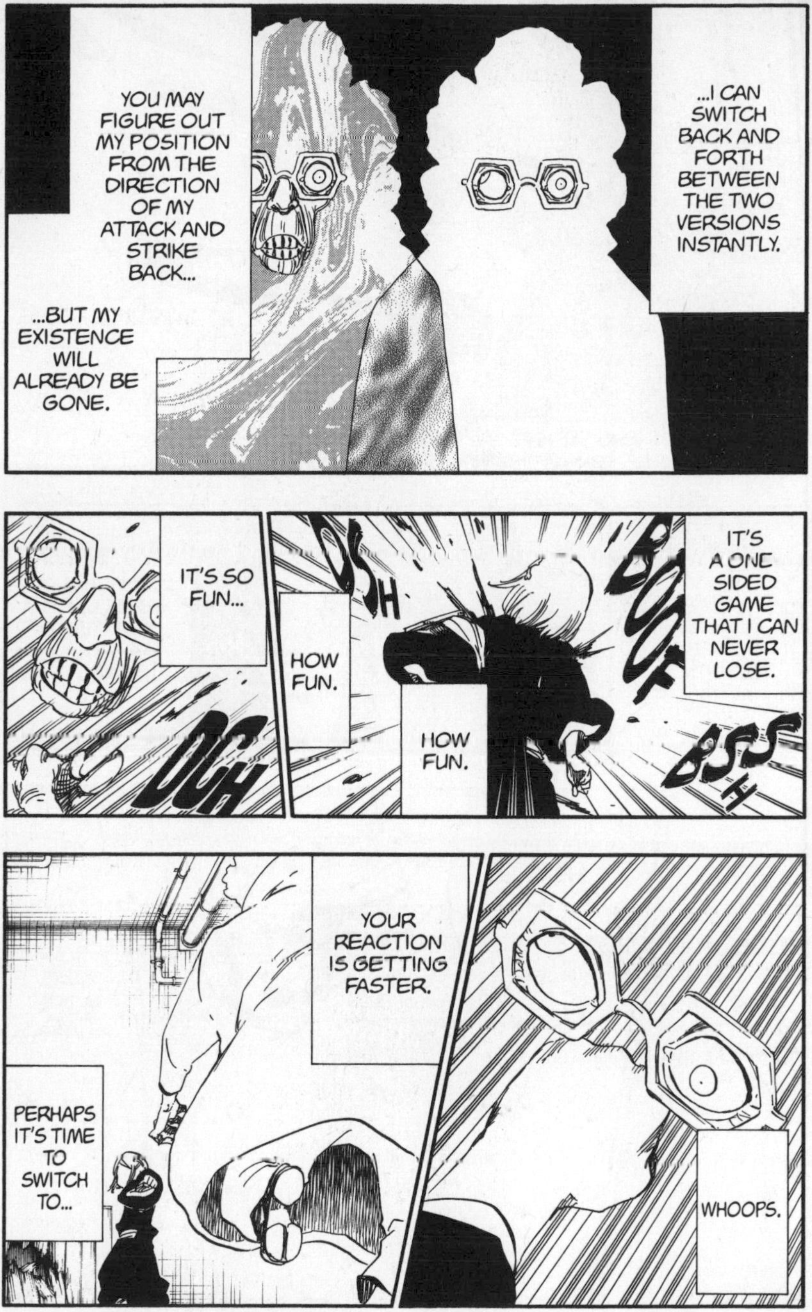
...I CAN SWITCH BACK AND FORTH BETWEEN THE TWO VERSIONS INSTANTLY.
YOU MAY FIGURE OUT MY POSITION FROM THE DIRECTION OF MY ATTACK AND STRIKE BACK...
...BUT MY EXISTENCE WILL ALREADY BE GONE.
IT'S A ONE SIDED GAME THAT I CAN NEVER LOSE.
BOOF
BSH
HOW FUN.
HOW FUN.
BSSH
IT'S SO FUN...
DCH
WHOOPS.
YOUR REACTION IS GETTING FASTER.
PERHAPS IT'S TIME TO SWITCH TO...

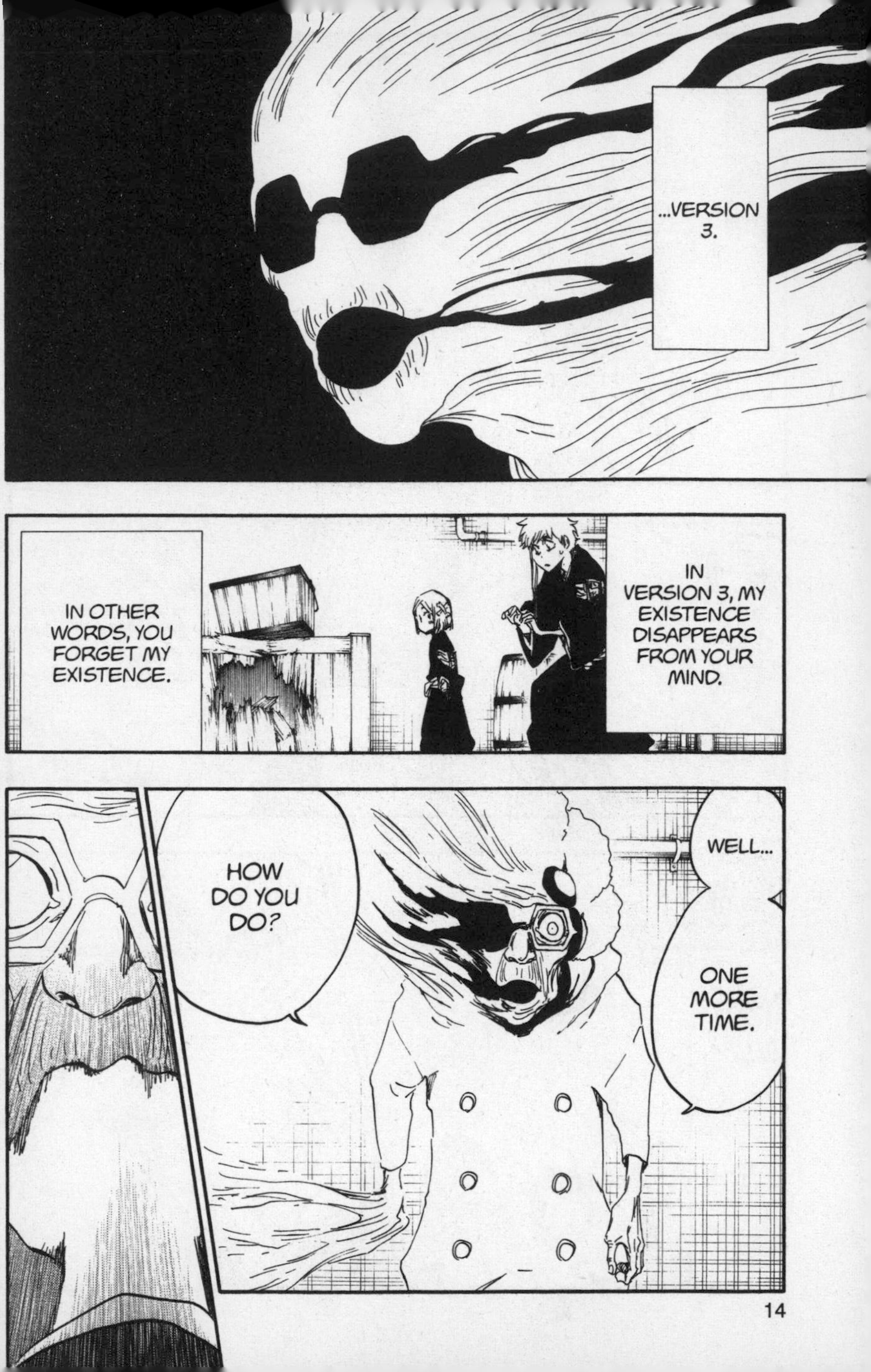
...VERSION 3.
IN VERSION 3, MY EXISTENCE DISAPPEARS FROM YOUR MIND.
IN OTHER WORDS, YOU FORGET MY EXISTENCE.
WELL...
ONE MORE TIME.
HOW DO YOU DO?

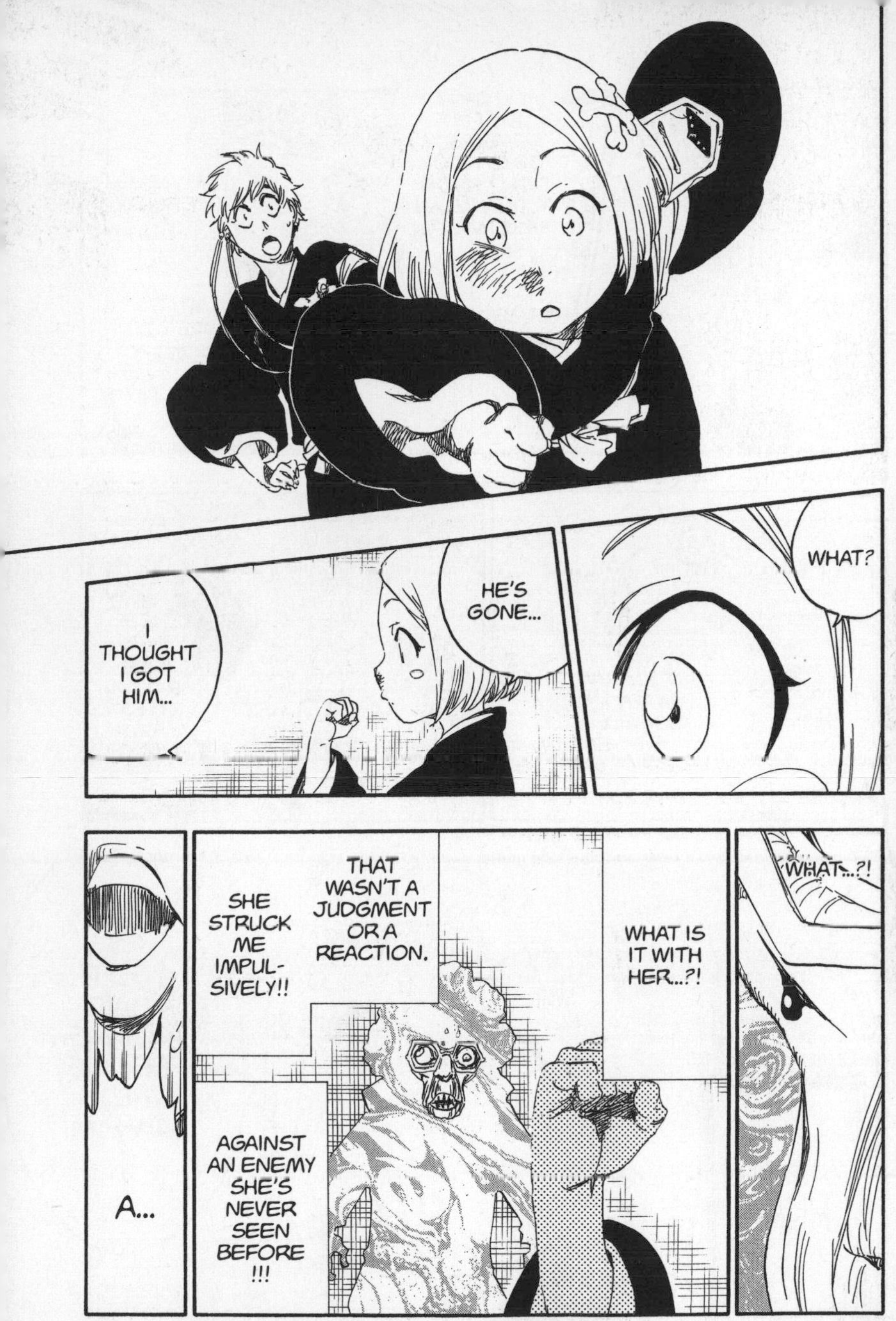
WHAT?
HE'S GONE...
I THOUGHT I GOT HIM...
WHAT...?!
WHAT IS IT WITH HER...?!
THAT WASN'T A JUDGMENT OR A REACTION.
SHE STRUCK ME IMPULSIVELY!!
AGAINST AN ENEMY SHE'S NEVER SEEN BEFORE!!!
A...

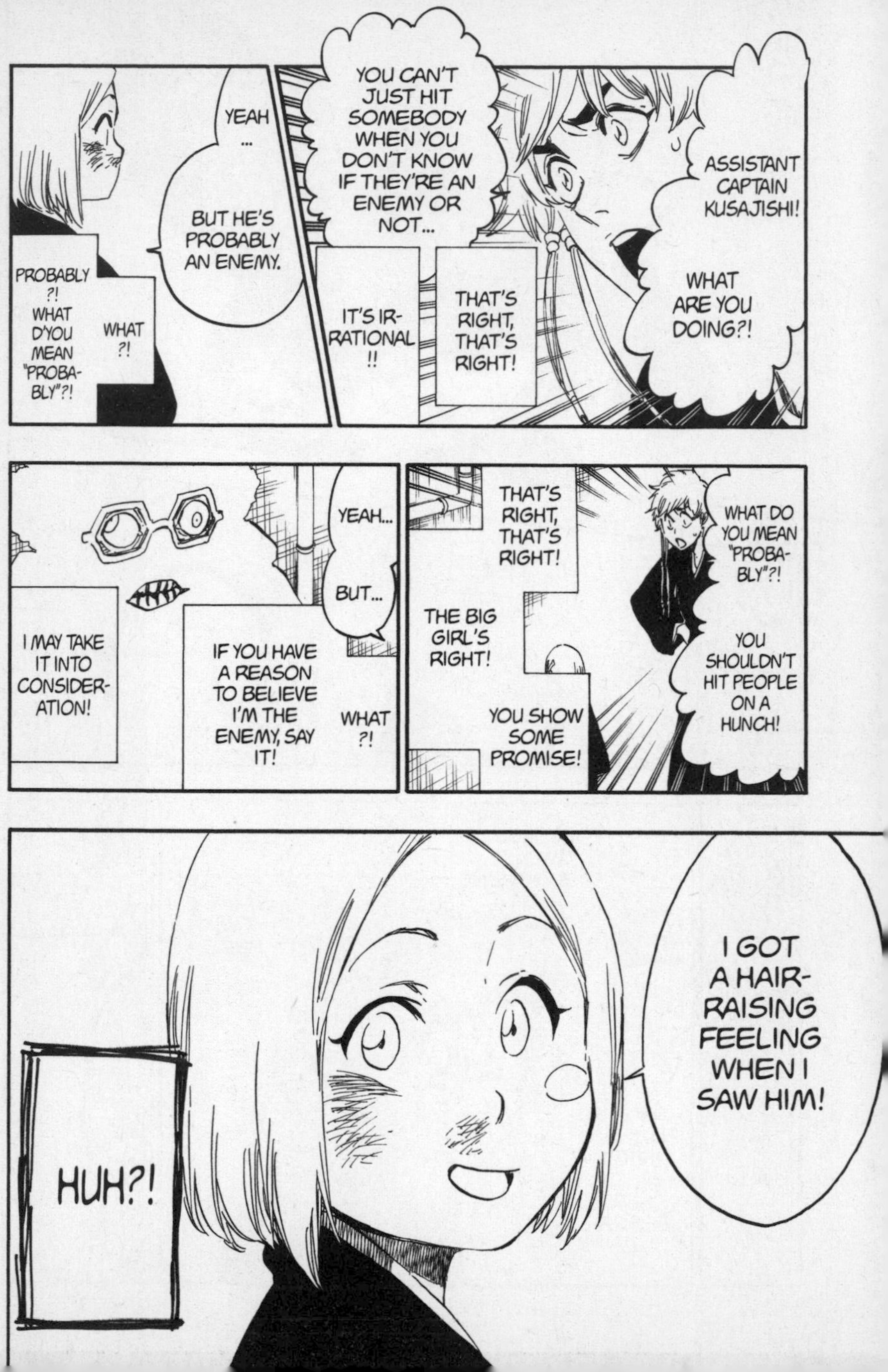
ASSISTANT CAPTAIN KUSAJISHI!
WHAT ARE YOU DOING?!
YOU CAN'T JUST HIT SOMEBODY WHEN YOU DON'T KNOW IF THEY'RE AN ENEMY OR NOT...
THAT'S RIGHT, THAT'S RIGHT!
IT'S IR-RATIONAL!!
YEAH ...
BUT HE'S PROBABLY AN ENEMY.
WHAT?!
PROBABLY?! WHAT D'YOU MEAN "PROBABLY"?!
WHAT DO YOU MEAN "PROBABLY"?!
YOU SHOULDN'T HIT PEOPLE ON A HUNCH!
THAT'S RIGHT, THAT'S RIGHT!
THE BIG GIRL'S RIGHT!
YOU SHOW SOME PROMISE!
YEAH...
BUT...
WHAT?!
IF YOU HAVE A REASON TO BELIEVE I'M THE ENEMY, SAY IT!
I MAY TAKE IT INTO CONSIDERATION!
I GOT A HAIR-RAISING FEELING WHEN I SAW HIM!
HUH?!

READ THIS WAY

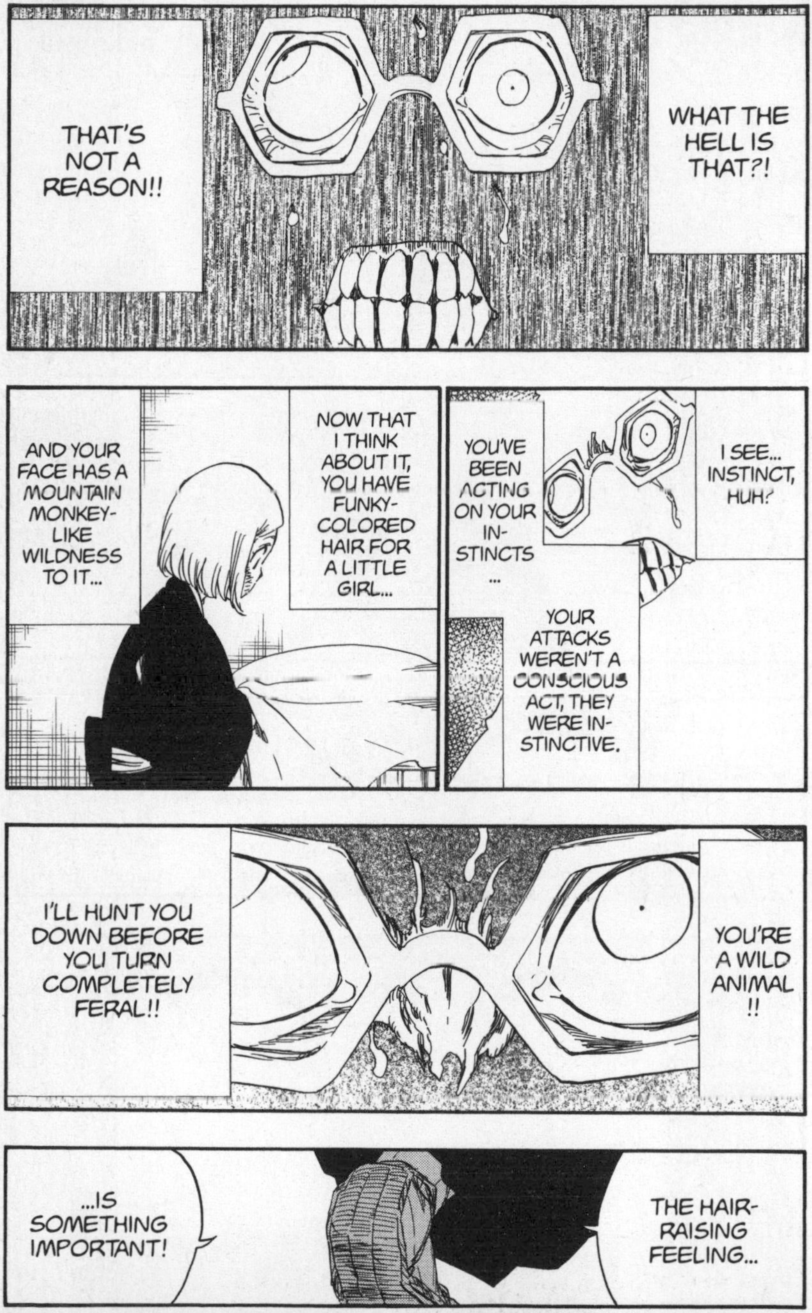
WHAT THE HELL IS THAT?!
THAT'S NOT A REASON!!
I SEE... INSTINCT, HUH?
YOU'VE BEEN ACTING ON YOUR INSTINCTS ...
YOUR ATTACKS WEREN'T A CONSCIOUS ACT, THEY WERE INSTINCTIVE.
NOW THAT I THINK ABOUT IT, YOU HAVE FUNKY-COLORED HAIR FOR A LITTLE GIRL...
AND YOUR FACE HAS A MOUNTAIN MONKEY-LIKE WILDNESS TO IT...
YOU'RE A WILD ANIMAL!!
I'LL HUNT YOU DOWN BEFORE YOU TURN COMPLETELY FERAL!!
THE HAIR-RAISING FEELING...
...IS SOMETHING IMPORTANT!

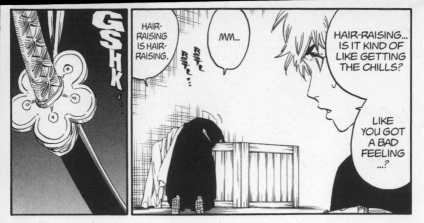

HAIR-RAISING... IS IT KIND OF LIKE GETTING THE CHILLS?
LIKE YOU GOT A BAD FEELING ...?
MM...
RSTL RSTL...
HAIR-RAISING IS HAIR-RAISING.
GSHK...
HAIR-RAISING IS...
...LIKE FEELING COLD OR HOT OR HAPPY.
IT'S KINDA LIKE THAT.
WHEN I FIND SOMEBODY LIKE THAT, I CAN'T HELP MYSELF FROM SLAYING HIM.
THAT'S WHAT KEN SAYS.
HE'S NOT HERE RIGHT NOW...
...SO HE WON'T GET MAD...
...IF I SLAY HIM, RIGHT?

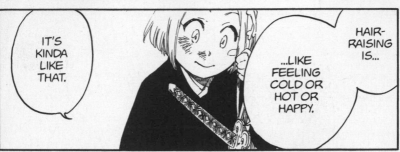

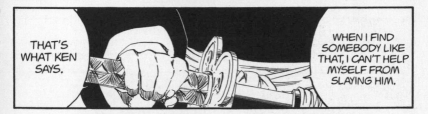

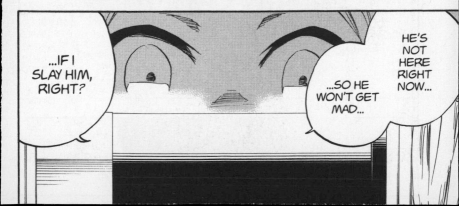

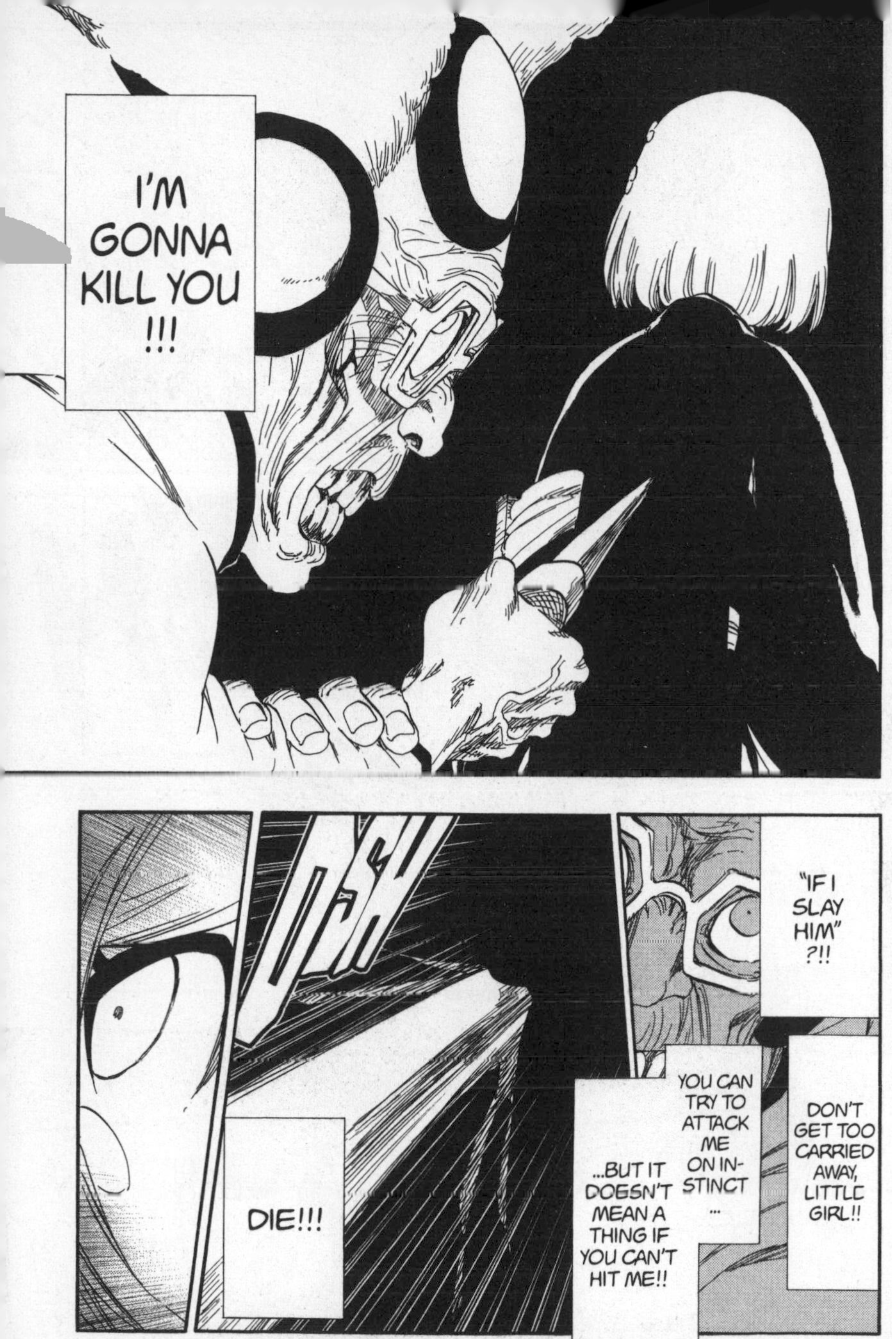
I'M GONNA KILL YOU !!!
"IF I SLAY HIM" ?!!
DON'T GET TOO CARRIED AWAY, LITTLE GIRL!!
YOU CAN TRY TO ATTACK ME ON IN-STINCT ...
...BUT IT DOESN'T MEAN A THING IF YOU CAN'T HIT ME!!
DIE!!!

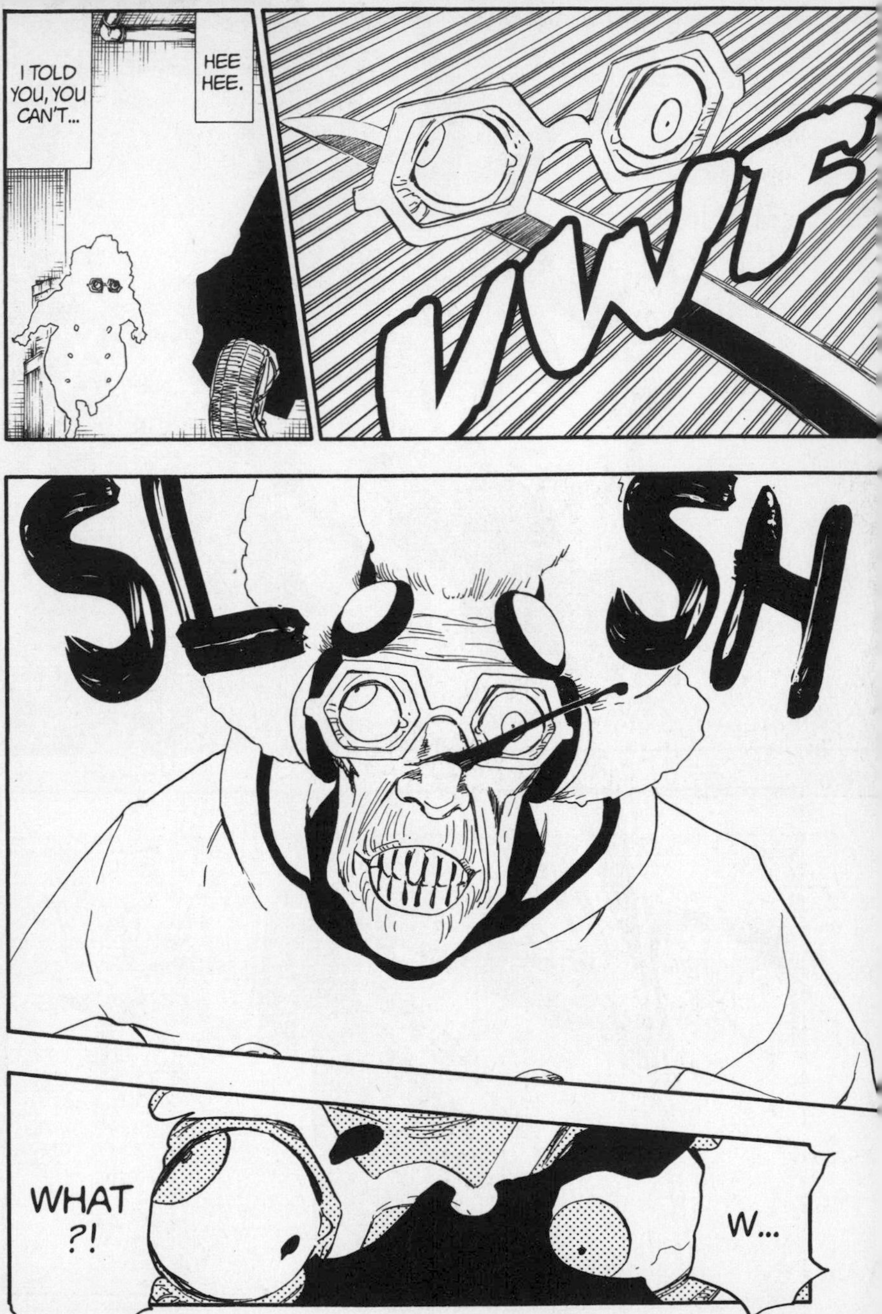
VWIF
HEE HEE.
I TOLD YOU, YOU CAN'T...
SL SH
W...
WHAT ?!

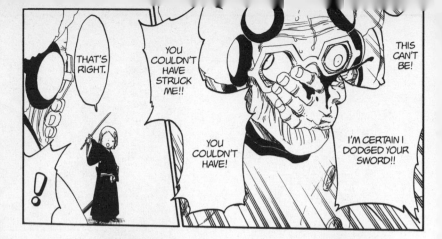

THIS CAN'T BE!
I'M CERTAIN I DODGED YOUR SWORD!!
YOU COULDN'T HAVE!
YOU COULDN'T HAVE STRUCK ME!!
THAT'S RIGHT.
!
MY SWORD...
...STRIKES WHETHER YOU DODGE IT OR NOT.
WHAT ...
...DID YOU SAY?
YOU SEE, MY SWORD ...
...IS A COPYCAT SWORD.
THERE ARE COPY-CATS ON THE...
...FRONT AND BACK OF MY SWORD.
SO...
...THE MORE YOU GAUGE THE TIMING, THE MORE YOUR TIMING GETS THROWN OFF...
...AND THE MORE LIKELY YOU'LL BE HIT.
IT'S OKAY.
COME ON OUT...

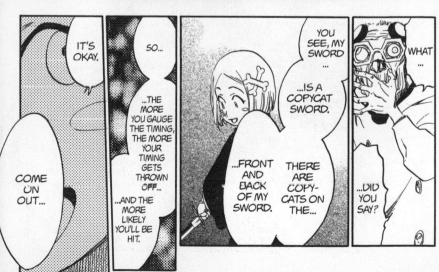

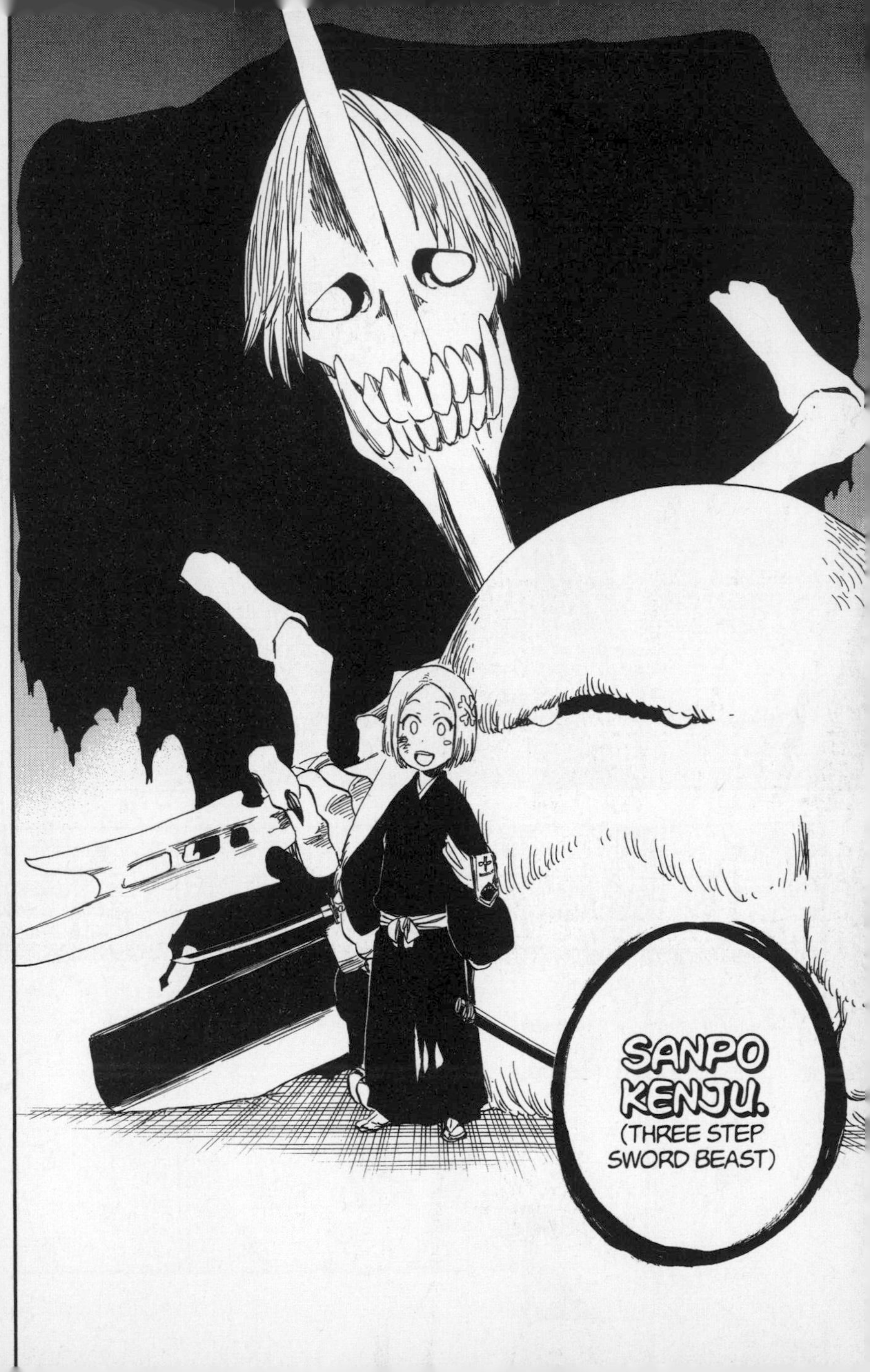
SANPO KENJU. (THREE STEP SWORD BEAST)

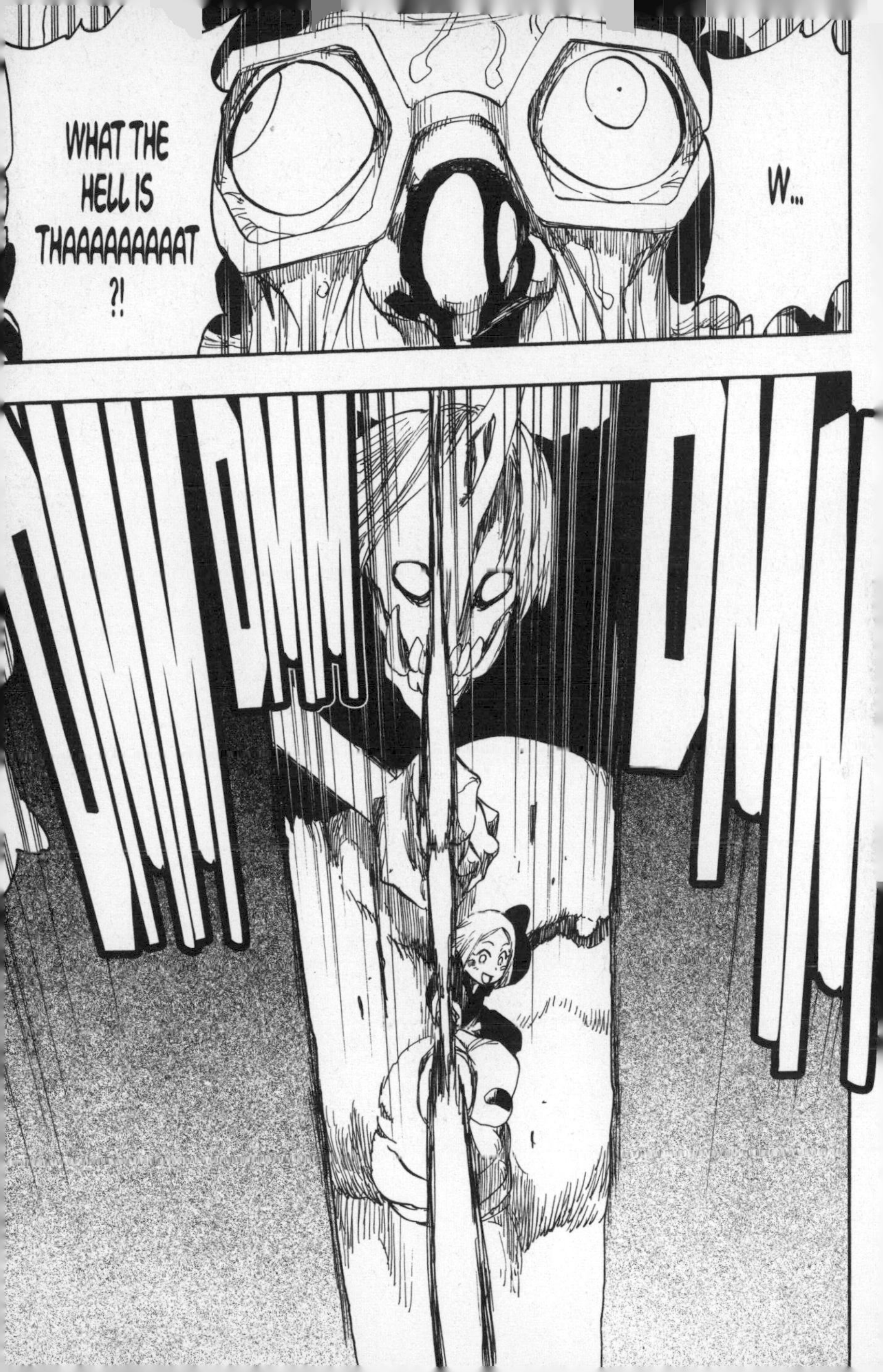
W...
WHAT THE HELL IS THAAAAAAAAAT ?!

FRONT BEAST
(MOKO MOKO)
&
BACK BEAST
(HONE HONE)

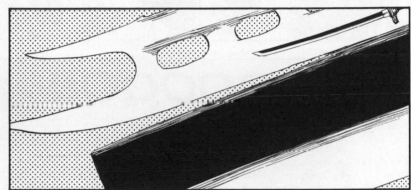

READY...

GET
SET...

572. THE BLASTER

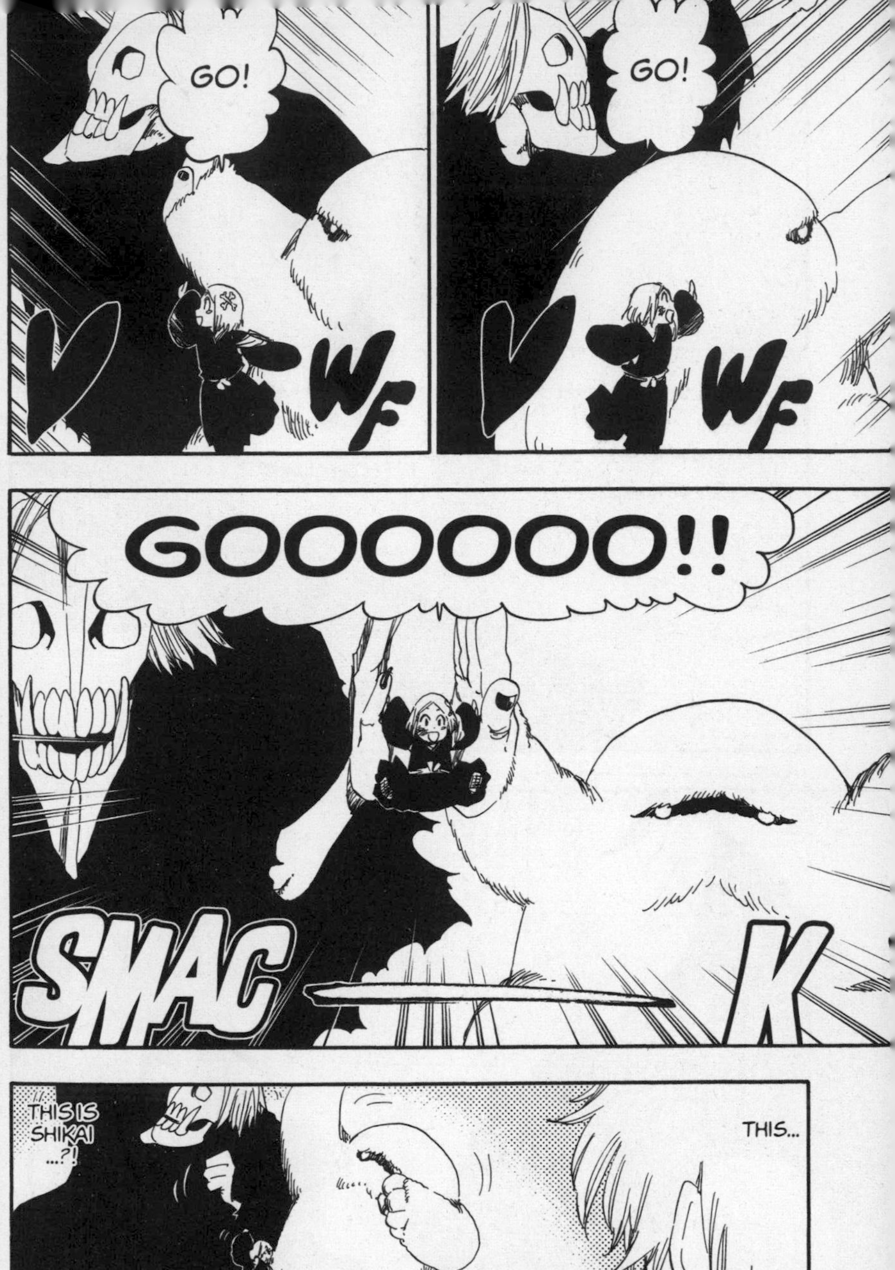
GO!
WF
GO!
WF
GOOOOOO!!
SMAC
K
THIS...
THIS IS SHIKAI ...?!

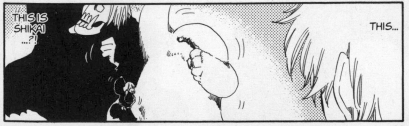

READ THIS WAY

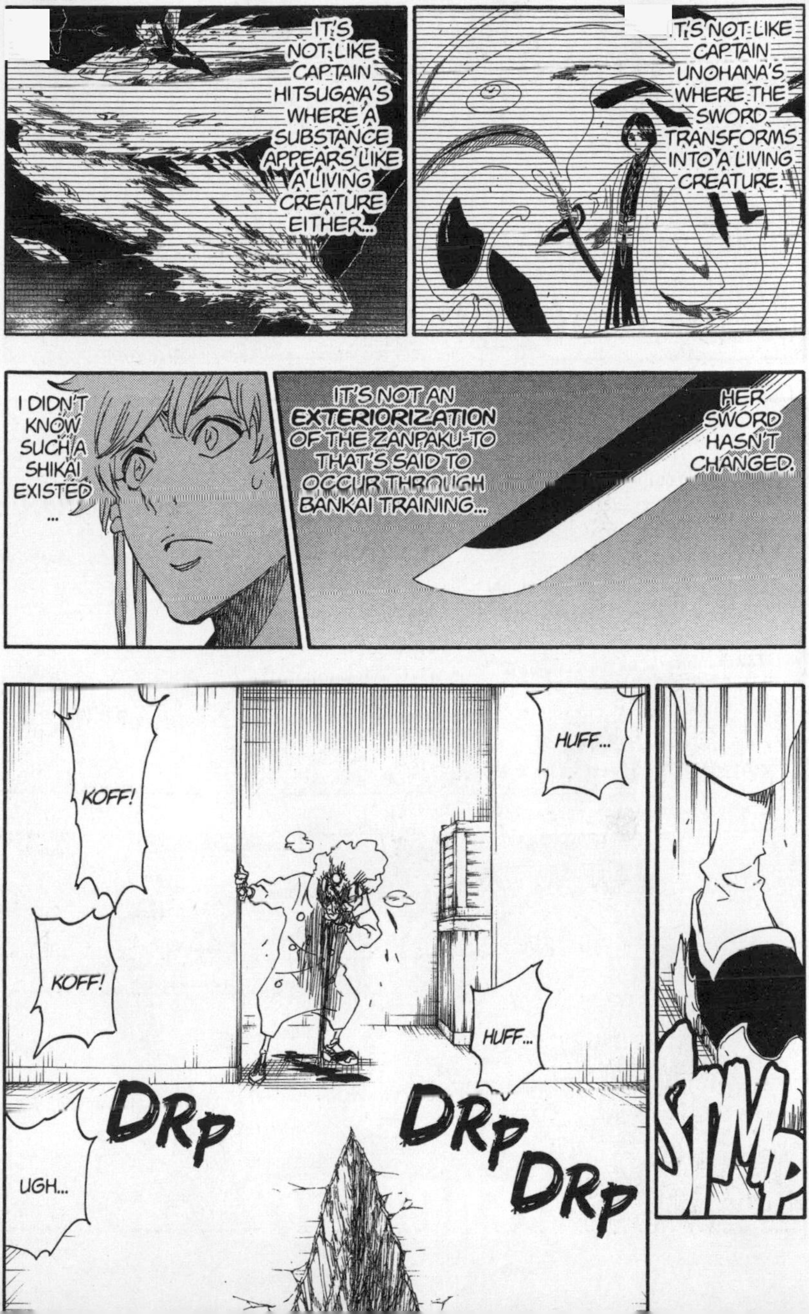

IT'S NOT LIKE CAPTAIN UNOHANA'S WHERE THE SWORD TRANSFORMS INTO A LIVING CREATURE.
IT'S NOT LIKE CAPTAIN HITSUGAYA'S WHERE A SUBSTANCE APPEARS LIKE A LIVING CREATURE EITHER...
HER SWORD HASN'T CHANGED.
IT'S NOT AN **EXTERIORIZATION** OF THE ZANPAKU-TO THAT'S SAID TO OCCUR THROUGH BANKAI TRAINING...
I DIDN'T KNOW SUCH A SHIKAI EXISTED...
STMP
HUFF...
HUFF...
KOFF!
KOFF!
DRP
DRP
DRP
UGH...

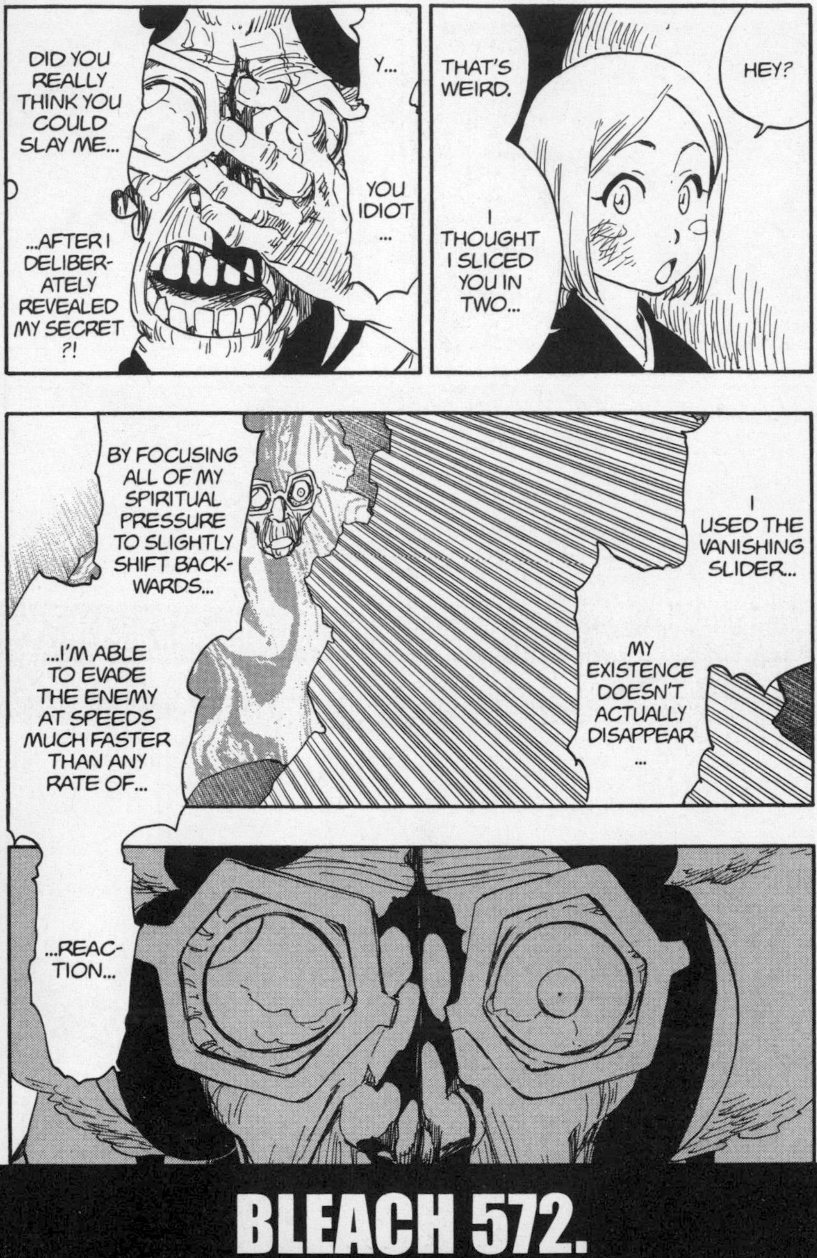
HEY?
THAT'S WEIRD.
I THOUGHT I SLICED YOU IN TWO...
Y...
YOU IDIOT ...
DID YOU REALLY THINK YOU COULD SLAY ME...
...AFTER I DELIBER-ATELY REVEALED MY SECRET ?!
I USED THE VANISHING SLIDER...
MY EXISTENCE DOESN'T ACTUALLY DISAPPEAR ...
BY FOCUSING ALL OF MY SPIRITUAL PRESSURE TO SLIGHTLY SHIFT BACK-WARDS...
...I'M ABLE TO EVADE THE ENEMY AT SPEEDS MUCH FASTER THAN ANY RATE OF...
...REAC-TION...

BLEACH 572.

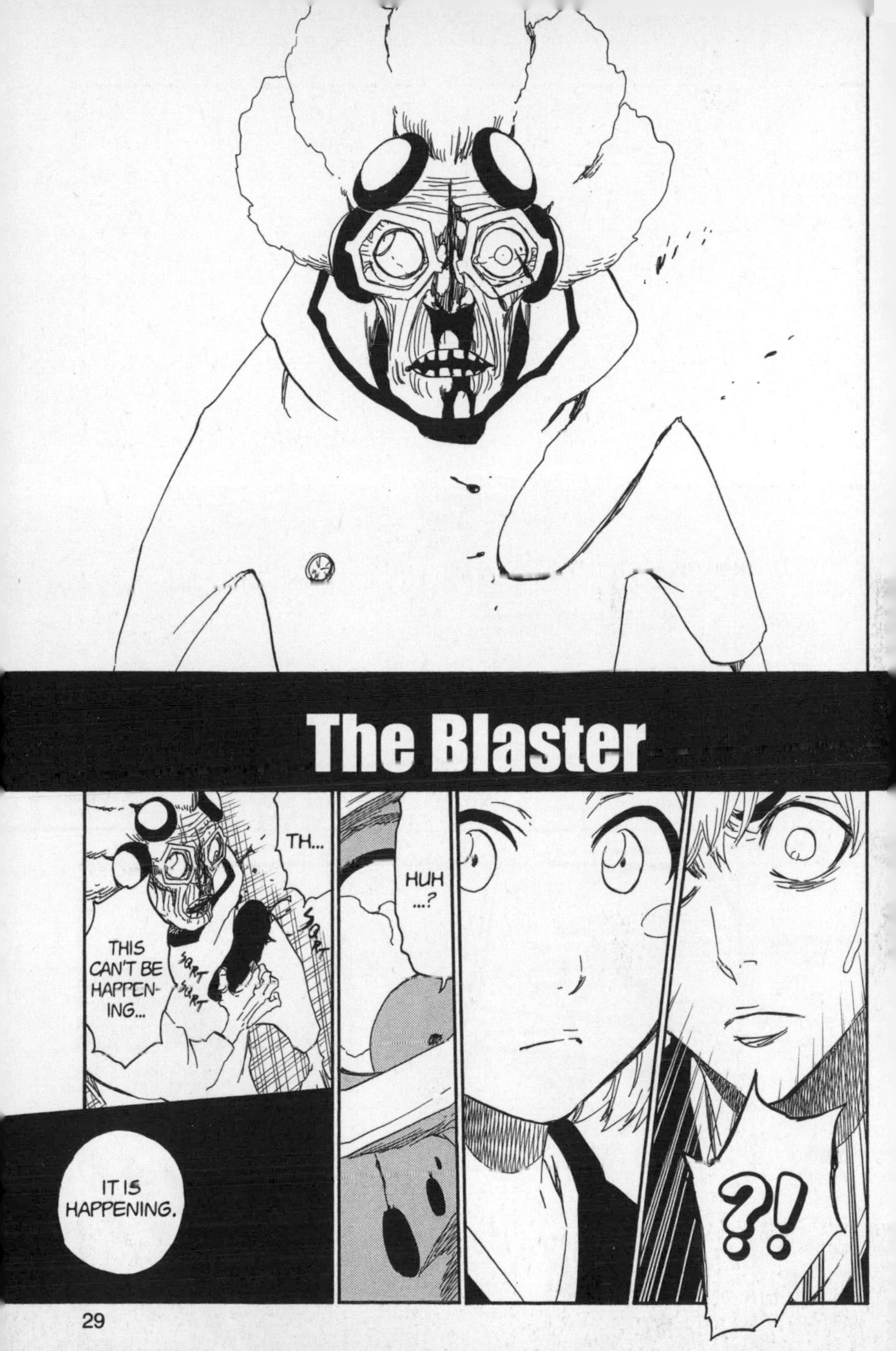
The Blaster
?!
HUH ...?
TH...
SQRT
THIS CAN'T BE HAPPENING...
SQRT SQRT
IT IS HAPPENING.

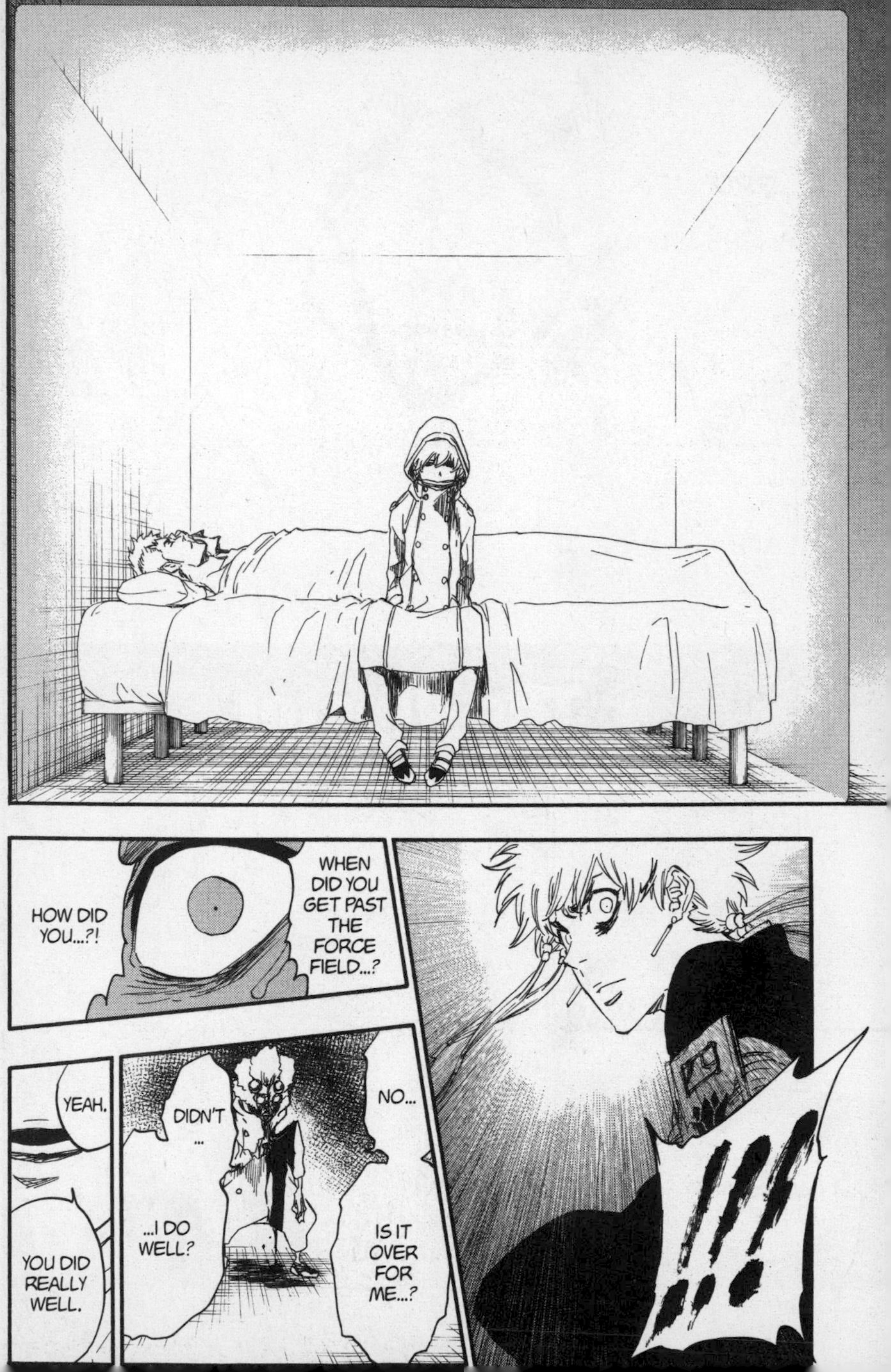
!!
WHEN DID YOU GET PAST THE FORCE FIELD...?
HOW DID YOU...?!
NO...
IS IT OVER FOR ME...?
DIDN'T ...
...I DO WELL?
YEAH.
YOU DID REALLY WELL.

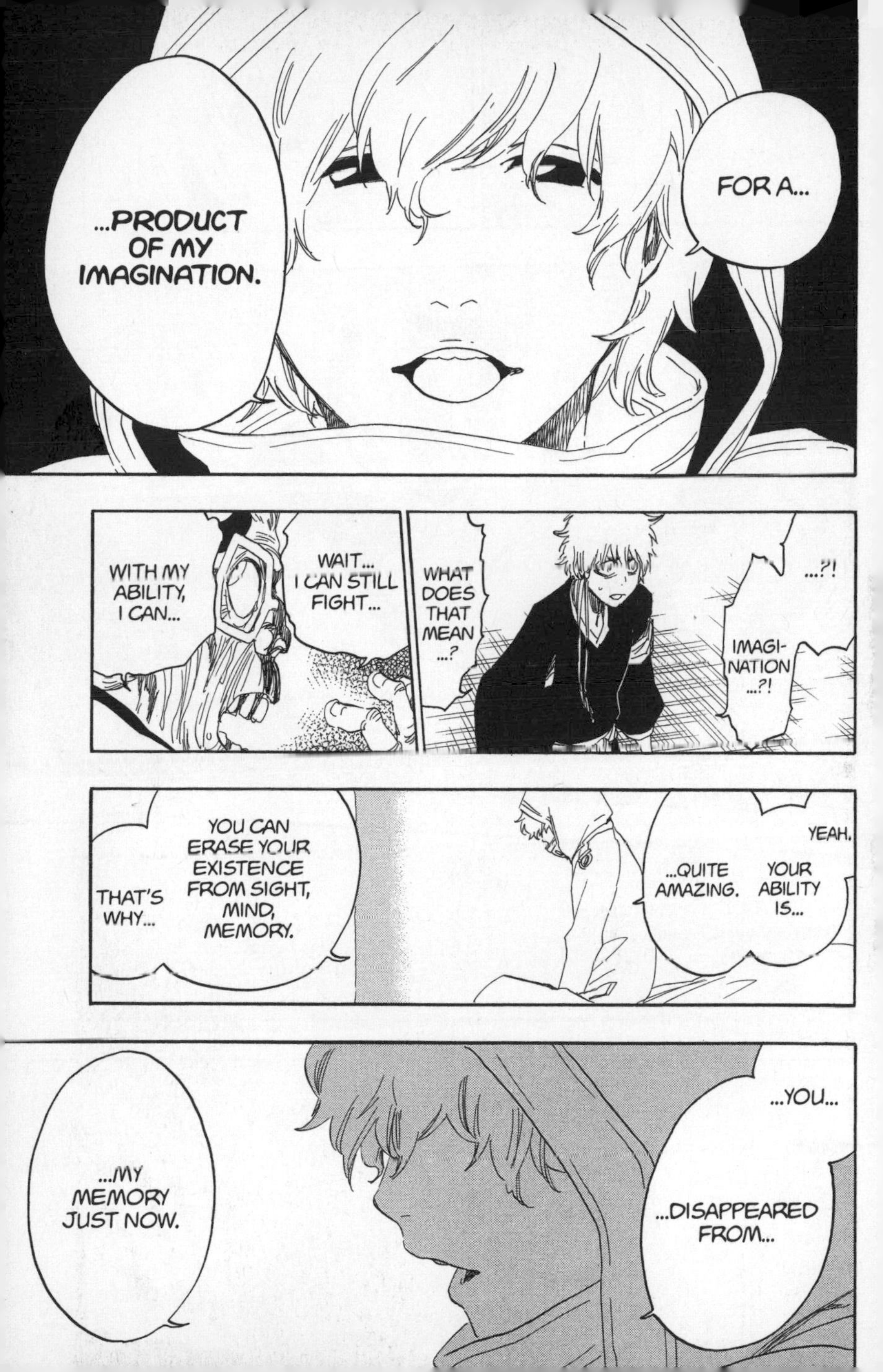
FOR A...
...PRODUCT OF MY IMAGINATION.
...?!
IMAGINATION...?!
WHAT DOES THAT MEAN...?
WAIT... I CAN STILL FIGHT...
WITH MY ABILITY, I CAN...
YEAH.
YOUR ABILITY IS...
...QUITE AMAZING.
YOU CAN ERASE YOUR EXISTENCE FROM SIGHT, MIND, MEMORY.
THAT'S WHY...
...YOU...
...DISAPPEARED FROM...
...MY MEMORY JUST NOW.

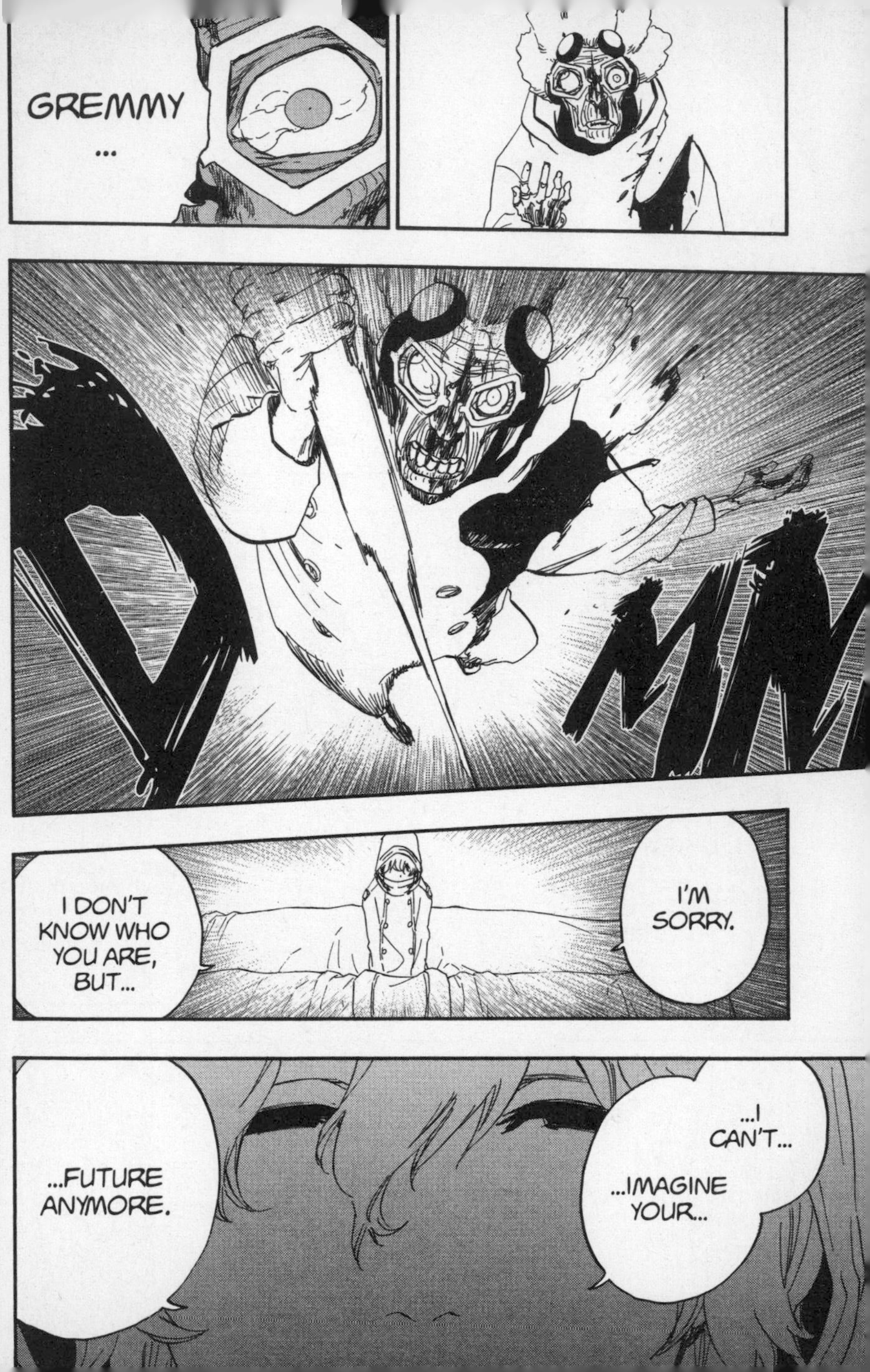
GREMMY ...
DMM
I'M SORRY.
I DON'T KNOW WHO YOU ARE, BUT...
...I CAN'T...
...IMAGINE YOUR...
...FUTURE ANYMORE.

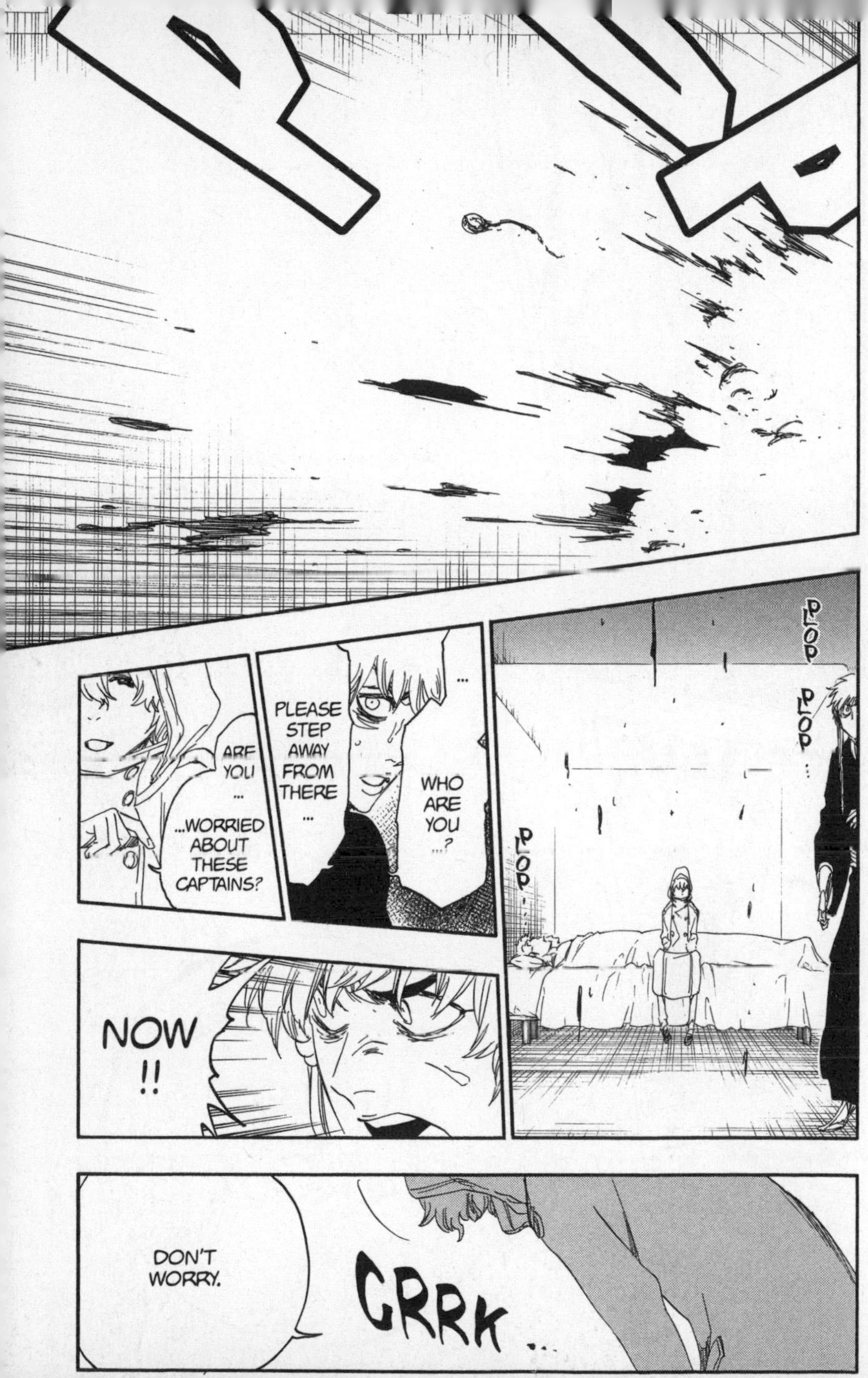
PLOP
PLOP...
PLOP...
WHO ARE YOU ...?
...
PLEASE STEP AWAY FROM THERE ...
ARE YOU ...
...WORRIED ABOUT THESE CAPTAINS?
NOW !!
GRRK...
DON'T WORRY.

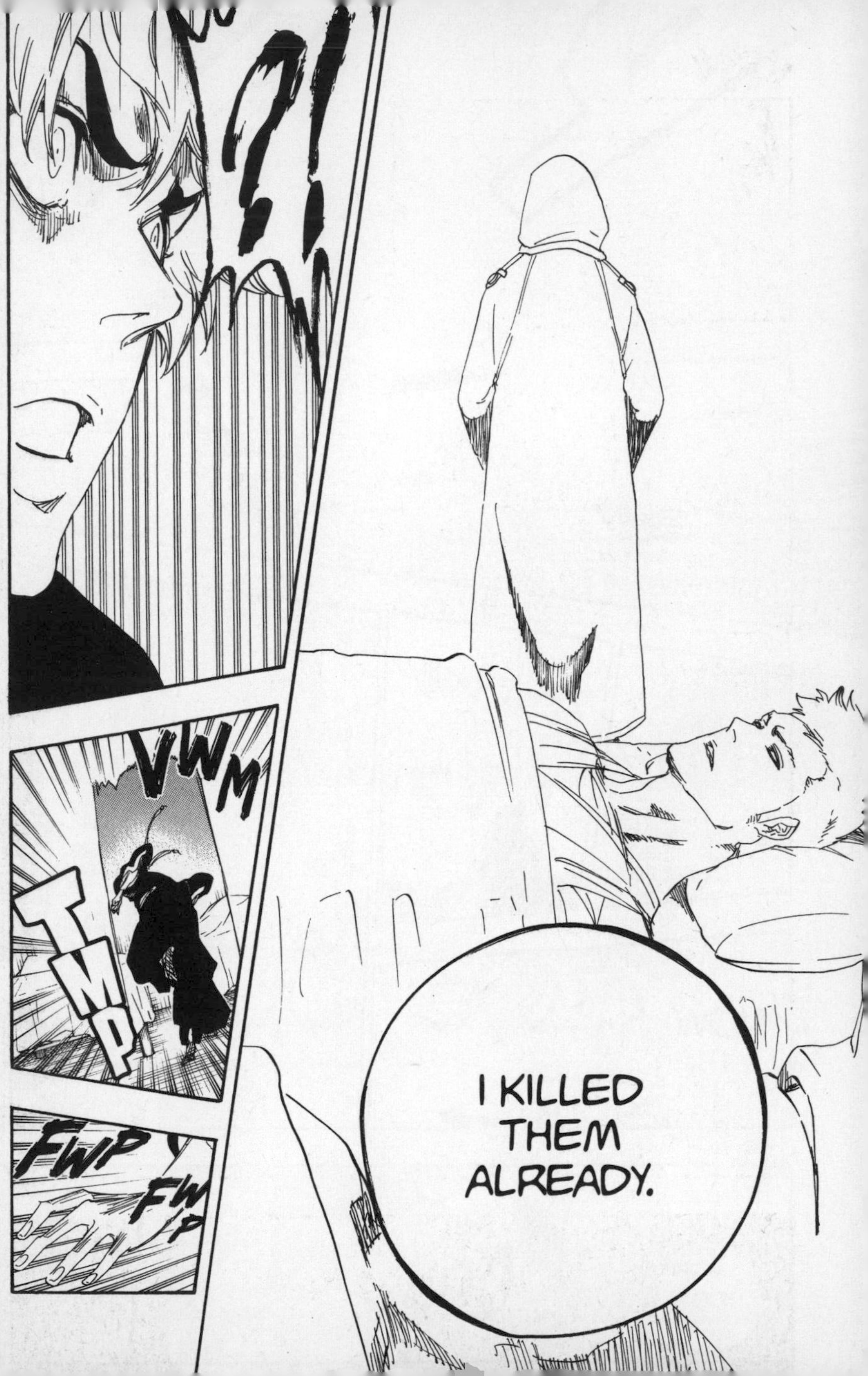
I KILLED THEM ALREADY.
?!
VWM
TMP
FWP
FWP

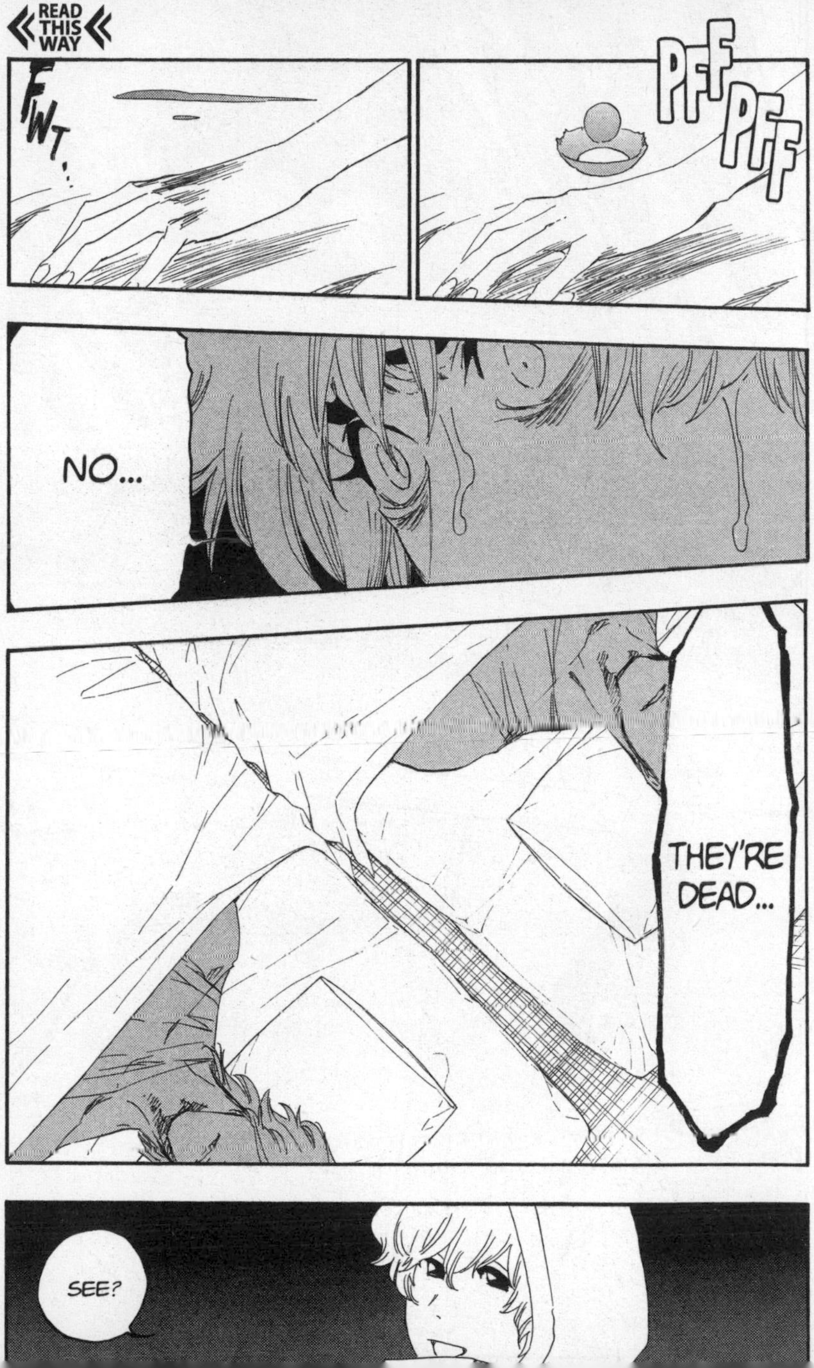
READ THIS WAY
PFF PFF
FWT..
NO...
THEY'RE DEAD...
SEE?

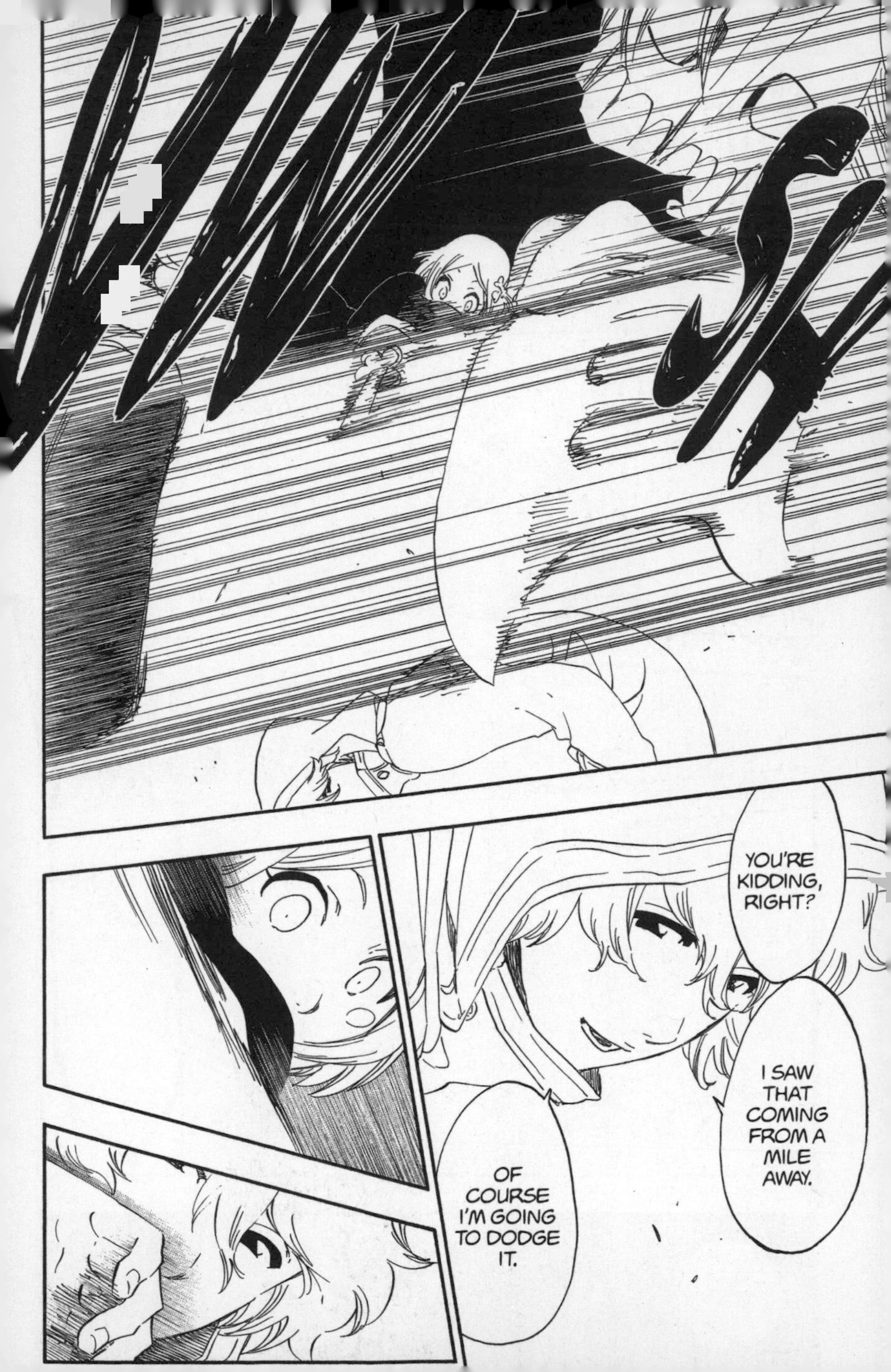

YOU'RE KIDDING, RIGHT?
I SAW THAT COMING FROM A MILE AWAY.
OF COURSE I'M GOING TO DODGE IT.

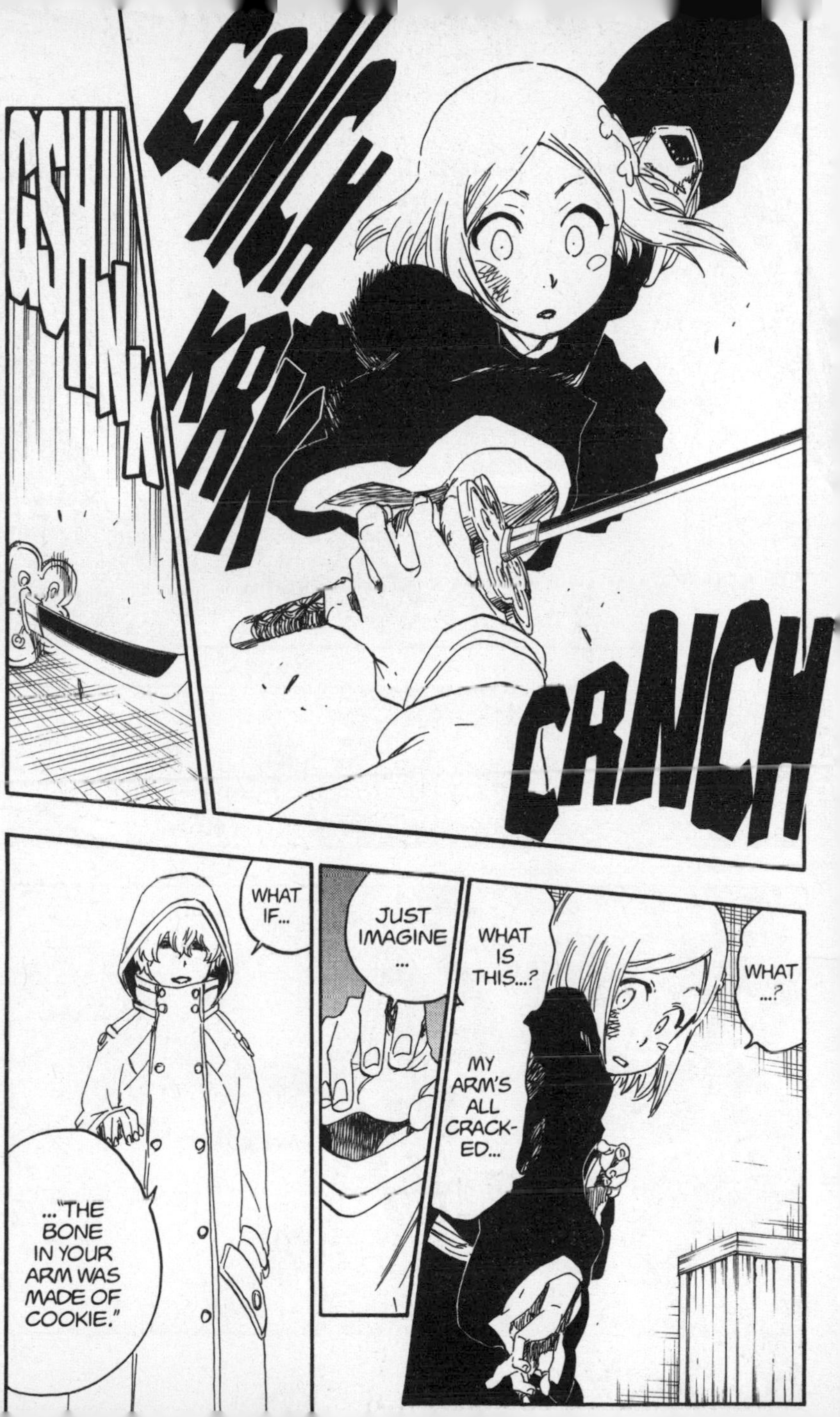
CRNCH
KRK
CRNCH
GSHNK
WHAT ...?
WHAT IS THIS...?
MY ARM'S ALL CRACKED...
JUST IMAGINE ...
WHAT IF...
..."THE BONE IN YOUR ARM WAS MADE OF COOKIE."

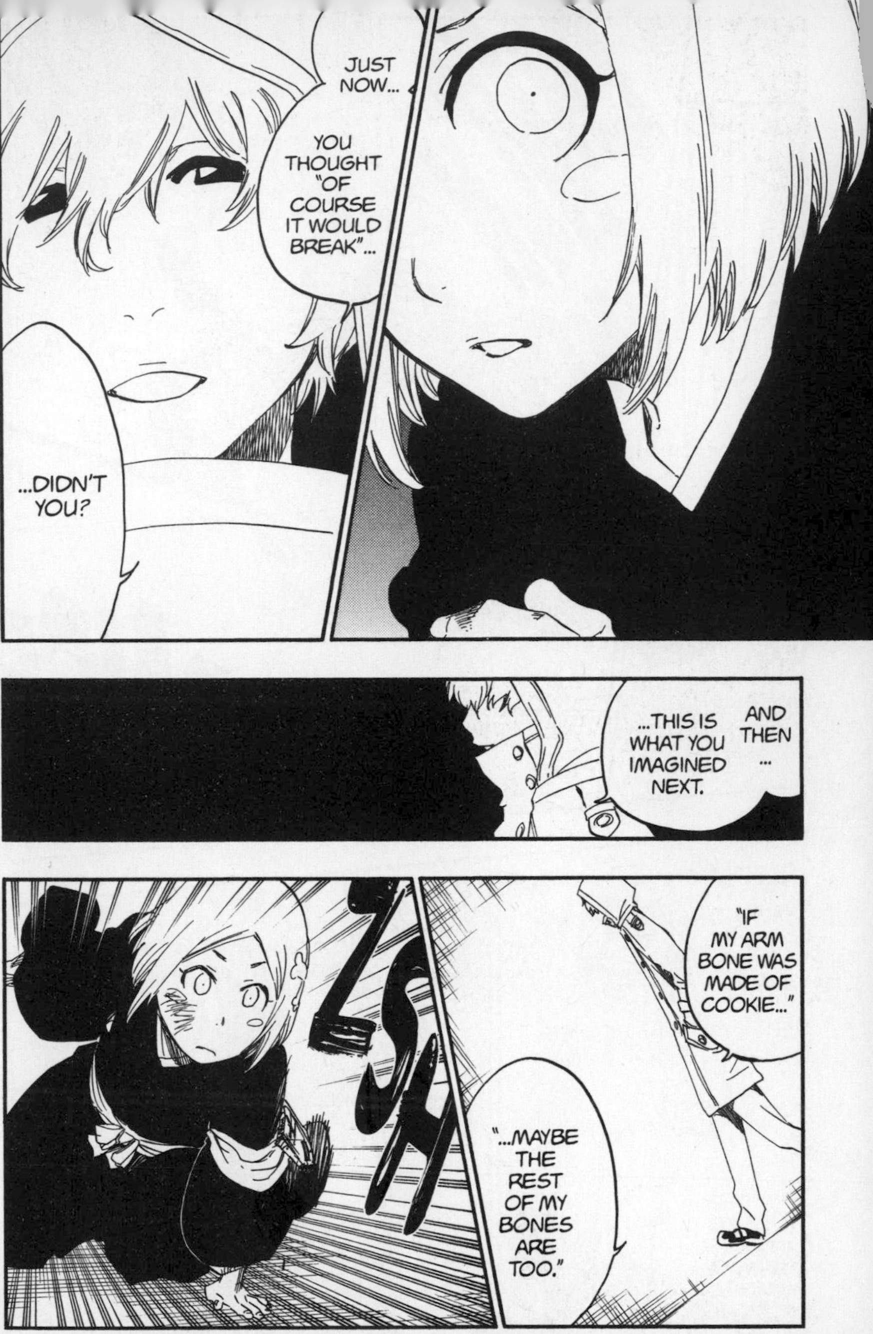
JUST NOW...
YOU THOUGHT "OF COURSE IT WOULD BREAK"...
...DIDN'T YOU?
AND THEN ...
...THIS IS WHAT YOU IMAGINED NEXT.
"IF MY ARM BONE WAS MADE OF COOKIE..."
"...MAYBE THE REST OF MY BONES ARE TOO."

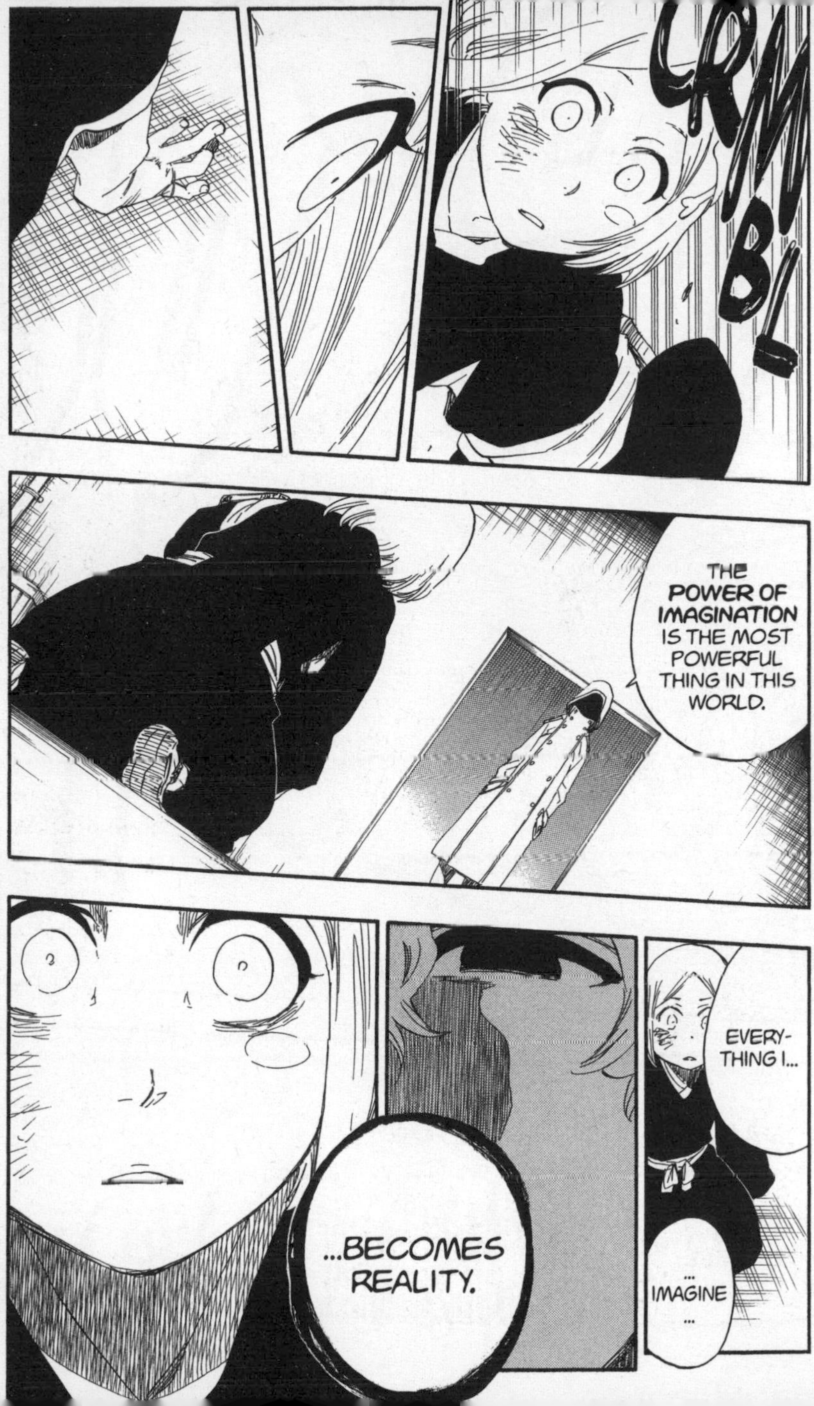
CRMBL
THE POWER OF IMAGINATION IS THE MOST POWERFUL THING IN THIS WORLD.
EVERY-THING I...
...IMAGINE...
...BECOMES REALITY.

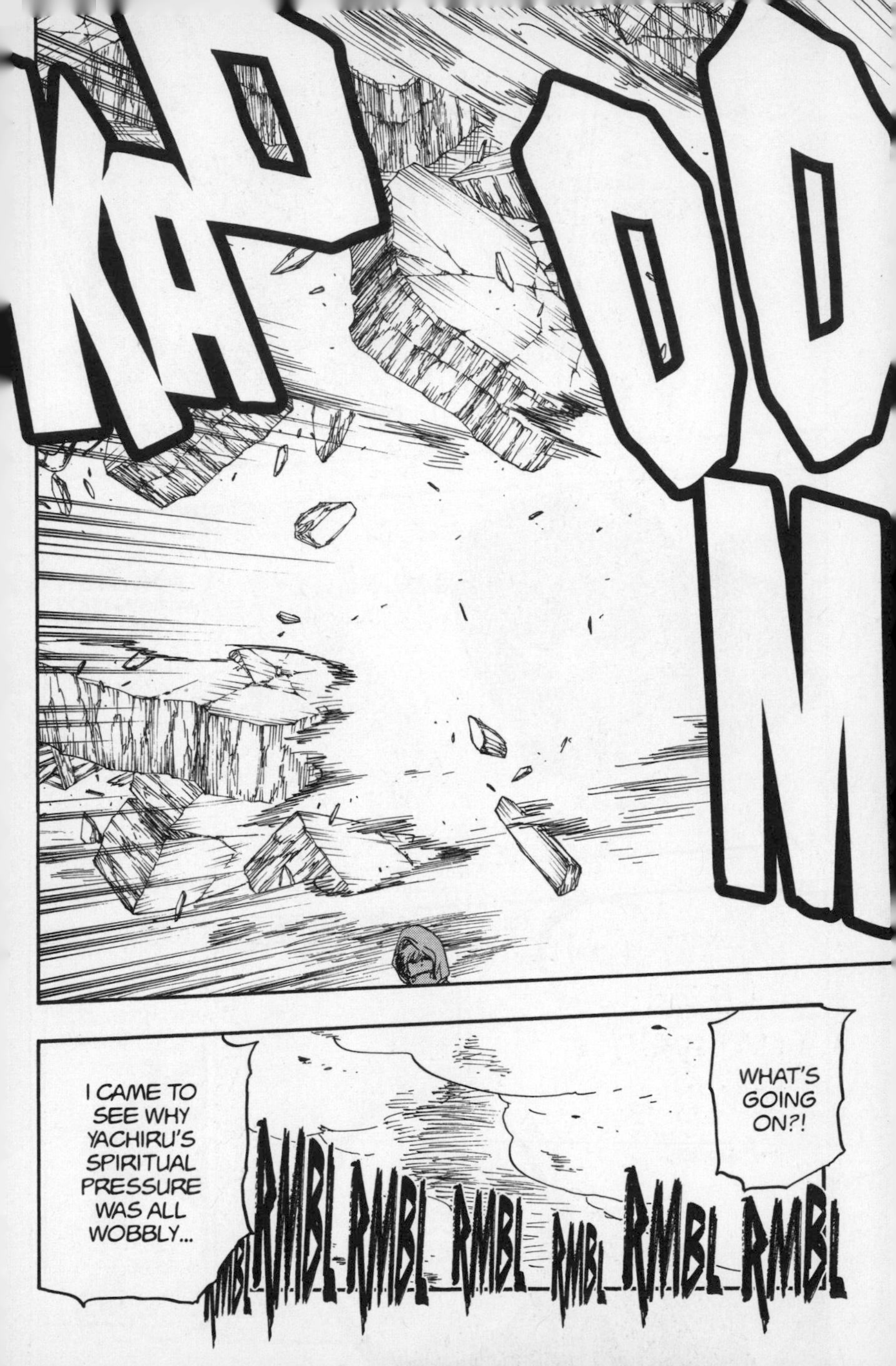
WHAT'S GOING ON?!
I CAME TO SEE WHY YACHIRU'S SPIRITUAL PRESSURE WAS ALL WOBBLY...
RMBL RMBL RMBL RMBL RMBL RMBL RMBL

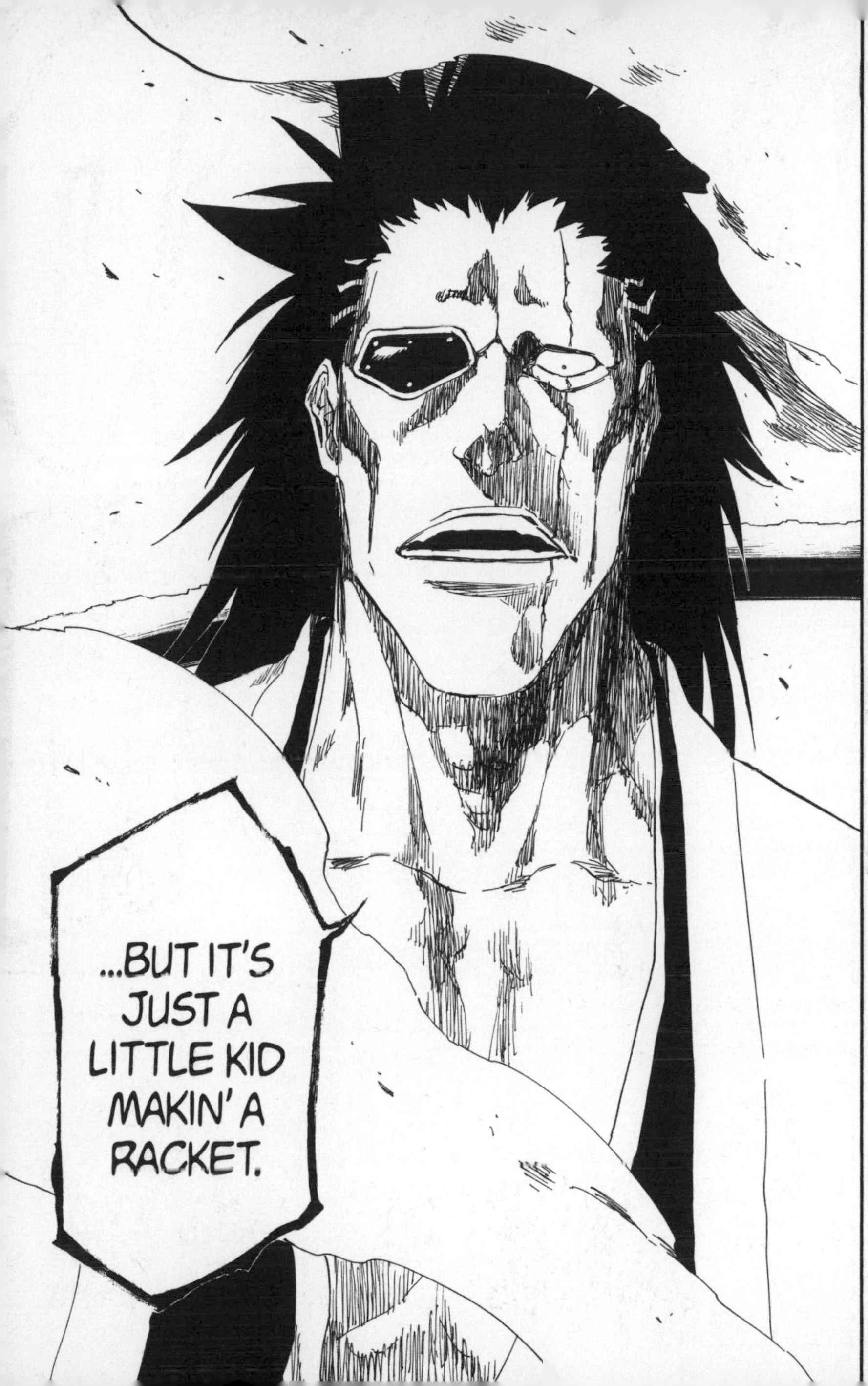
...BUT IT'S JUST A LITTLE KID MAKIN' A RACKET.

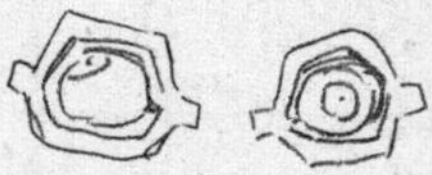

FAREWELL

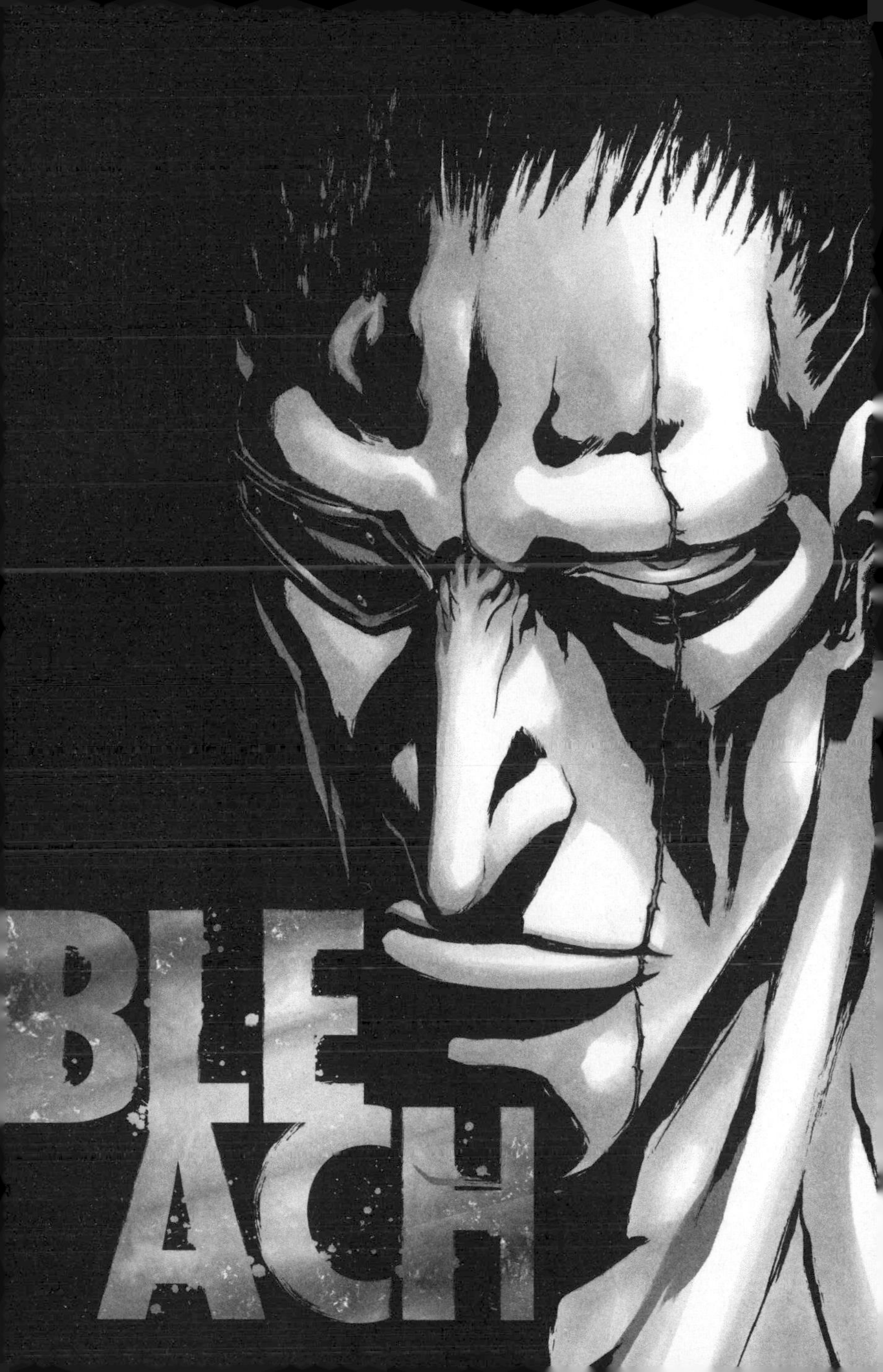
BLE
ACH

BLEACH
ブリーチ

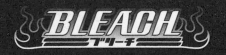

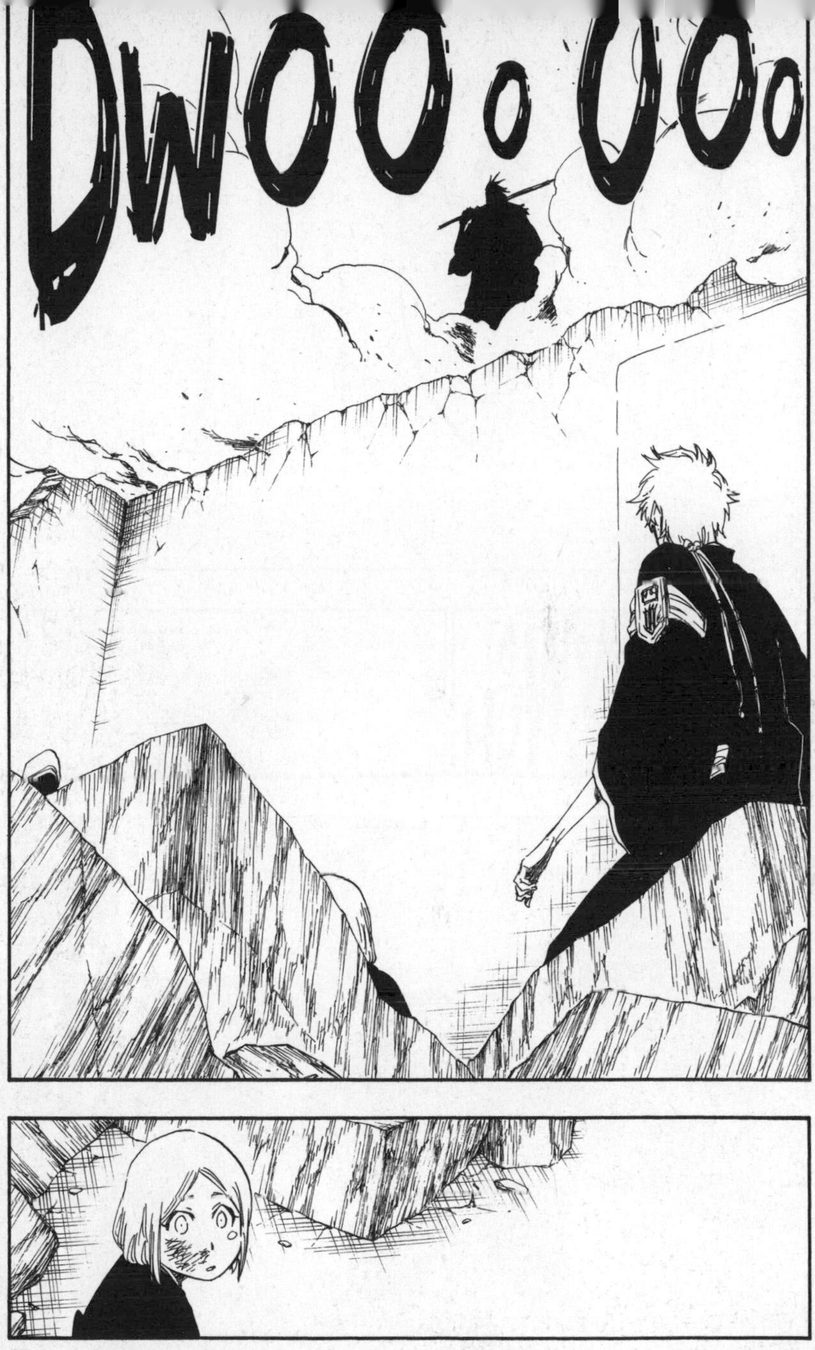
DWOOOOOOO

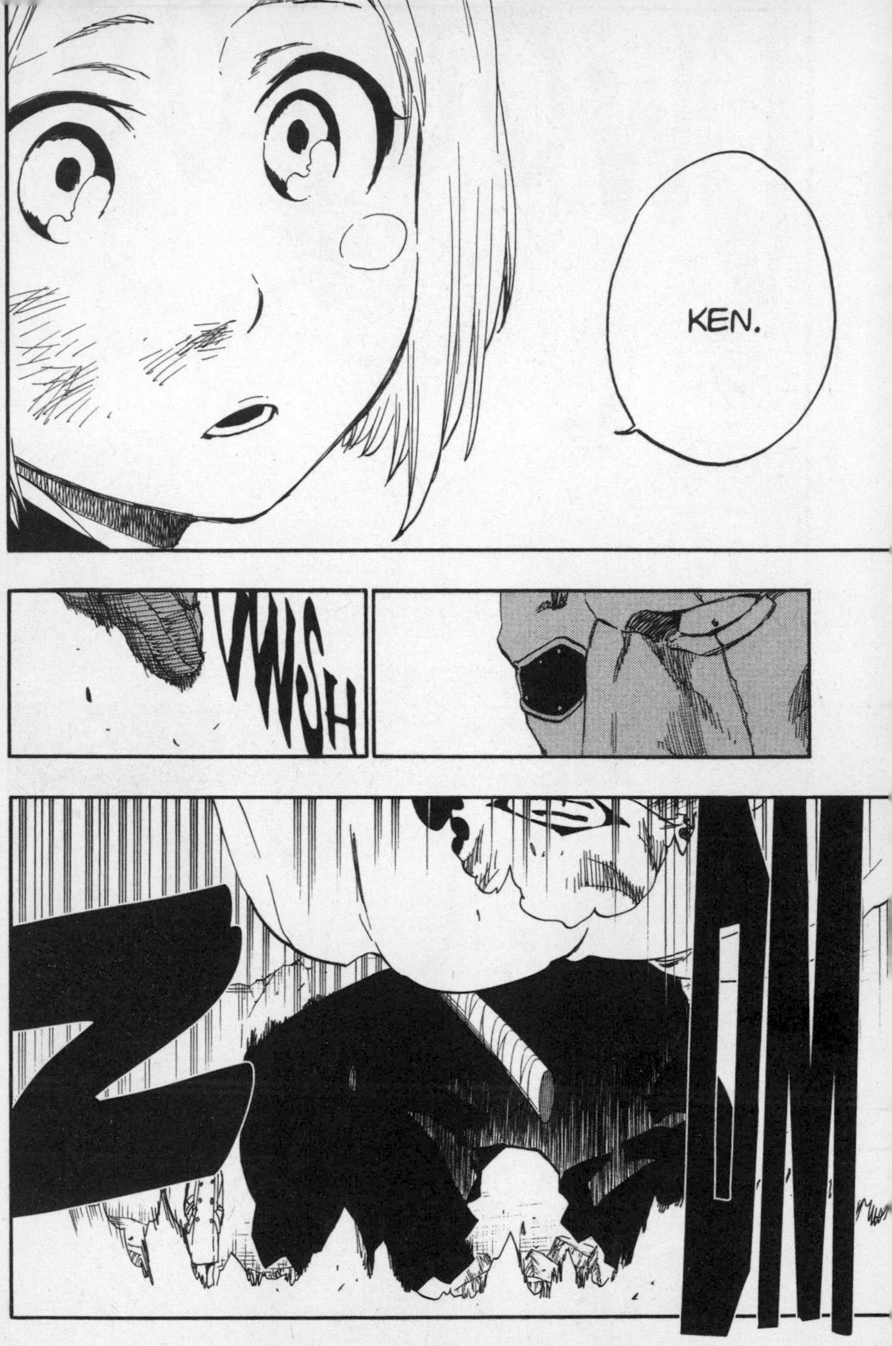
KEN.
VWSH

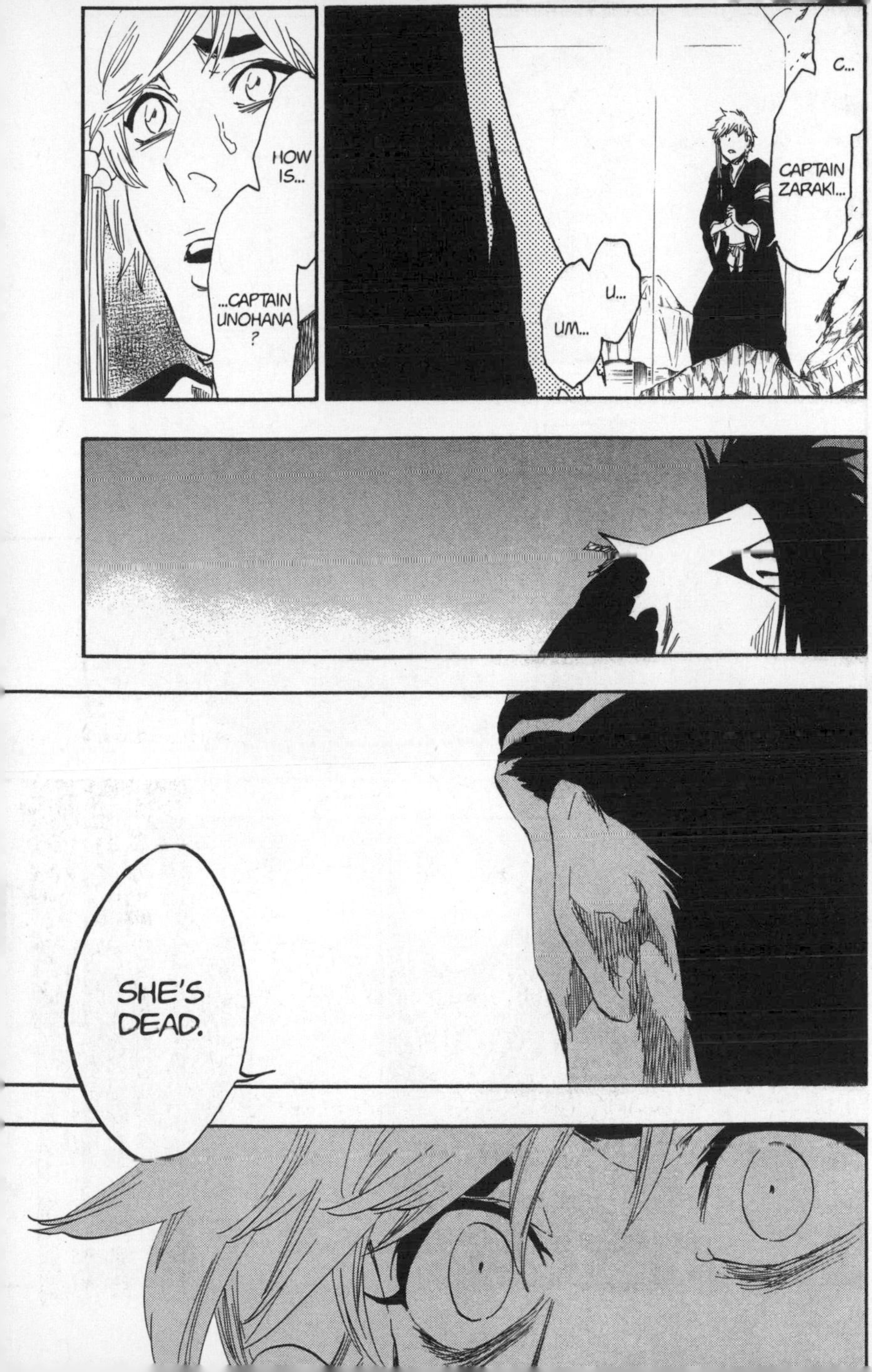
C...
CAPTAIN ZARAKI...
U...
UM...
HOW IS...
...CAPTAIN UNOHANA ?
SHE'S DEAD.

I...

...SEE.

I KILLED HER.

PLOP

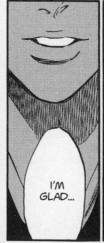

I'M GLAD...

IF YOU HATE ME...

GO AHEAD AND SLAY ME.

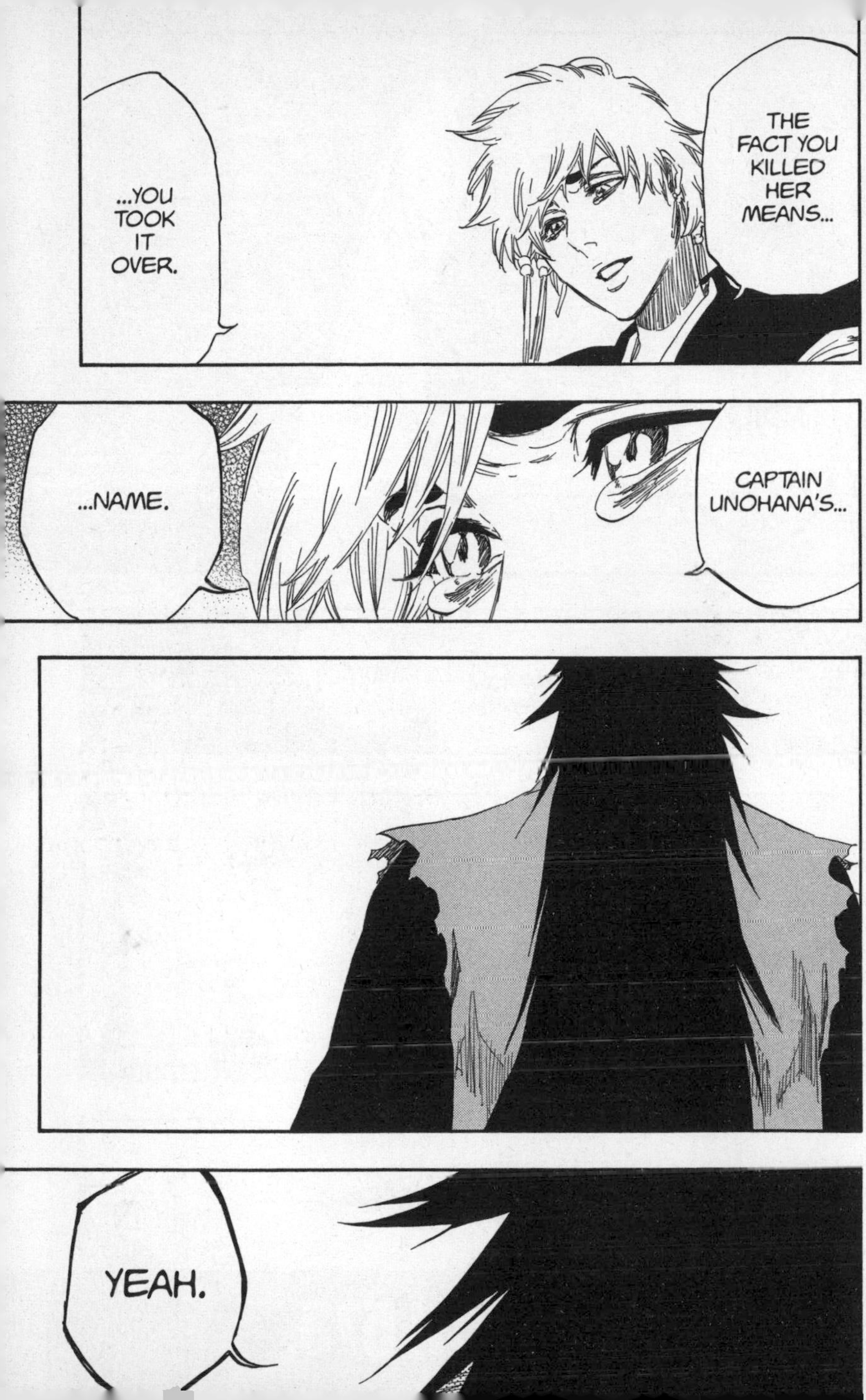
THE FACT YOU KILLED HER MEANS...
...YOU TOOK IT OVER.
CAPTAIN UNOHANA'S...
...NAME.
YEAH.

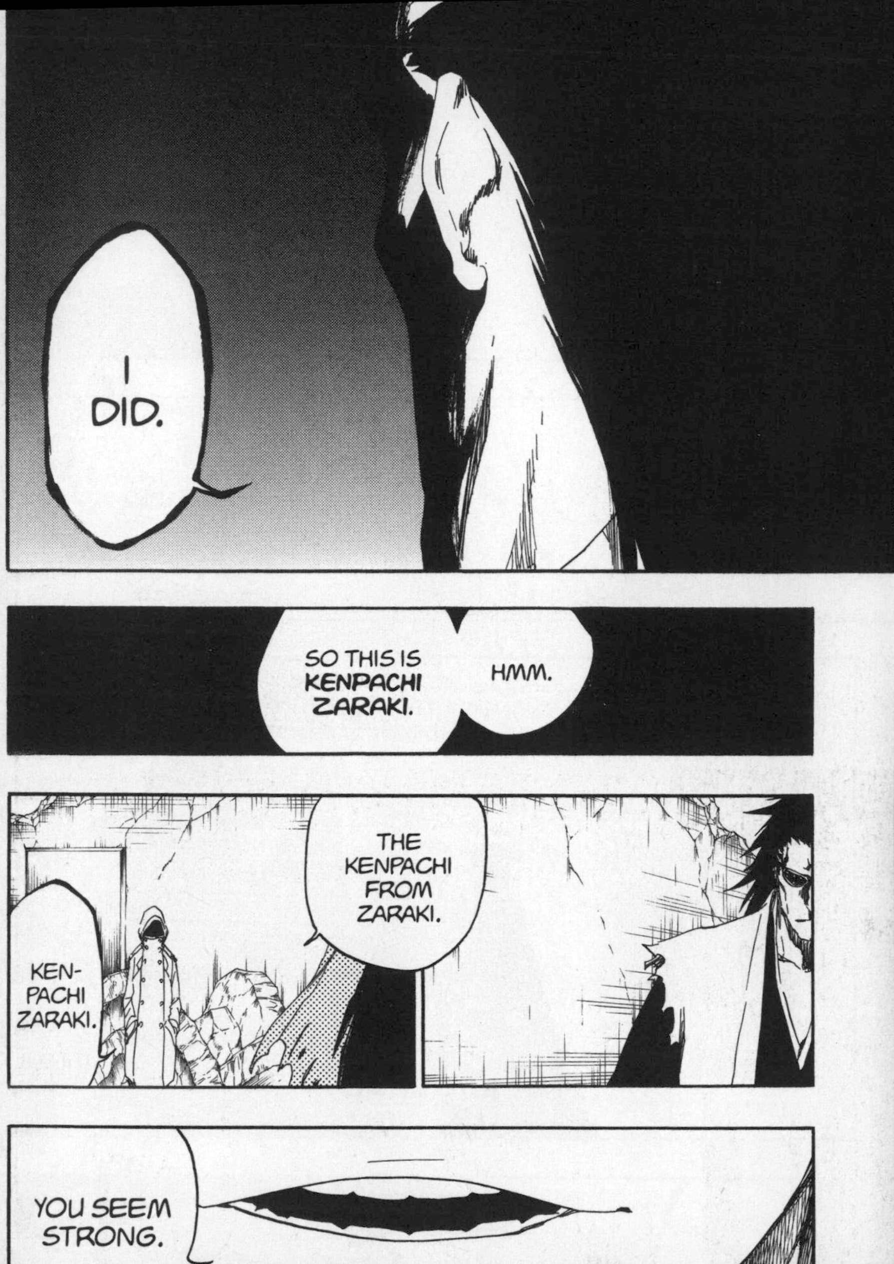
I DID.
HMM.
SO THIS IS KENPACHI ZARAKI.
THE KENPACHI FROM ZARAKI.
KEN-PACHI ZARAKI.
YOU SEEM STRONG.

BLEACH 573.

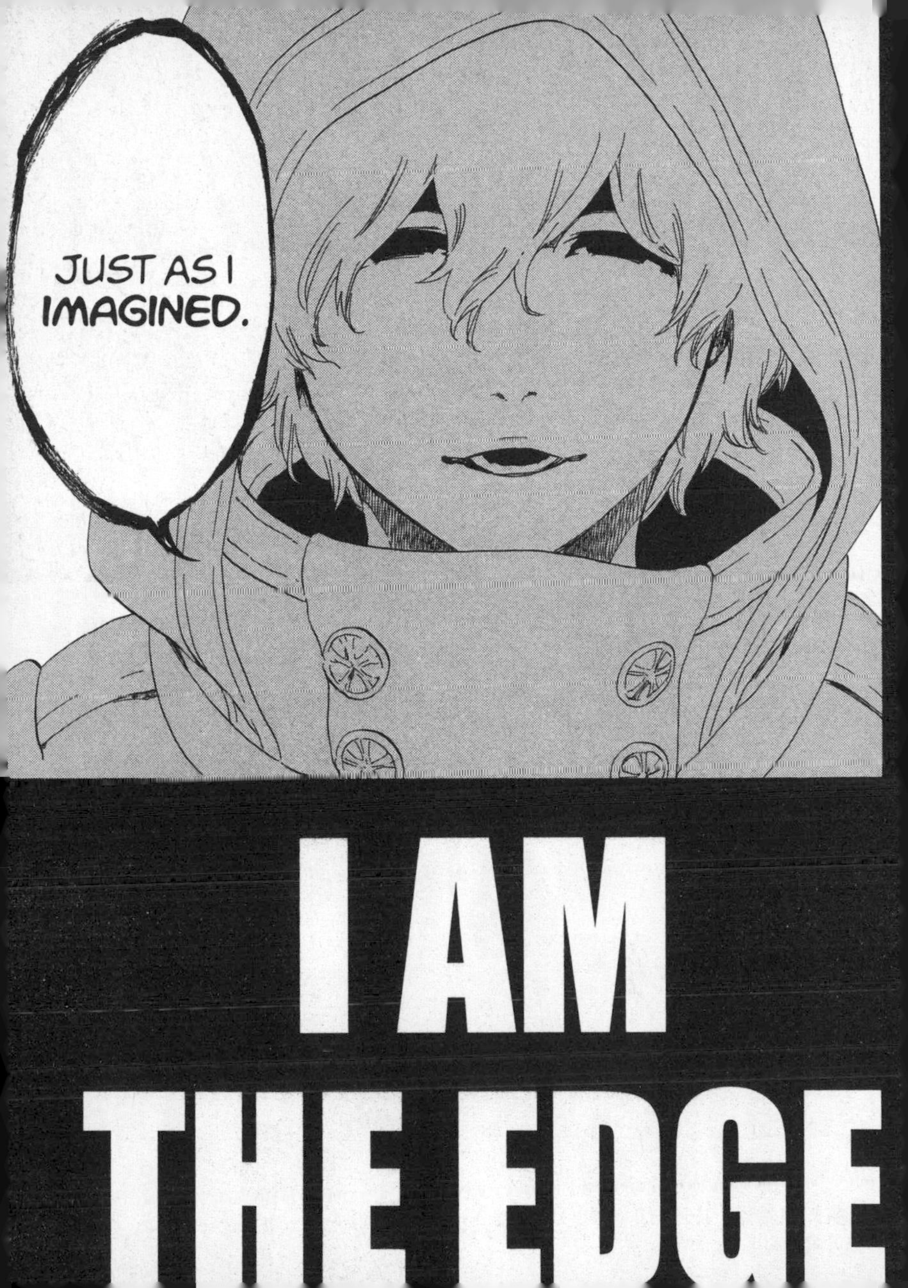
JUST AS I IMAGINED.
I AM THE EDGE

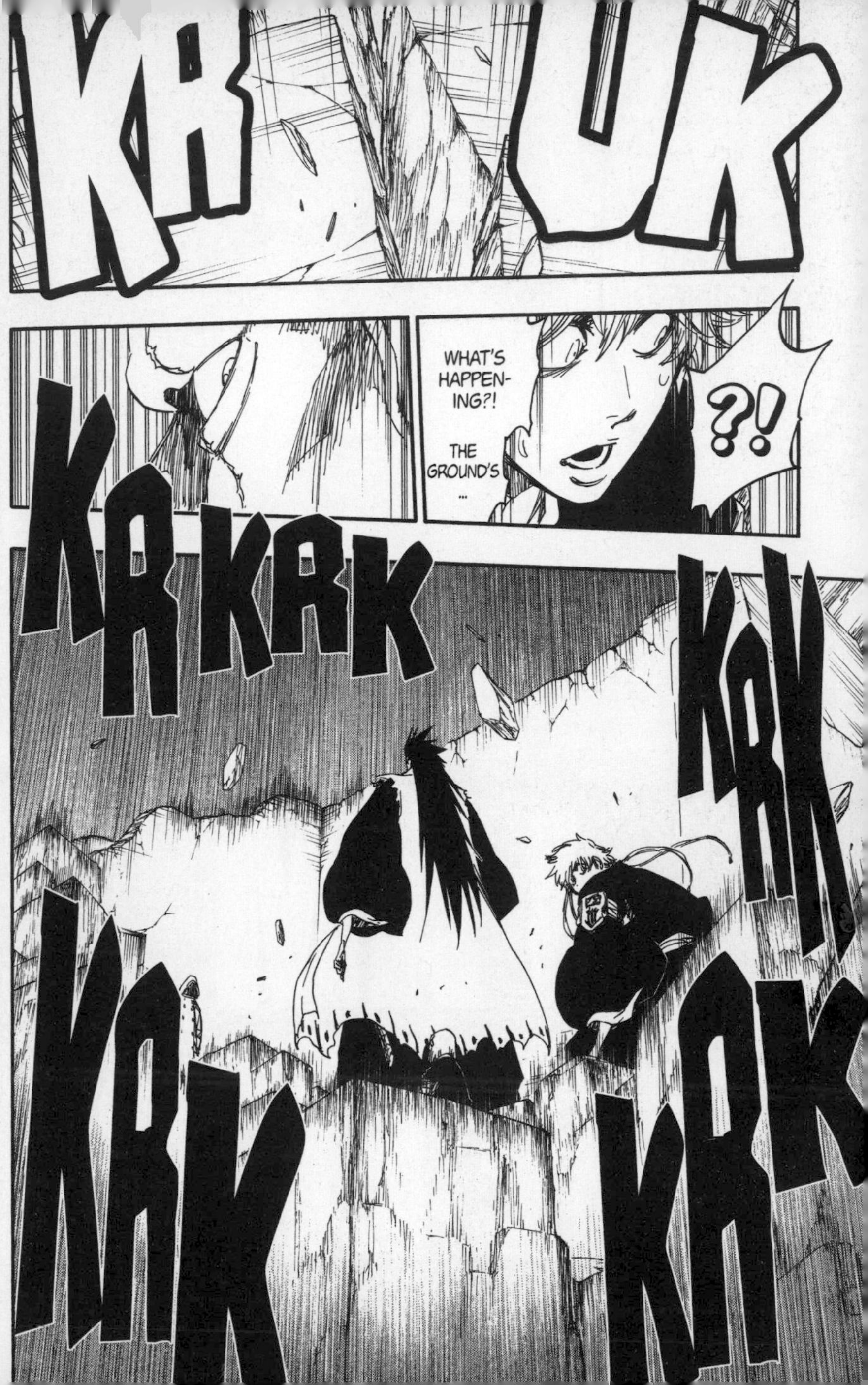
KA
UK
?!
WHAT'S HAPPEN-ING?!
THE GROUND'S ...
KRKRK
KRK
KRK
KRK
KRK

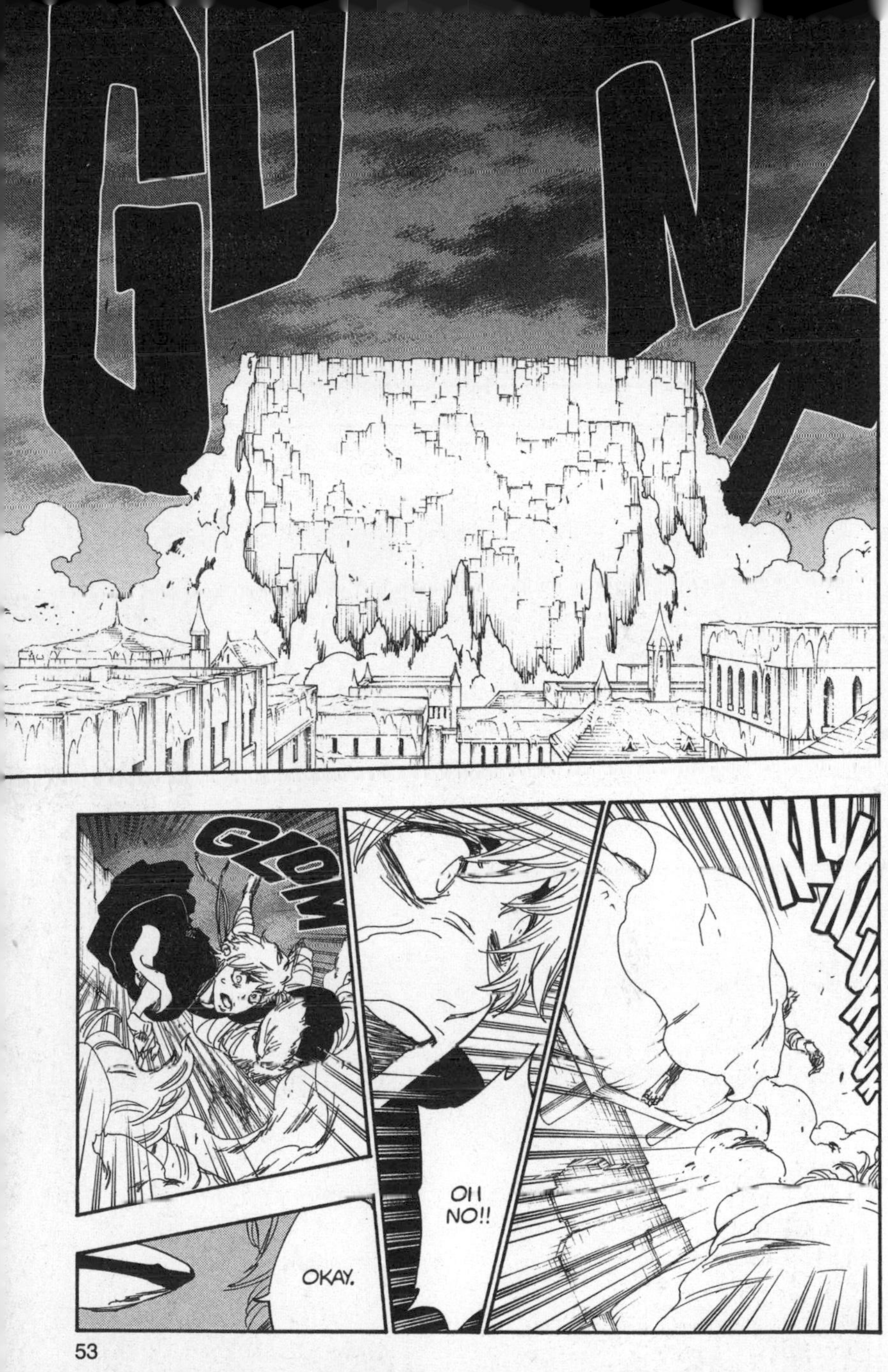
GUN
KLUK KLUK KLUK
OH NO!!
GLOM
OKAY.

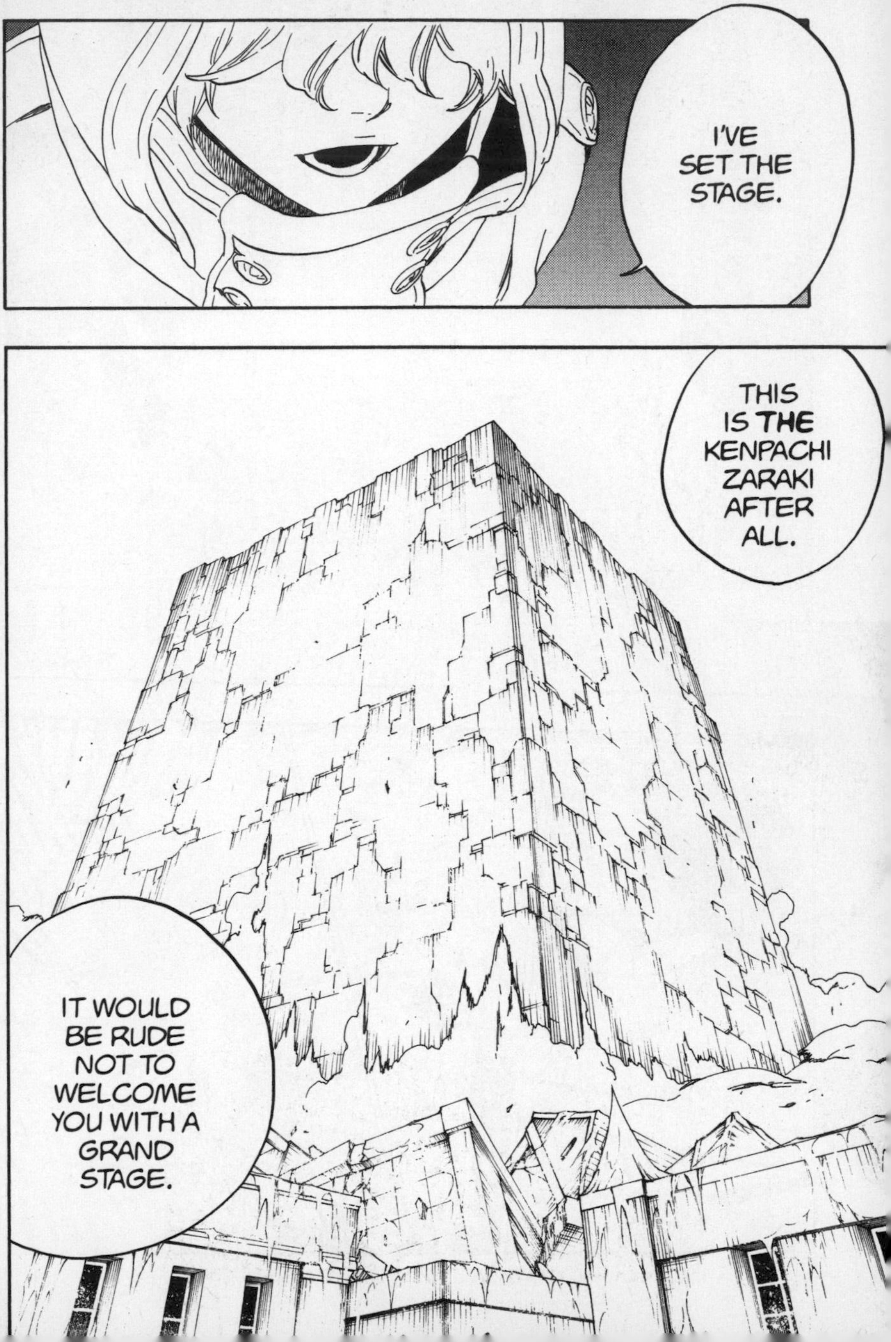
I'VE SET THE STAGE.
THIS IS THE KENPACHI ZARAKI AFTER ALL.
IT WOULD BE RUDE NOT TO WELCOME YOU WITH A GRAND STAGE.

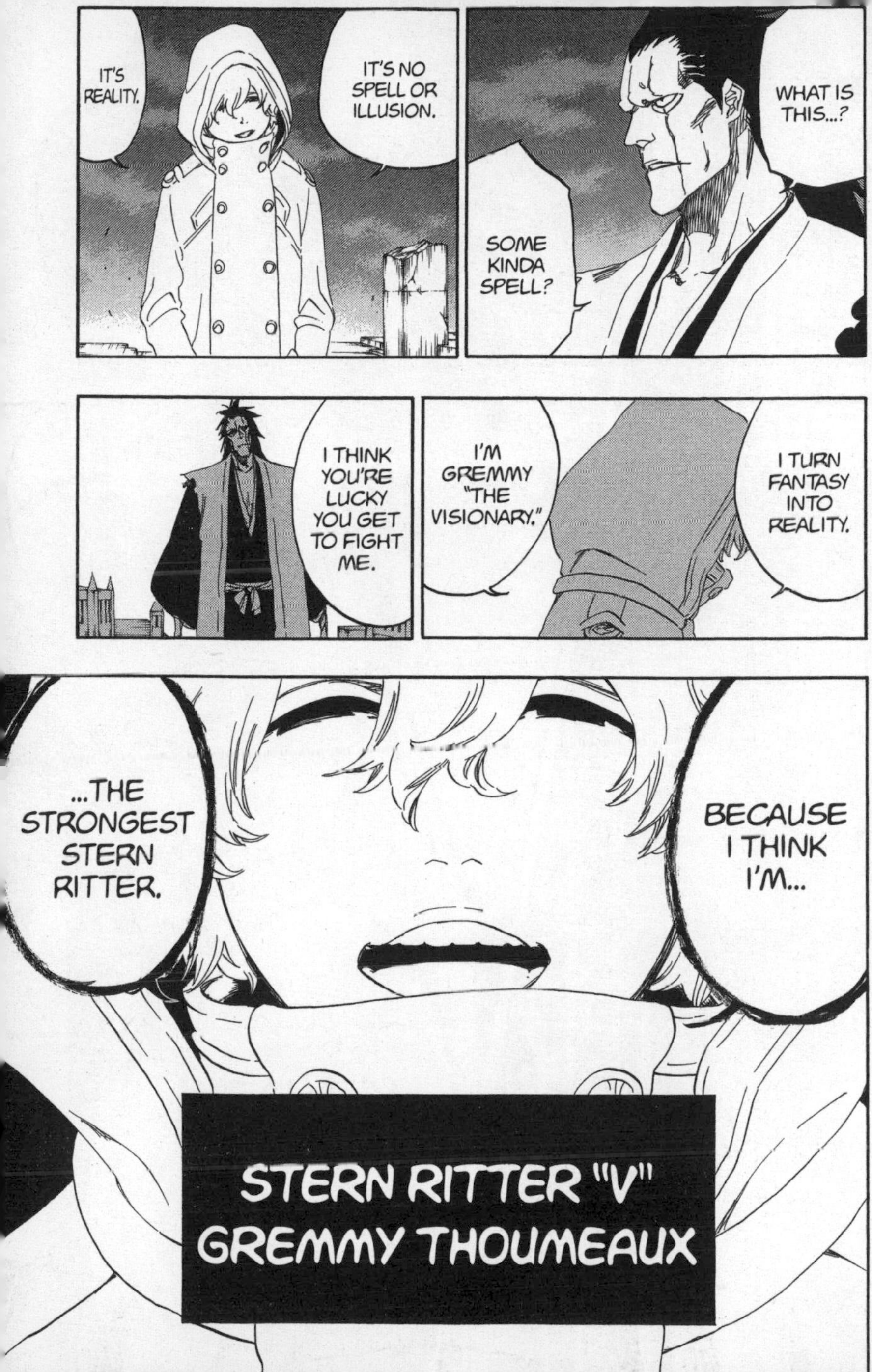
WHAT IS THIS...?
SOME KINDA SPELL?
IT'S NO SPELL OR ILLUSION.
IT'S REALITY.
I TURN FANTASY INTO REALITY.
I'M GREMMY "THE VISIONARY."
I THINK YOU'RE LUCKY YOU GET TO FIGHT ME.
BECAUSE I THINK I'M...
...THE STRONGEST STERN RITTER.
STERN RITTER "V" GREMMY THOUMEAUX

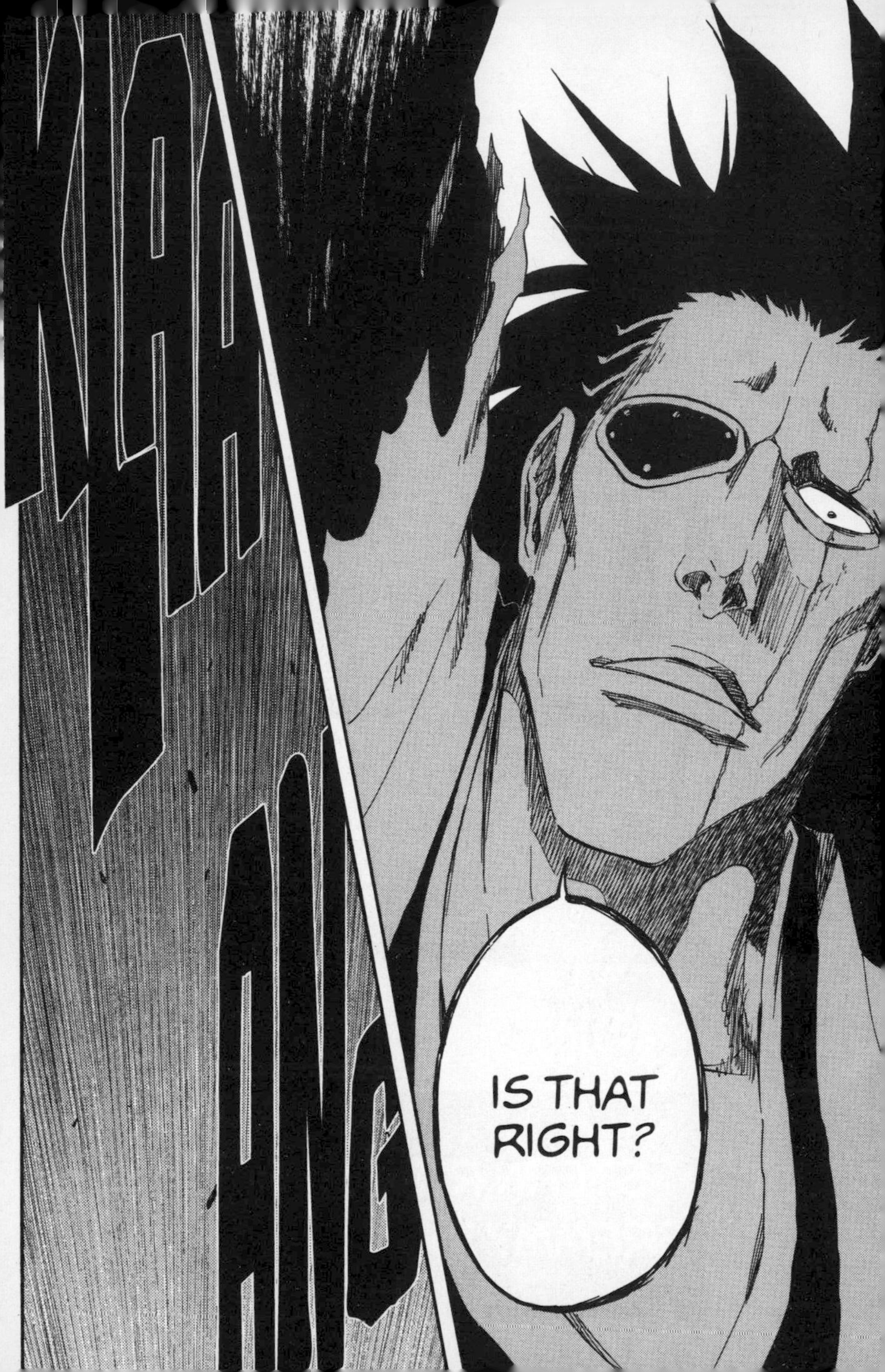
IS THAT RIGHT?

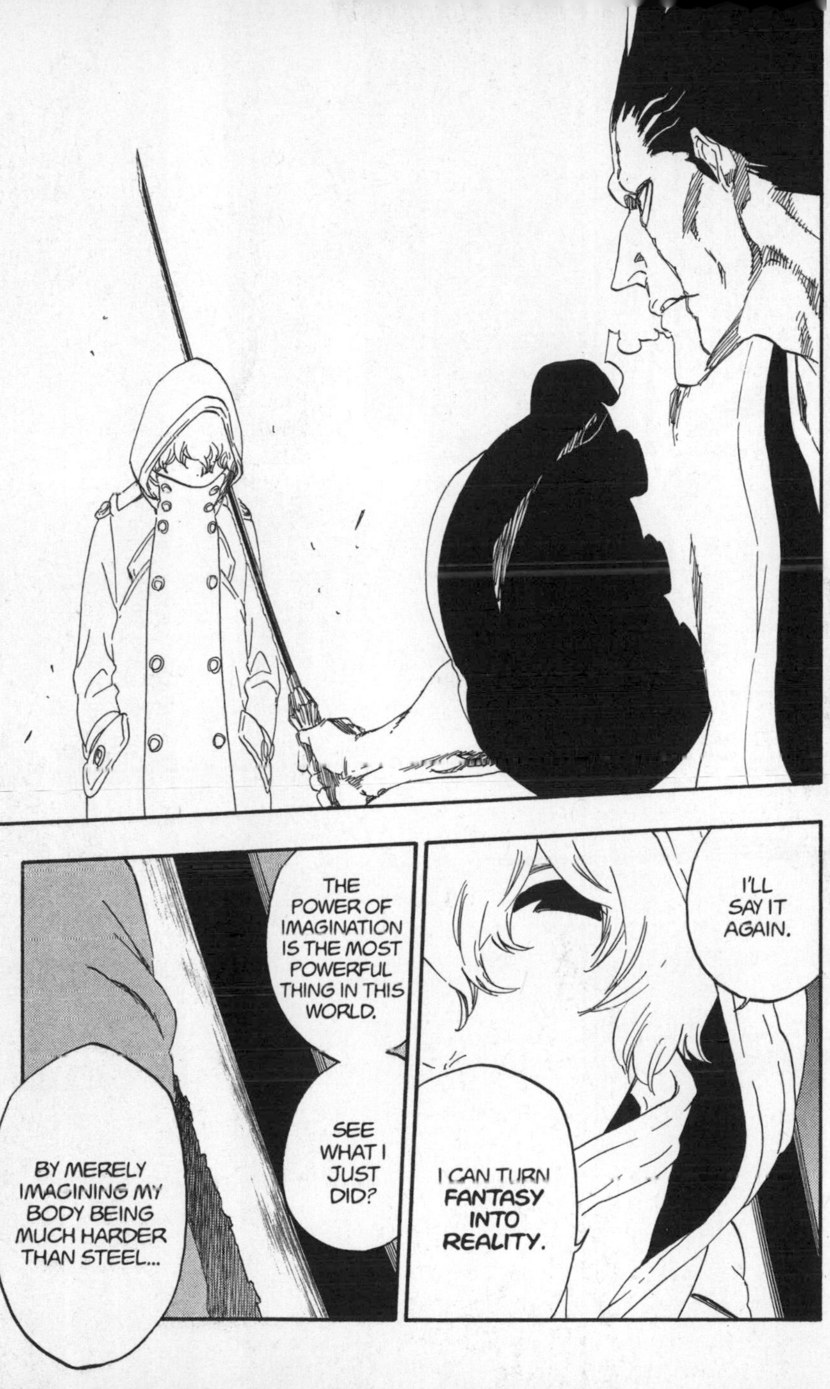
I'LL SAY IT AGAIN.
I CAN TURN FANTASY INTO REALITY.
THE POWER OF IMAGINATION IS THE MOST POWERFUL THING IN THIS WORLD.
SEE WHAT I JUST DID?
BY MERELY IMAGINING MY BODY BEING MUCH HARDER THAN STEEL...

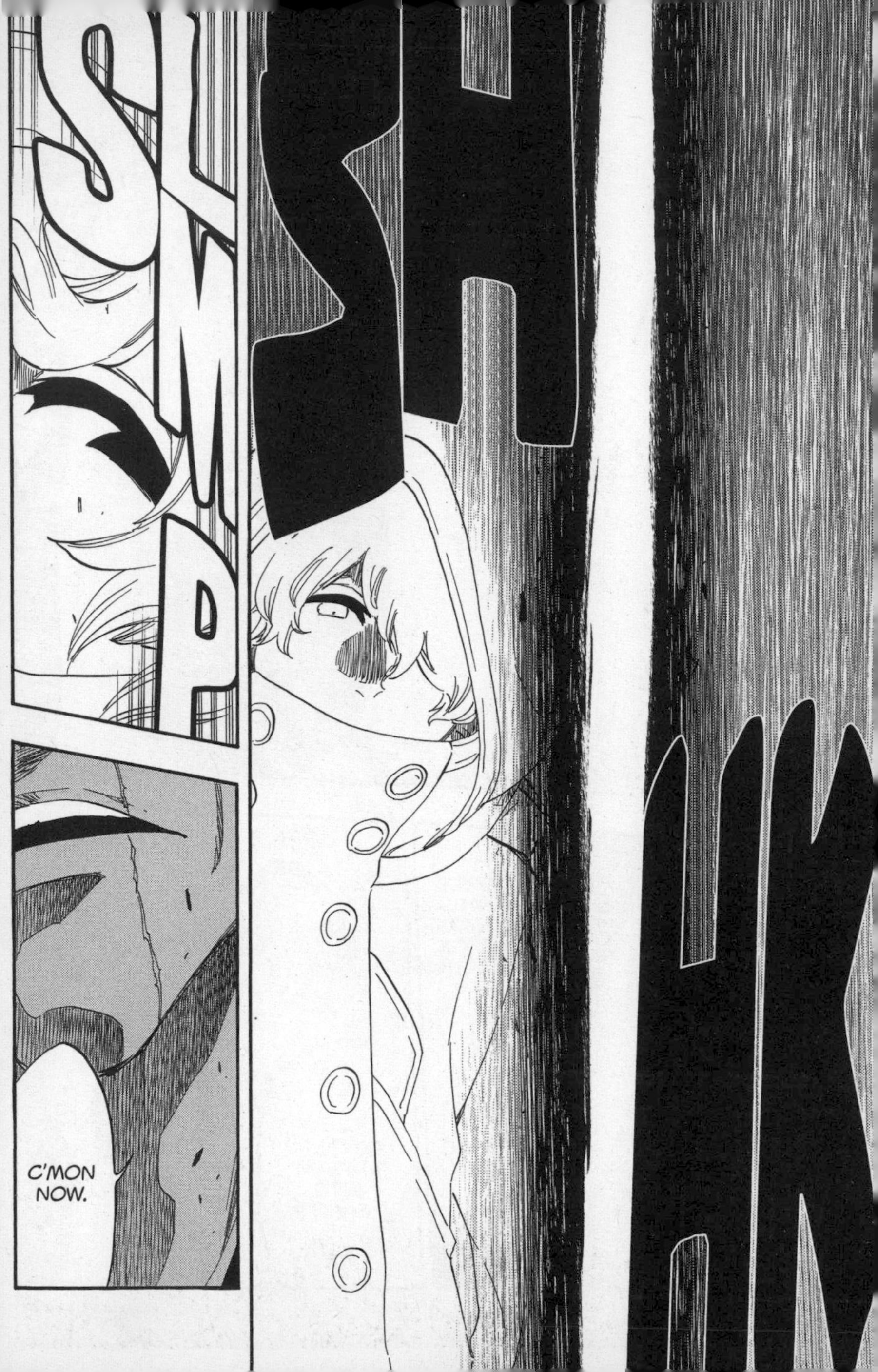
C'MON NOW.

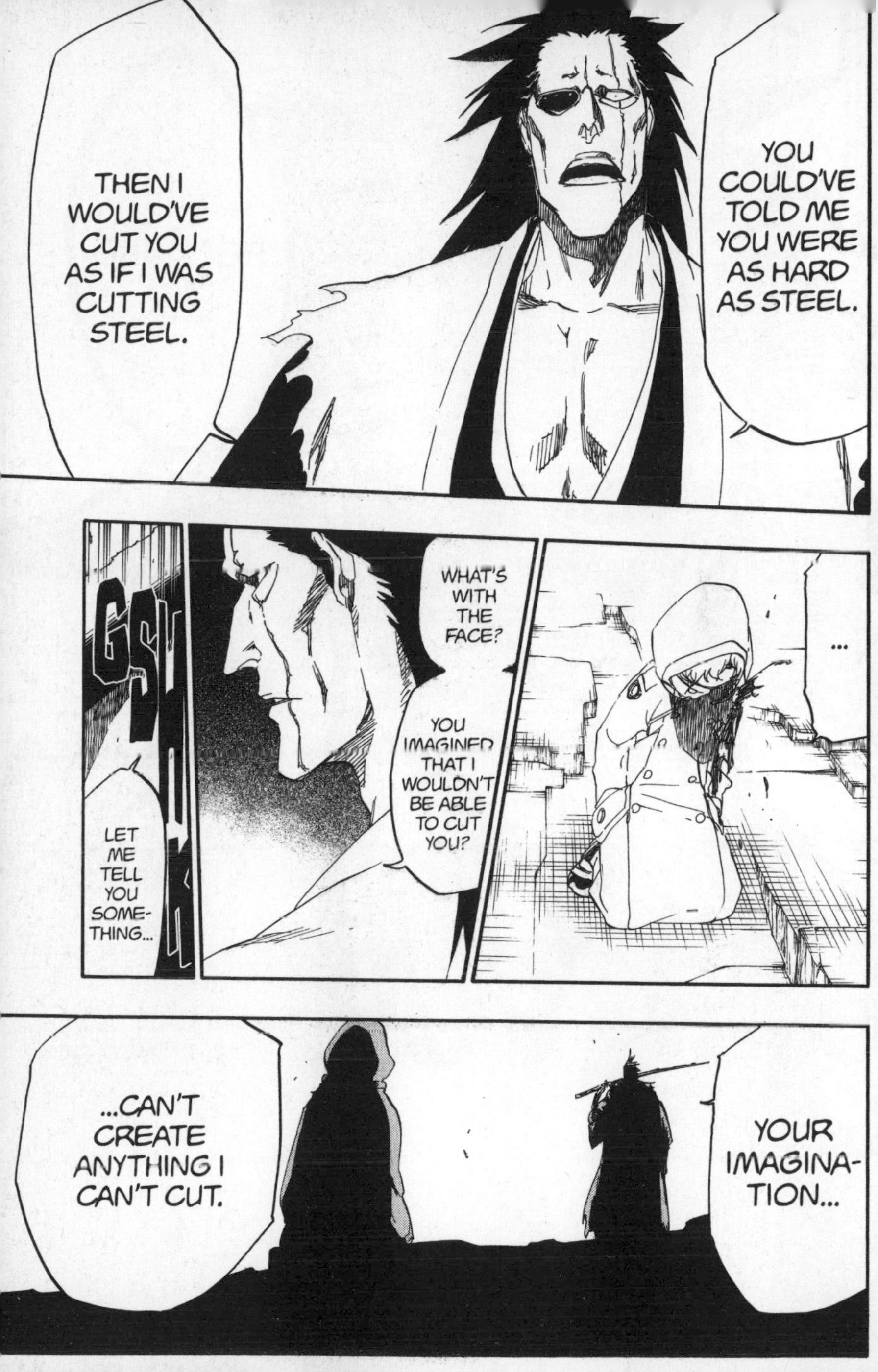
YOU COULD'VE TOLD ME YOU WERE AS HARD AS STEEL.
THEN I WOULD'VE CUT YOU AS IF I WAS CUTTING STEEL.
...
WHAT'S WITH THE FACE?
YOU IMAGINED THAT I WOULDN'T BE ABLE TO CUT YOU?
LET ME TELL YOU SOME-THING...
YOUR IMAGINA-TION...
...CAN'T CREATE ANYTHING I CAN'T CUT.

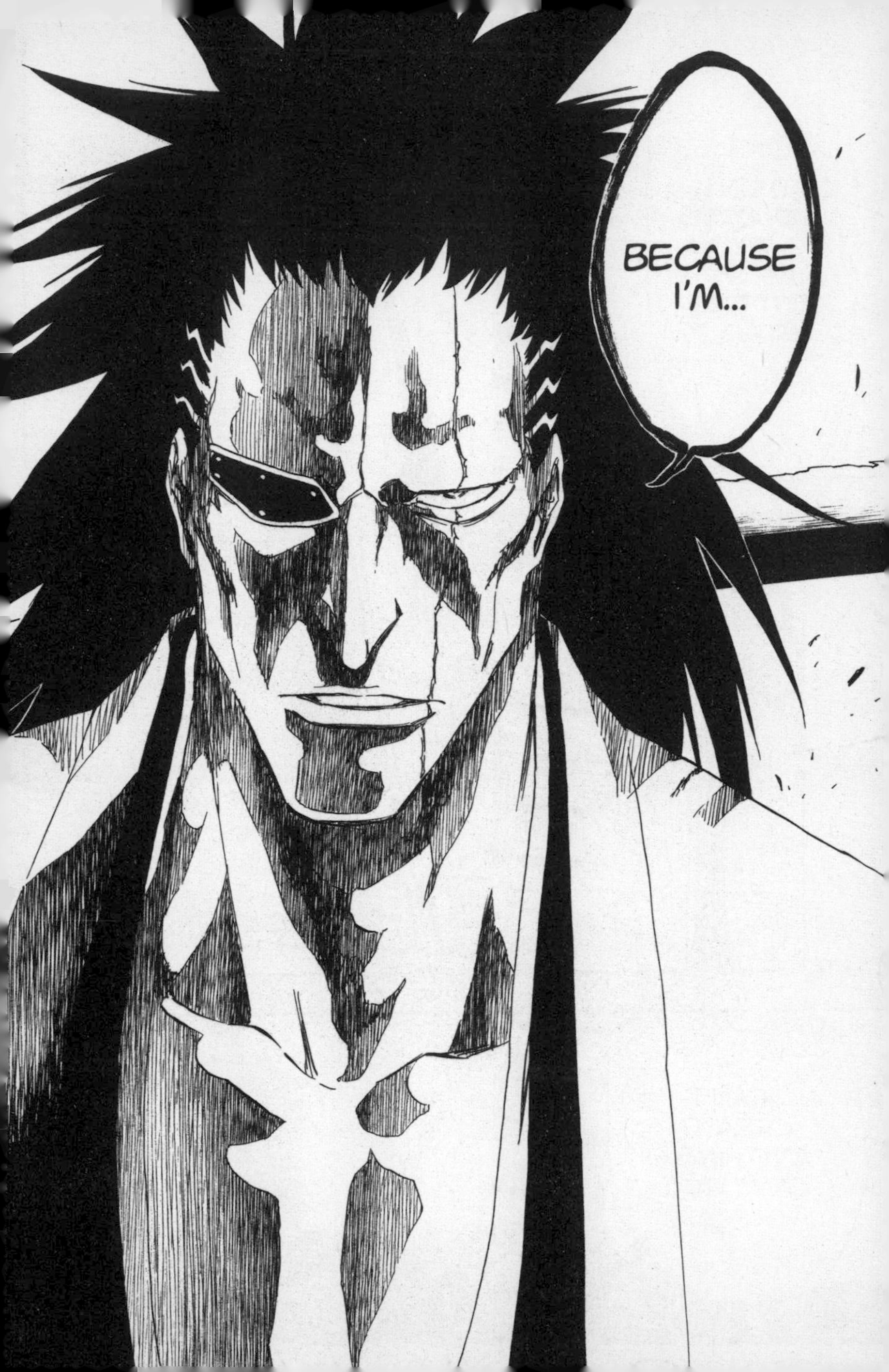
BECAUSE I'M...

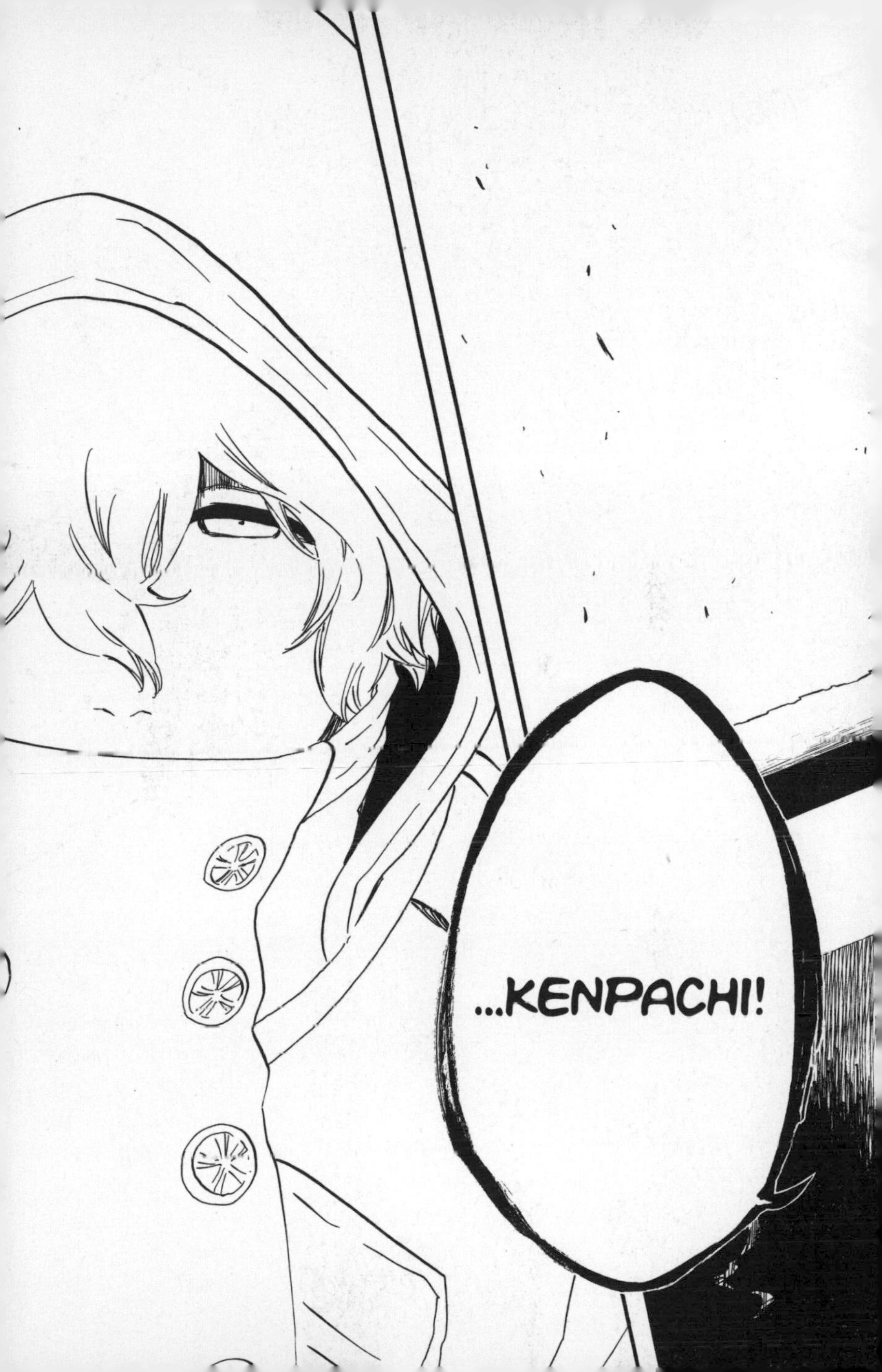
...KENPACHI!

574. DEATH IN VISION

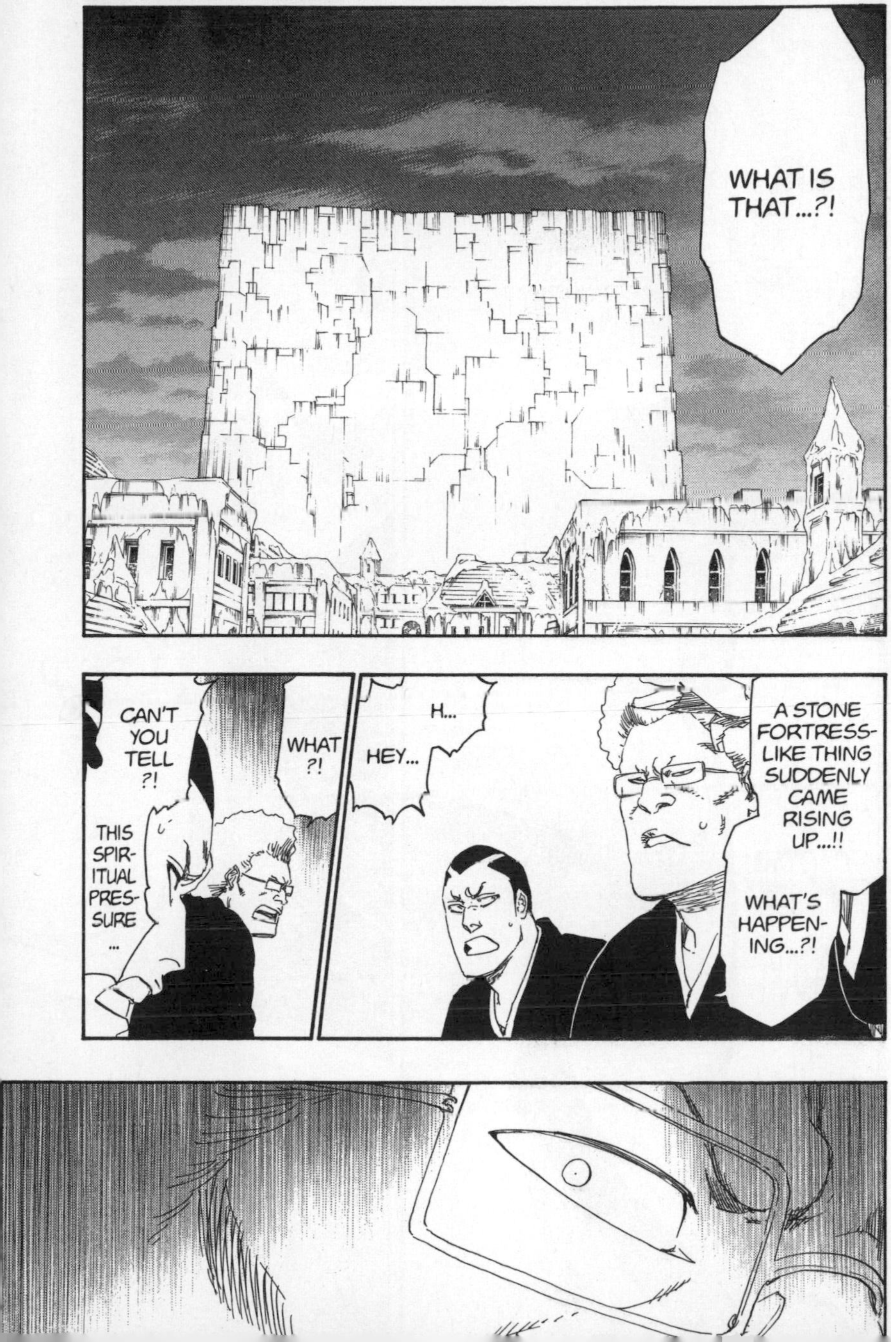
WHAT IS THAT...?!
A STONE FORTRESS-LIKE THING SUDDENLY CAME RISING UP...!!
WHAT'S HAPPENING...?!
H... HEY...
WHAT?!
CAN'T YOU TELL?!
THIS SPIRITUAL PRESSURE...

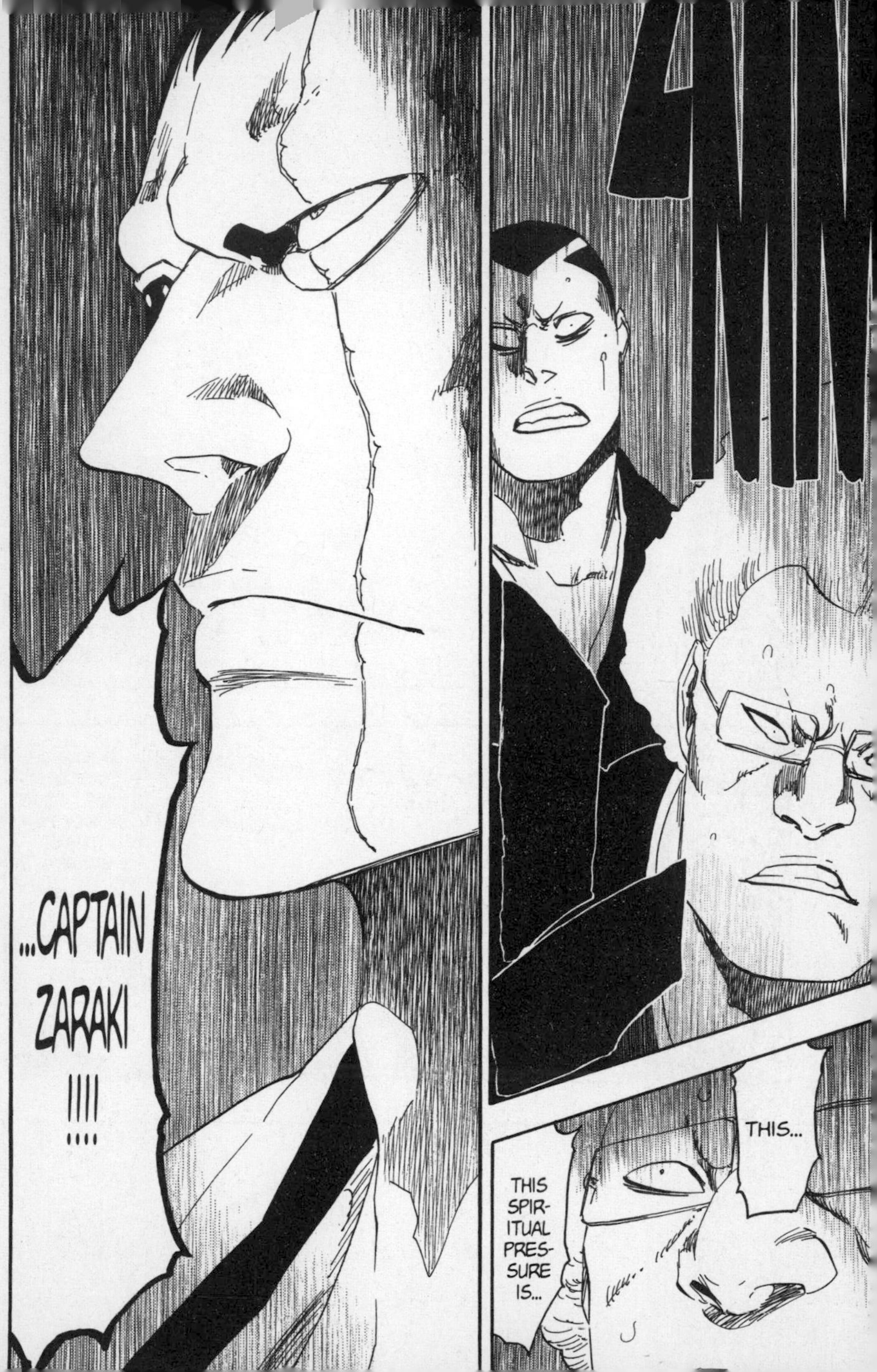
THIS...
THIS SPIRITUAL PRESSURE IS...
...CAPTAIN ZARAKI !!!!

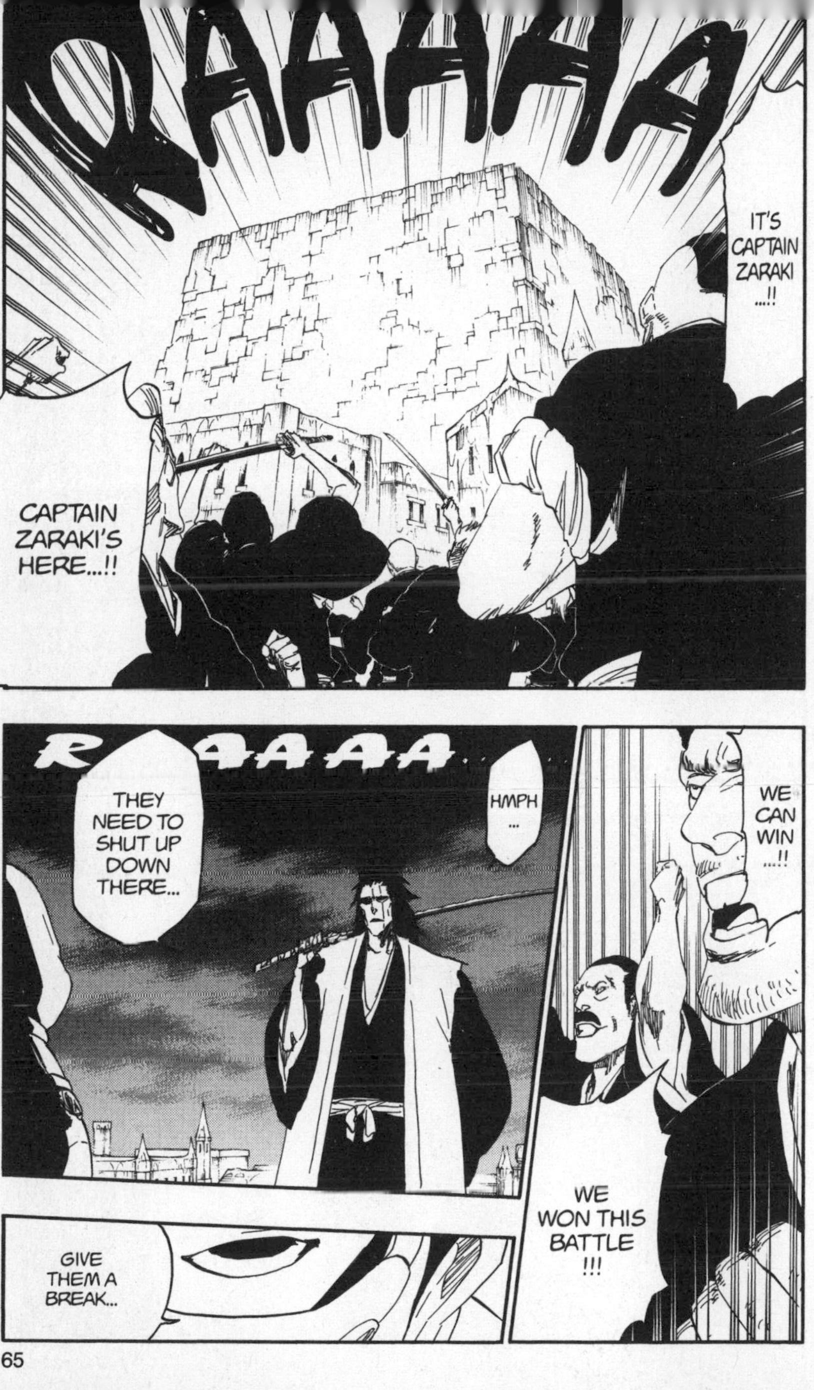
AAAAAA
IT'S CAPTAIN ZARAKI ...!!
CAPTAIN ZARAKI'S HERE...!!
WE CAN WIN ...!!
WE WON THIS BATTLE !!!
R AAAAA...
HMPH ...
THEY NEED TO SHUT UP DOWN THERE...
GIVE THEM A BREAK...

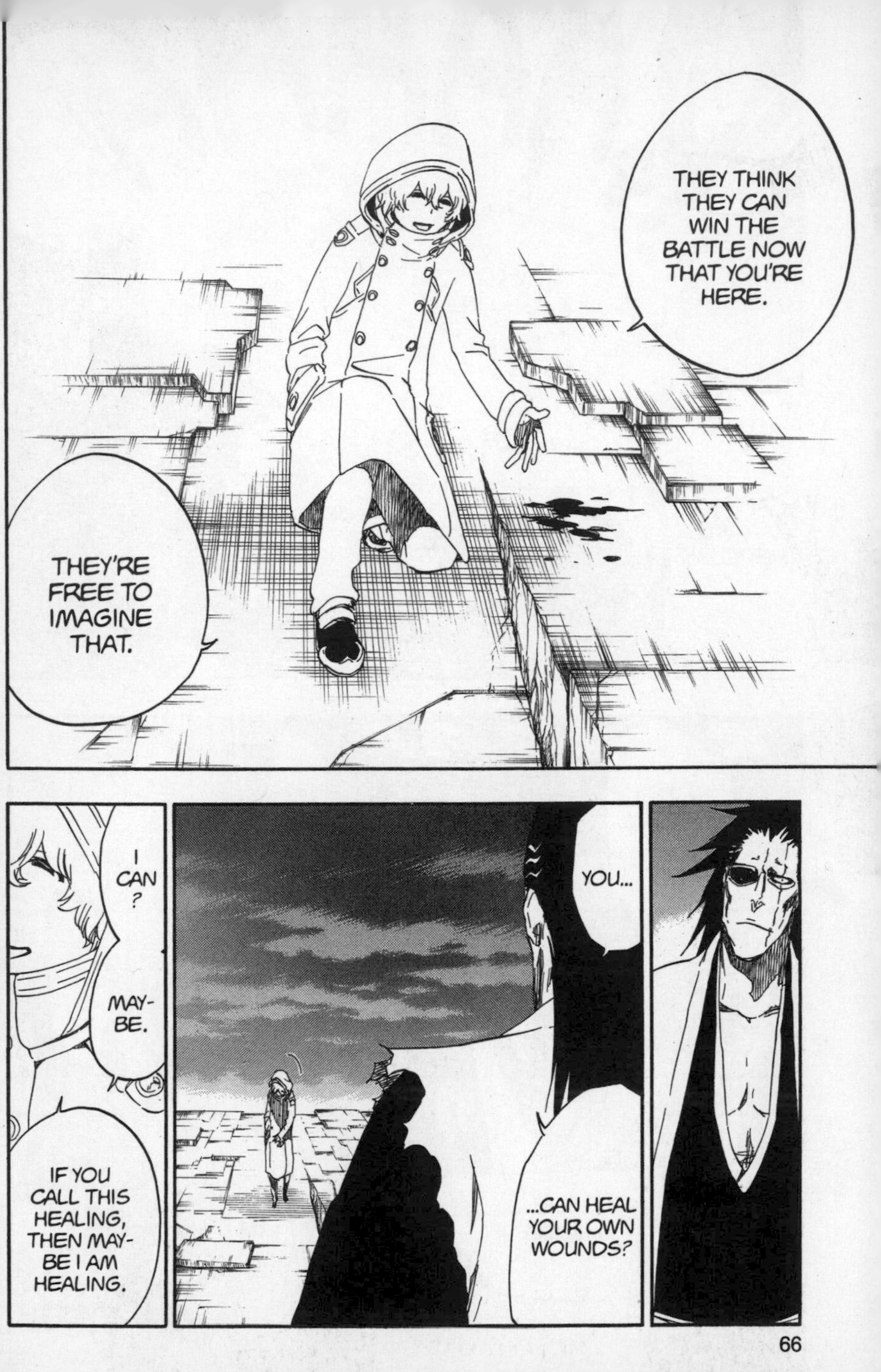
THEY THINK THEY CAN WIN THE BATTLE NOW THAT YOU'RE HERE.
THEY'RE FREE TO IMAGINE THAT.
YOU...
...CAN HEAL YOUR OWN WOUNDS?
I CAN ?
MAY-BE.
IF YOU CALL THIS HEALING, THEN MAY-BE I AM HEALING.

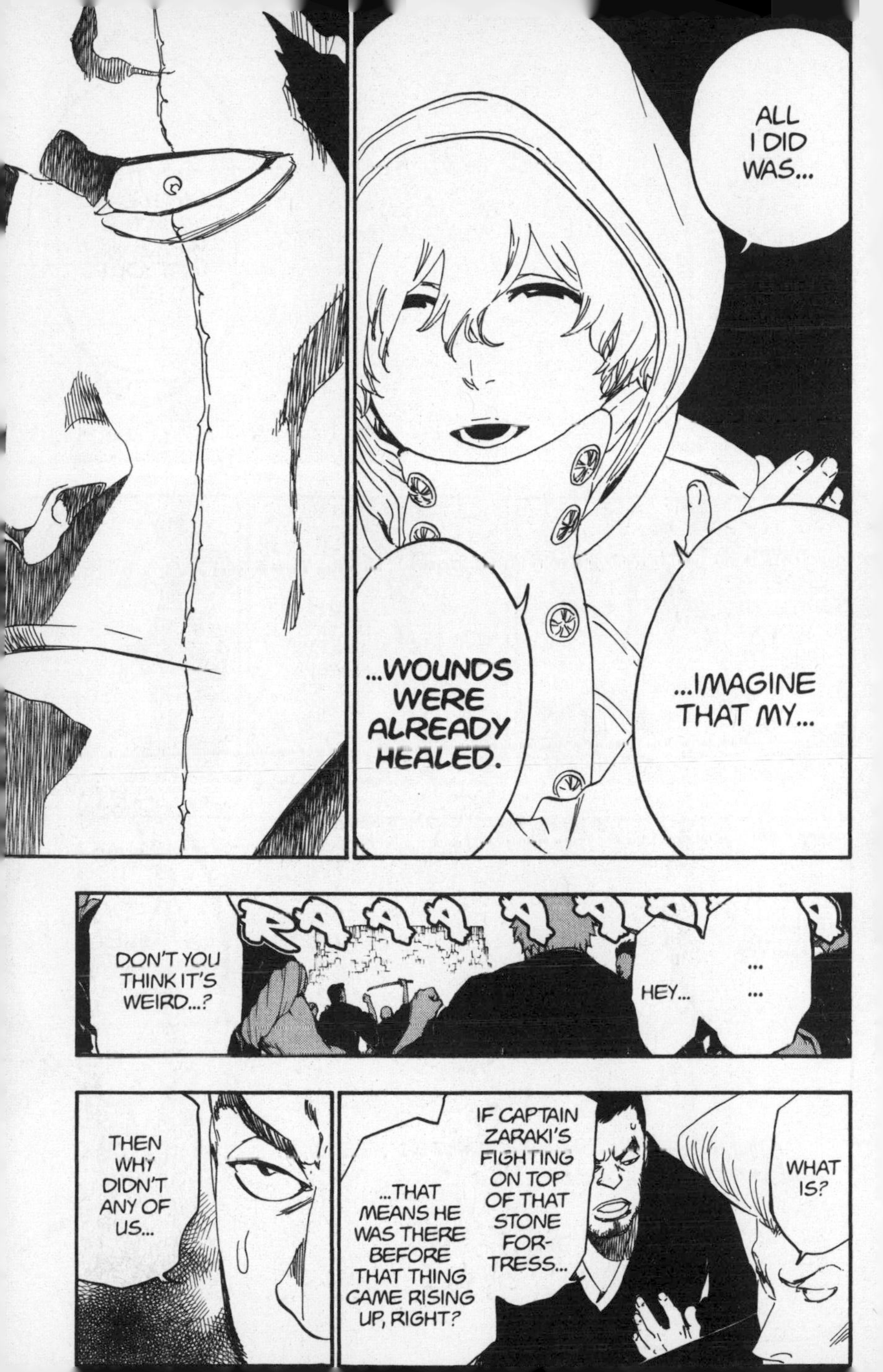
ALL I DID WAS...
...IMAGINE THAT MY...
...WOUNDS WERE ALREADY HEALED.
...
...
RAAAAAAAA
HEY...
DON'T YOU THINK IT'S WEIRD...?
WHAT IS?
IF CAPTAIN ZARAKI'S FIGHTING ON TOP OF THAT STONE FOR-TRESS...
...THAT MEANS HE WAS THERE BEFORE THAT THING CAME RISING UP, RIGHT?
THEN WHY DIDN'T ANY OF US...

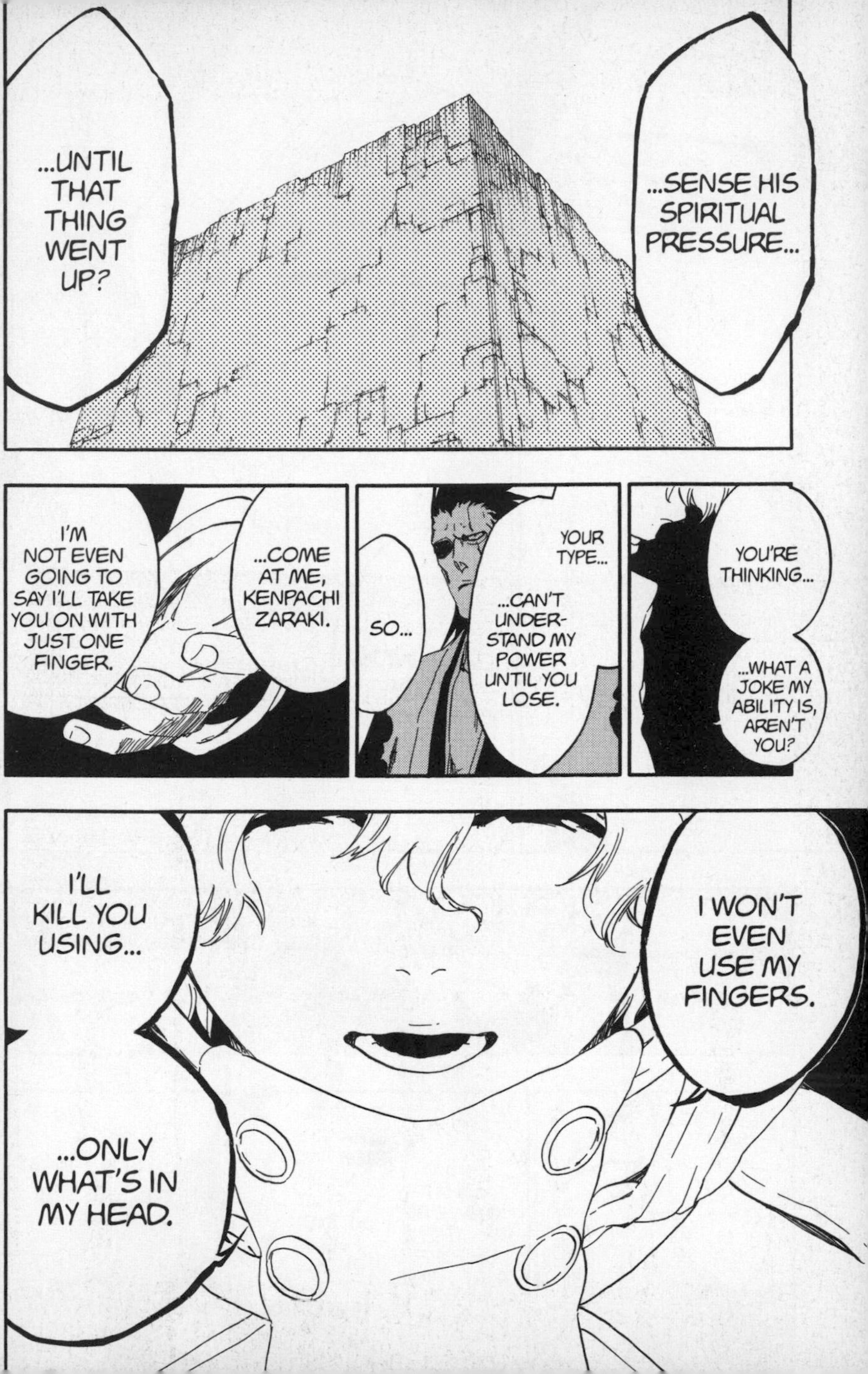
...SENSE HIS SPIRITUAL PRESSURE...
...UNTIL THAT THING WENT UP?
YOU'RE THINKING...
...WHAT A JOKE MY ABILITY IS, AREN'T YOU?
YOUR TYPE...
...CAN'T UNDER-STAND MY POWER UNTIL YOU LOSE.
SO...
...COME AT ME, KENPACHI ZARAKI.
I'M NOT EVEN GOING TO SAY I'LL TAKE YOU ON WITH JUST ONE FINGER.
I WON'T EVEN USE MY FINGERS.
I'LL KILL YOU USING...
...ONLY WHAT'S IN MY HEAD.

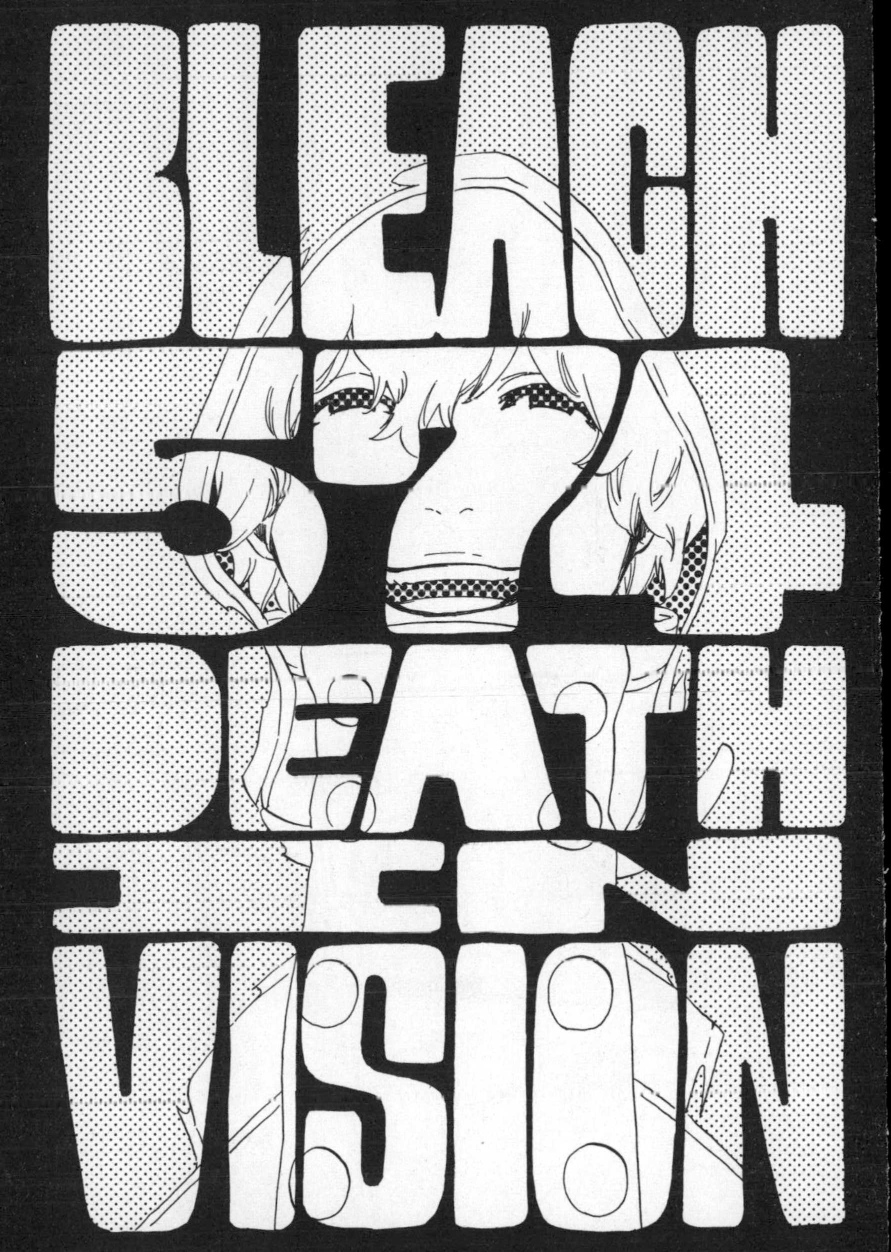
BLEACH
574
DEATH
VISION

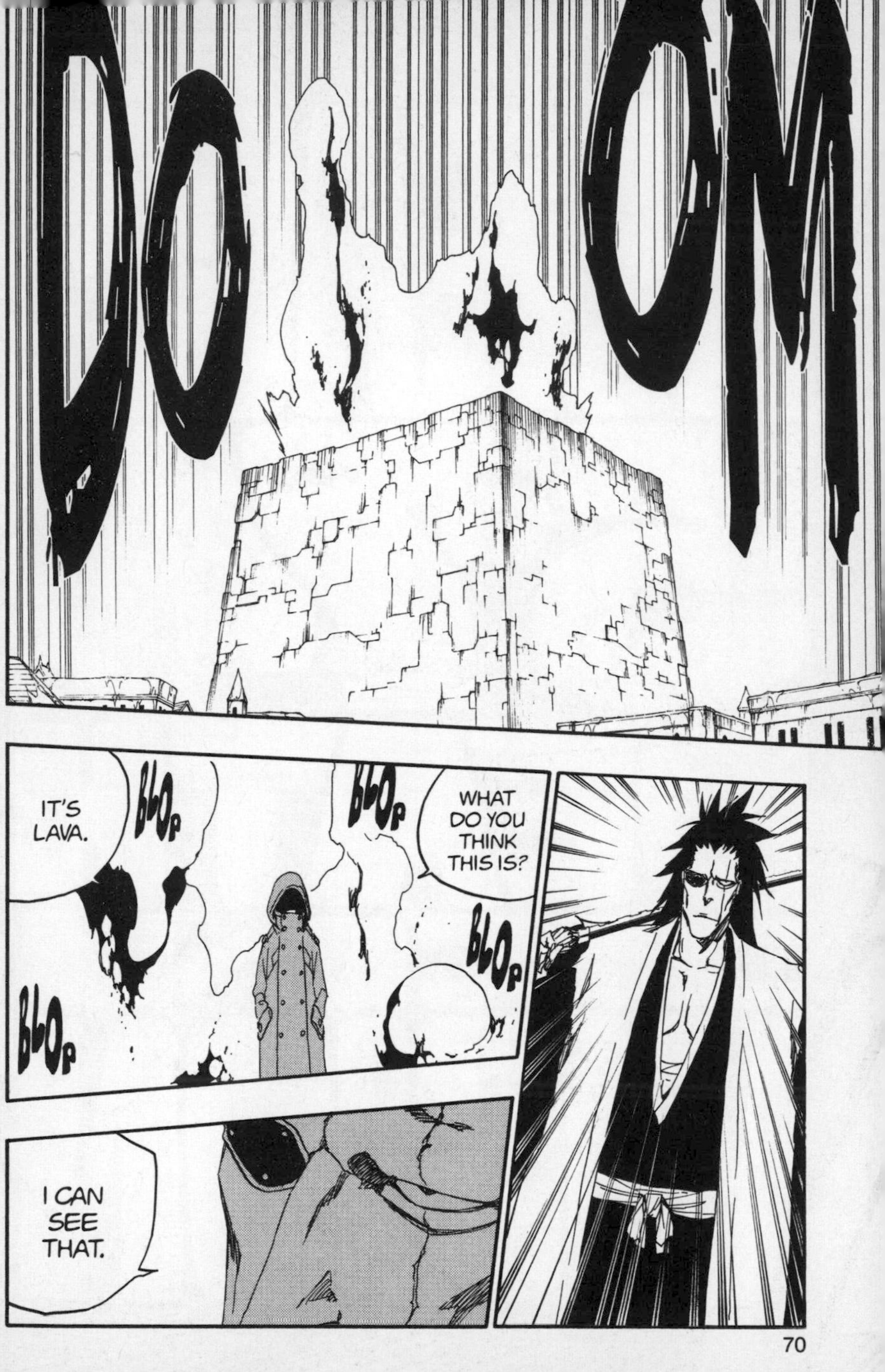
DO-OM
WHAT DO YOU THINK THIS IS?
BLOP
BLOP
IT'S LAVA.
BLOP
BLOP
I CAN SEE THAT.

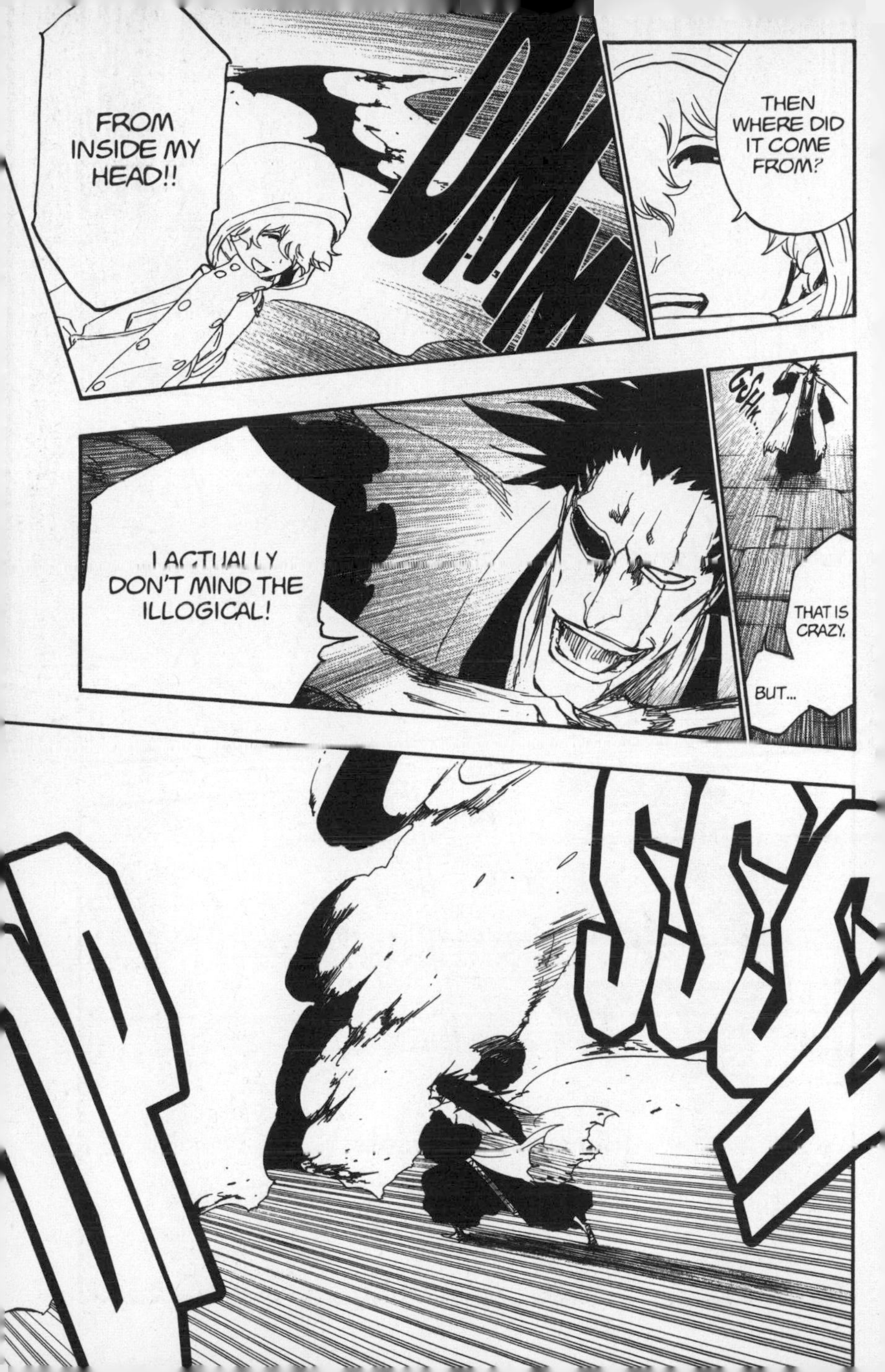
THEN WHERE DID IT COME FROM?
FROM INSIDE MY HEAD!!
THAT IS CRAZY.
BUT...
I ACTUALLY DON'T MIND THE ILLOGICAL!

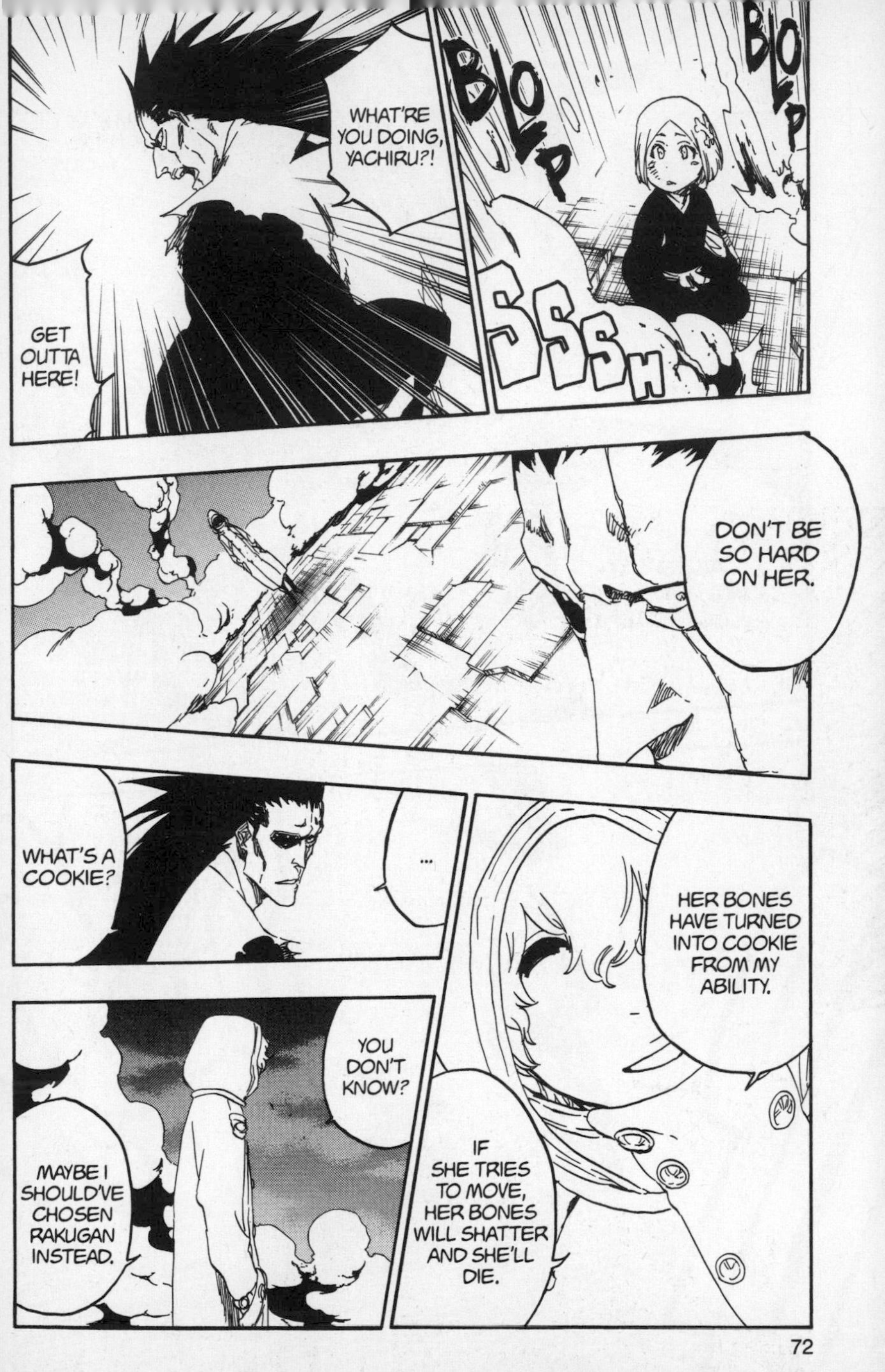
BLOOP
BLOOP
SSSH
WHAT'RE YOU DOING, YACHIRU?!
GET OUTTA HERE!
DON'T BE SO HARD ON HER.
HER BONES HAVE TURNED INTO COOKIE FROM MY ABILITY.
IF SHE TRIES TO MOVE, HER BONES WILL SHATTER AND SHE'LL DIE.
...
WHAT'S A COOKIE?
YOU DON'T KNOW?
MAYBE I SHOULD'VE CHOSEN RAKUGAN INSTEAD.

READ THIS WAY

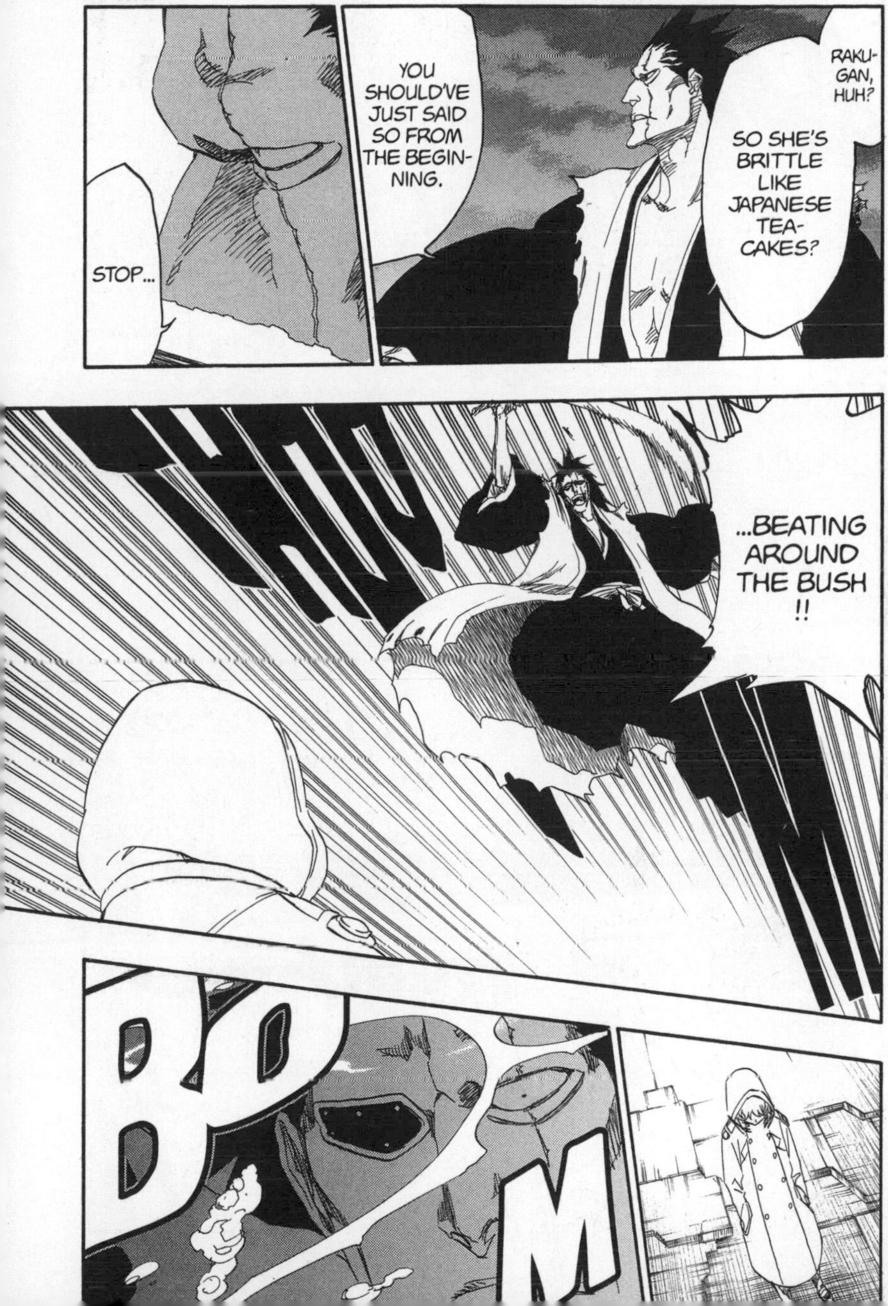
RAKU-GAN, HUH?
SO SHE'S BRITTLE LIKE JAPANESE TEA-CAKES?
YOU SHOULD'VE JUST SAID SO FROM THE BEGIN-NING.
STOP...
...BEATING AROUND THE BUSH !!

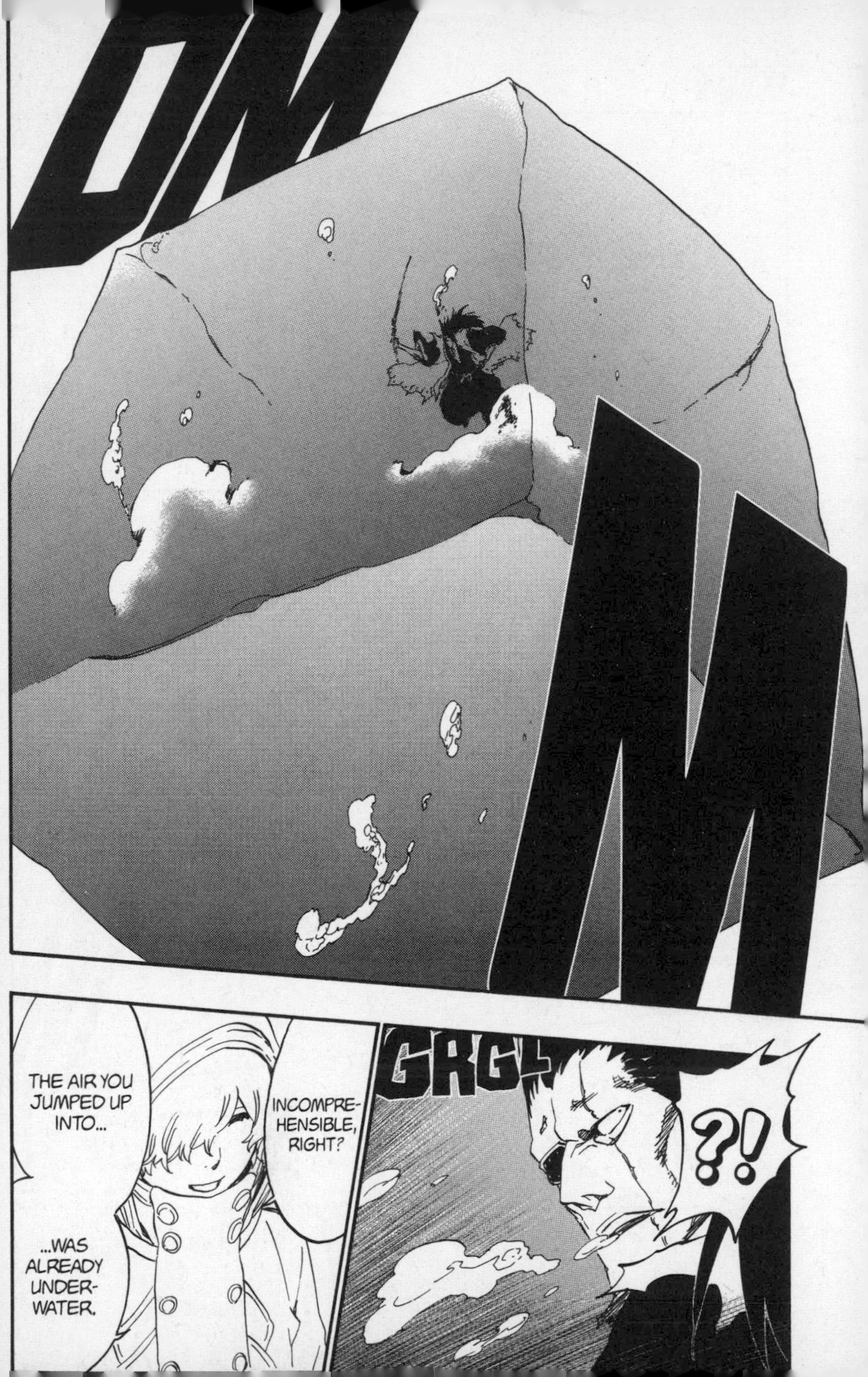
DOM
GRGL
?!
INCOMPRE-
HENSIBLE,
RIGHT?
THE AIR YOU
JUMPED UP
INTO...
...WAS
ALREADY
UNDER-
WATER.

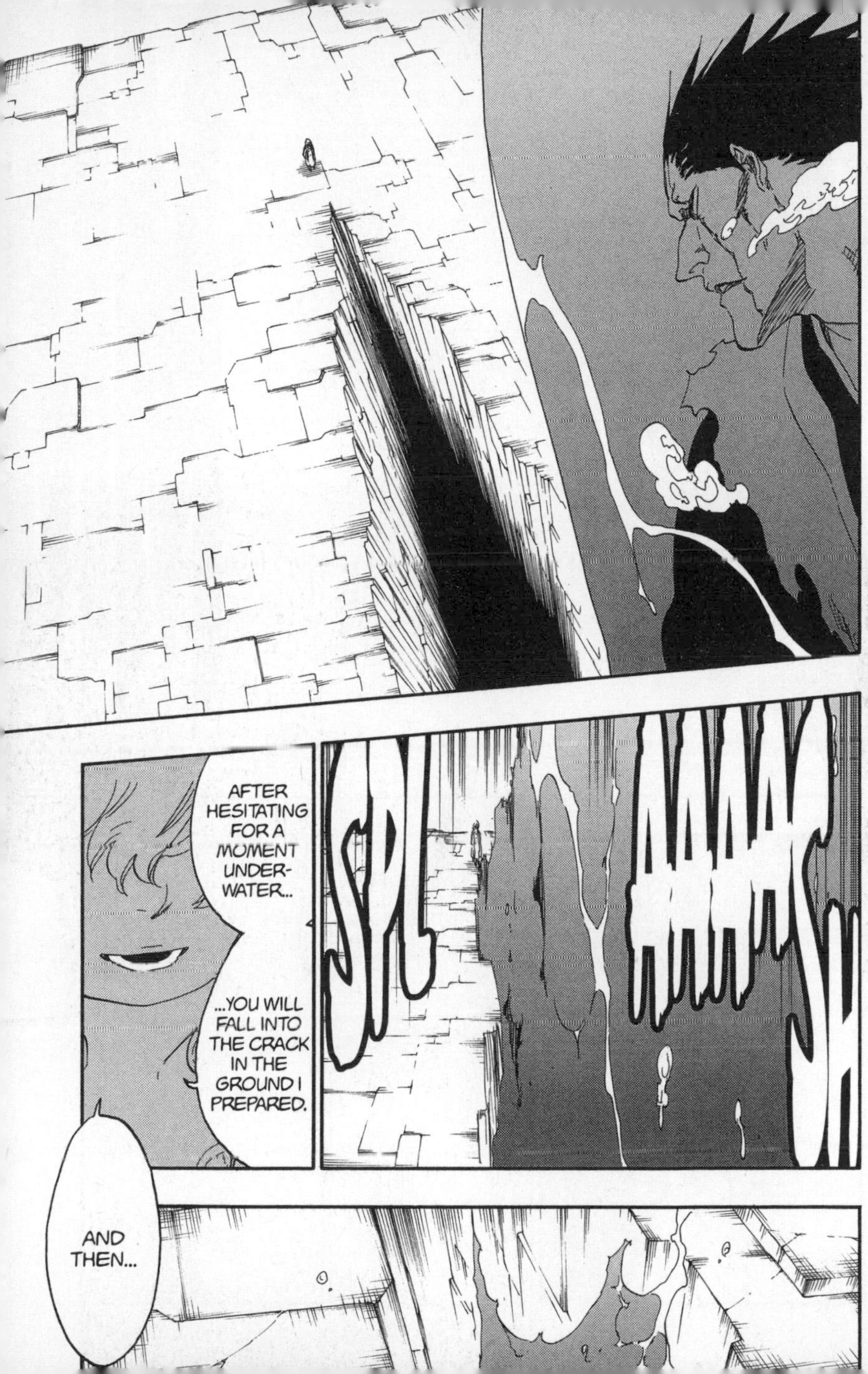
AFTER HESITATING FOR A MOMENT UNDER-WATER...
...YOU WILL FALL INTO THE CRACK IN THE GROUND I PREPARED.
AND THEN...

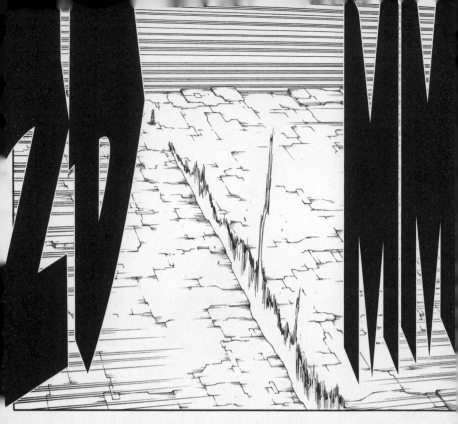

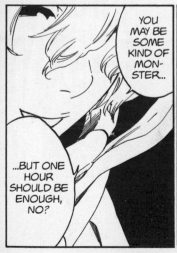

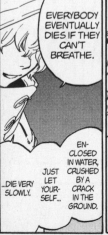

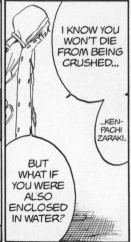

I KNOW YOU WON'T DIE FROM BEING CRUSHED...
...KEN-PACHI ZARAKI.
BUT WHAT IF YOU WERE ALSO ENCLOSED IN WATER?
EVERYBODY EVENTUALLY DIES IF THEY CAN'T BREATHE.
EN-CLOSED IN WATER, CRUSHED BY A CRACK IN THE GROUND.
JUST LET YOUR-SELF...
...DIE VERY SLOWLY.
YOU MAY BE SOME KIND OF MON-STER...
...BUT ONE HOUR SHOULD BE ENOUGH, NO?

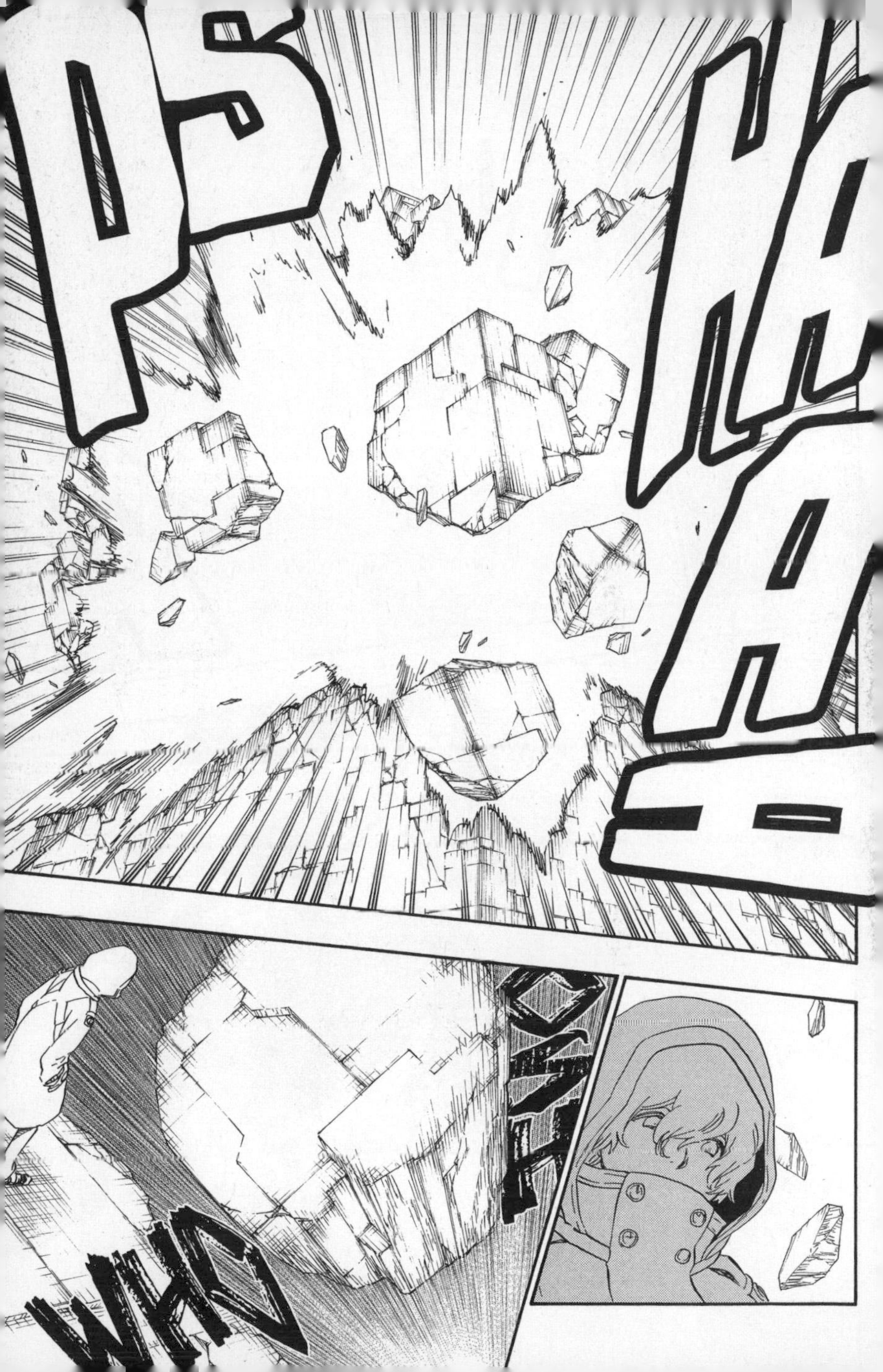

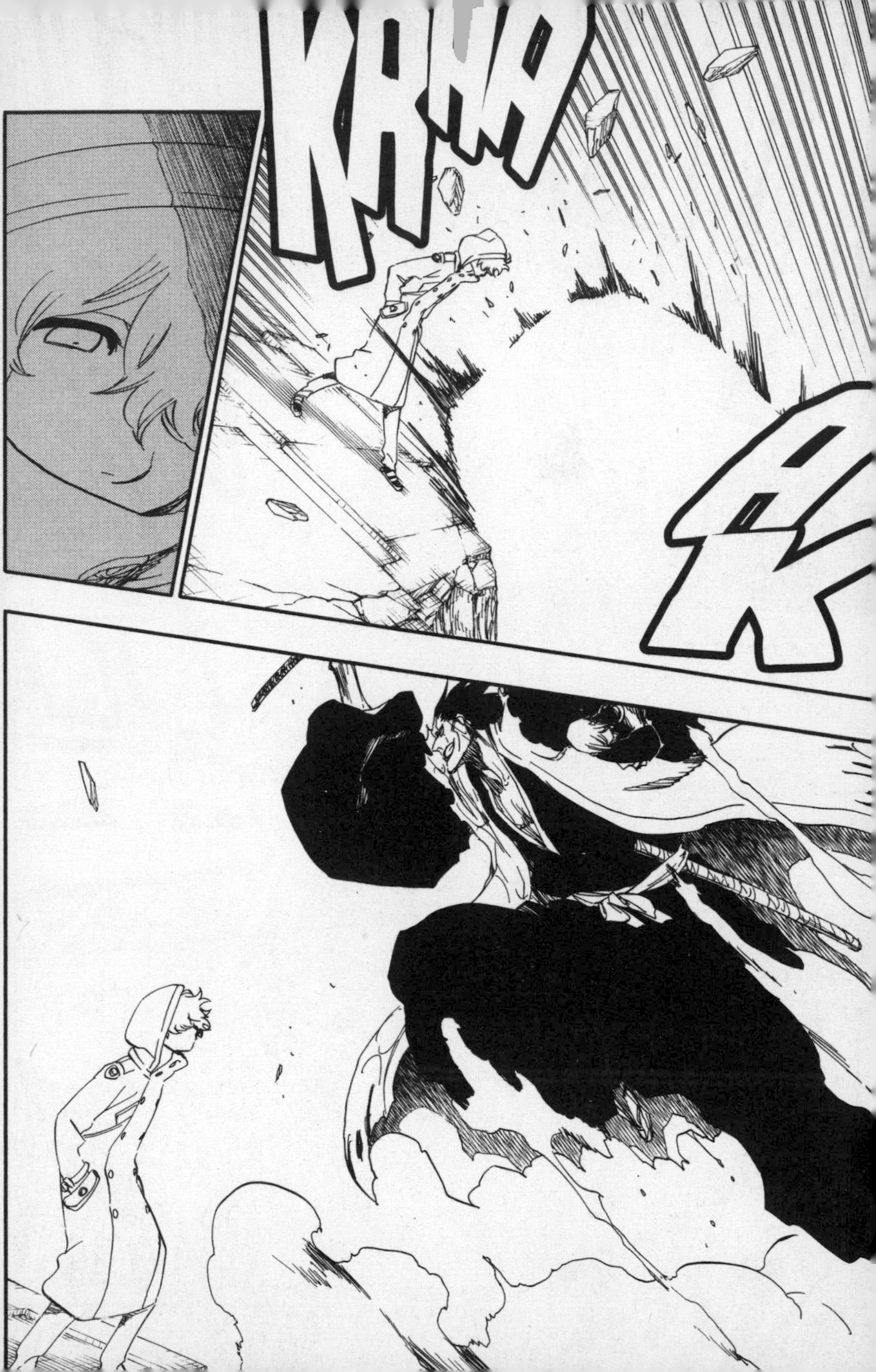

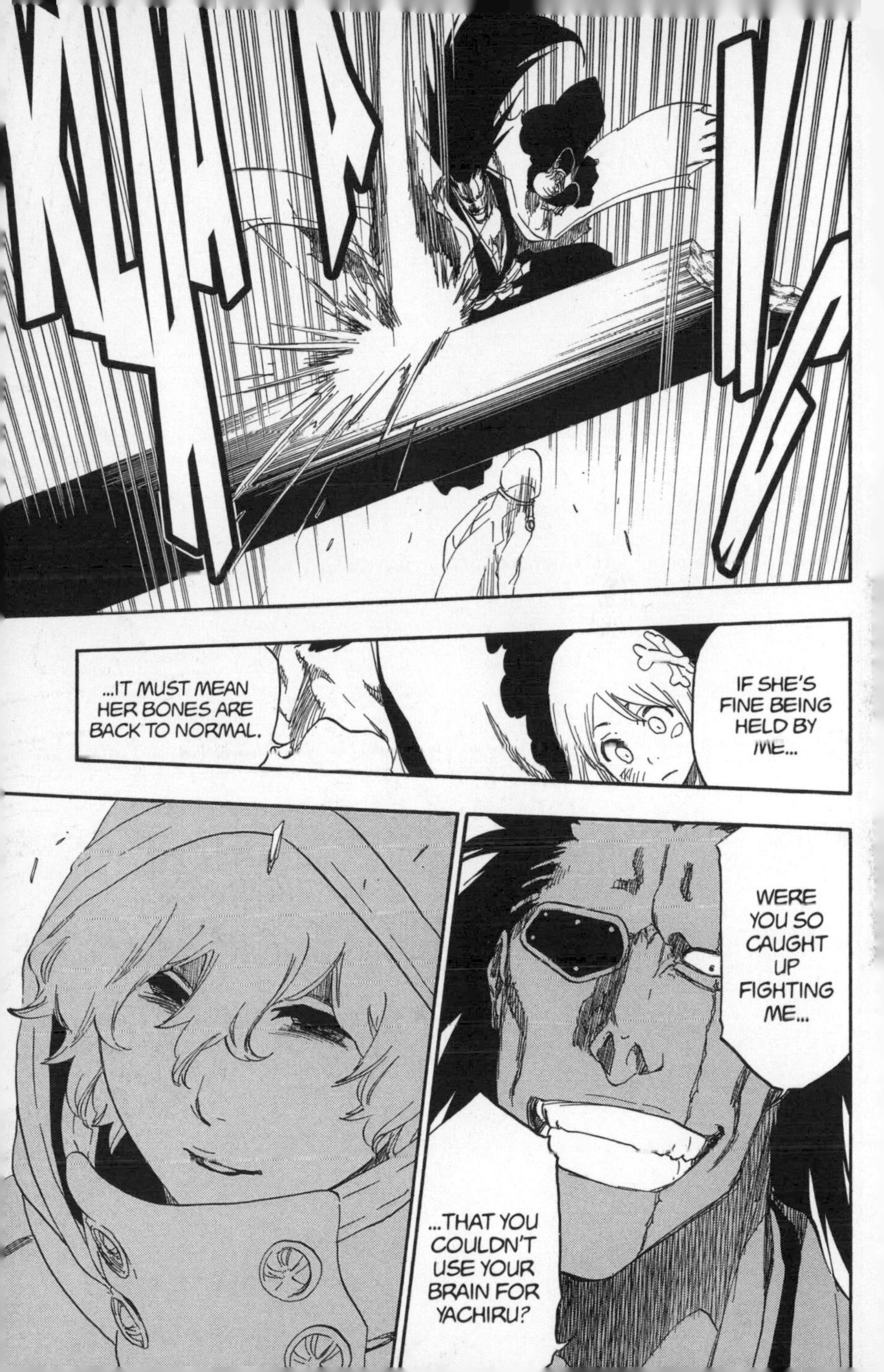
IF SHE'S FINE BEING HELD BY ME...
...IT MUST MEAN HER BONES ARE BACK TO NORMAL.
WERE YOU SO CAUGHT UP FIGHTING ME...
...THAT YOU COULDN'T USE YOUR BRAIN FOR YACHIRU?

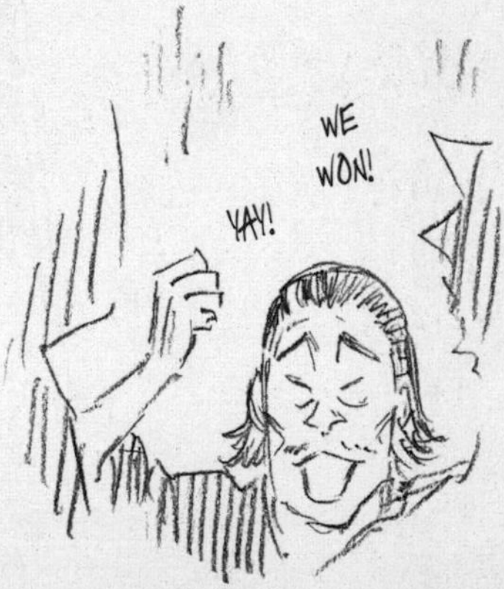
WE WON!
YAY!

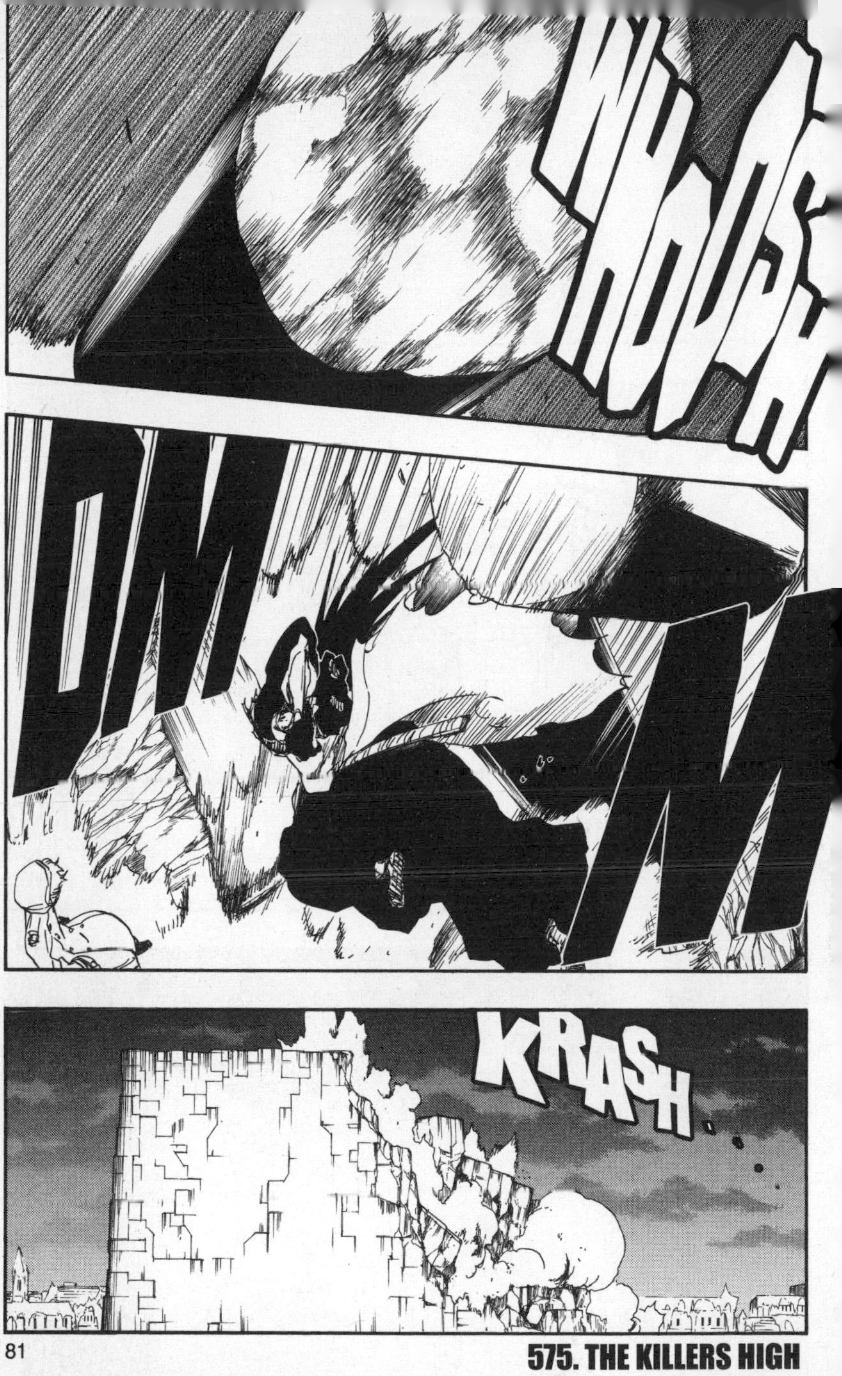
KRASH

575. THE KILLERS HIGH

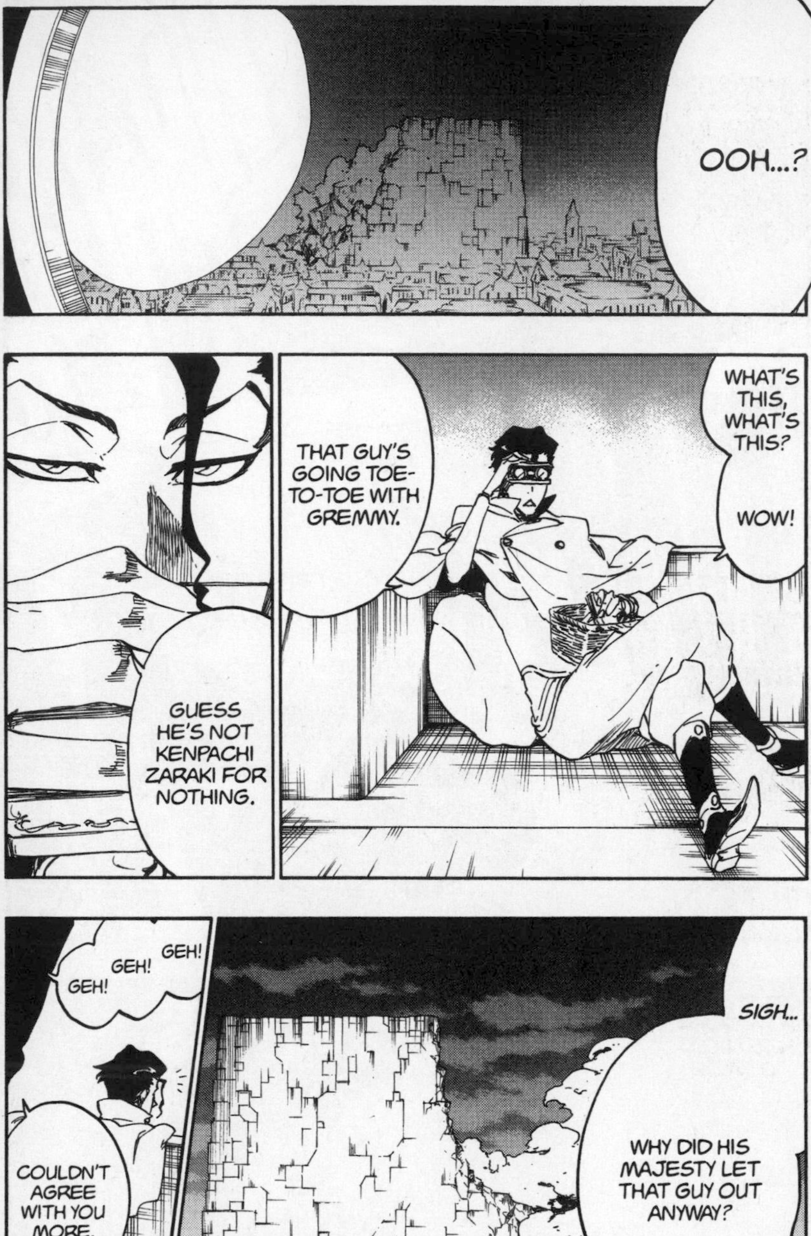
OOH...?
WHAT'S THIS, WHAT'S THIS?
WOW!
THAT GUY'S GOING TOE-TO-TOE WITH GREMMY.
GUESS HE'S NOT KENPACHI ZARAKI FOR NOTHING.
SIGH...
WHY DID HIS MAJESTY LET THAT GUY OUT ANYWAY?
GEH! GEH! GEH!
COULDN'T AGREE WITH YOU MORE. ♡

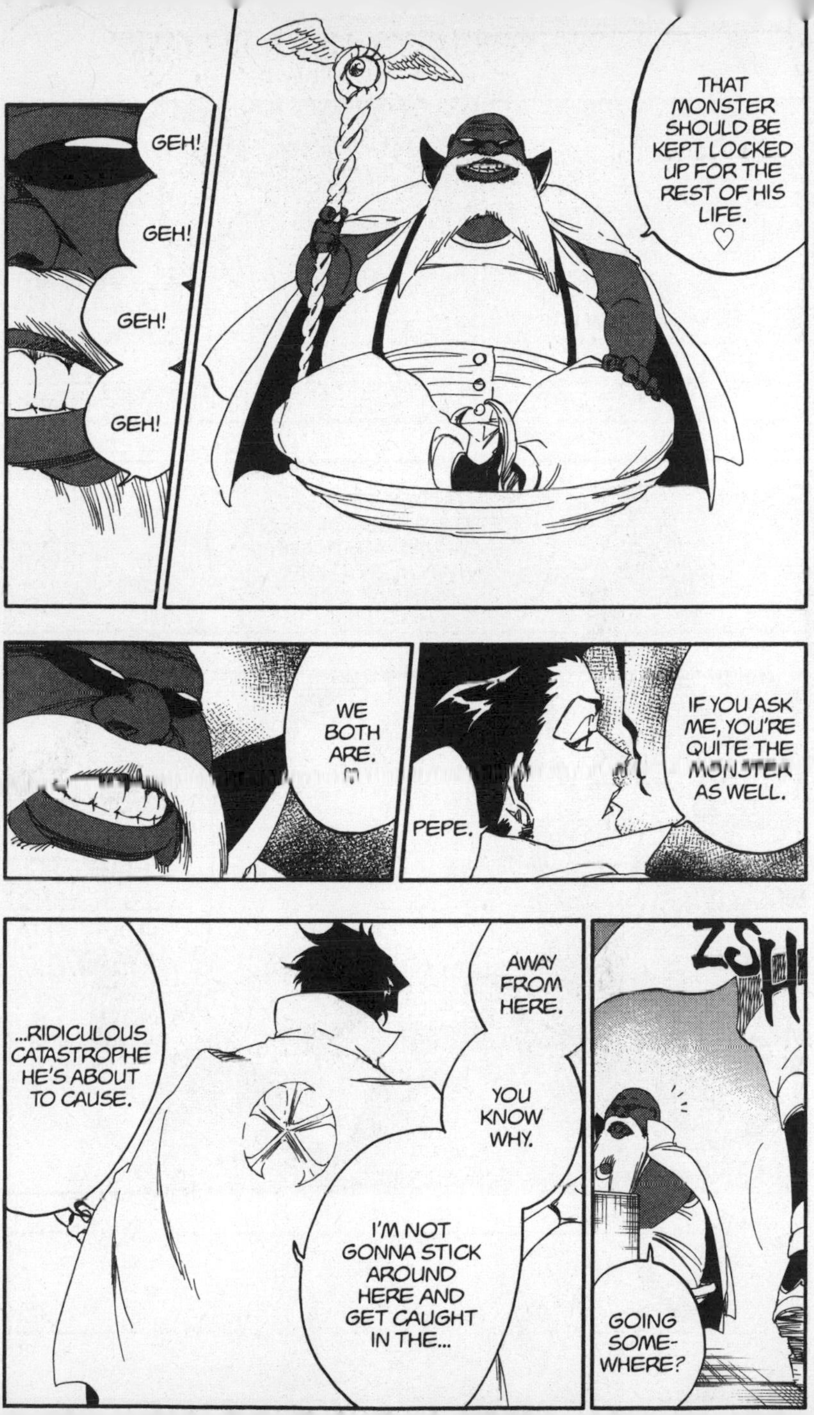

THAT MONSTER SHOULD BE KEPT LOCKED UP FOR THE REST OF HIS LIFE. ♡
GEH!
GEH!
GEH!
GEH!
IF YOU ASK ME, YOU'RE QUITE THE MONSTER AS WELL.
PEPE.
WE BOTH ARE.
ZSHH
GOING SOME-WHERE?
AWAY FROM HERE.
YOU KNOW WHY.
I'M NOT GONNA STICK AROUND HERE AND GET CAUGHT IN THE...
...RIDICULOUS CATASTROPHE HE'S ABOUT TO CAUSE.

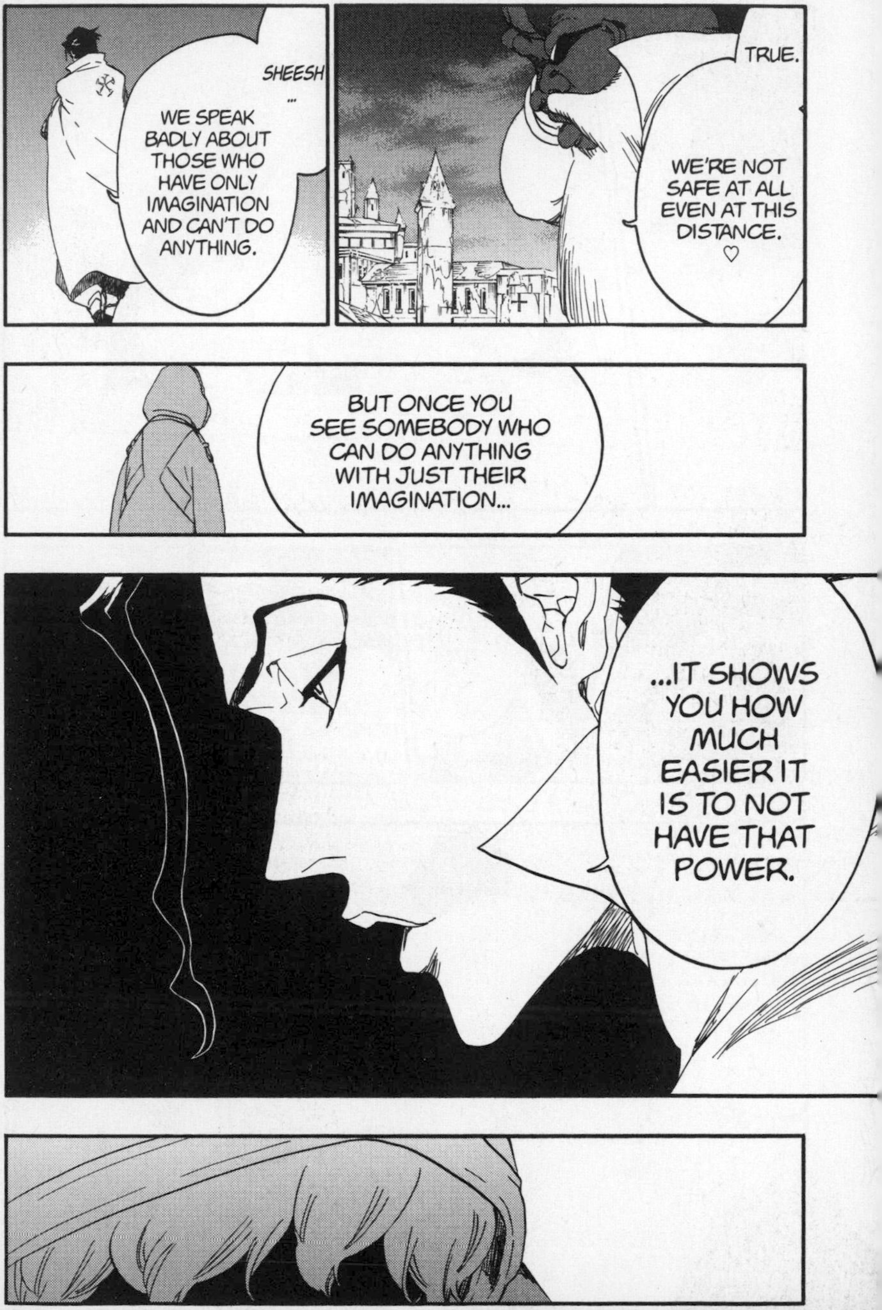
TRUE.
WE'RE NOT SAFE AT ALL EVEN AT THIS DISTANCE. ♡
SHEESH...
WE SPEAK BADLY ABOUT THOSE WHO HAVE ONLY IMAGINATION AND CAN'T DO ANYTHING.
BUT ONCE YOU SEE SOMEBODY WHO CAN DO ANYTHING WITH JUST THEIR IMAGINATION...
...IT SHOWS YOU HOW MUCH EASIER IT IS TO NOT HAVE THAT POWER.

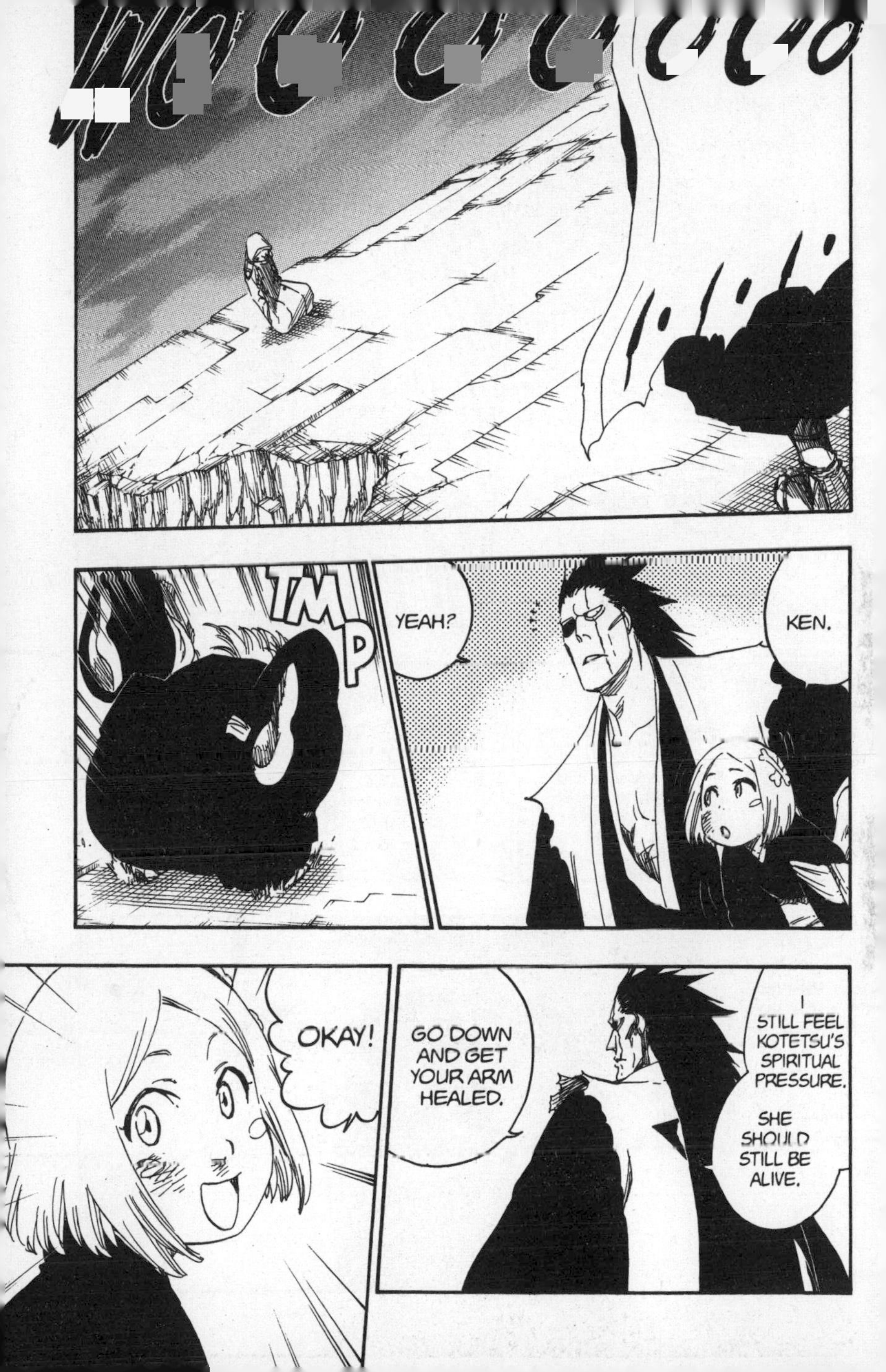
KEN.
YEAH?
TMP
I STILL FEEL KOTETSU'S SPIRITUAL PRESSURE.
SHE SHOULD STILL BE ALIVE.
GO DOWN AND GET YOUR ARM HEALED.
OKAY!

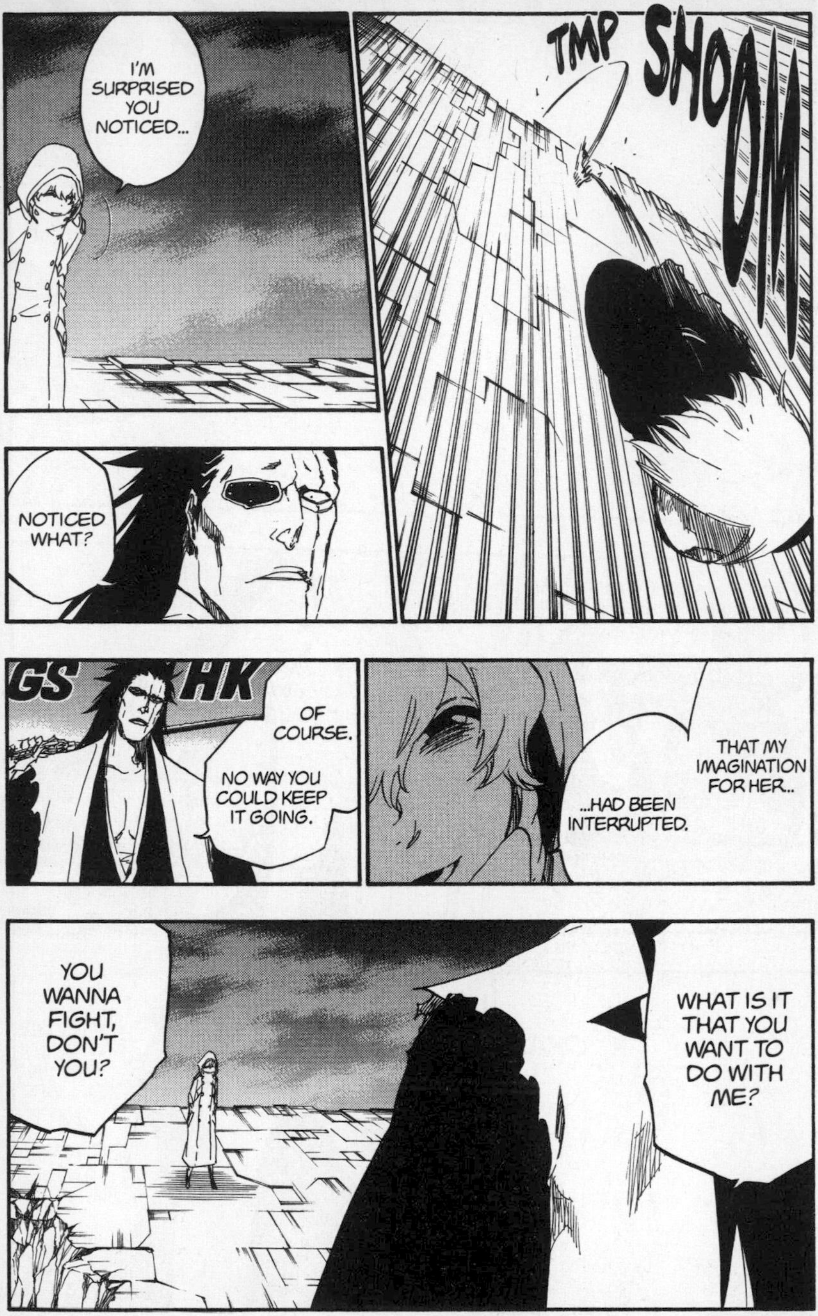
TMP
SHOOM
I'M SURPRISED YOU NOTICED...
NOTICED WHAT?
THAT MY IMAGINATION FOR HER...
...HAD BEEN INTERRUPTED.
OF COURSE.
NO WAY YOU COULD KEEP IT GOING.
WHAT IS IT THAT YOU WANT TO DO WITH ME?
YOU WANNA FIGHT, DON'T YOU?

FIGHT...?

WHAT DID...

...YOU CALL YOURSELF?

AREN'T YOU THE STRONGEST QUINCY?

IF YOU'RE THE STRONGEST...

...WOULDN'T YOU WANT TO CRUSH THE STRONGEST ?!

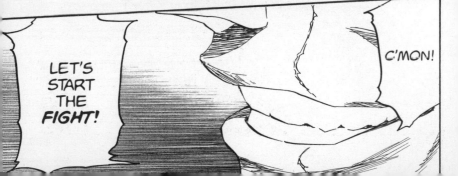

C'MON!

LET'S START THE *FIGHT!*

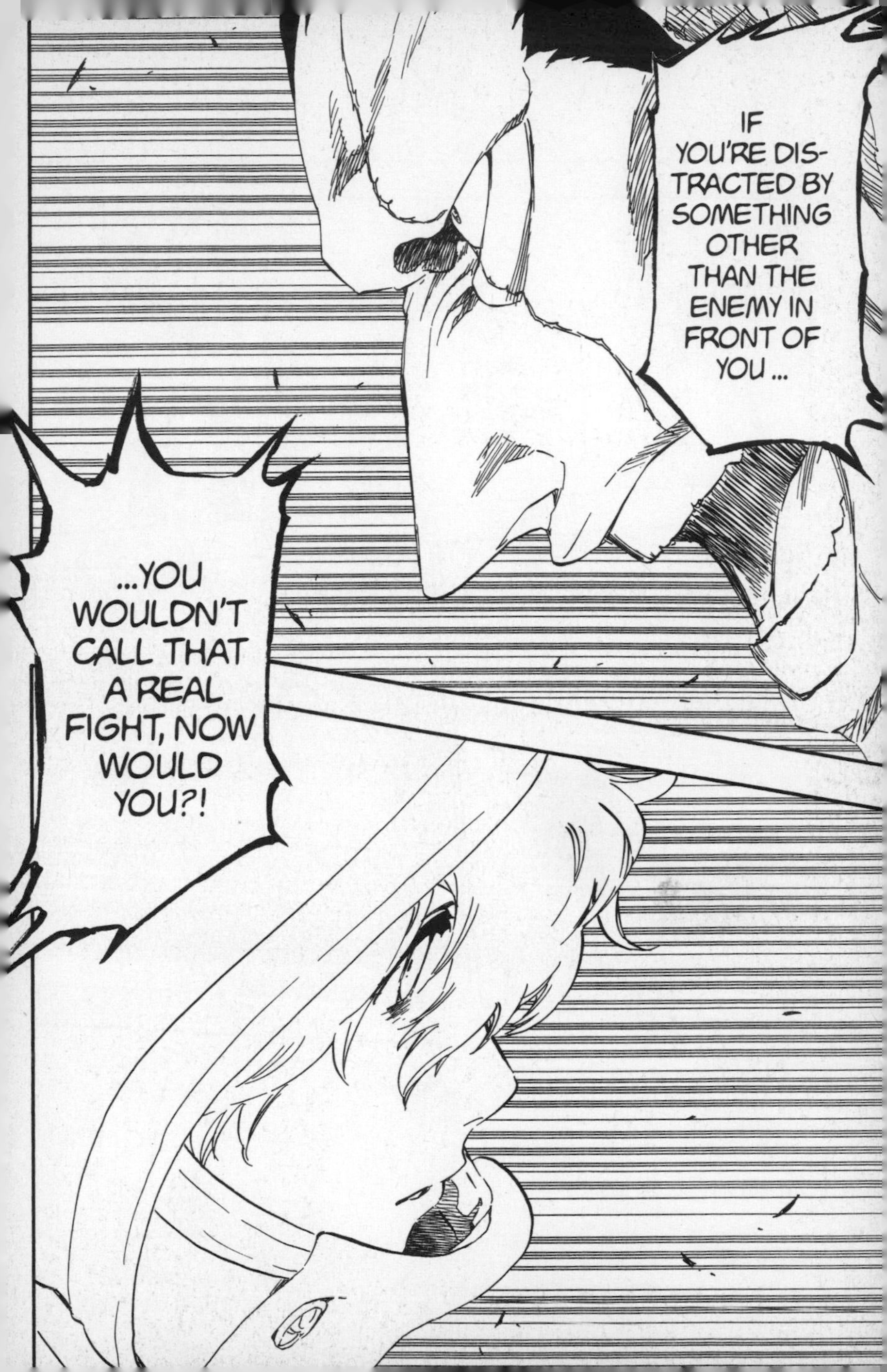
IF YOU'RE DIS-TRACTED BY SOMETHING OTHER THAN THE ENEMY IN FRONT OF YOU ...
...YOU WOULDN'T CALL THAT A REAL FIGHT, NOW WOULD YOU?!

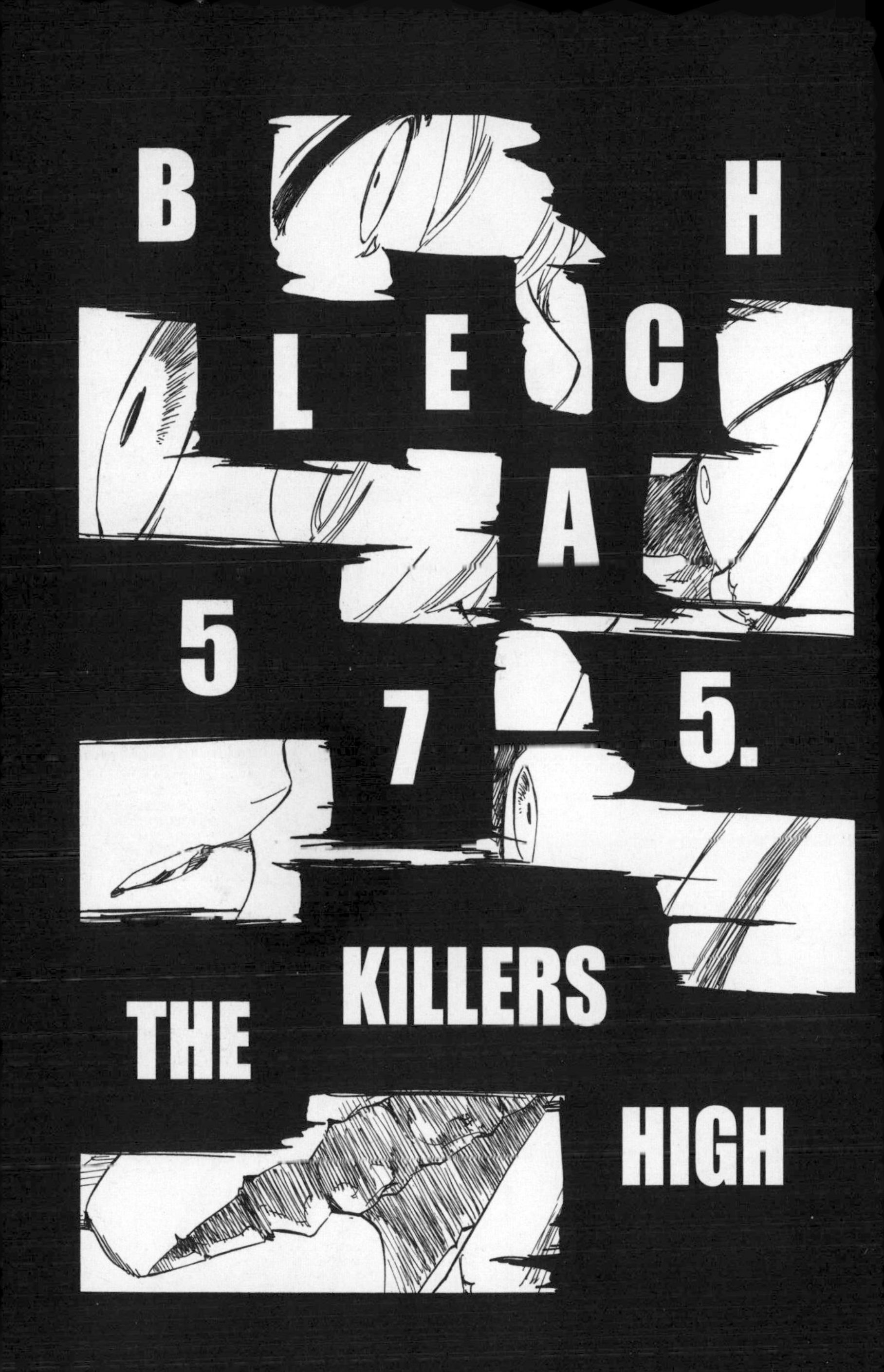
BLEACH
575.
THE KILLERS HIGH

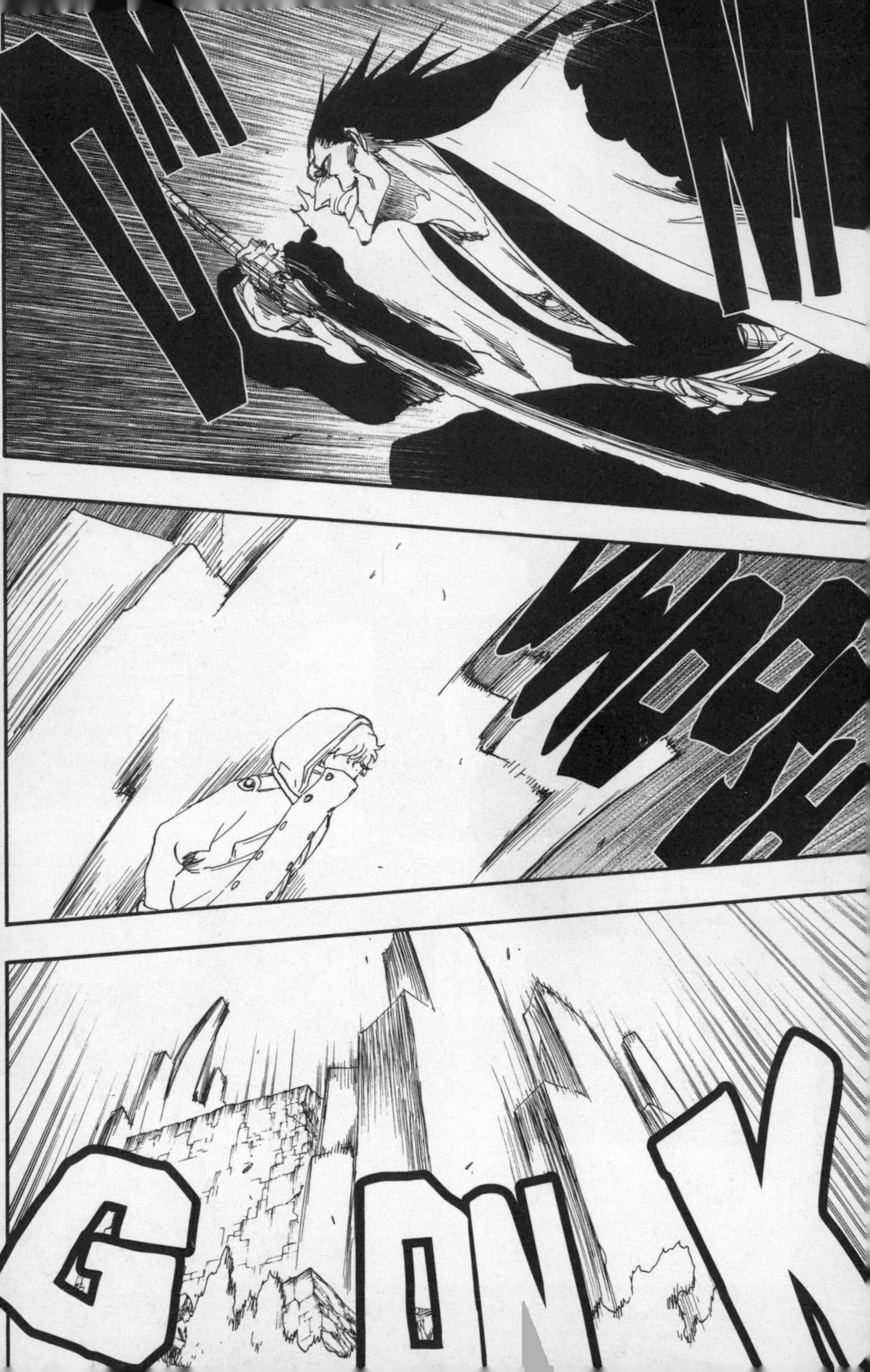
GONK

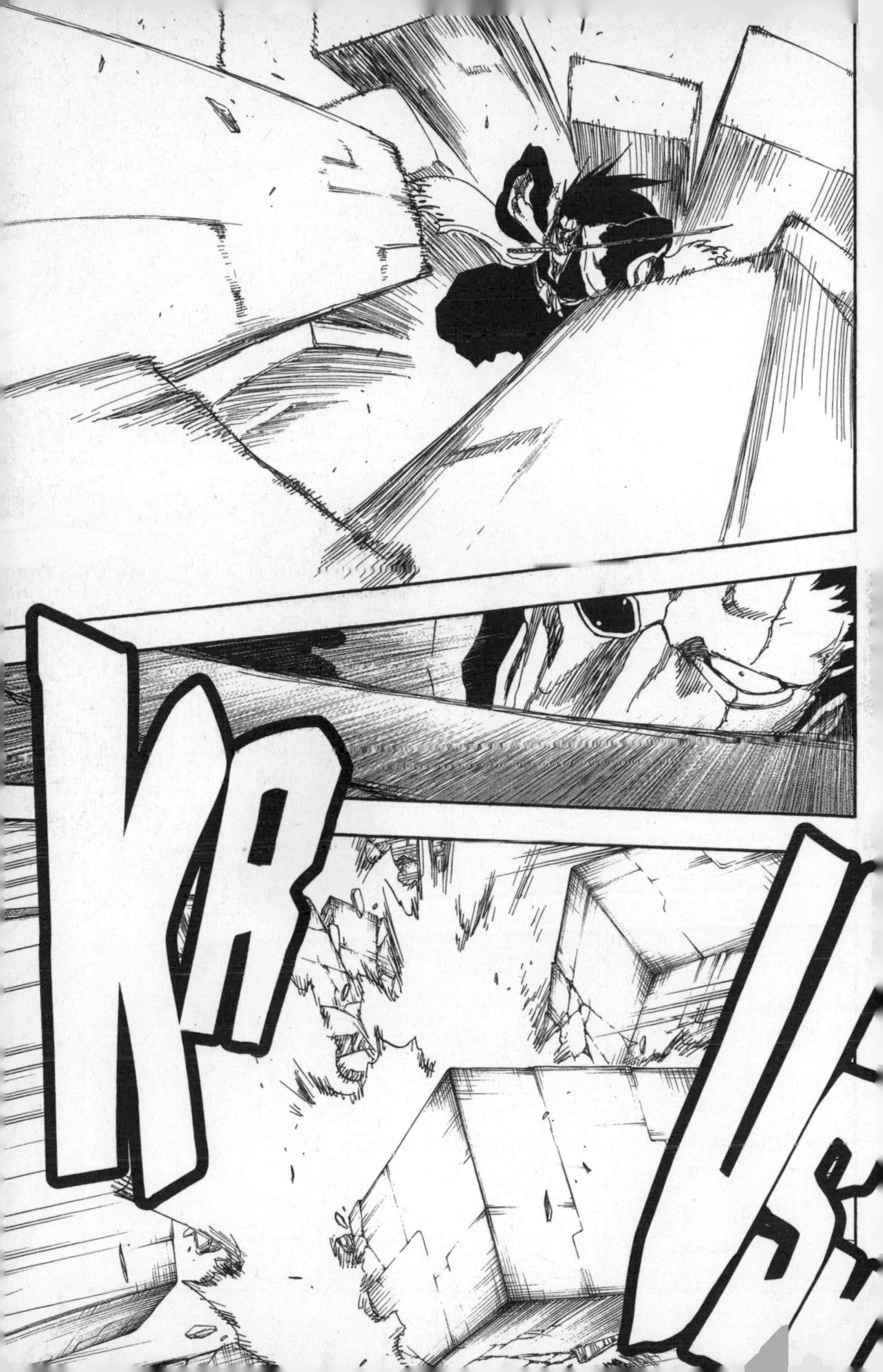
KA

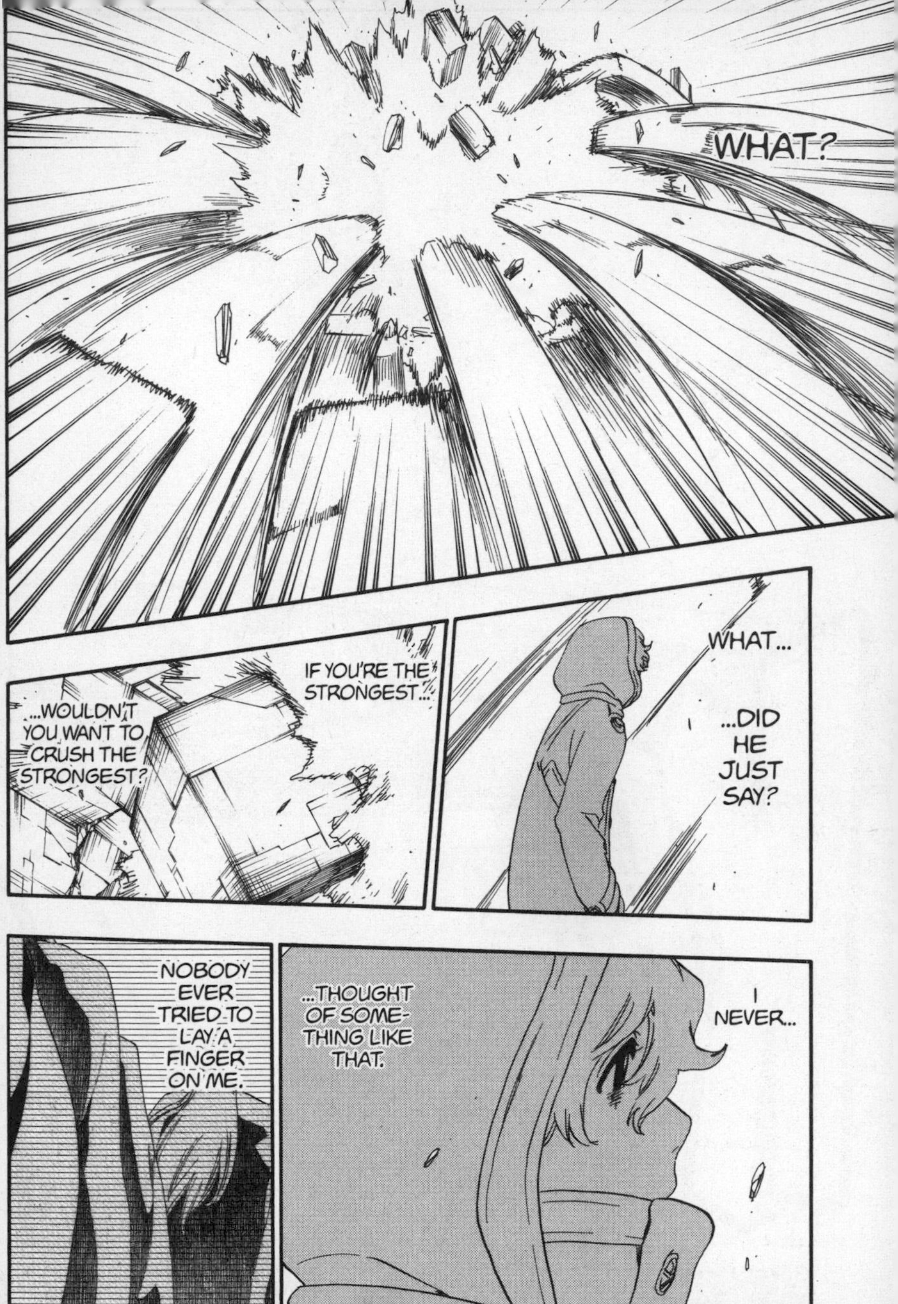
WHAT?
WHAT...
...DID HE JUST SAY?
IF YOU'RE THE STRONGEST...
...WOULDN'T YOU WANT TO CRUSH THE STRONGEST?
I NEVER...
...THOUGHT OF SOME-THING LIKE THAT.
NOBODY EVER TRIED TO LAY A FINGER ON ME.

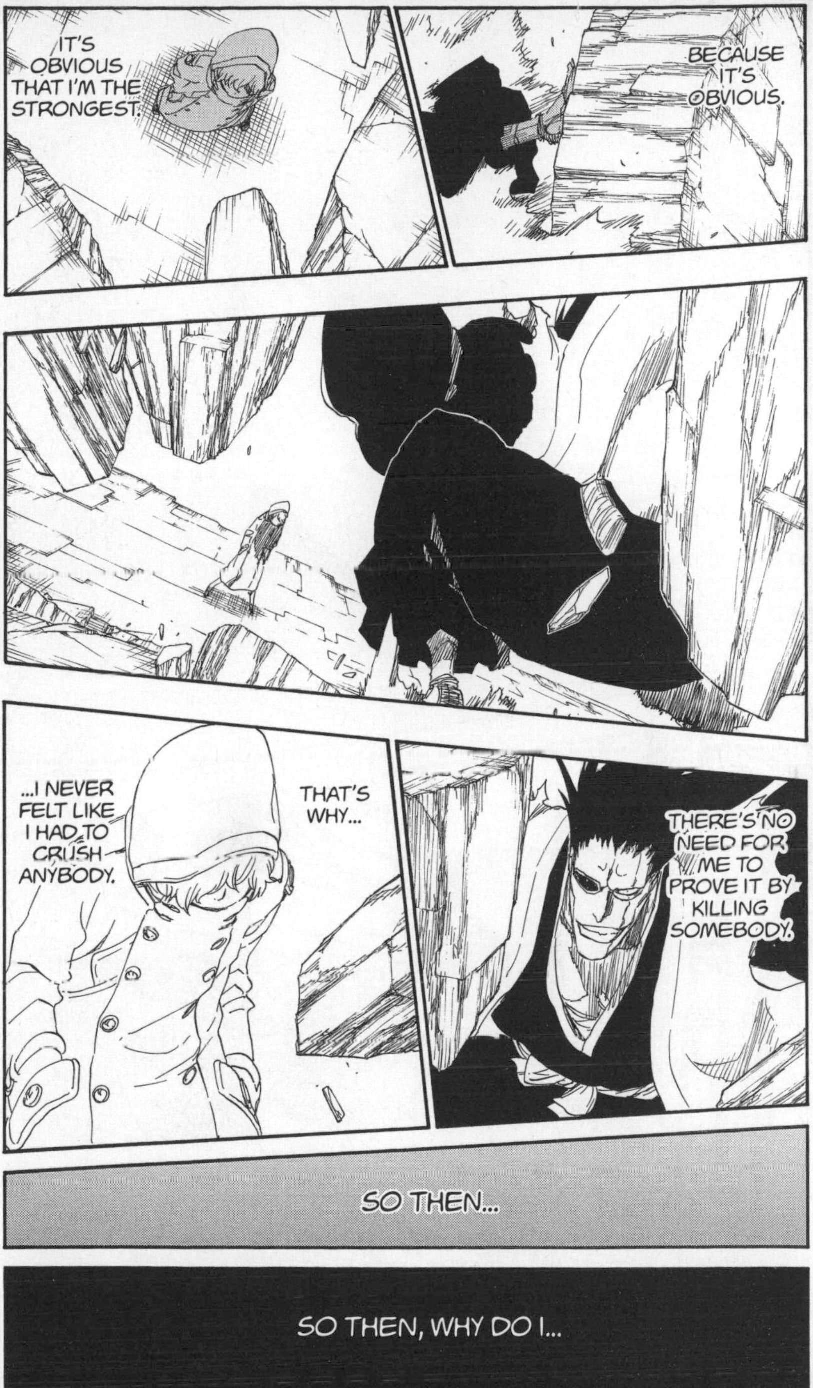
BECAUSE IT'S OBVIOUS.
IT'S OBVIOUS THAT I'M THE STRONGEST.
THERE'S NO NEED FOR ME TO PROVE IT BY KILLING SOMEBODY.
THAT'S WHY...
...I NEVER FELT LIKE I HAD TO CRUSH ANYBODY.
SO THEN...
SO THEN, WHY DO I...

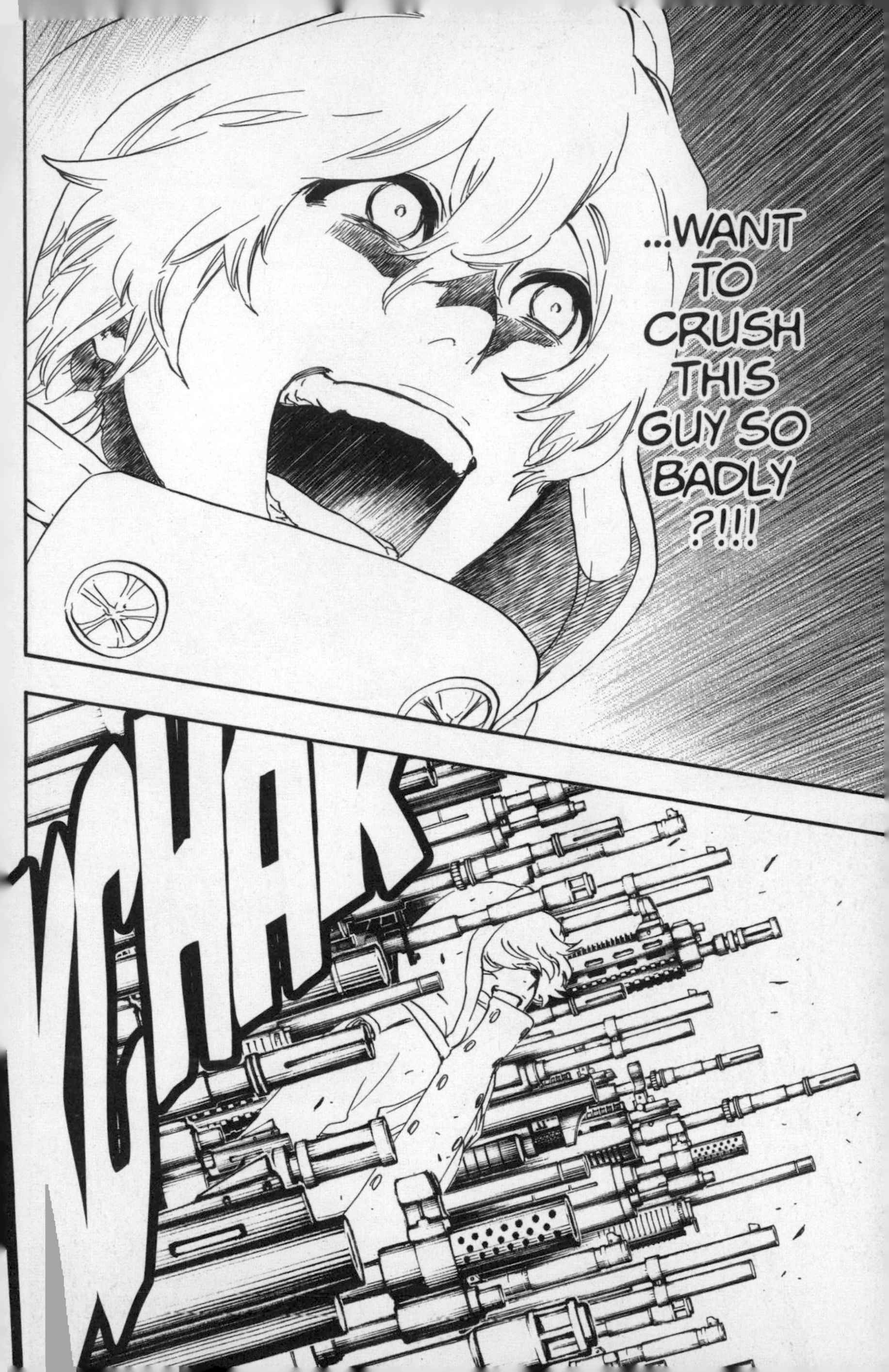
...WANT TO CRUSH THIS GUY SO BADLY ?!!!
CHAK

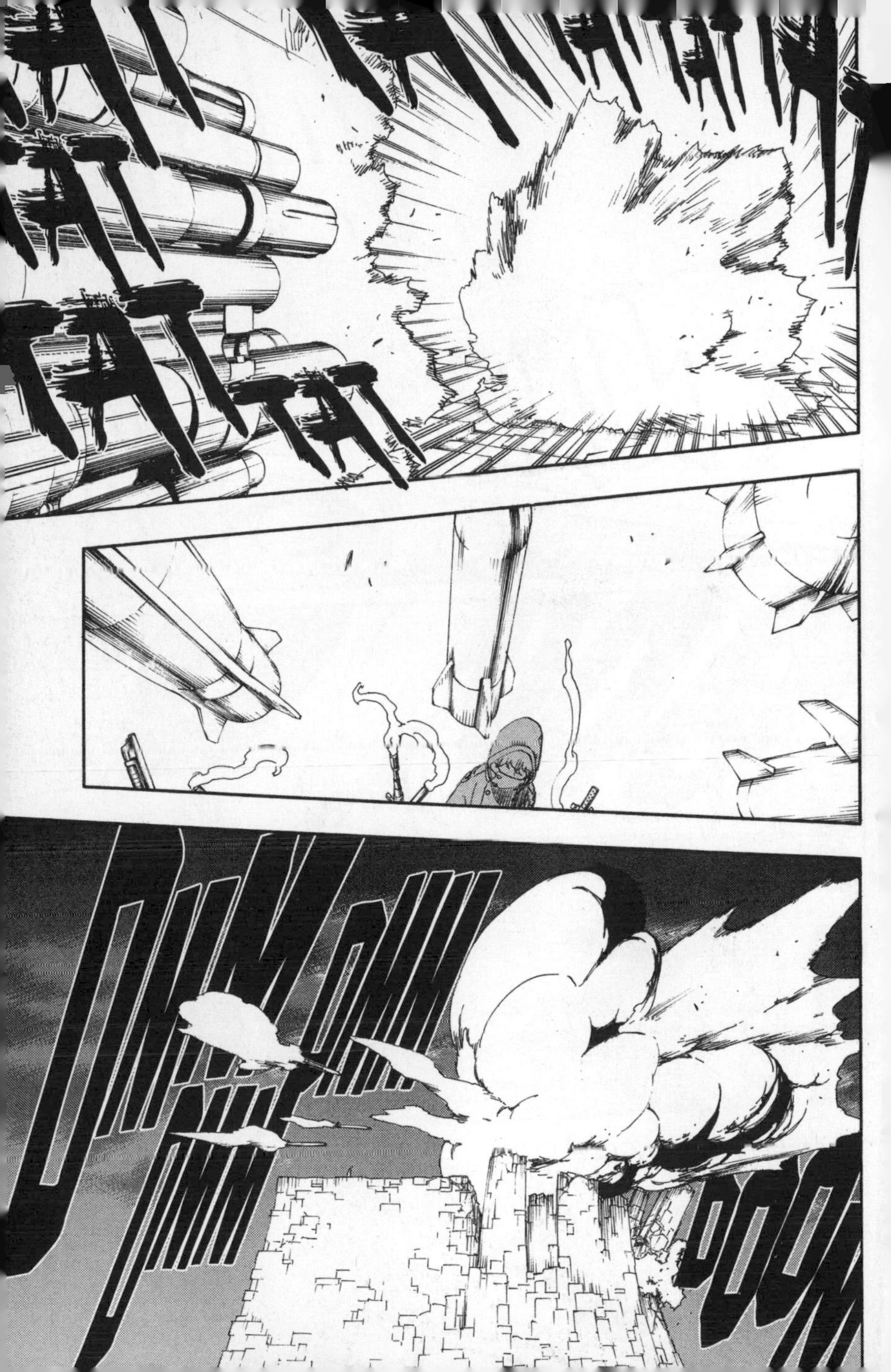

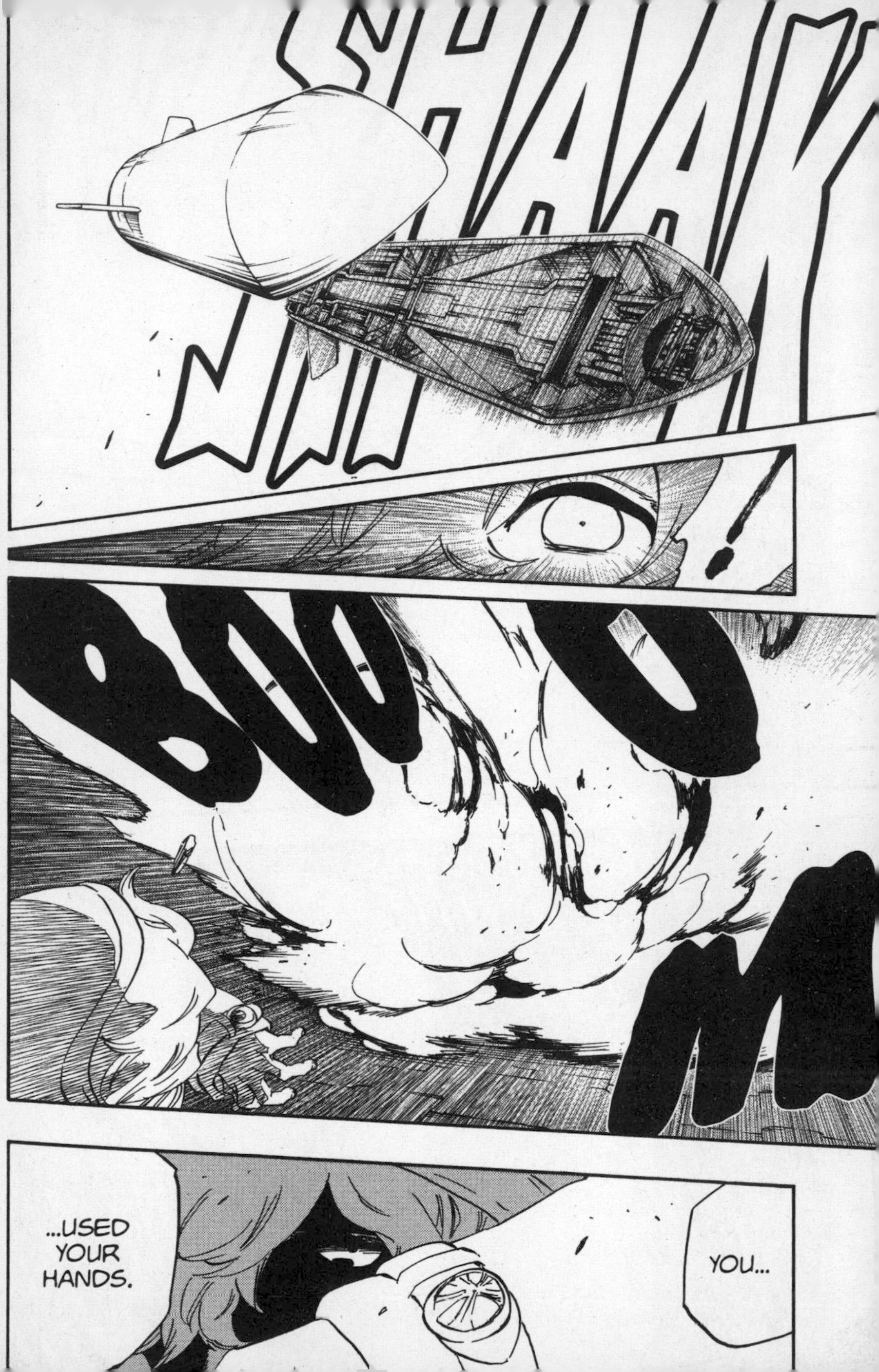
!
YOU...
...USED YOUR HANDS.

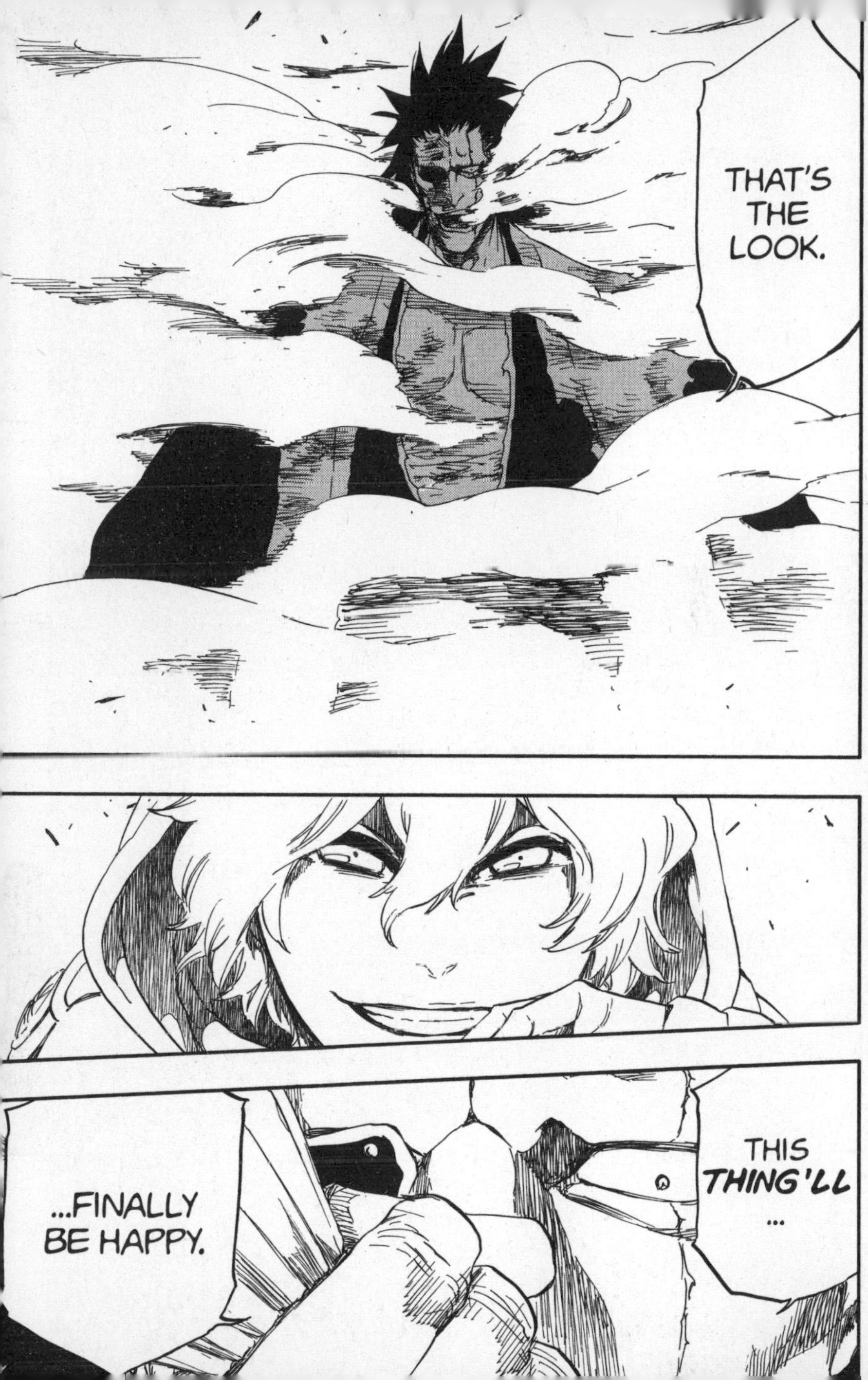
THAT'S THE LOOK.
THIS *THING'LL* ...
...FINALLY BE HAPPY.

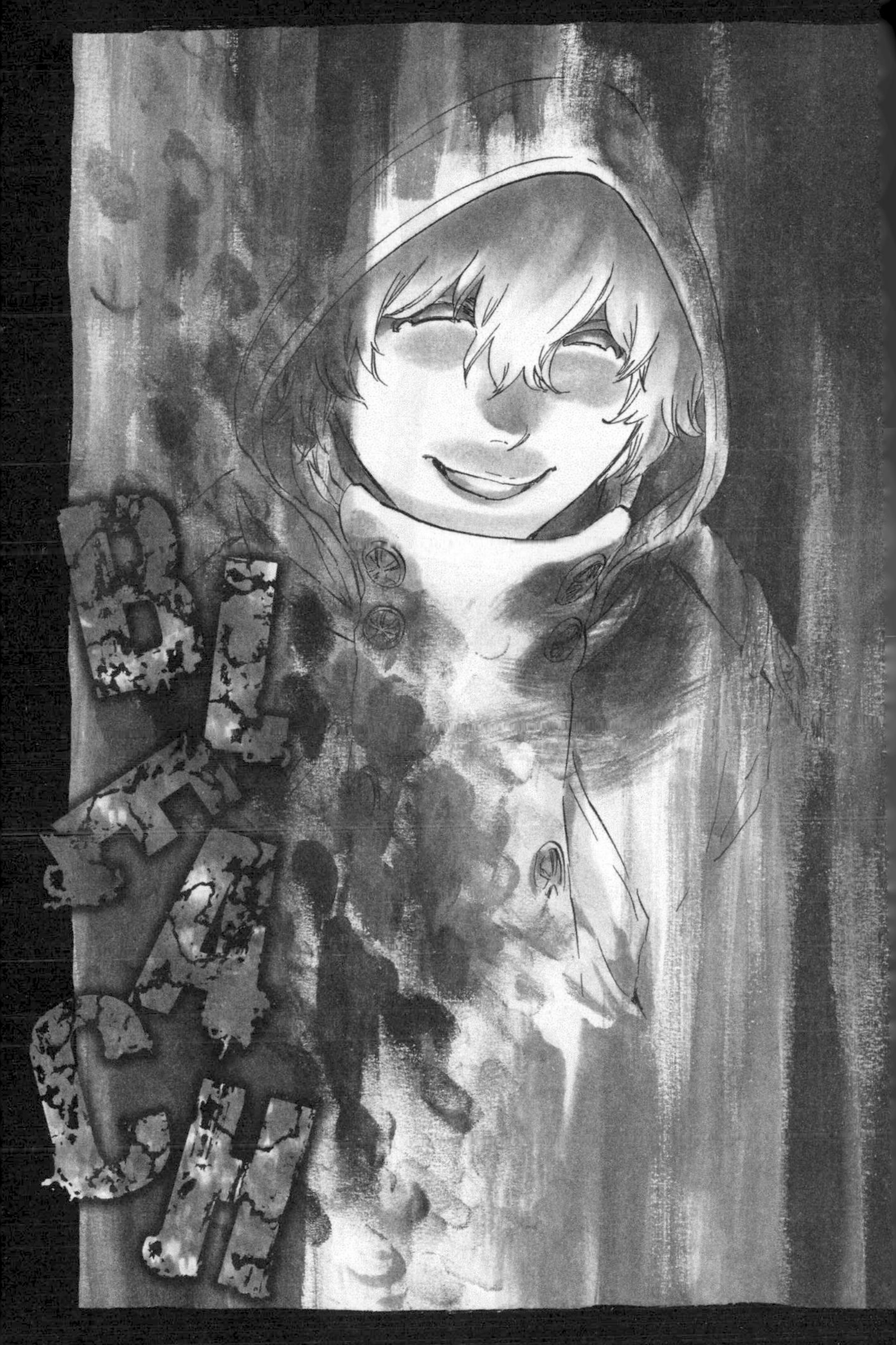
BLEACH

BLEACH
ブリーチ

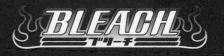

READ THIS WAY

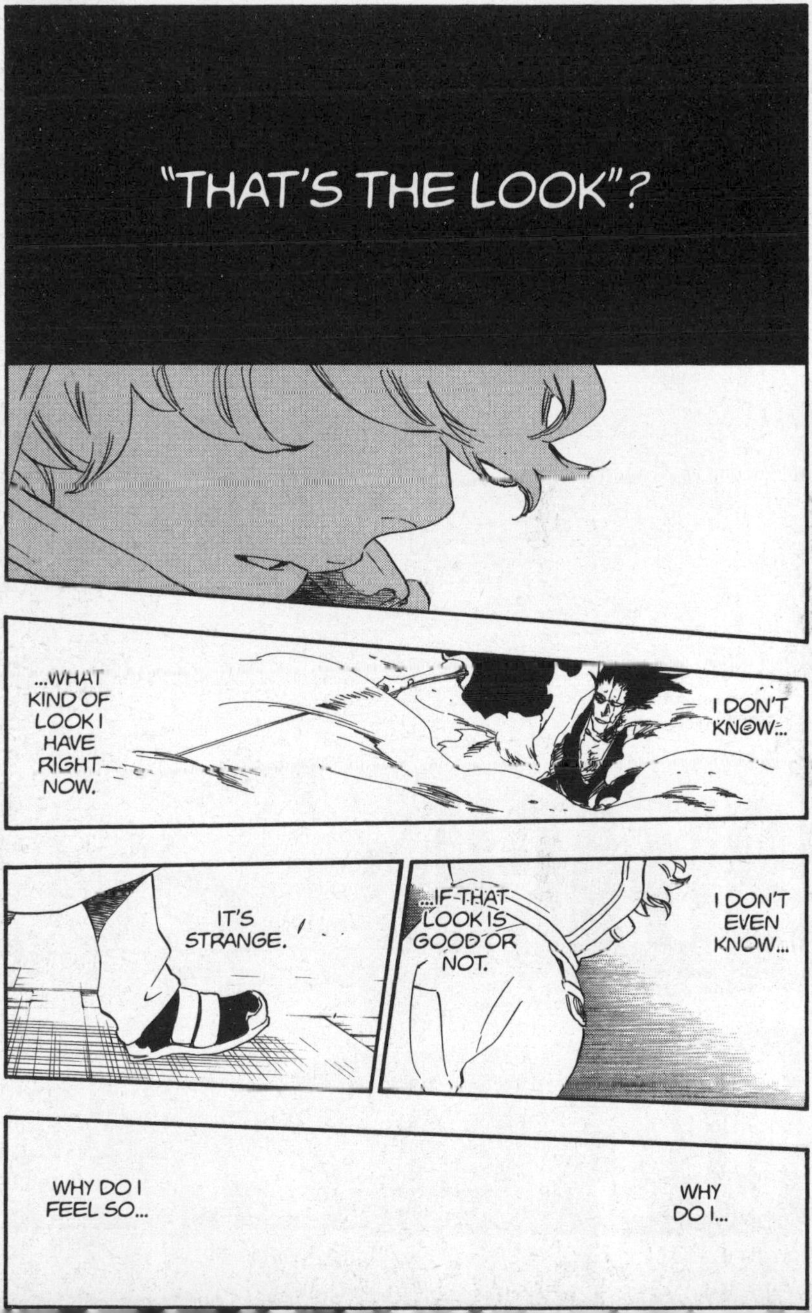
"THAT'S THE LOOK"?
I DON'T KNOW...
...WHAT KIND OF LOOK I HAVE RIGHT NOW.
I DON'T EVEN KNOW...
...IF THAT LOOK IS GOOD OR NOT.
IT'S STRANGE.
WHY DO I...
WHY DO I FEEL SO...

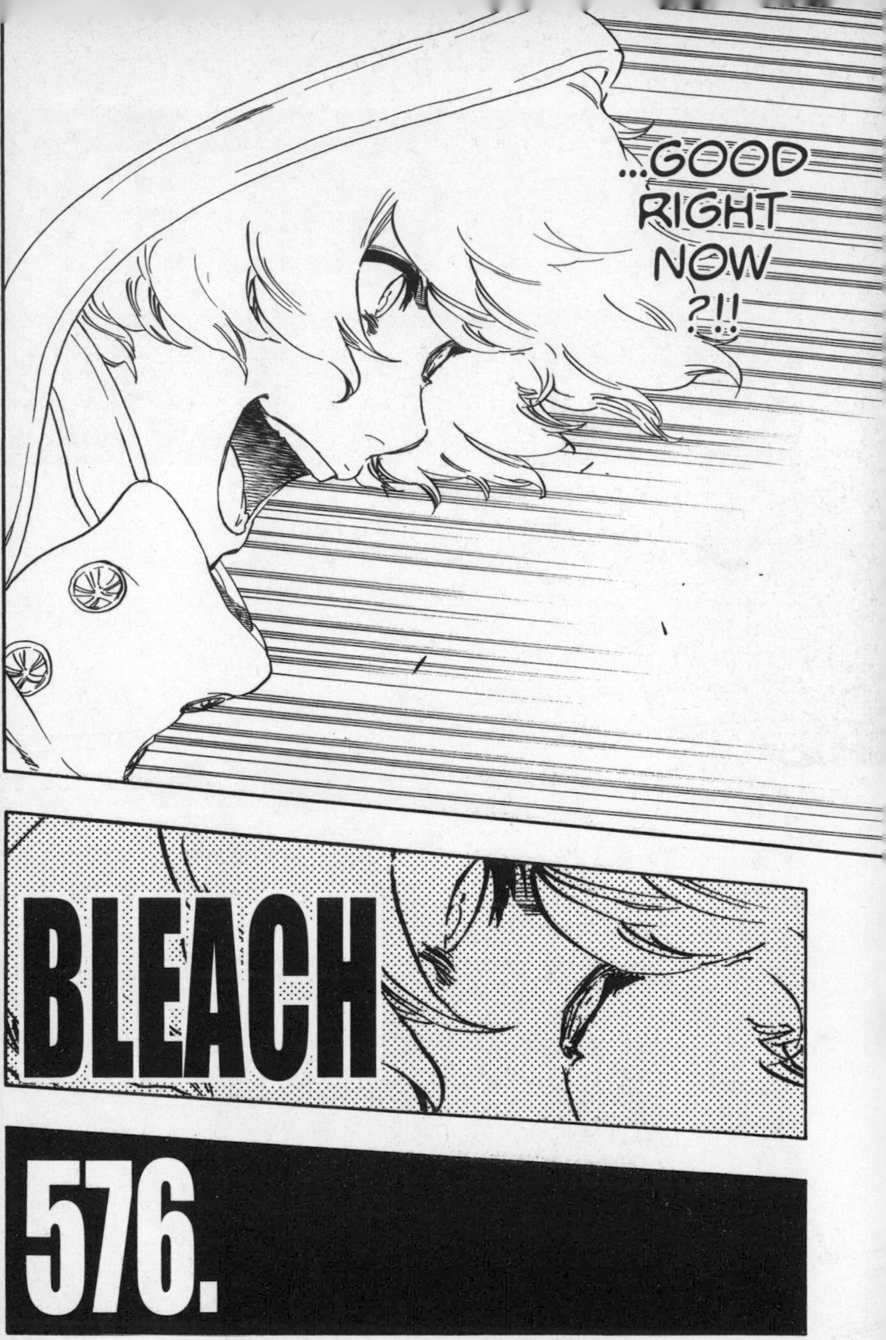
...GOOD RIGHT NOW ?!!
BLEACH
576.

THE KILLERS HIGH 2

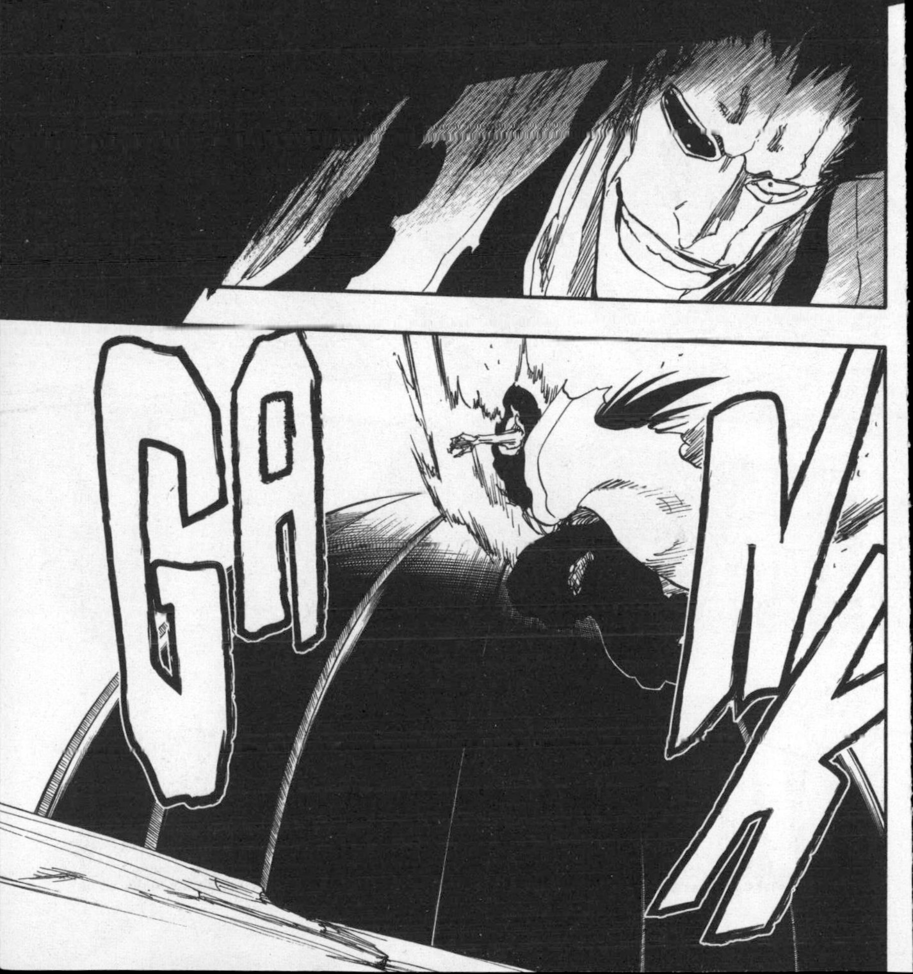
GA

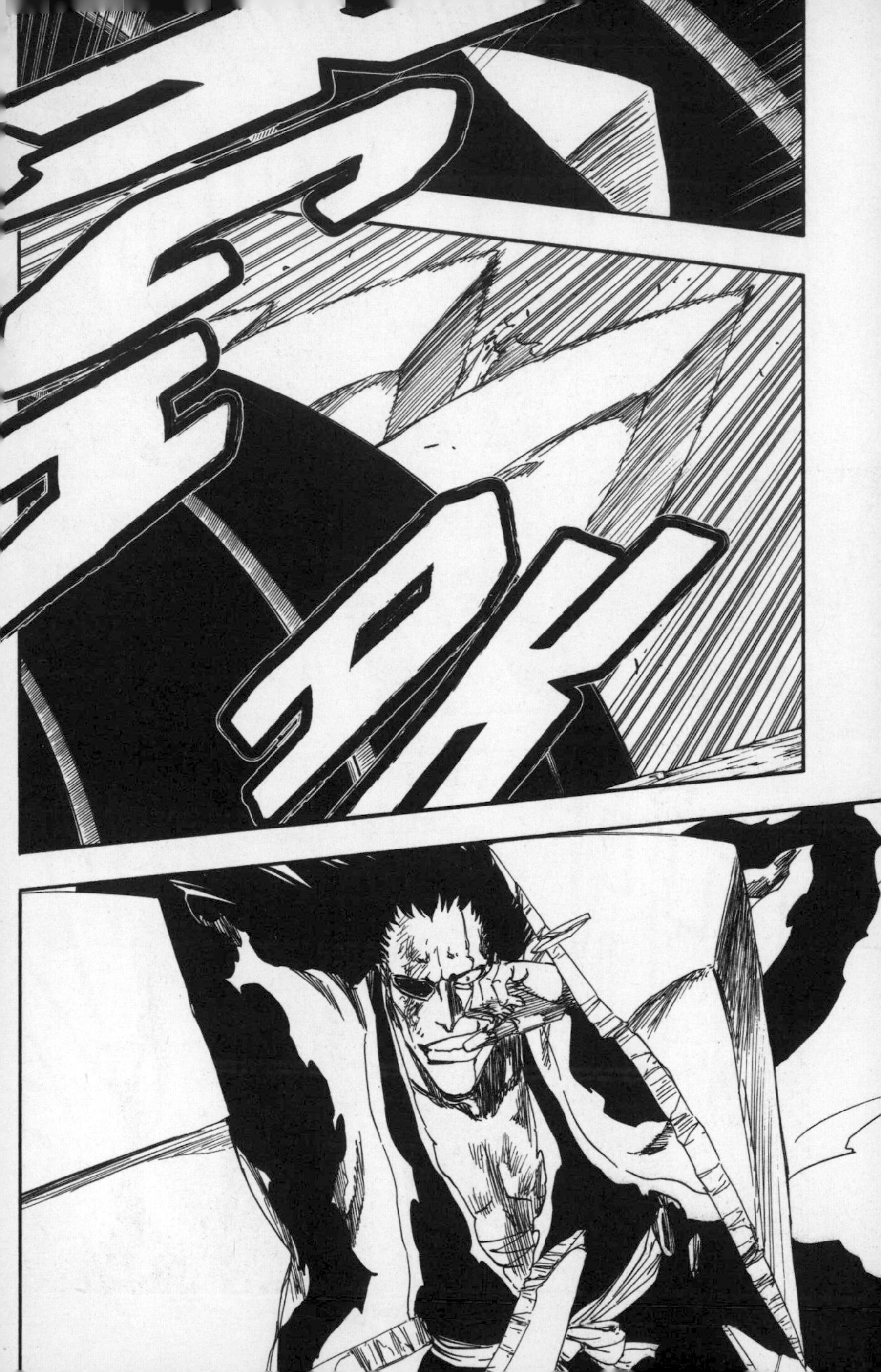

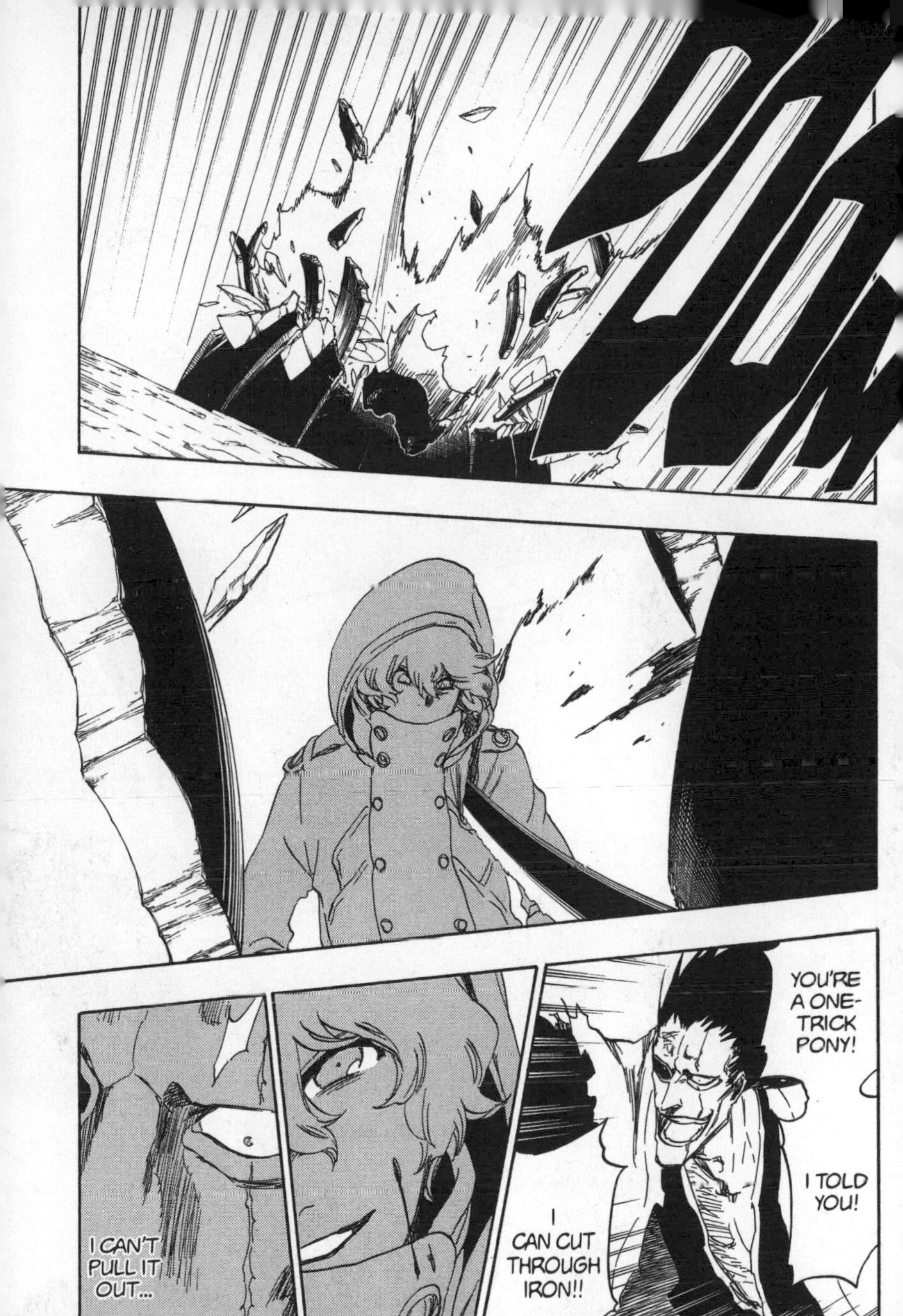
YOU'RE A ONE-TRICK PONY!
I TOLD YOU!
I CAN CUT THROUGH IRON!!
I CAN'T PULL IT OUT...

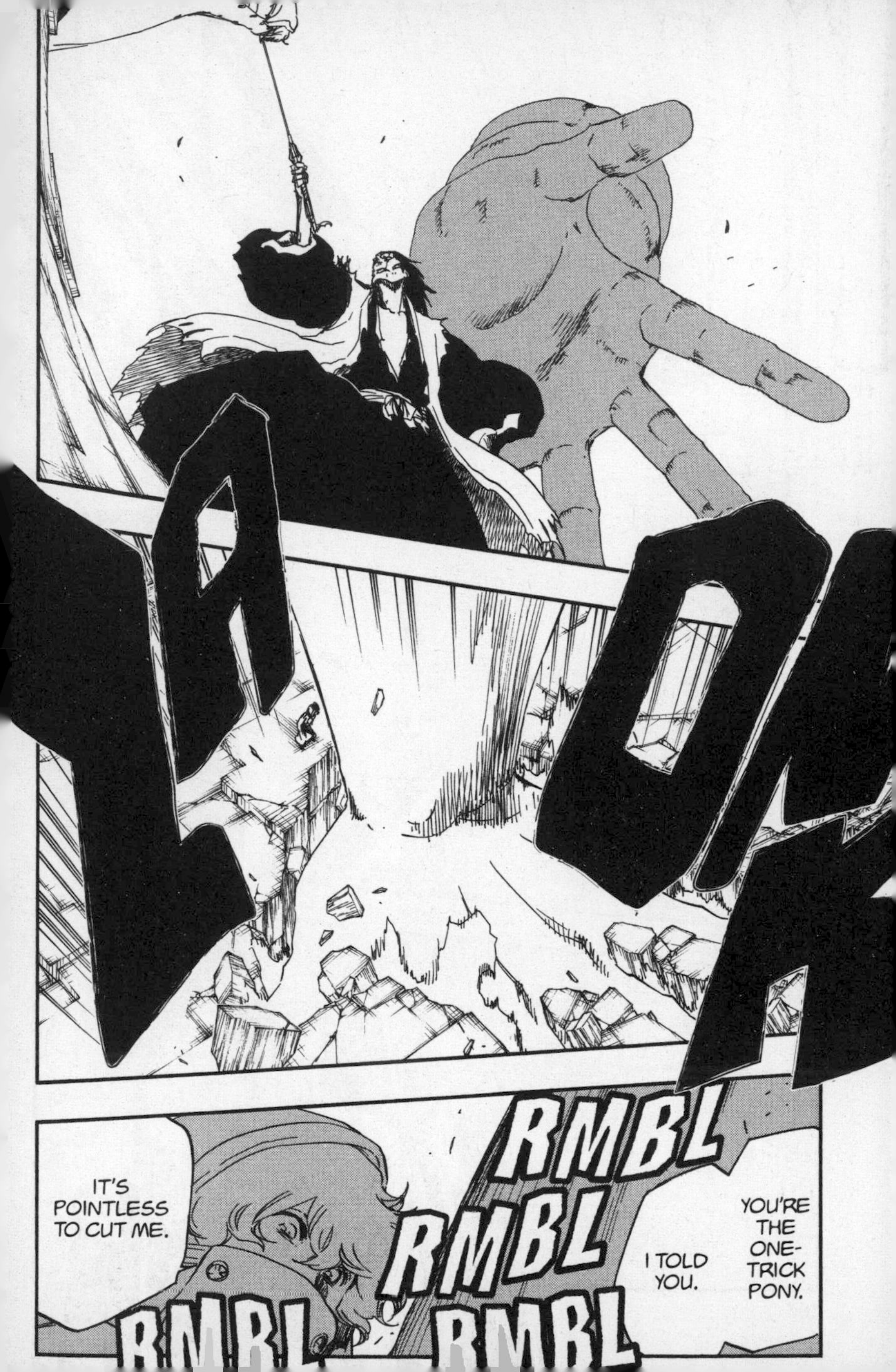
RMBL
YOU'RE THE ONE-TRICK PONY.
I TOLD YOU.
RMBL
IT'S POINTLESS TO CUT ME.
RMBL
RMBL

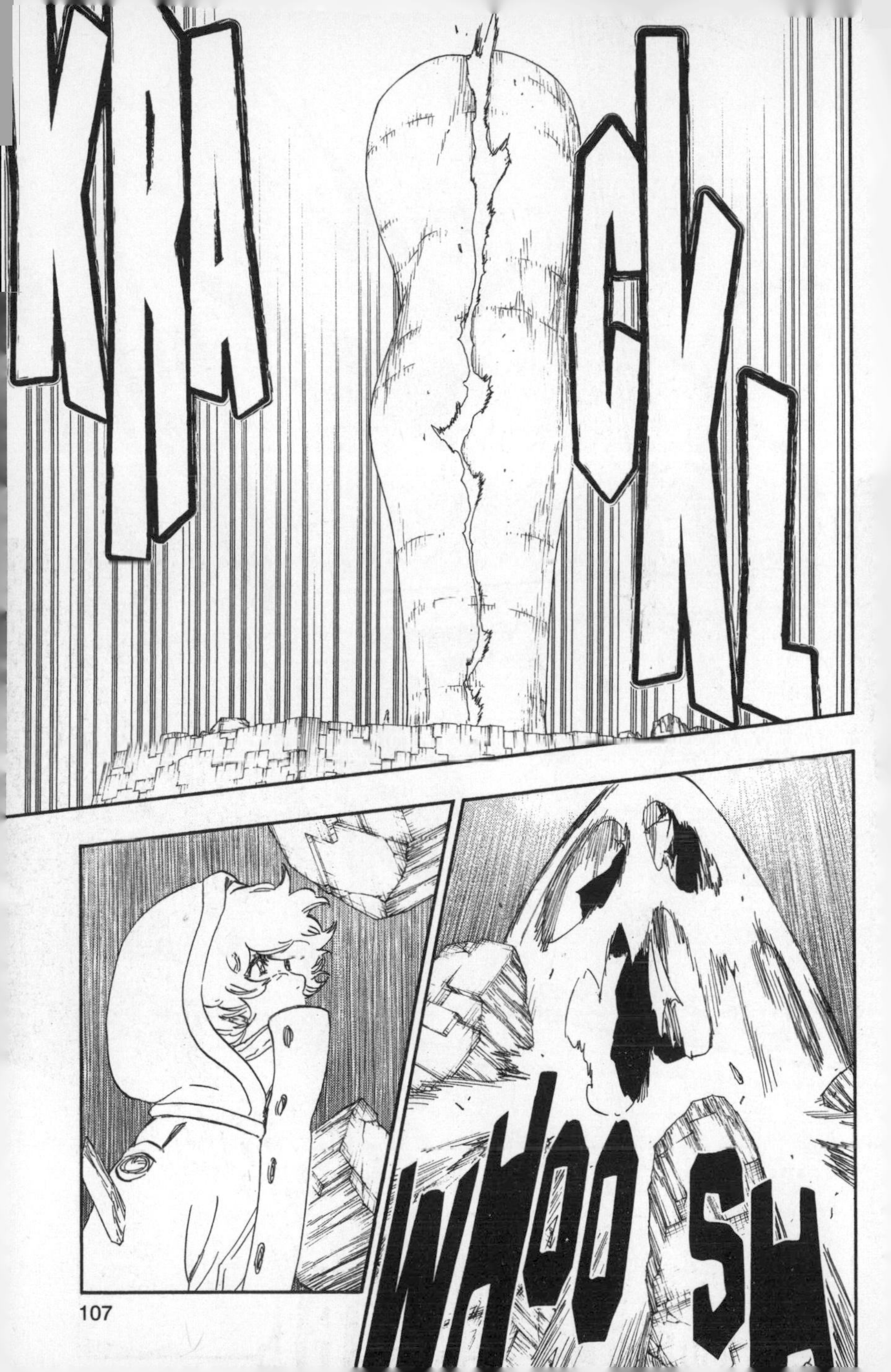
KRACK!!
WHOOSH

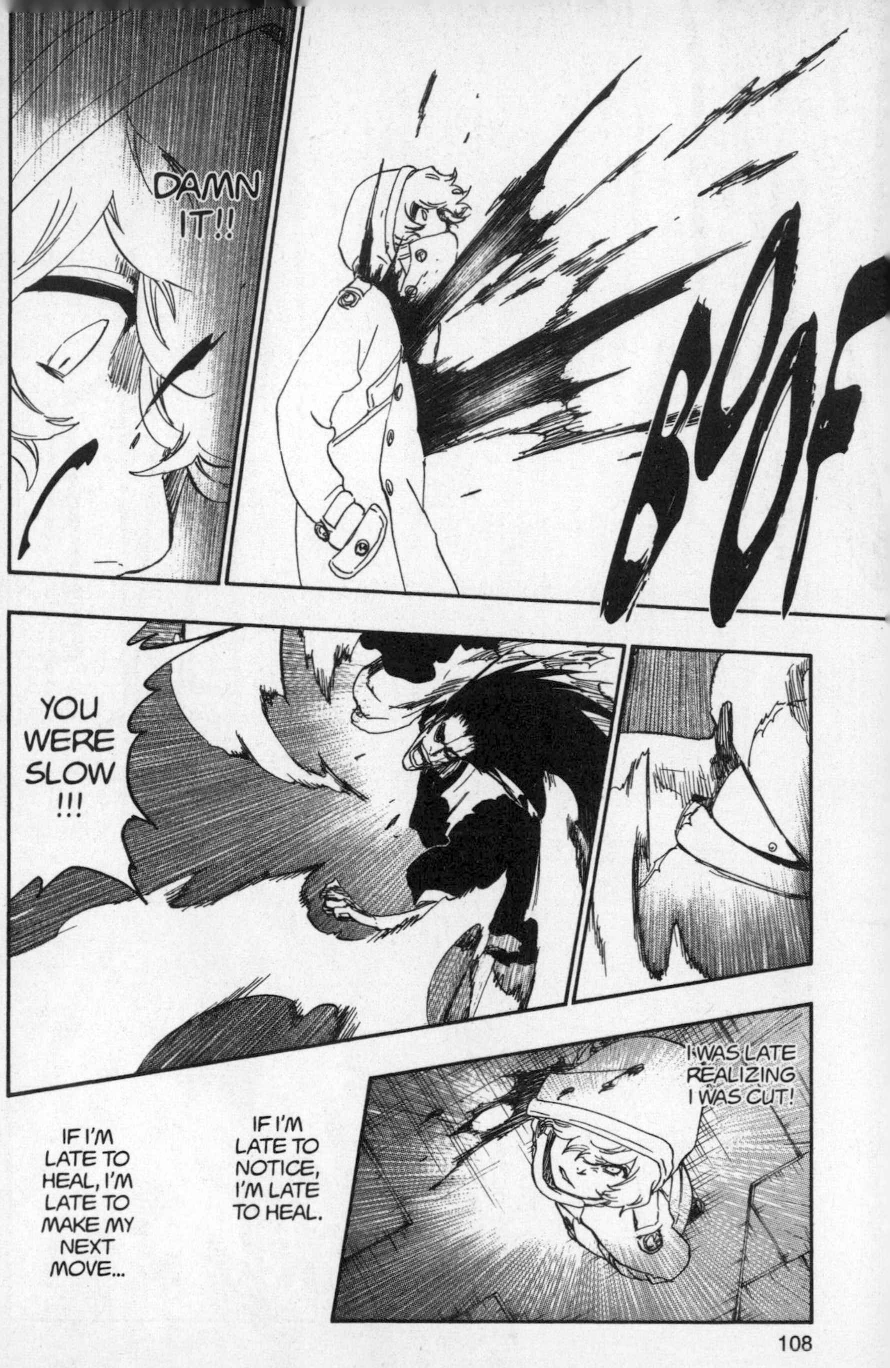
DAMN IT!!
YOU WERE SLOW !!!
I WAS LATE REALIZING I WAS CUT!
IF I'M LATE TO NOTICE, I'M LATE TO HEAL.
IF I'M LATE TO HEAL, I'M LATE TO MAKE MY NEXT MOVE...

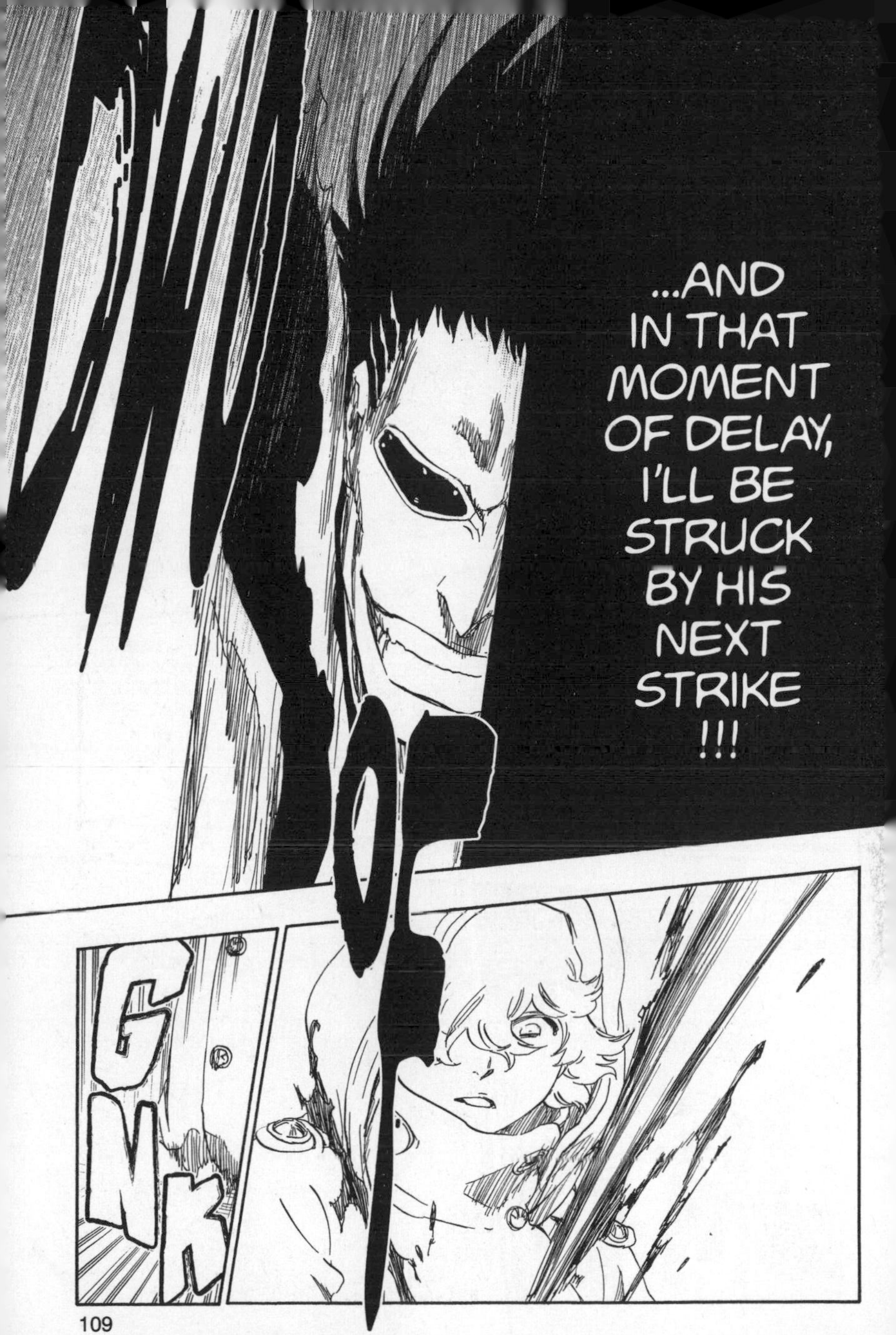
...AND IN THAT MOMENT OF DELAY, I'LL BE STRUCK BY HIS NEXT STRIKE !!!

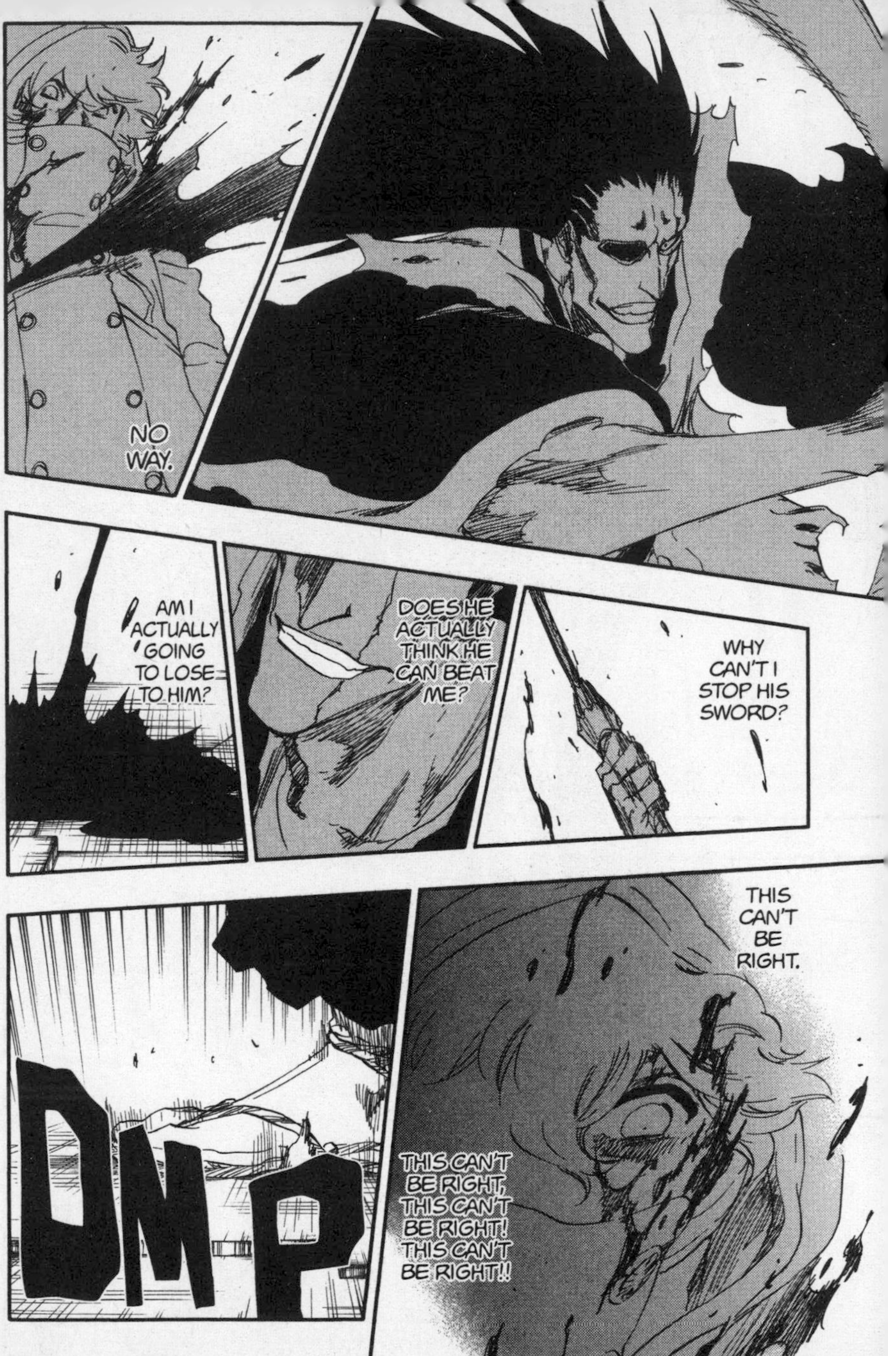
NO WAY.
WHY CAN'T I STOP HIS SWORD?
DOES HE ACTUALLY THINK HE CAN BEAT ME?
AM I ACTUALLY GOING TO LOSE TO HIM?
THIS CAN'T BE RIGHT.
THIS CAN'T BE RIGHT, THIS CAN'T BE RIGHT! THIS CAN'T BE RIGHT!!
DMP

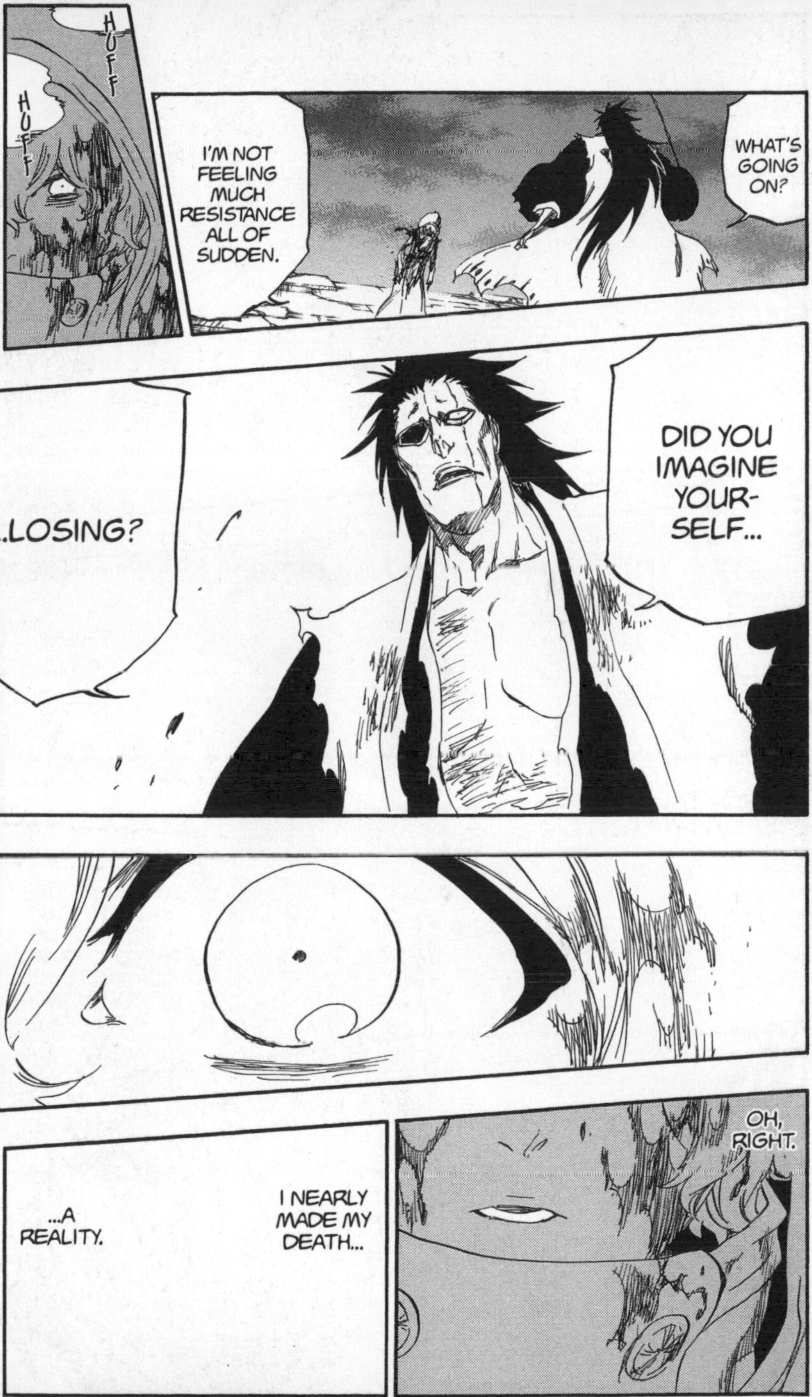
WHAT'S GOING ON?
I'M NOT FEELING MUCH RESISTANCE ALL OF SUDDEN.
HUFF
HUFF
DID YOU IMAGINE YOUR-SELF...
...LOSING?
OH, RIGHT.
I NEARLY MADE MY DEATH...
...A REALITY.

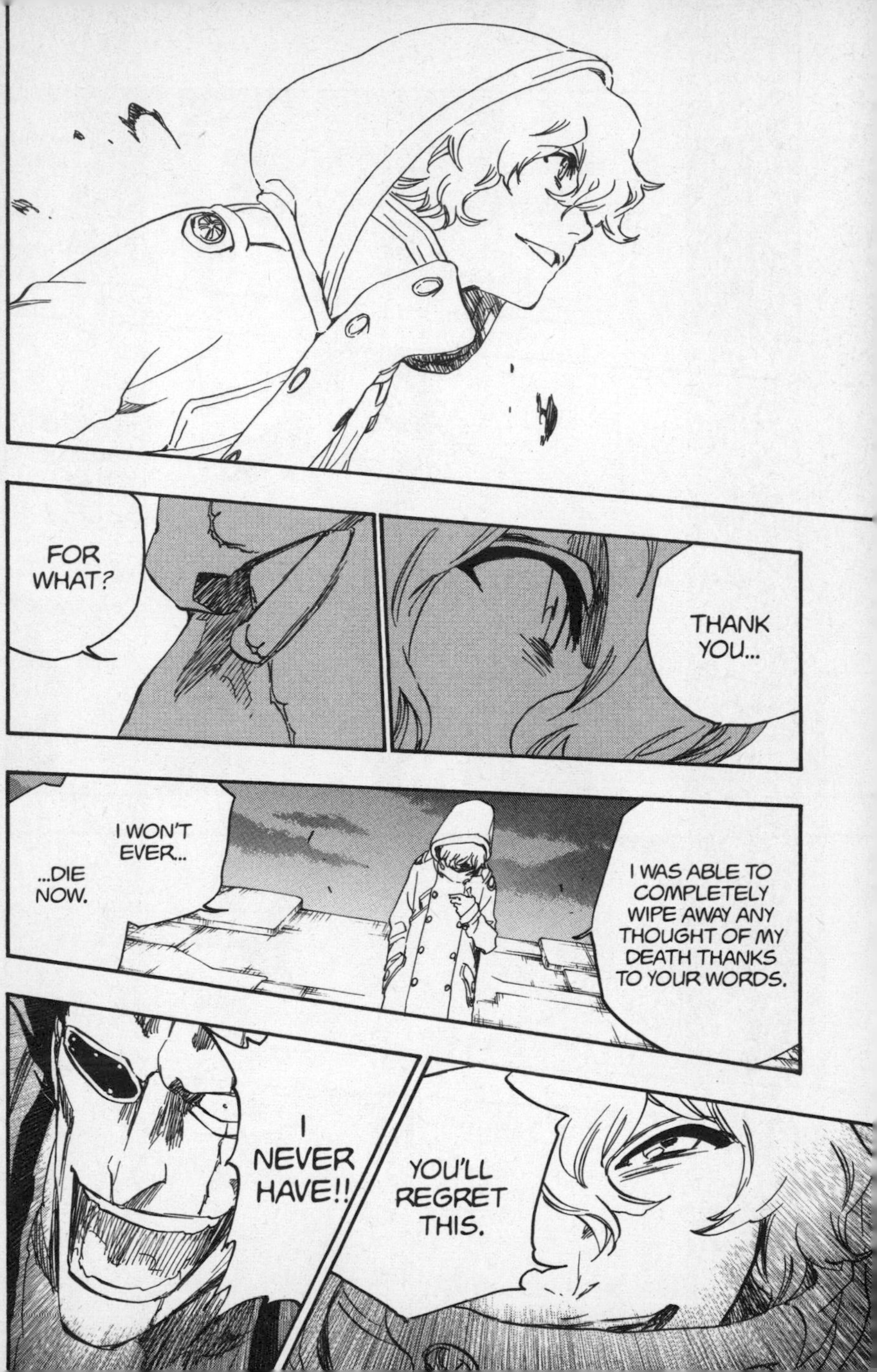
THANK YOU...
FOR WHAT?
I WAS ABLE TO COMPLETELY WIPE AWAY ANY THOUGHT OF MY DEATH THANKS TO YOUR WORDS.
I WON'T EVER...
...DIE NOW.
YOU'LL REGRET THIS.
I NEVER HAVE!!

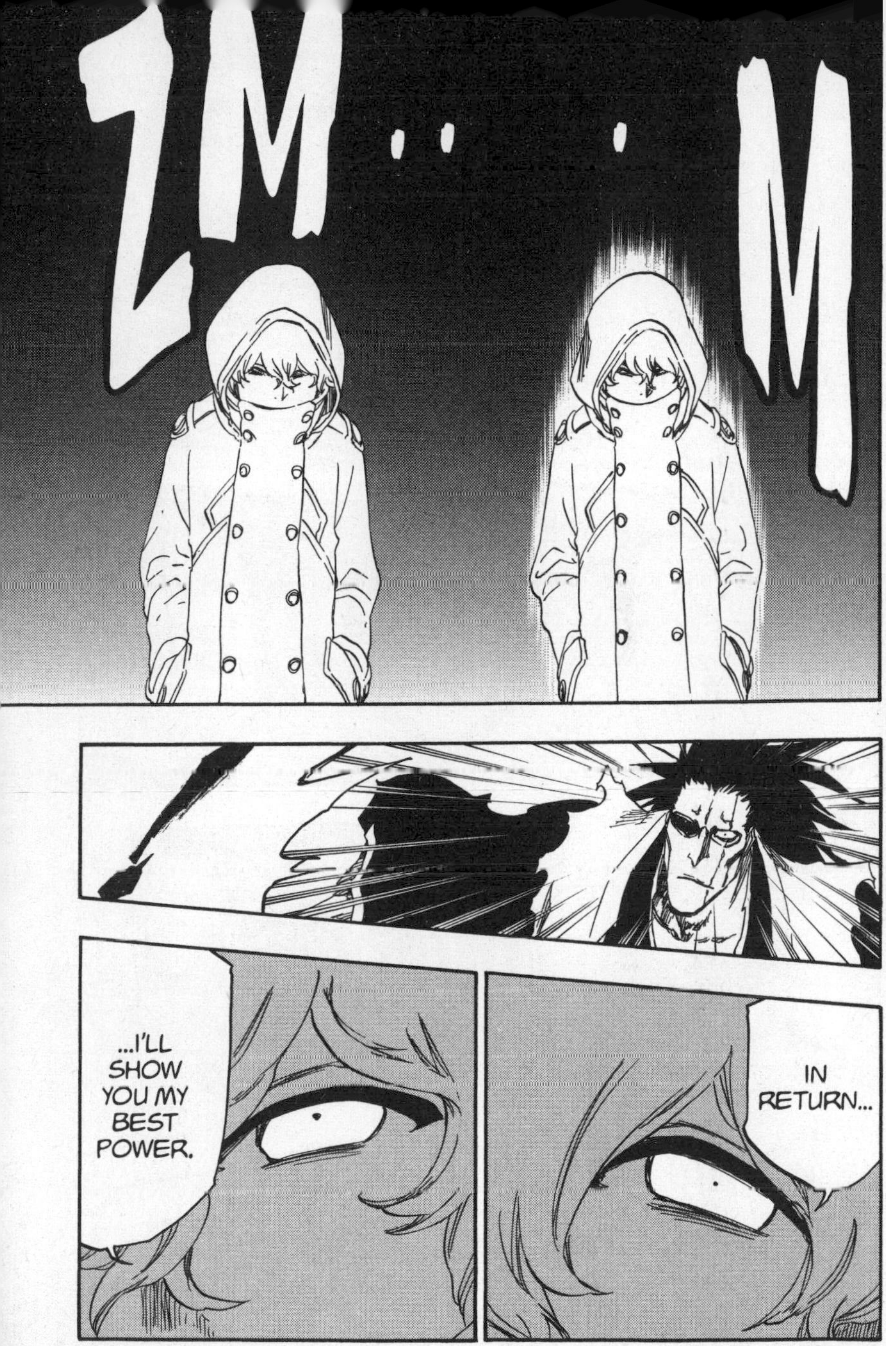
ZM... M
IN RETURN...
...I'LL SHOW YOU MY BEST POWER.

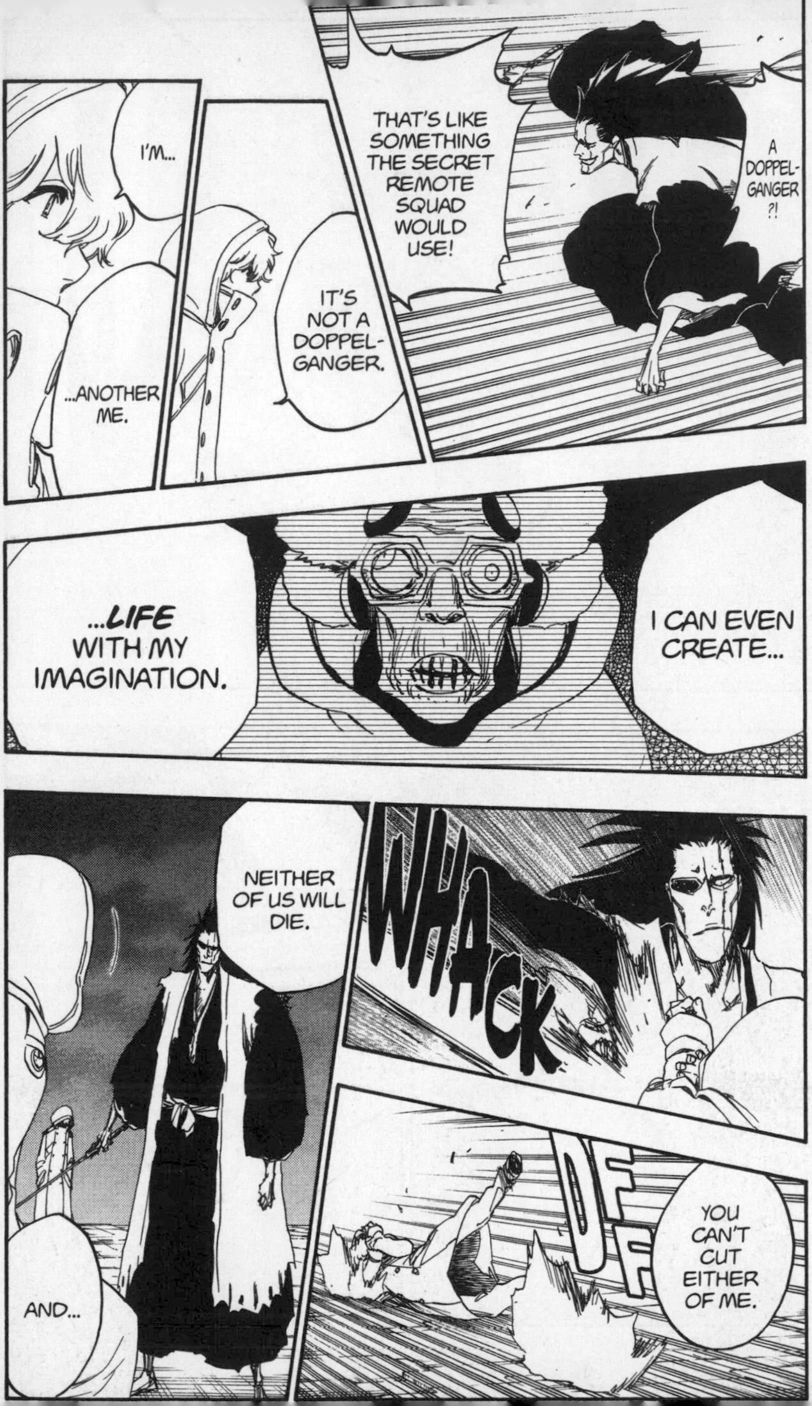
A DOPPEL-GANGER ?!
THAT'S LIKE SOMETHING THE SECRET REMOTE SQUAD WOULD USE!
IT'S NOT A DOPPEL-GANGER.
I'M...
...ANOTHER ME.
I CAN EVEN CREATE...
...**LIFE** WITH MY IMAGINATION.
WHACK
YOU CAN'T CUT EITHER OF ME.
NEITHER OF US WILL DIE.
AND...

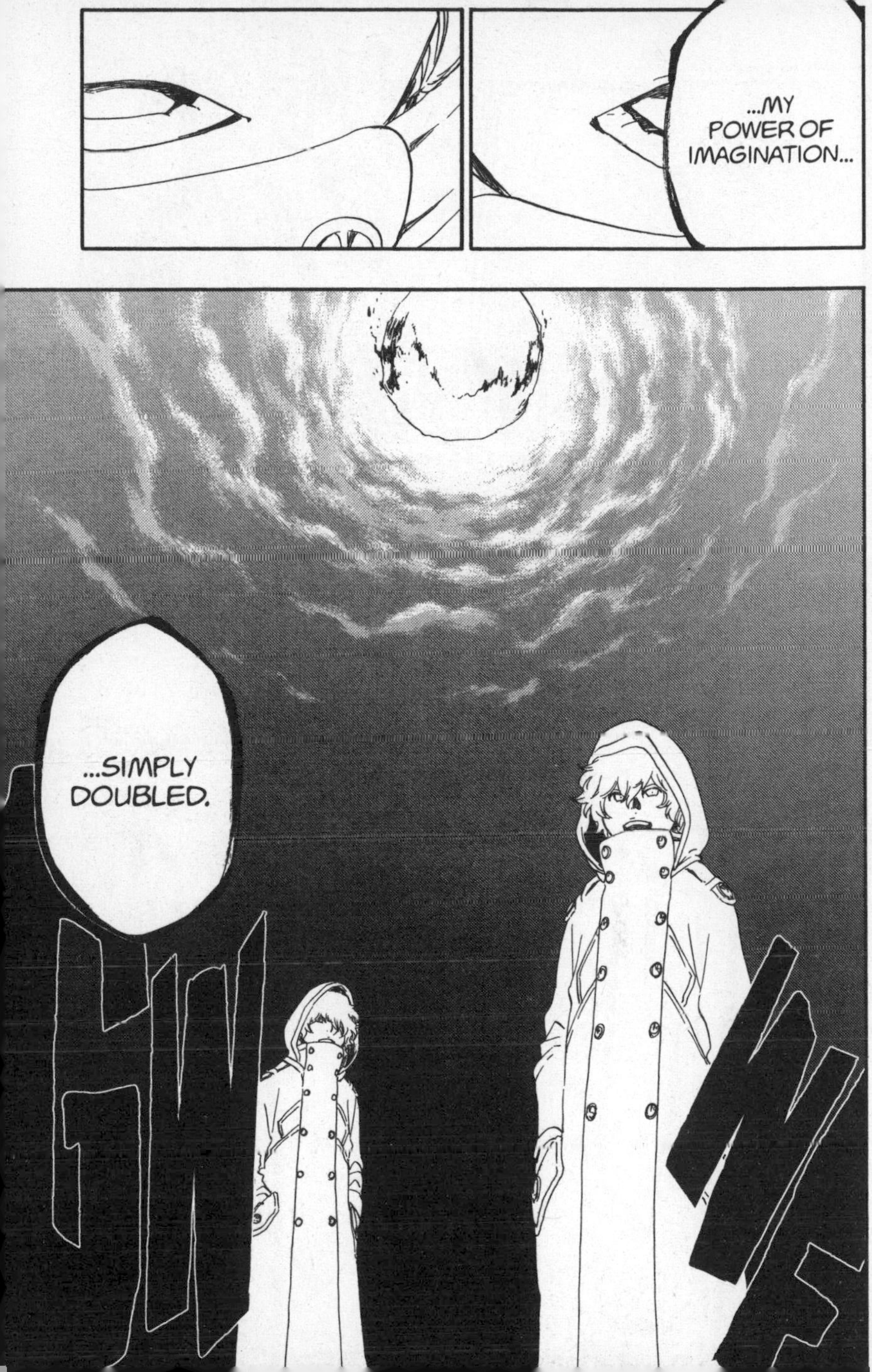
...MY POWER OF IMAGINATION...
...SIMPLY DOUBLED.

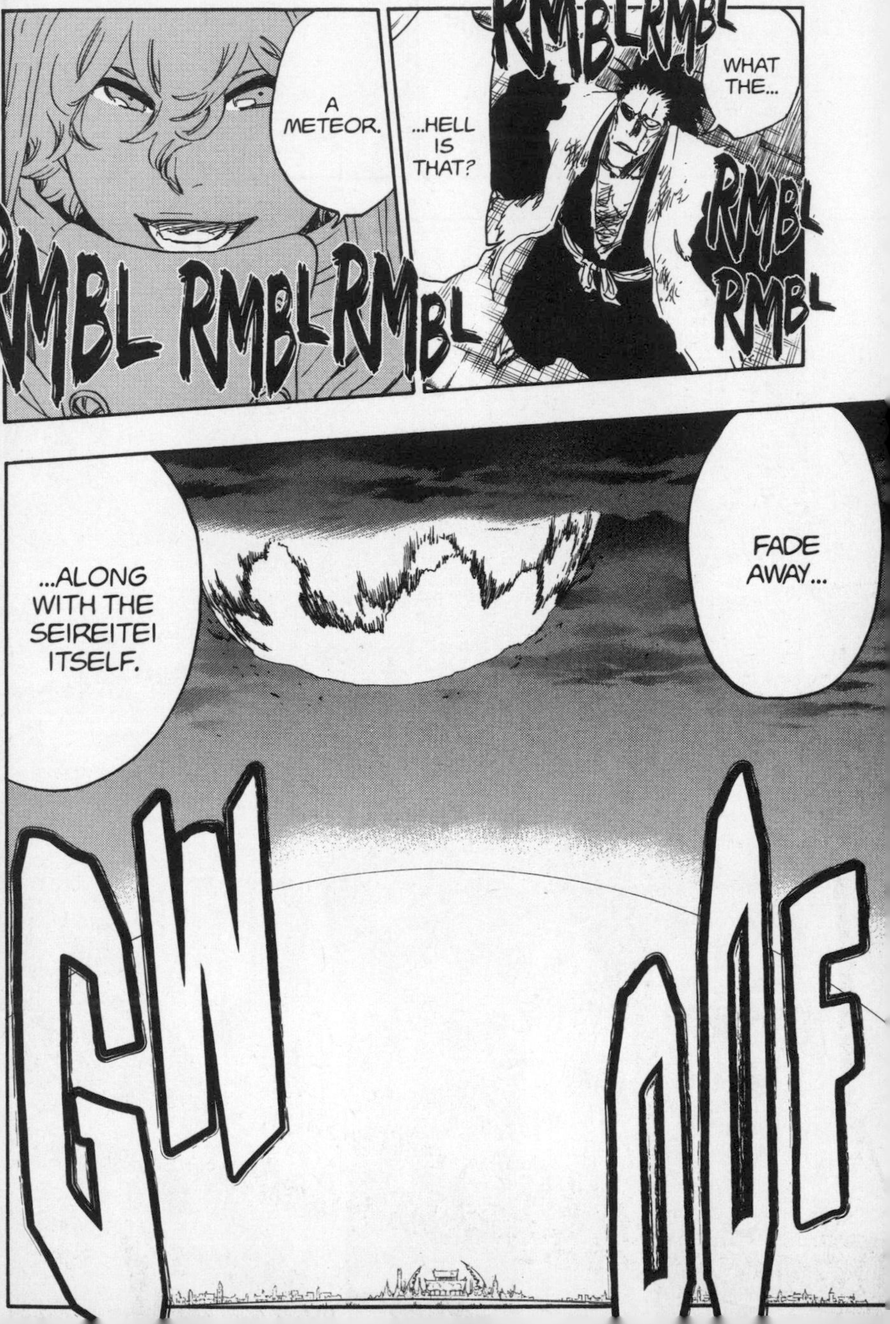

RMBL RMBL
WHAT THE...
RMBL RMBL
...HELL IS THAT?
A METEOR.
RMBL RMBL RMBL
FADE AWAY...
...ALONG WITH THE SEIREITEI ITSELF.

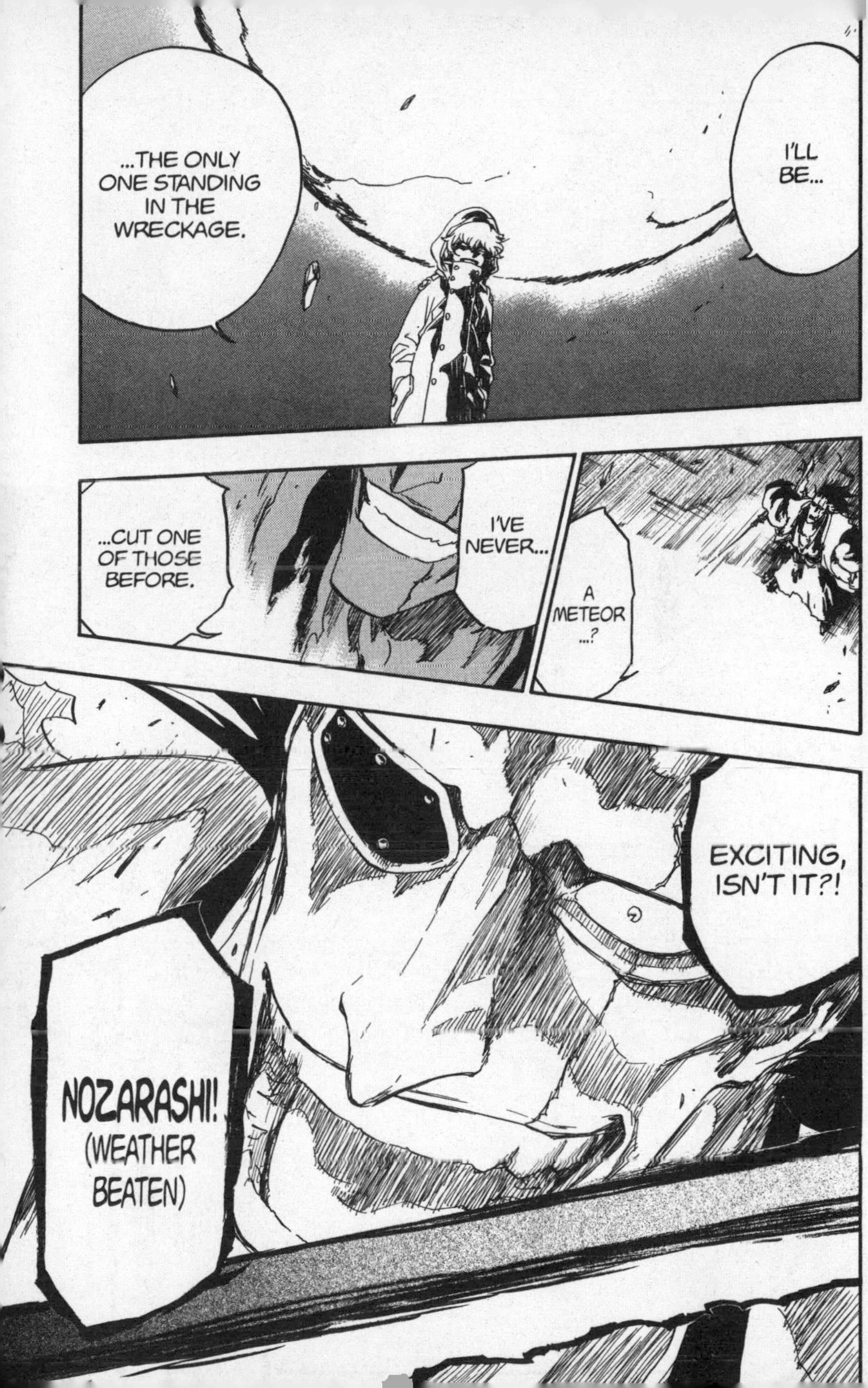
I'LL BE...
...THE ONLY ONE STANDING IN THE WRECKAGE.
A METEOR ...?
I'VE NEVER...
...CUT ONE OF THOSE BEFORE.
EXCITING, ISN'T IT?!
NOZARASHI! (WEATHER BEATEN)

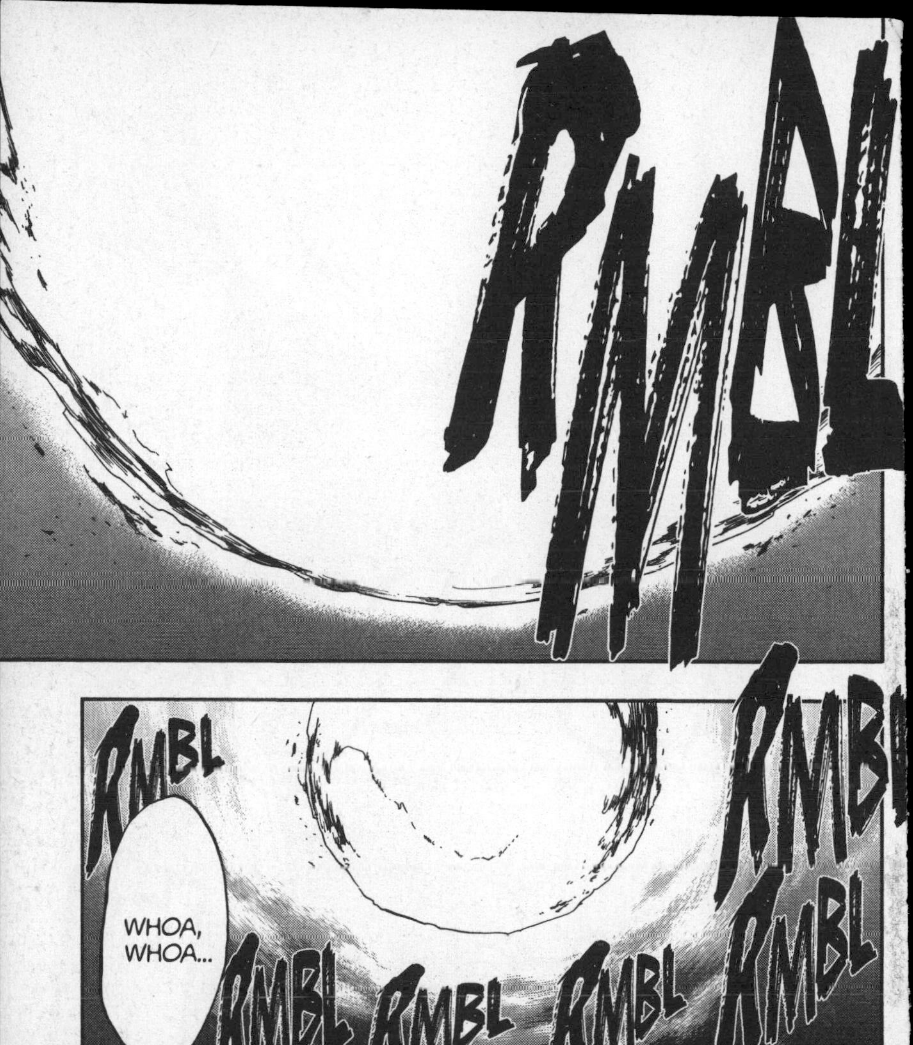
RMBL
RMBL
RMBL
RMBL
RMBL
RMBL
RMBL
RMBL
WHOA, WHOA...

BLEACH 577.

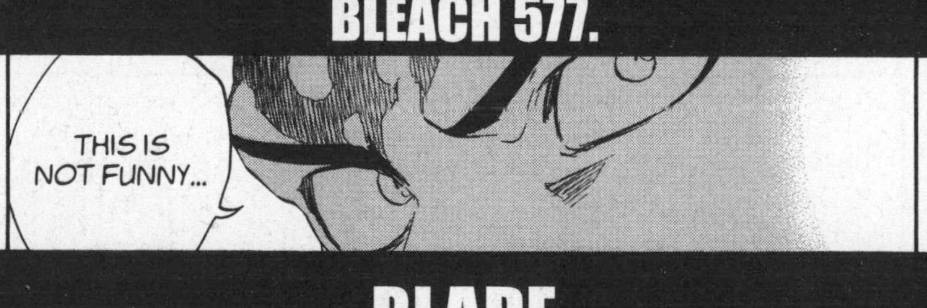
THIS IS NOT FUNNY...

BLADE

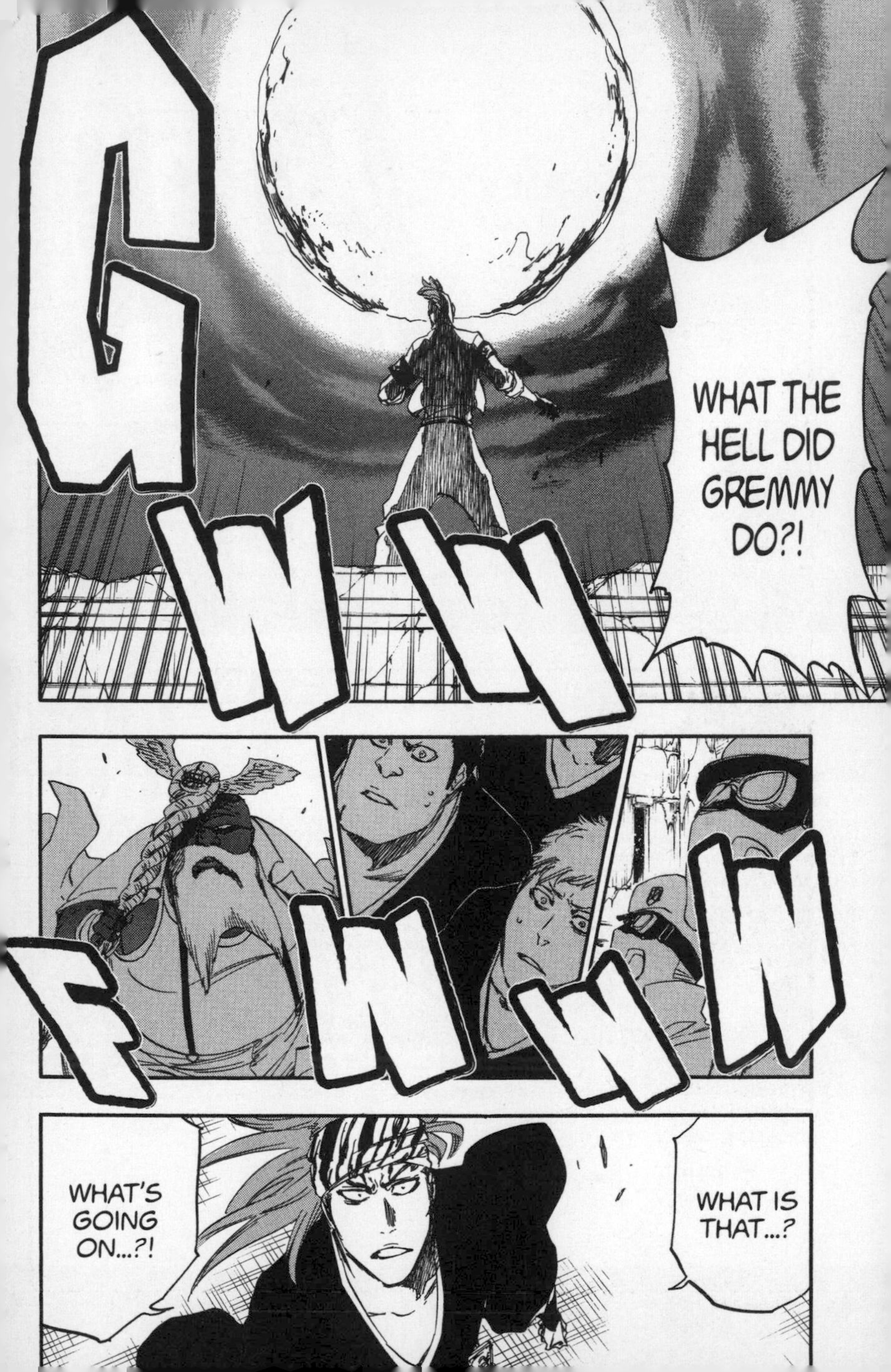
WHAT THE HELL DID GREMMY DO?!
GWW
FWWW
WHAT IS THAT...?
WHAT'S GOING ON...?!

READ THIS WAY

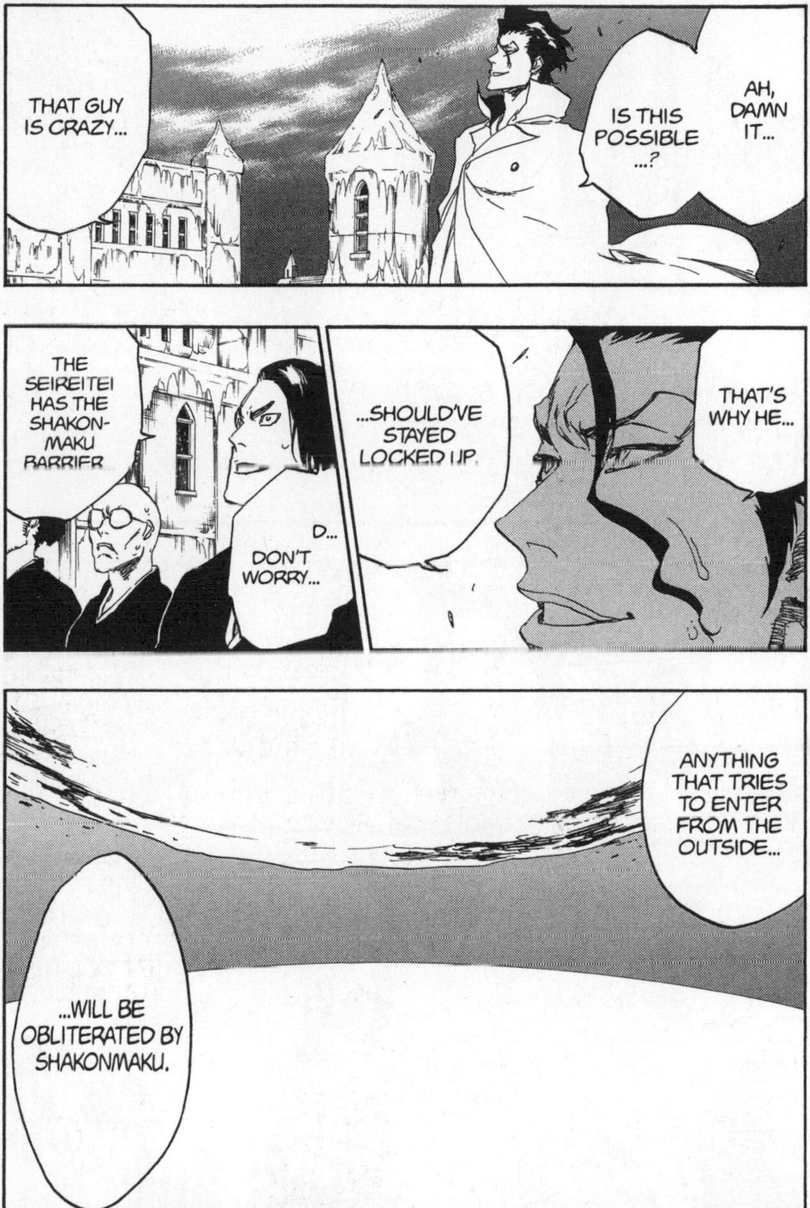
AH, DAMN IT...
IS THIS POSSIBLE ...?
THAT GUY IS CRAZY...
THAT'S WHY HE...
...SHOULD'VE STAYED LOCKED UP.
D... DON'T WORRY...
THE SEIREITEI HAS THE SHAKON-MAKU BARRIER
ANYTHING THAT TRIES TO ENTER FROM THE OUTSIDE...
...WILL BE OBLITERATED BY SHAKONMAKU.

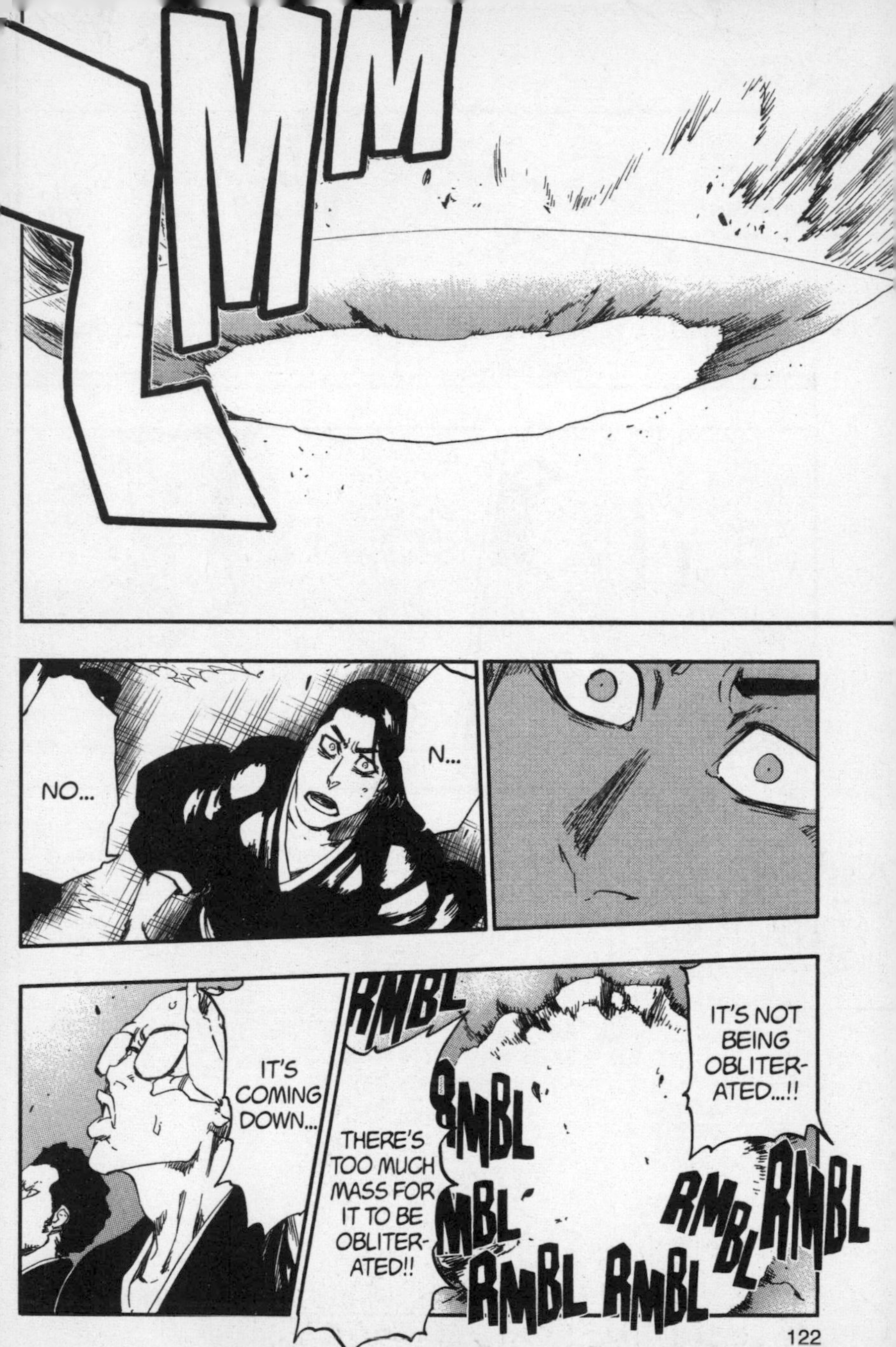
MM
N...
NO...
IT'S NOT BEING OBLITERATED...!!
RMBL
RMBL
RMBL
RMBL RMBL
RMBL
RMBL
RMBL
THERE'S TOO MUCH MASS FOR IT TO BE OBLITERATED!!
IT'S COMING DOWN...

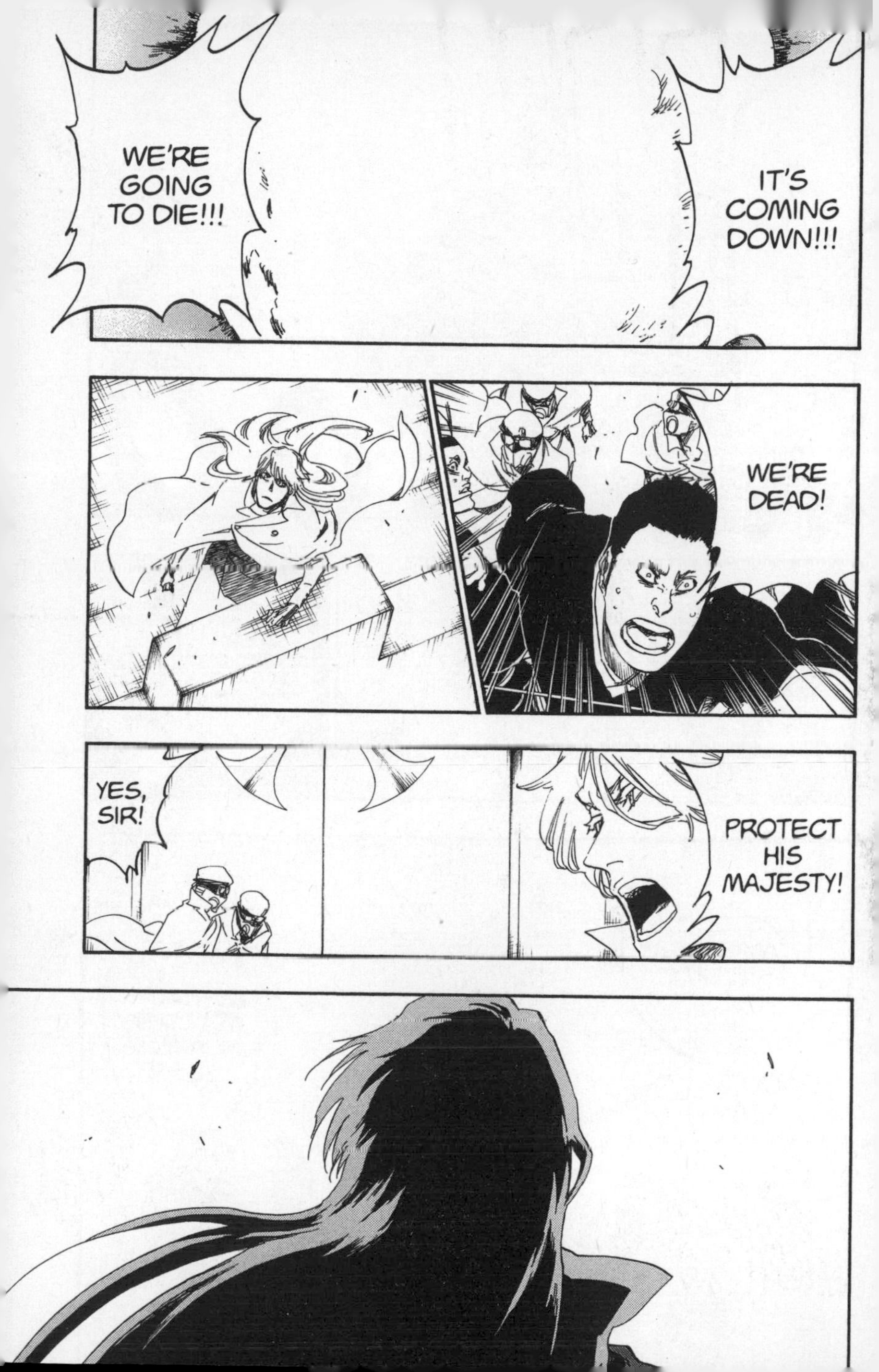
IT'S COMING DOWN!!!
WE'RE GOING TO DIE!!!
WE'RE DEAD!
PROTECT HIS MAJESTY!
YES, SIR!

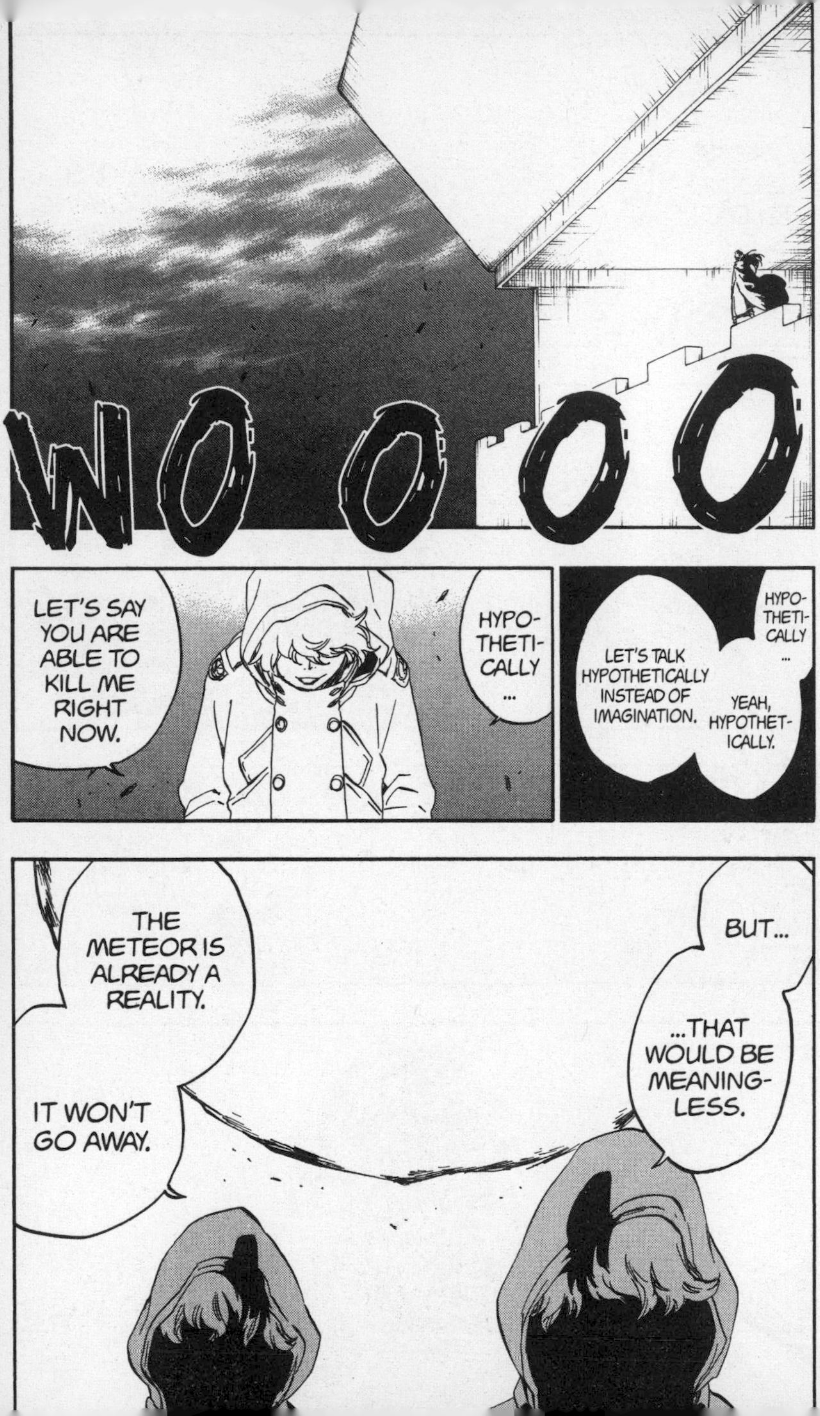
WOOOO
HYPO-THETI-CALLY ...
LET'S TALK HYPOTHETICALLY INSTEAD OF IMAGINATION.
YEAH, HYPOTHET-ICALLY.
HYPO-THETI-CALLY ...
LET'S SAY YOU ARE ABLE TO KILL ME RIGHT NOW.
BUT...
...THAT WOULD BE MEANING-LESS.
THE METEOR IS ALREADY A REALITY.
IT WON'T GO AWAY.

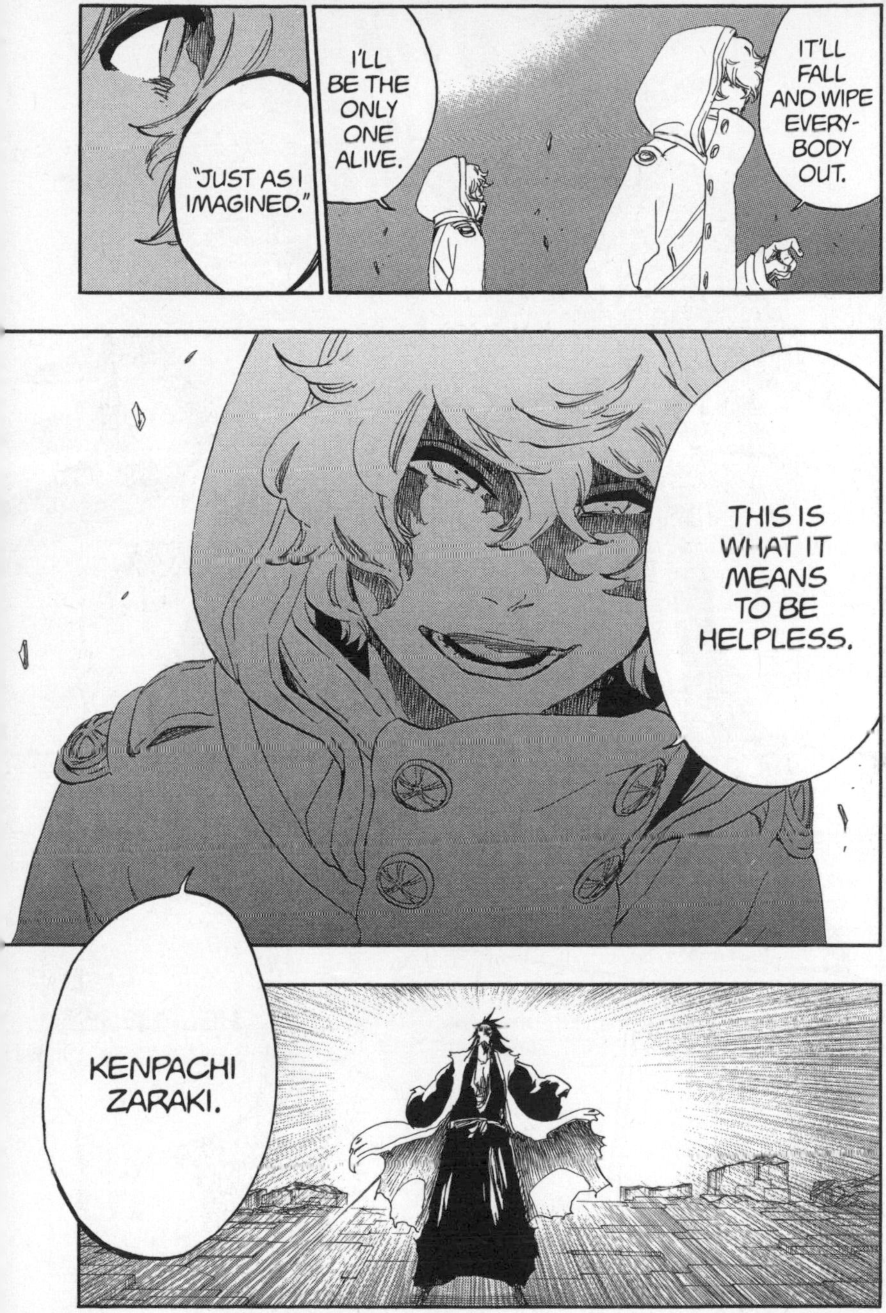
IT'LL FALL AND WIPE EVERYBODY OUT.
I'LL BE THE ONLY ONE ALIVE.
"JUST AS I IMAGINED."
THIS IS WHAT IT MEANS TO BE HELPLESS.
KENPACHI ZARAKI.

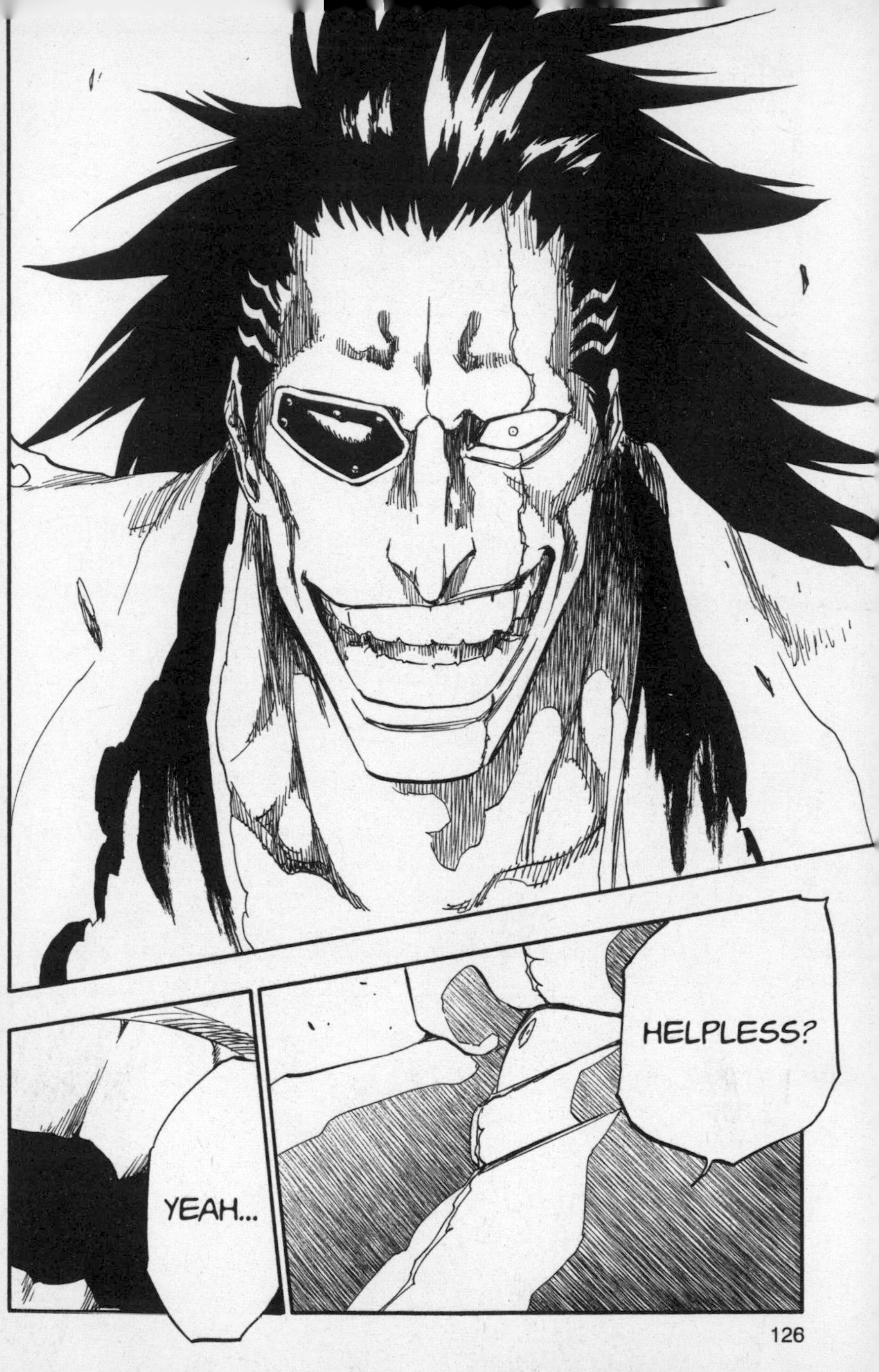
HELPLESS?
YEAH...

READ THIS WAY

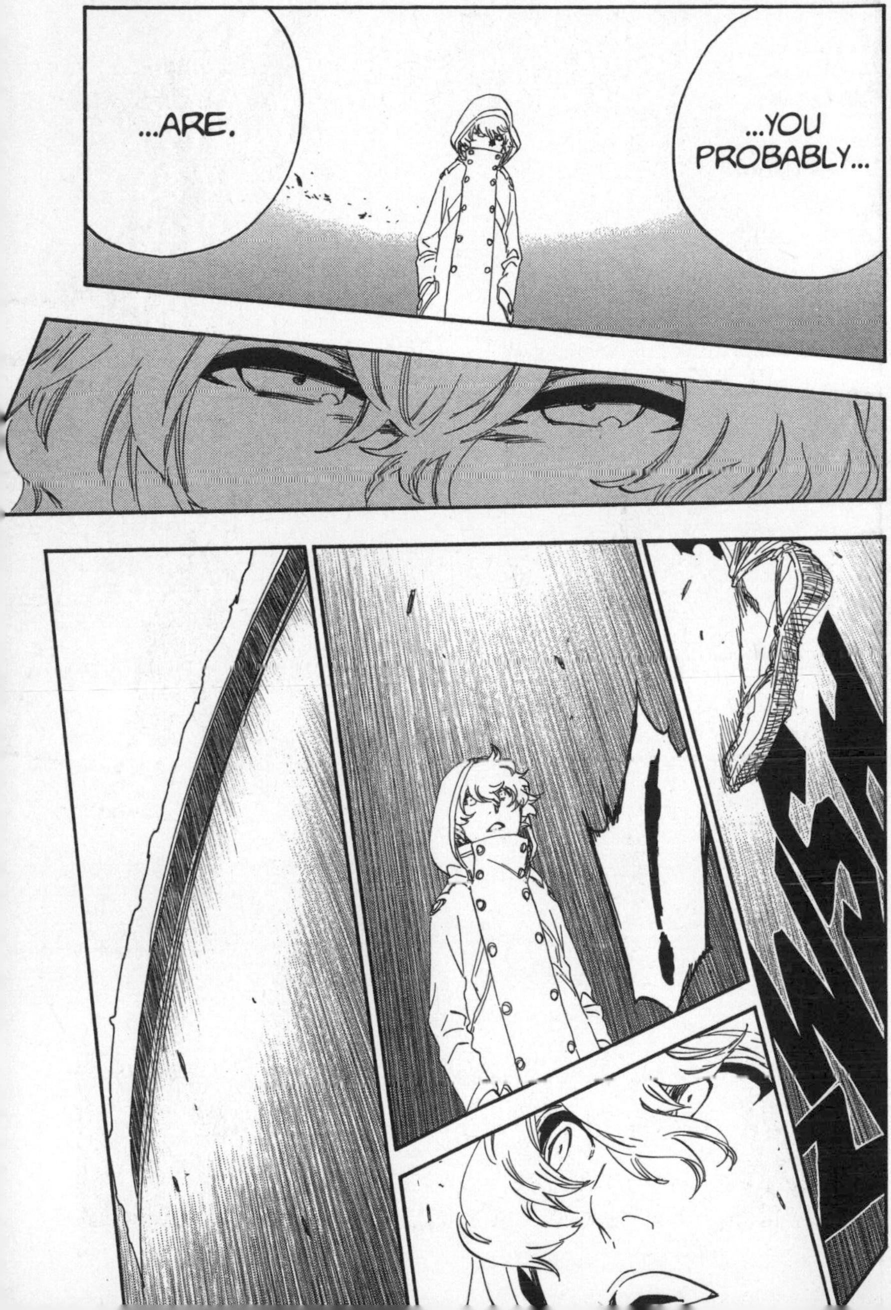
...YOU PROBABLY...
...ARE.

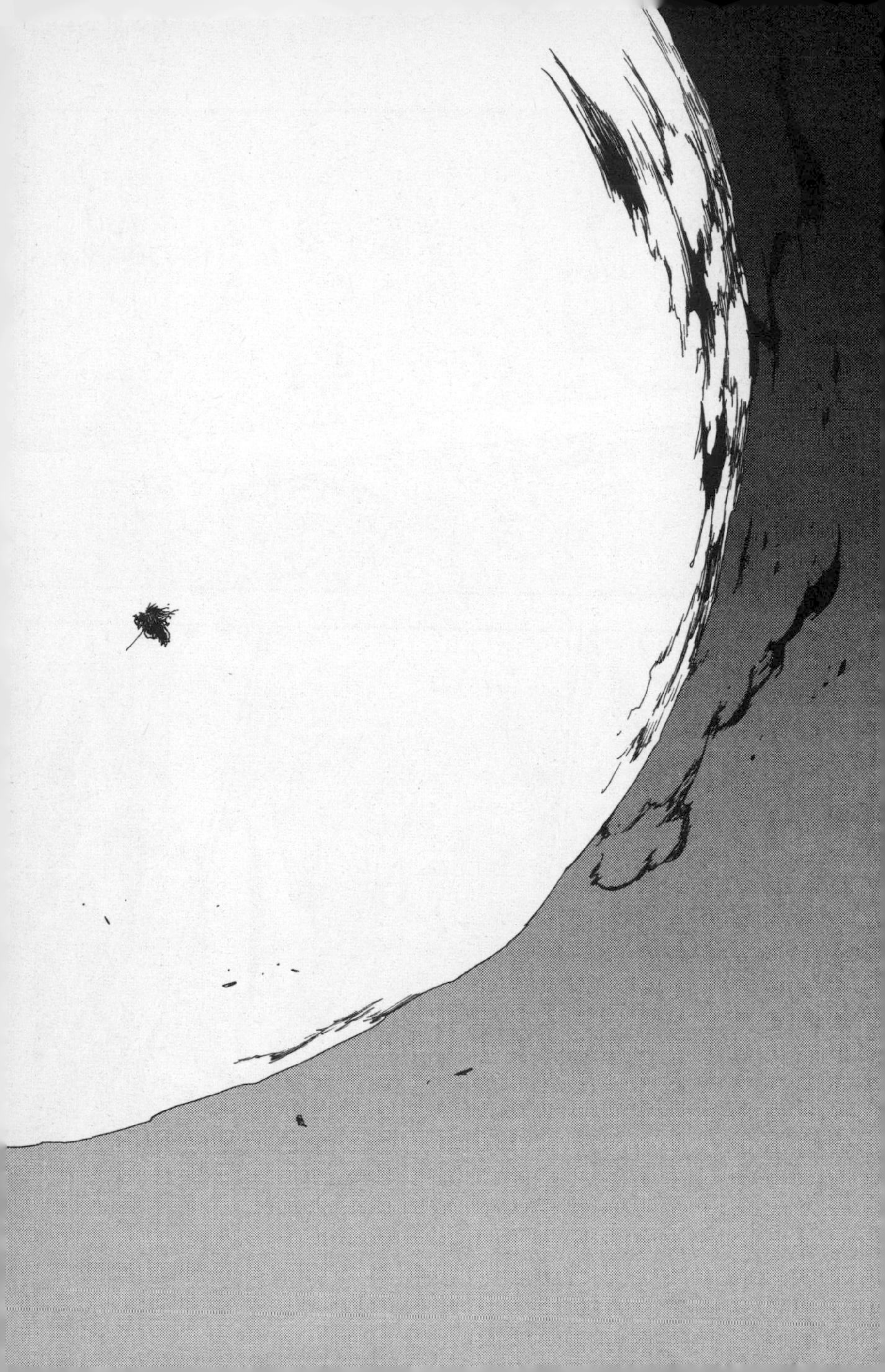

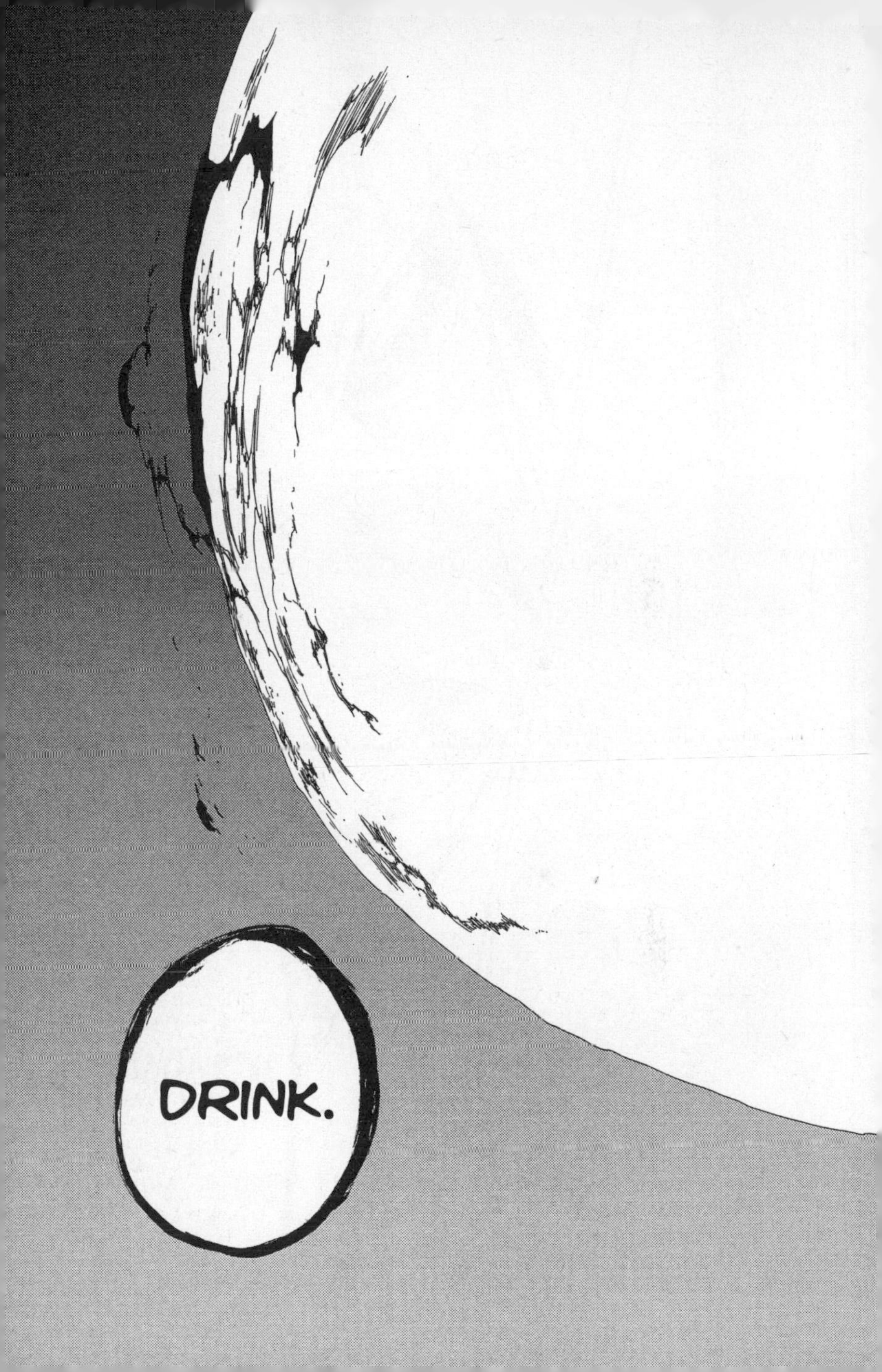
DRINK.

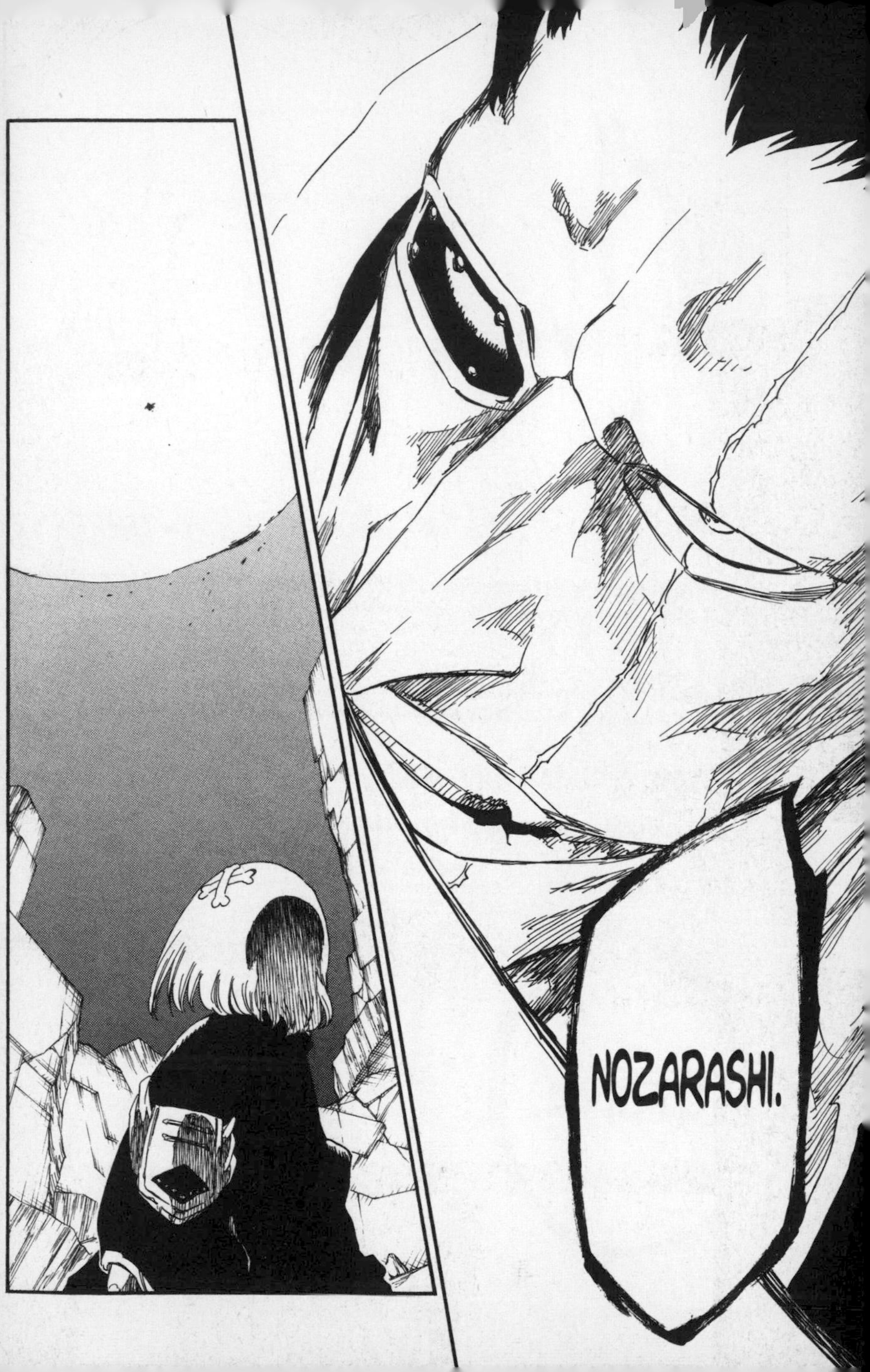
NOZARASHI.

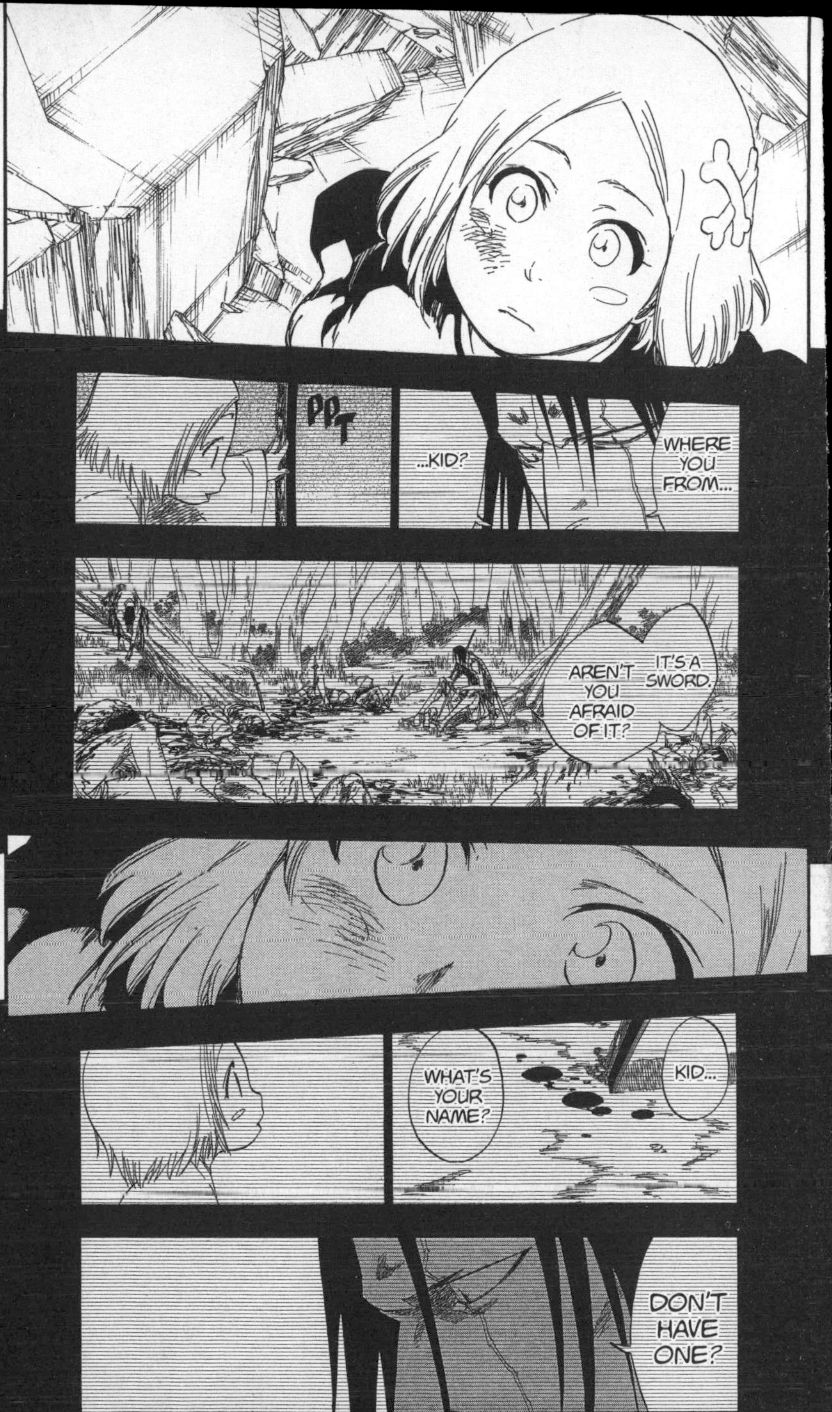
WHERE YOU FROM...
...KID?
PPT
IT'S A SWORD.
AREN'T YOU AFRAID OF IT?
KID...
WHAT'S YOUR NAME?
DON'T HAVE ONE?

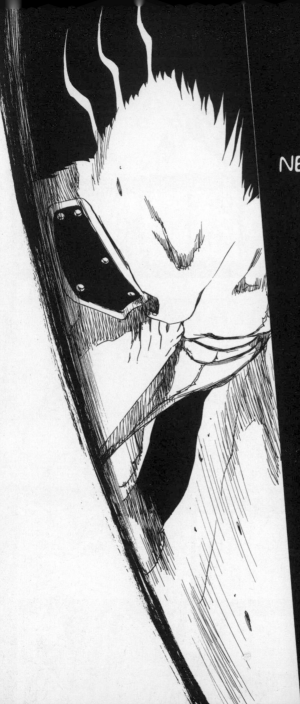

NEITHER
DO I.

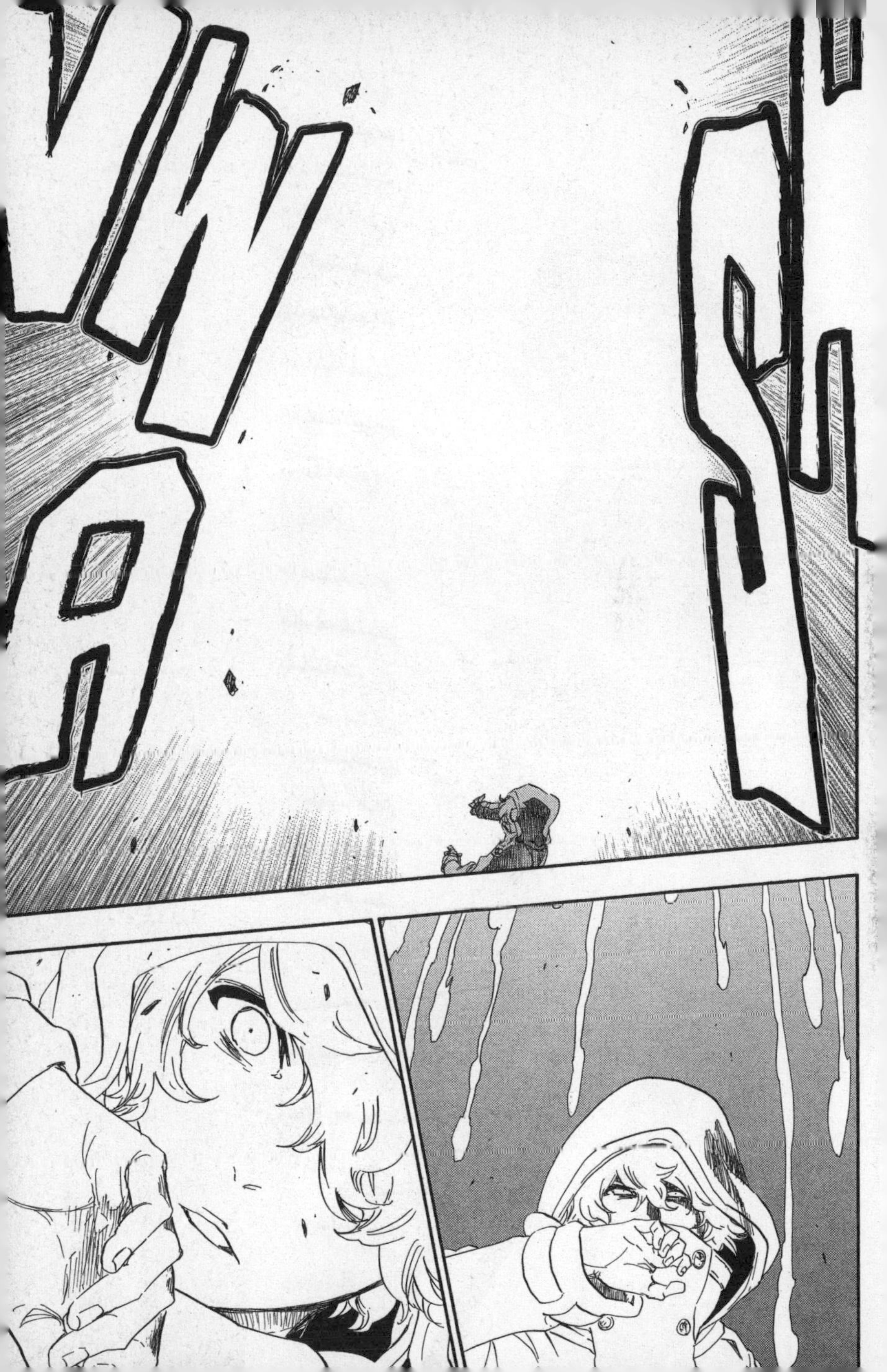

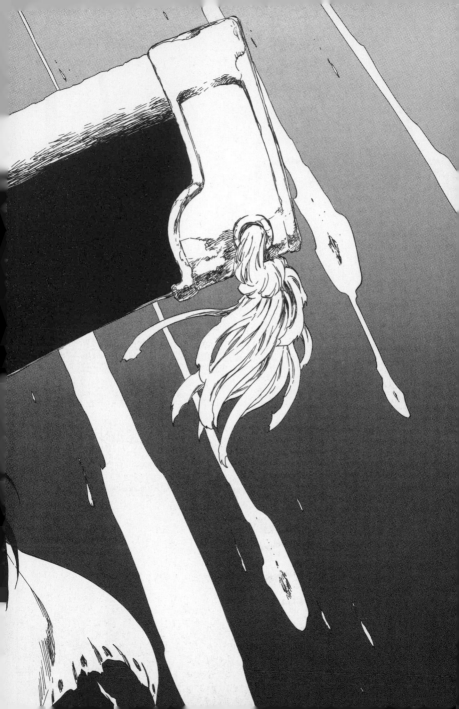

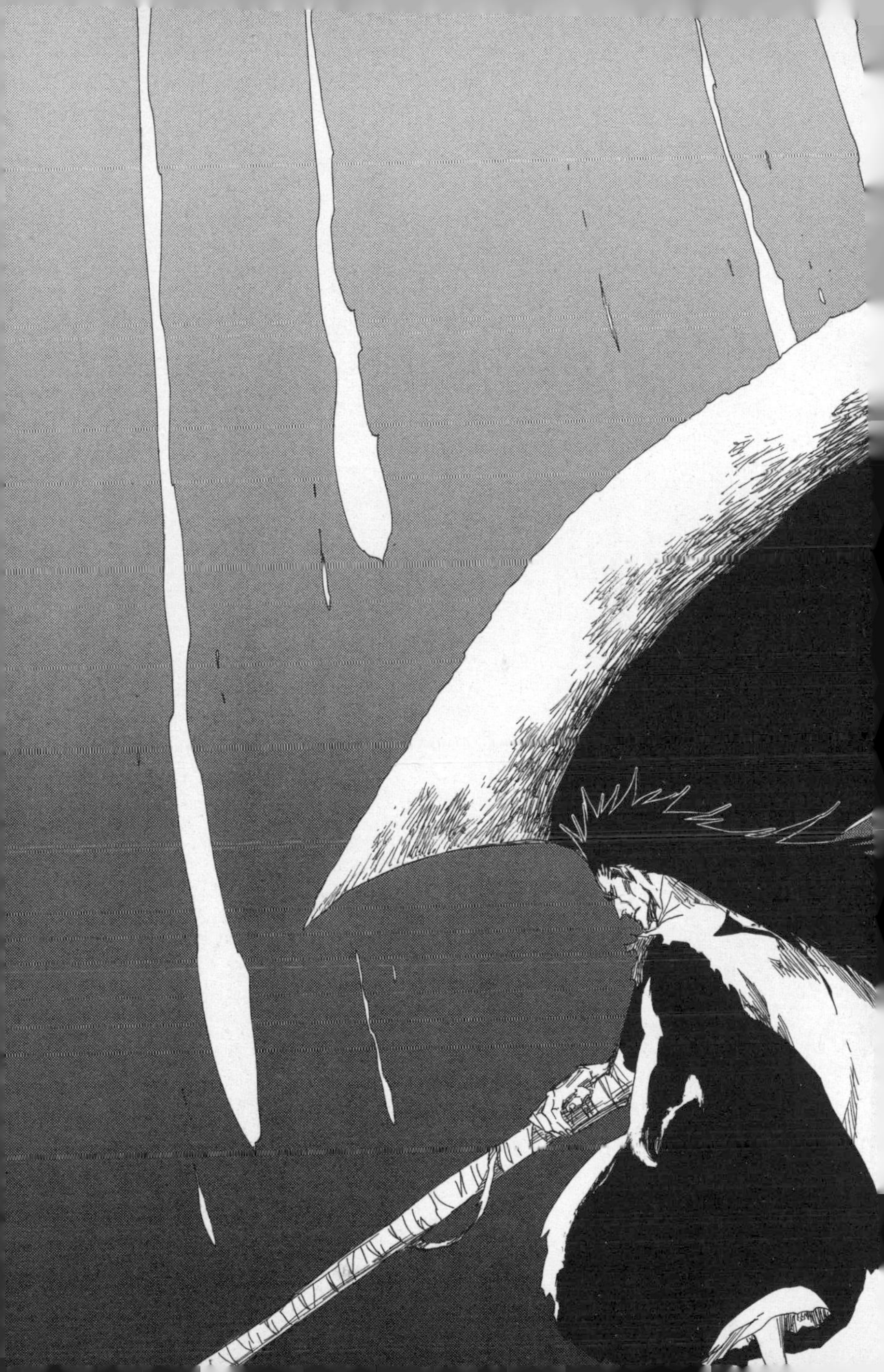

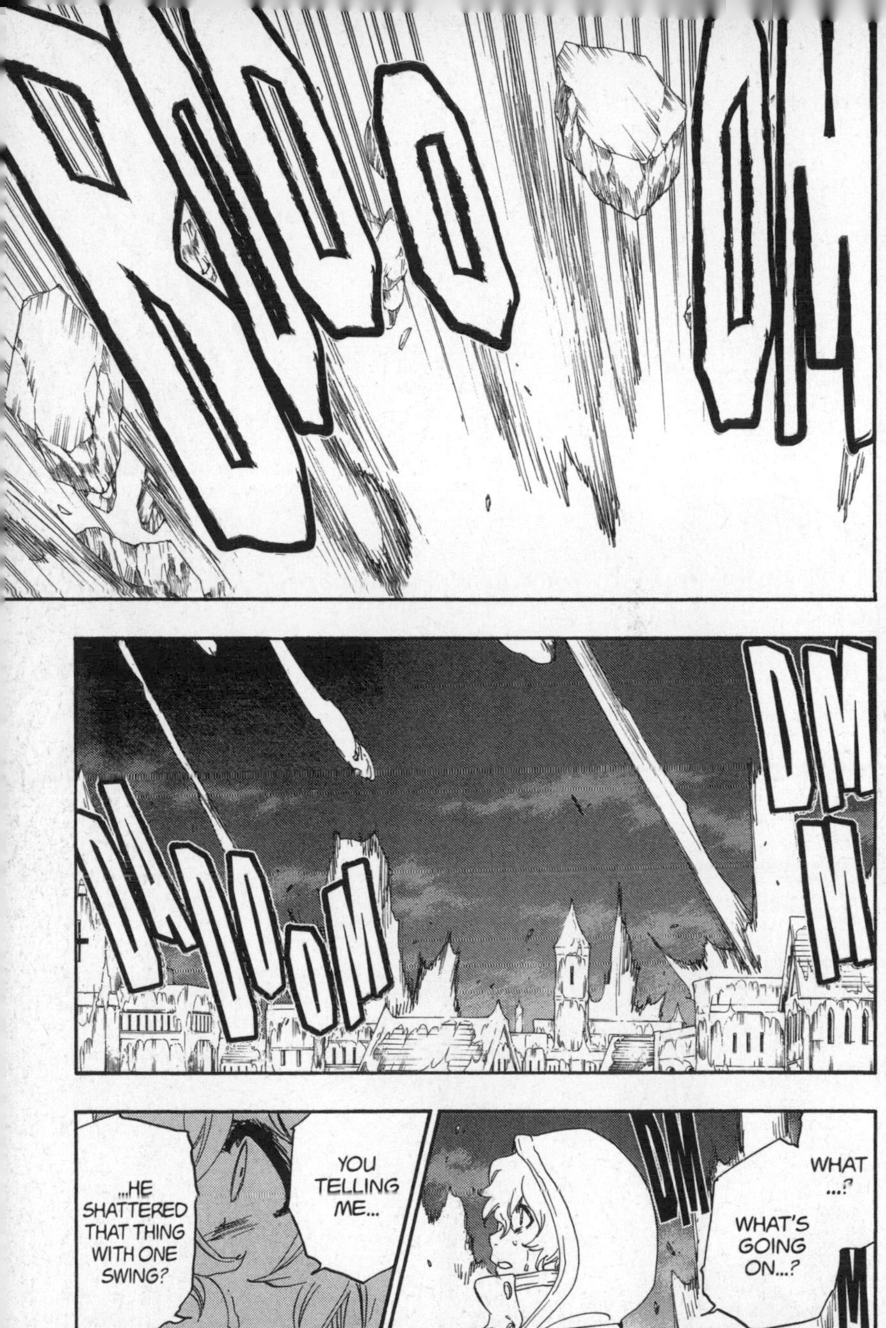
DMMM
WHAT ...?
WHAT'S GOING ON...?
YOU TELLING ME...
...HE SHATTERED THAT THING WITH ONE SWING?

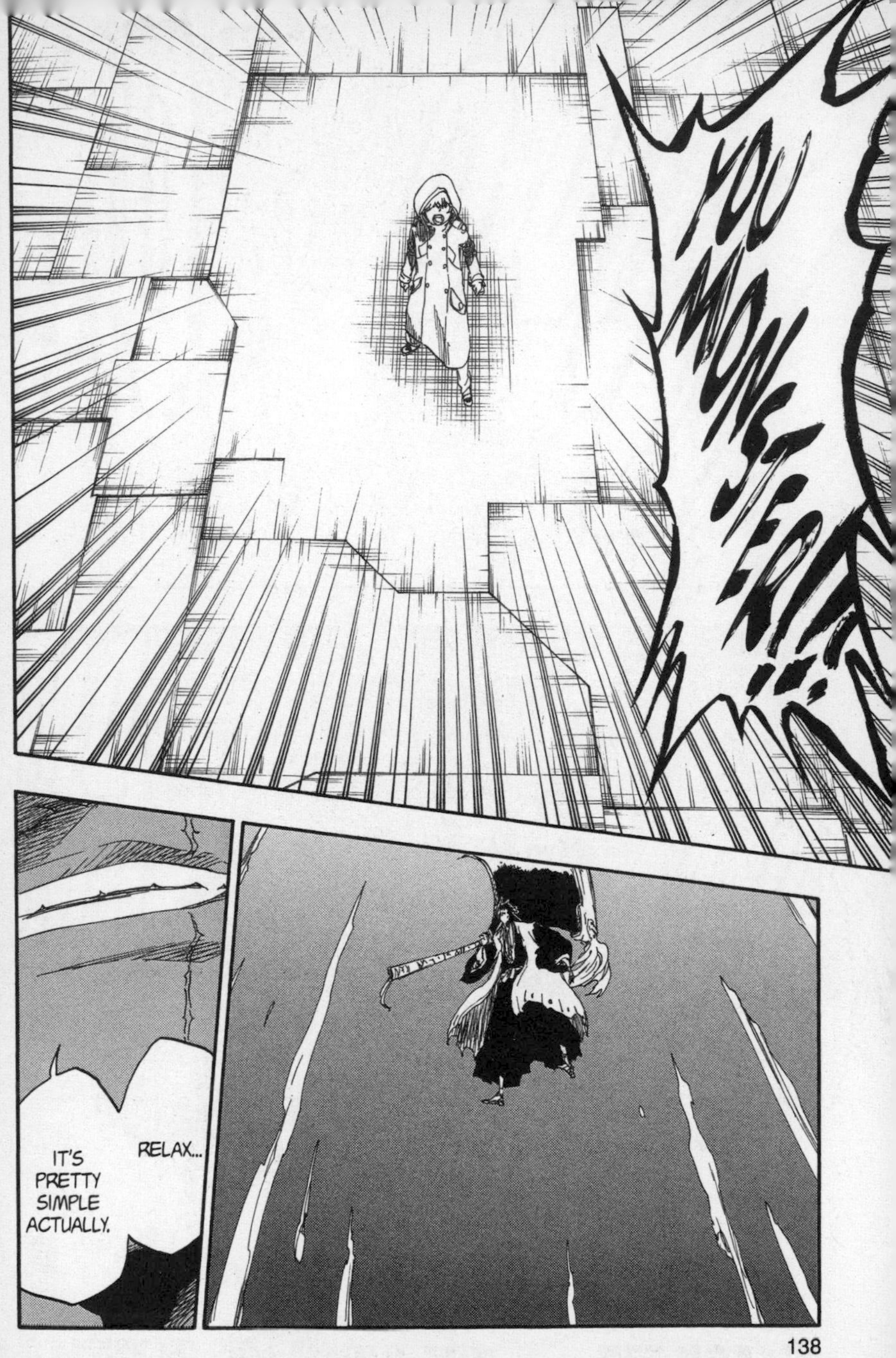
YOU MONSTER!!
RELAX...
IT'S PRETTY SIMPLE ACTUALLY.

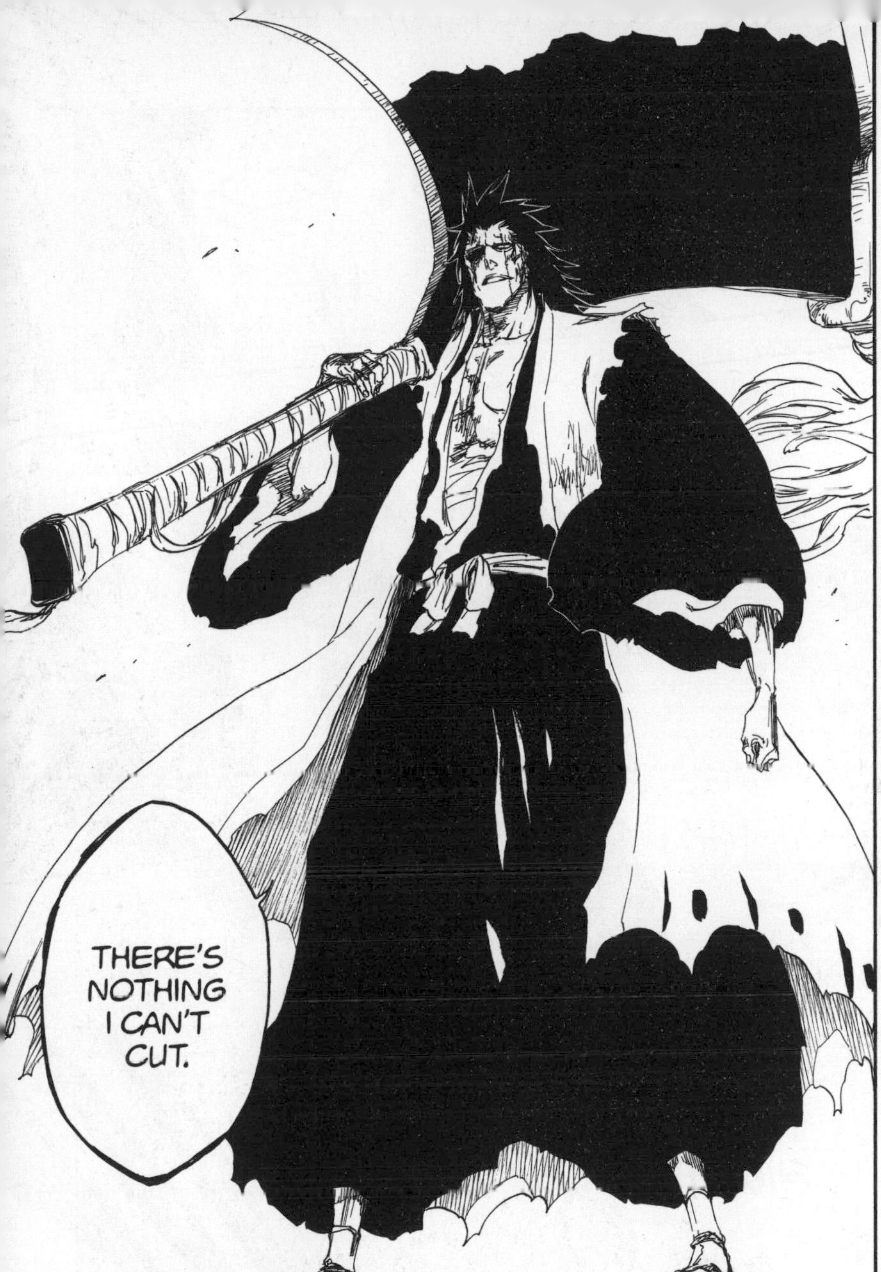
THERE'S NOTHING I CAN'T CUT.

BLEACH 578. THE UNDEAD 5

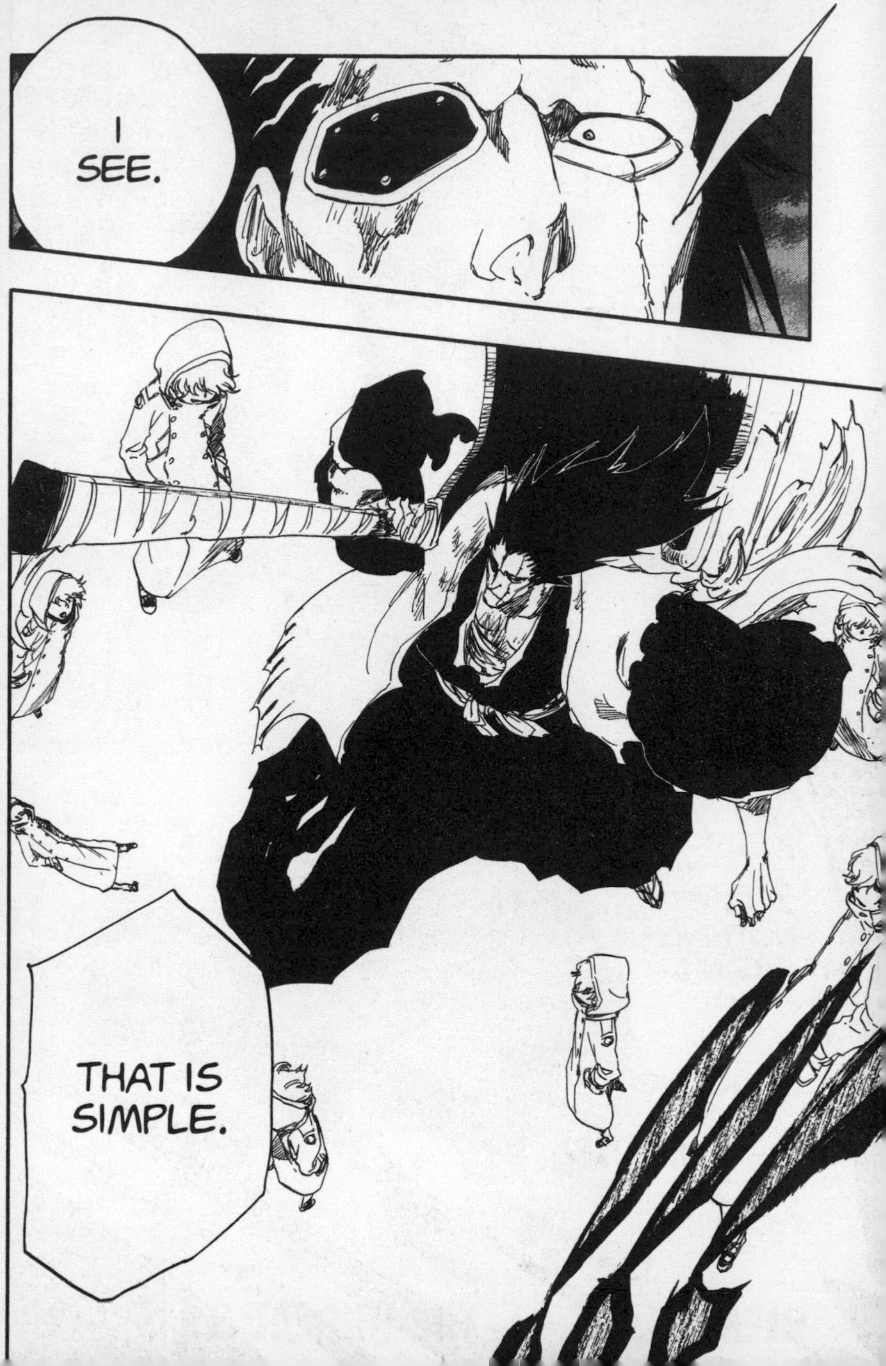
I SEE.
THAT IS SIMPLE.

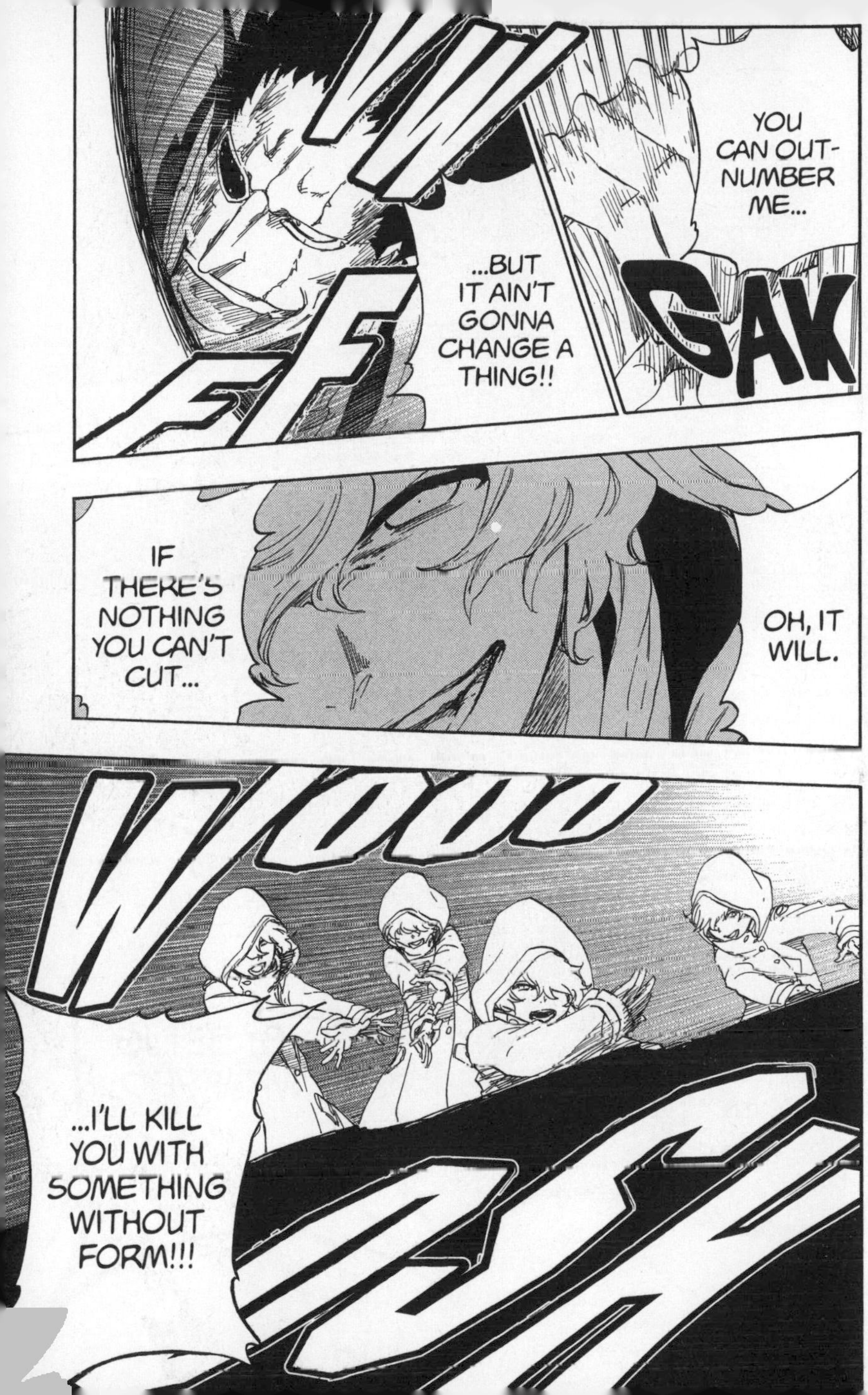
YOU CAN OUT-NUMBER ME...
GAK
...BUT IT AIN'T GONNA CHANGE A THING!!
OH, IT WILL.
IF THERE'S NOTHING YOU CAN'T CUT...
...I'LL KILL YOU WITH SOMETHING WITHOUT FORM!!!

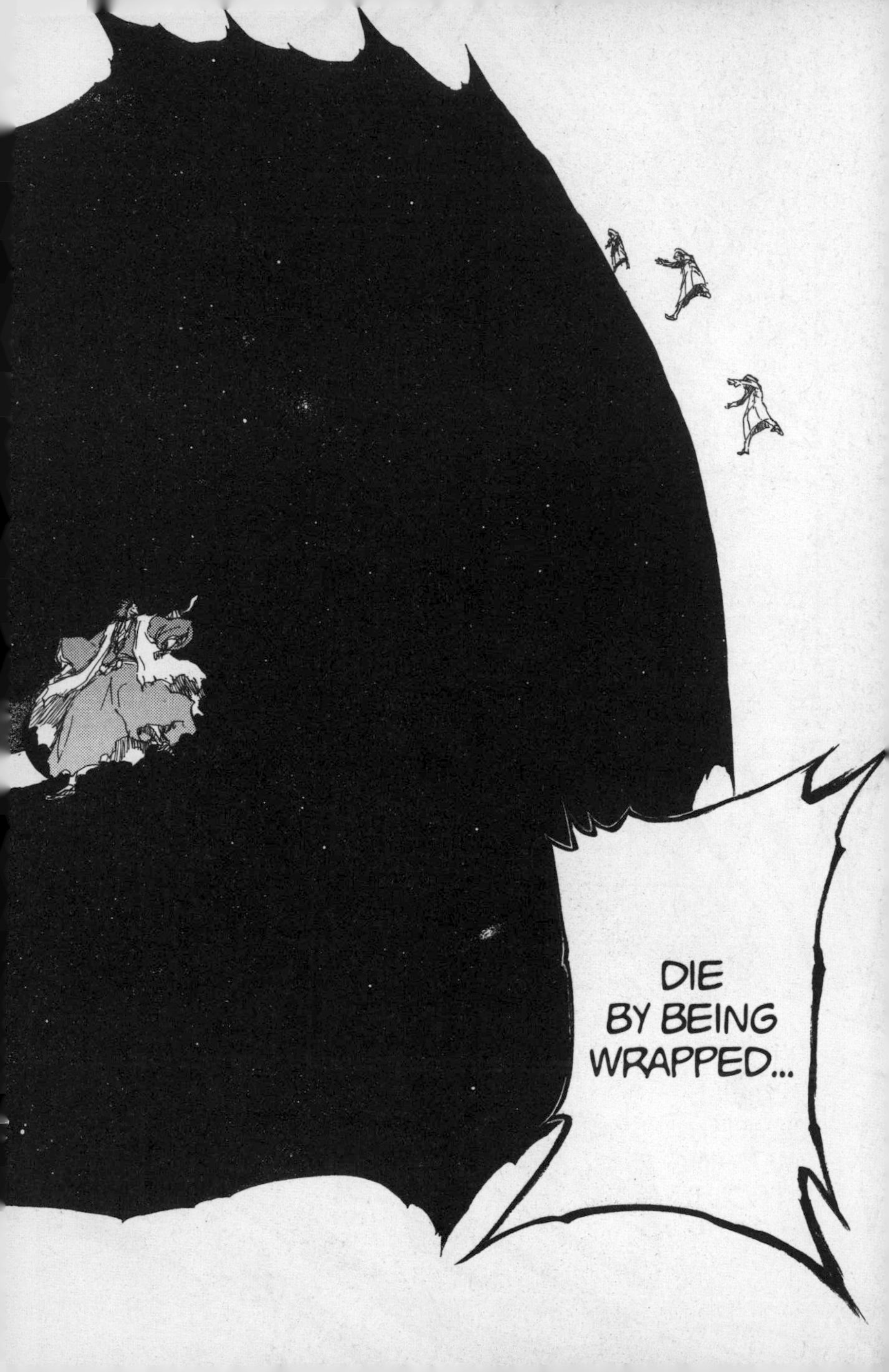
DIE BY BEING WRAPPED...

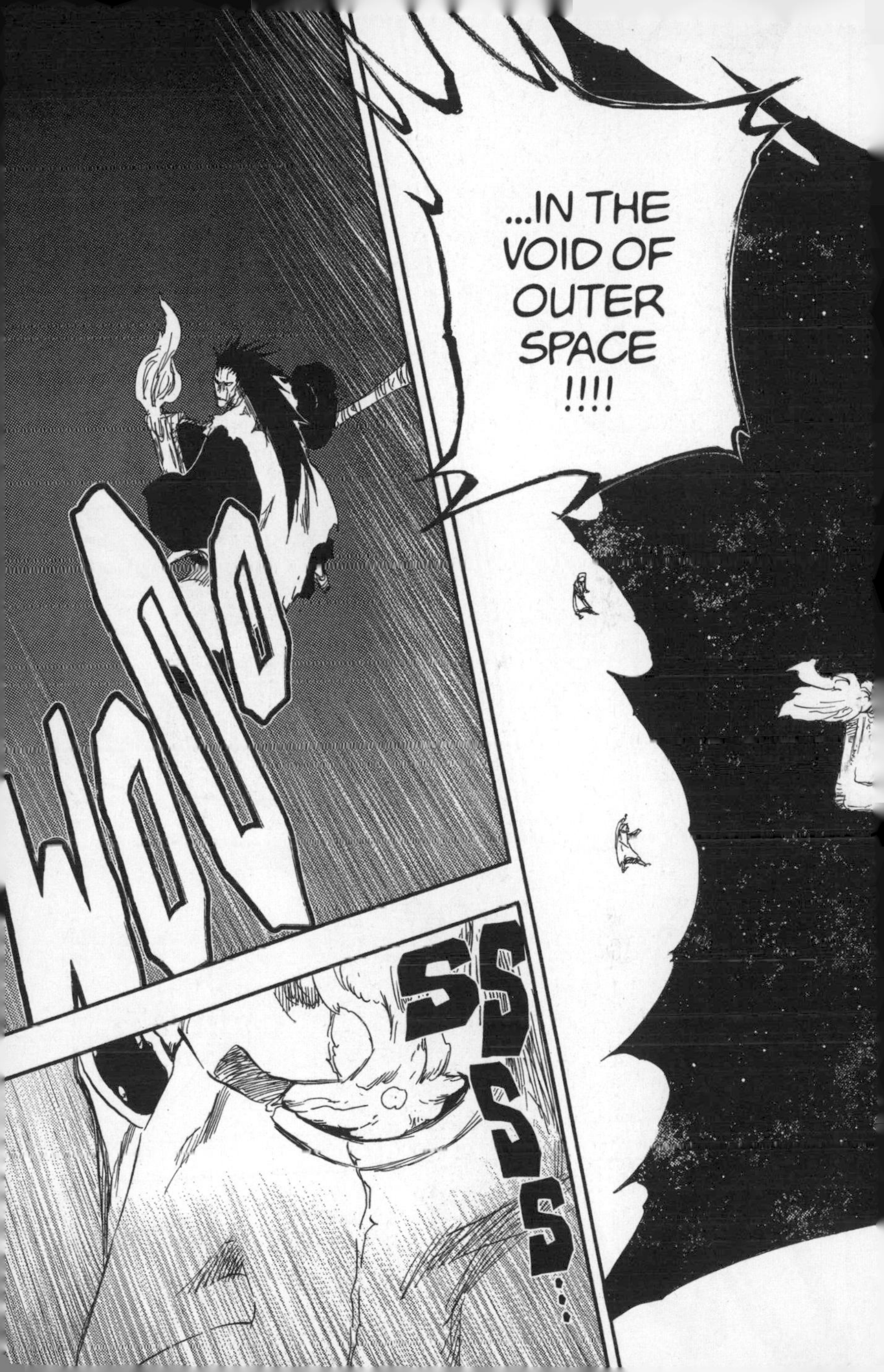
...IN THE VOID OF OUTER SPACE !!!!
WOOO
SSSS...

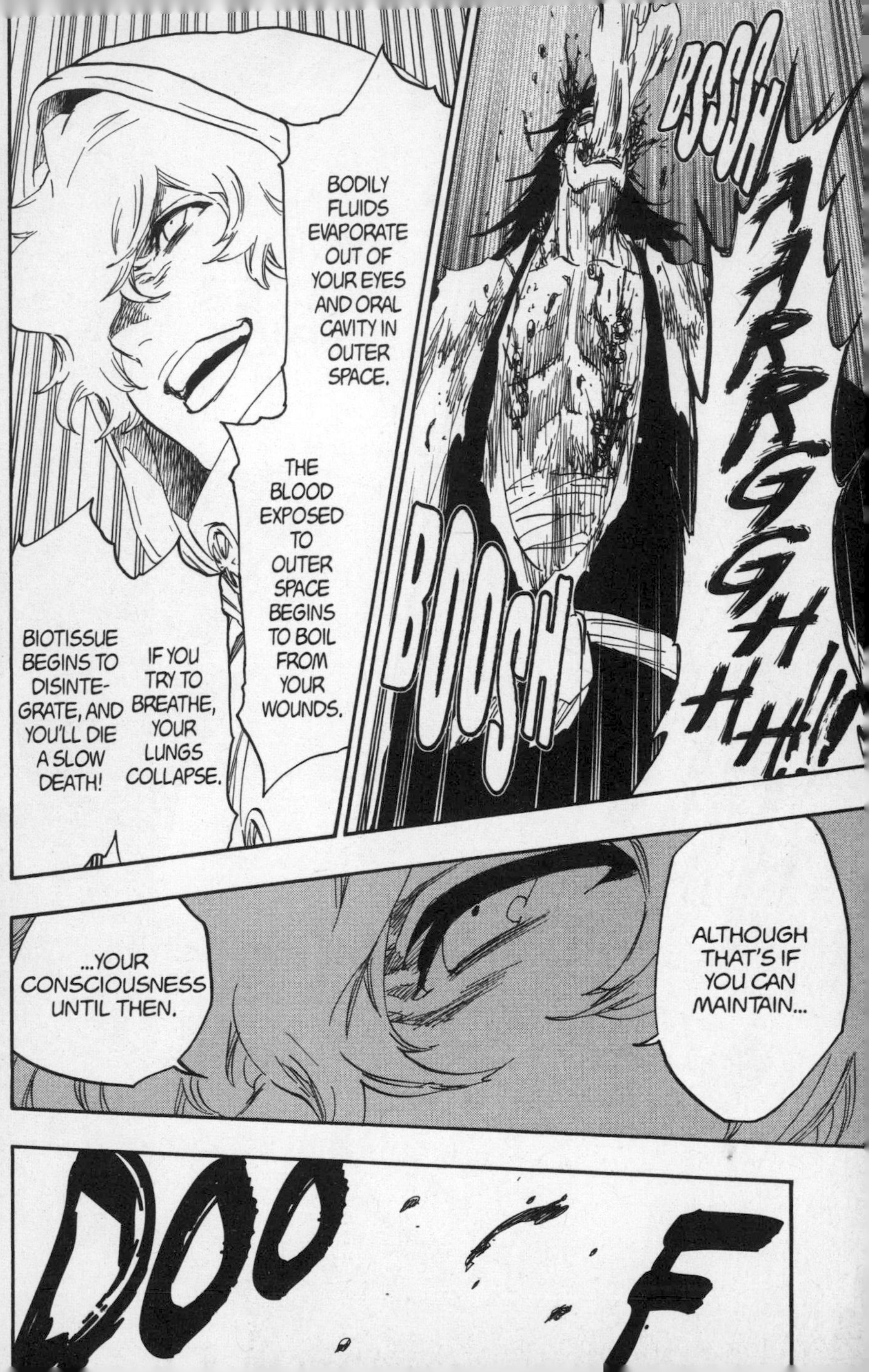
BSSSH
AARRGGHHH!!!
BOOSH
BODILY FLUIDS EVAPORATE OUT OF YOUR EYES AND ORAL CAVITY IN OUTER SPACE.
THE BLOOD EXPOSED TO OUTER SPACE BEGINS TO BOIL FROM YOUR WOUNDS.
IF YOU TRY TO BREATHE, YOUR LUNGS COLLAPSE.
BIOTISSUE BEGINS TO DISINTE-GRATE, AND YOU'LL DIE A SLOW DEATH!
ALTHOUGH THAT'S IF YOU CAN MAINTAIN...
...YOUR CONSCIOUSNESS UNTIL THEN.
DOOF

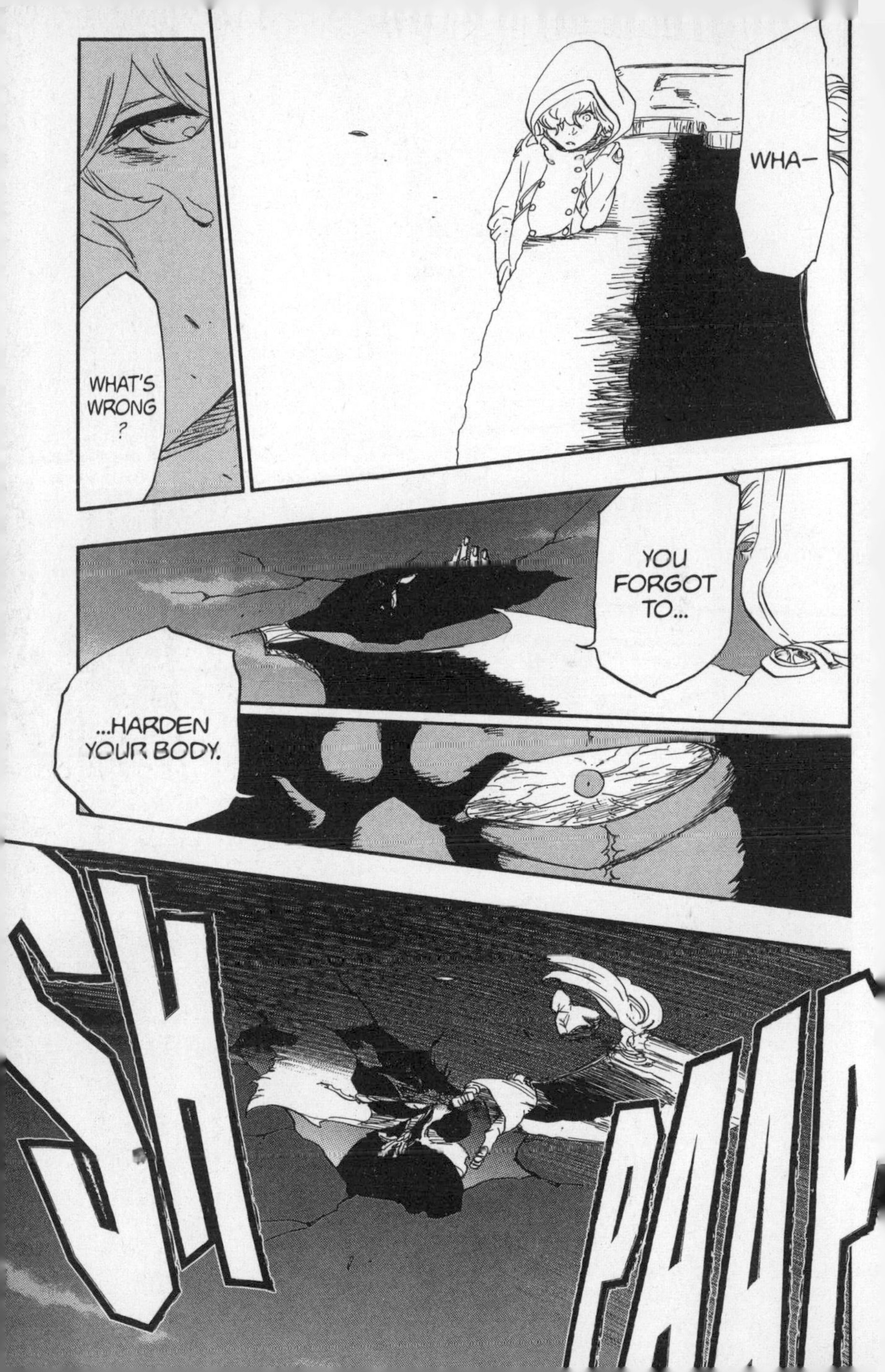
WHA-
WHAT'S WRONG?
YOU FORGOT TO...
...HARDEN YOUR BODY.
SHPAAP

WHAT...?

GSGSH
GSH
GSH

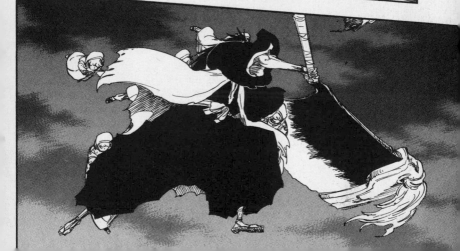

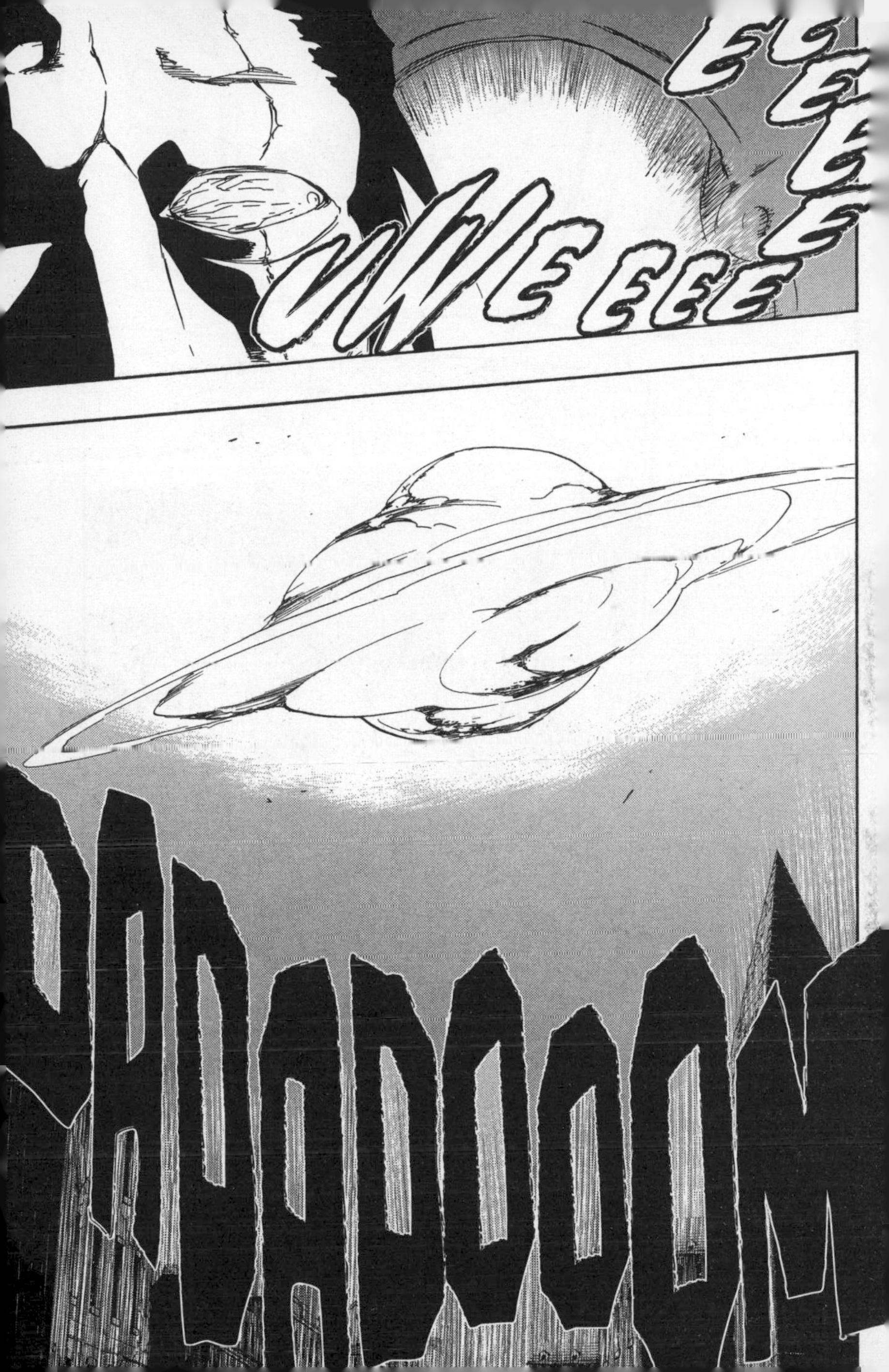
EEEEE
UWEEEE

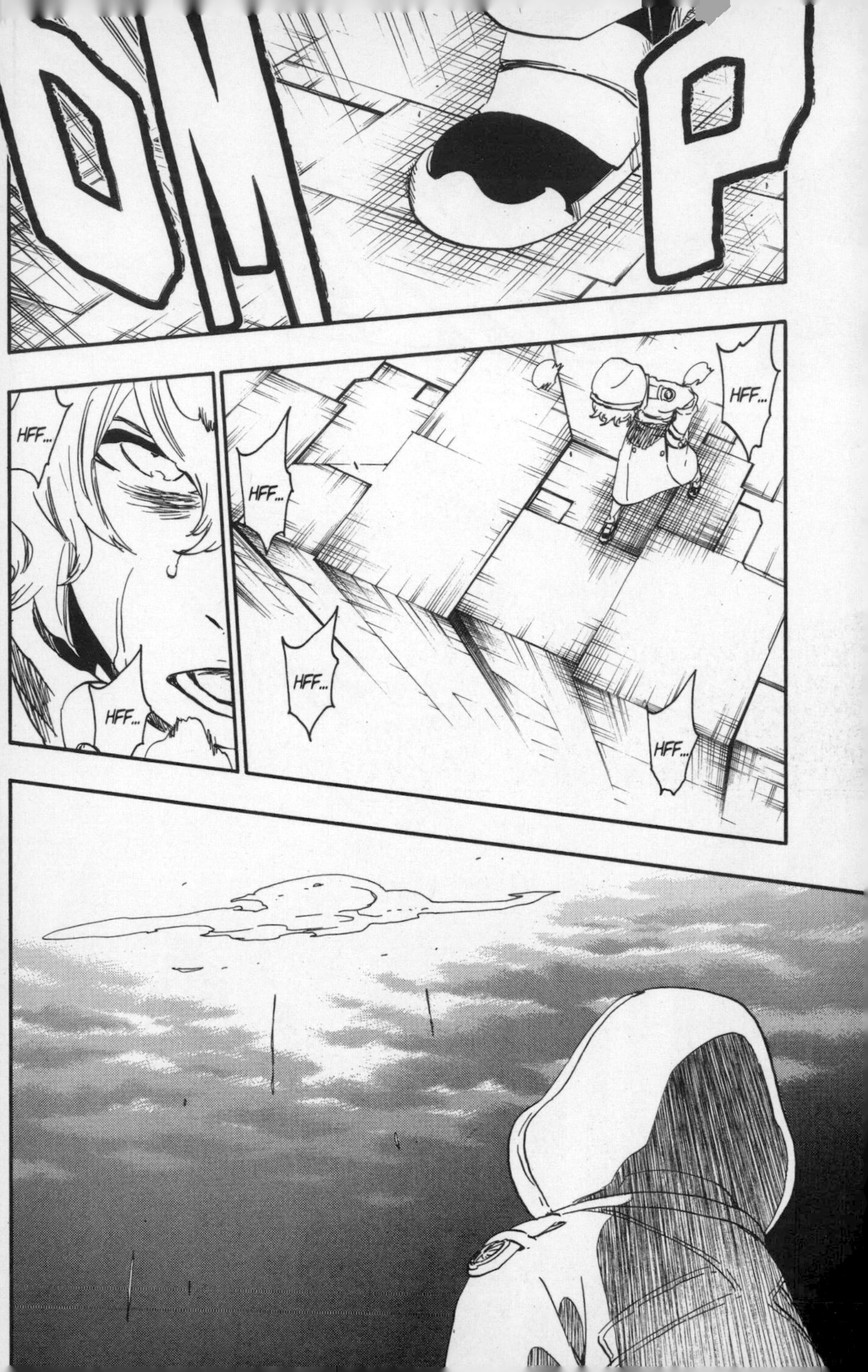

HFF...
HFF...
HFF...
HFF...
HFF...
HFF...

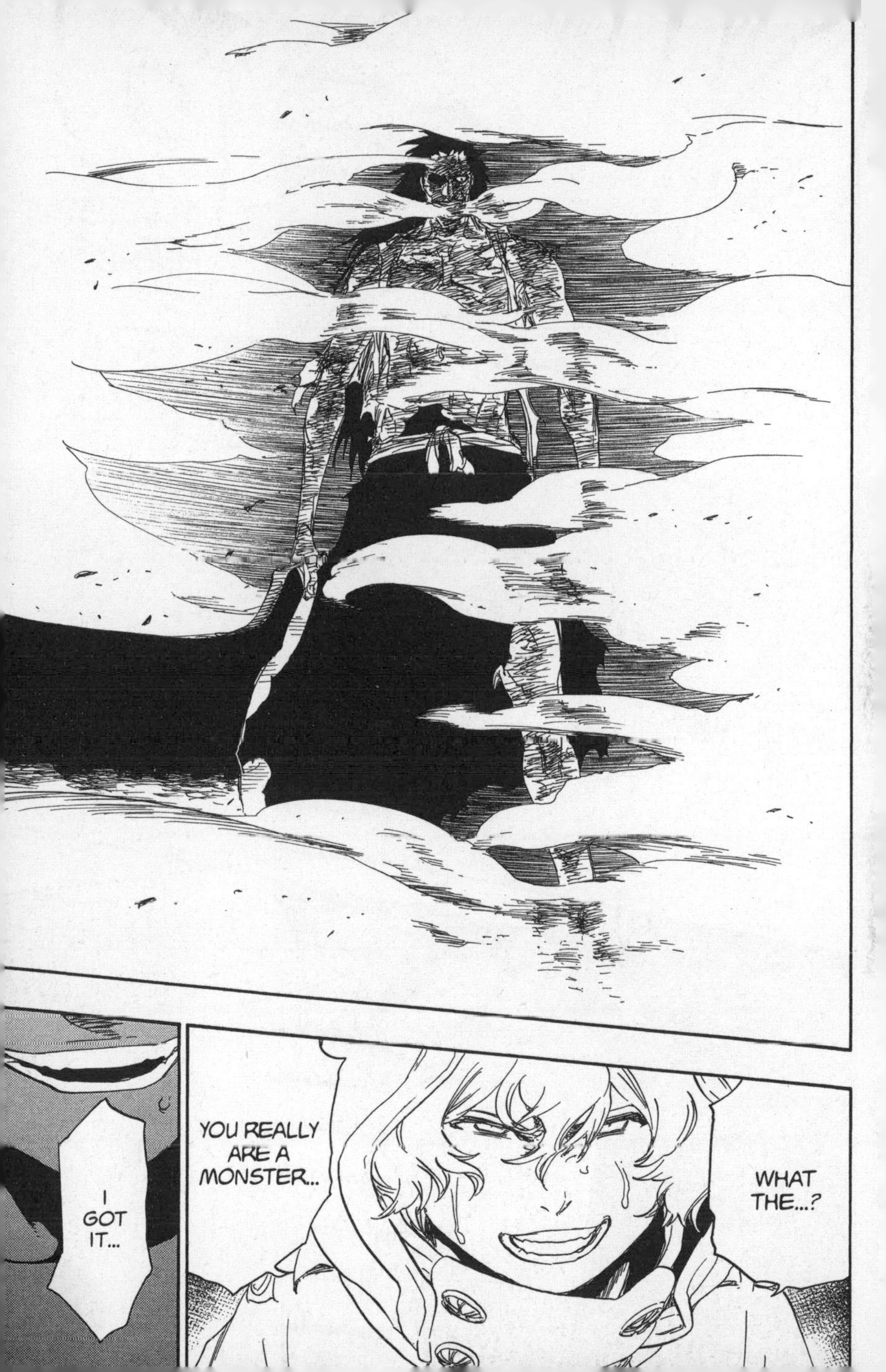
WHAT THE...?
YOU REALLY ARE A MONSTER...
I GOT IT...

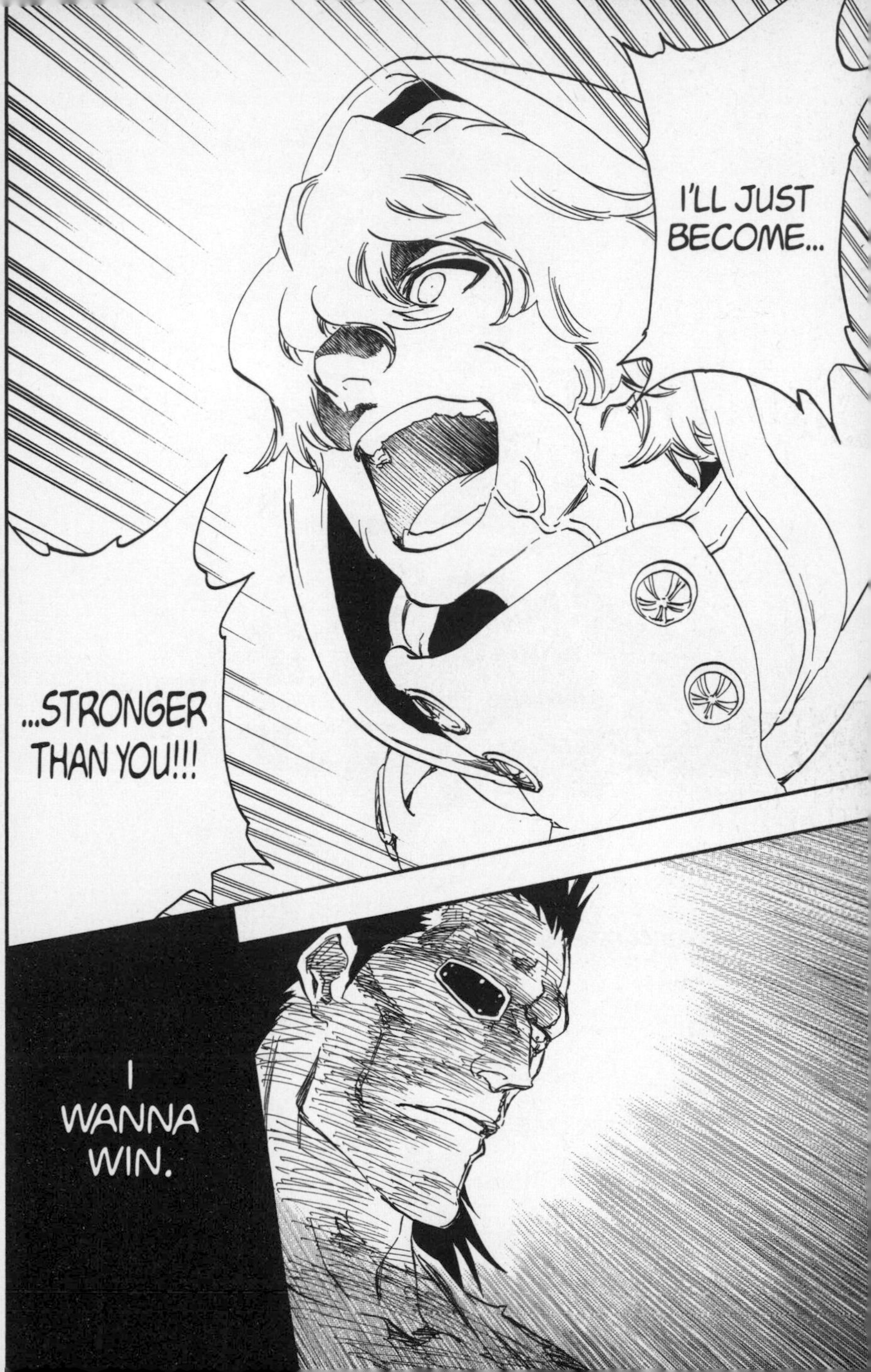
I'LL JUST BECOME...
...STRONGER THAN YOU!!!
I WANNA WIN.

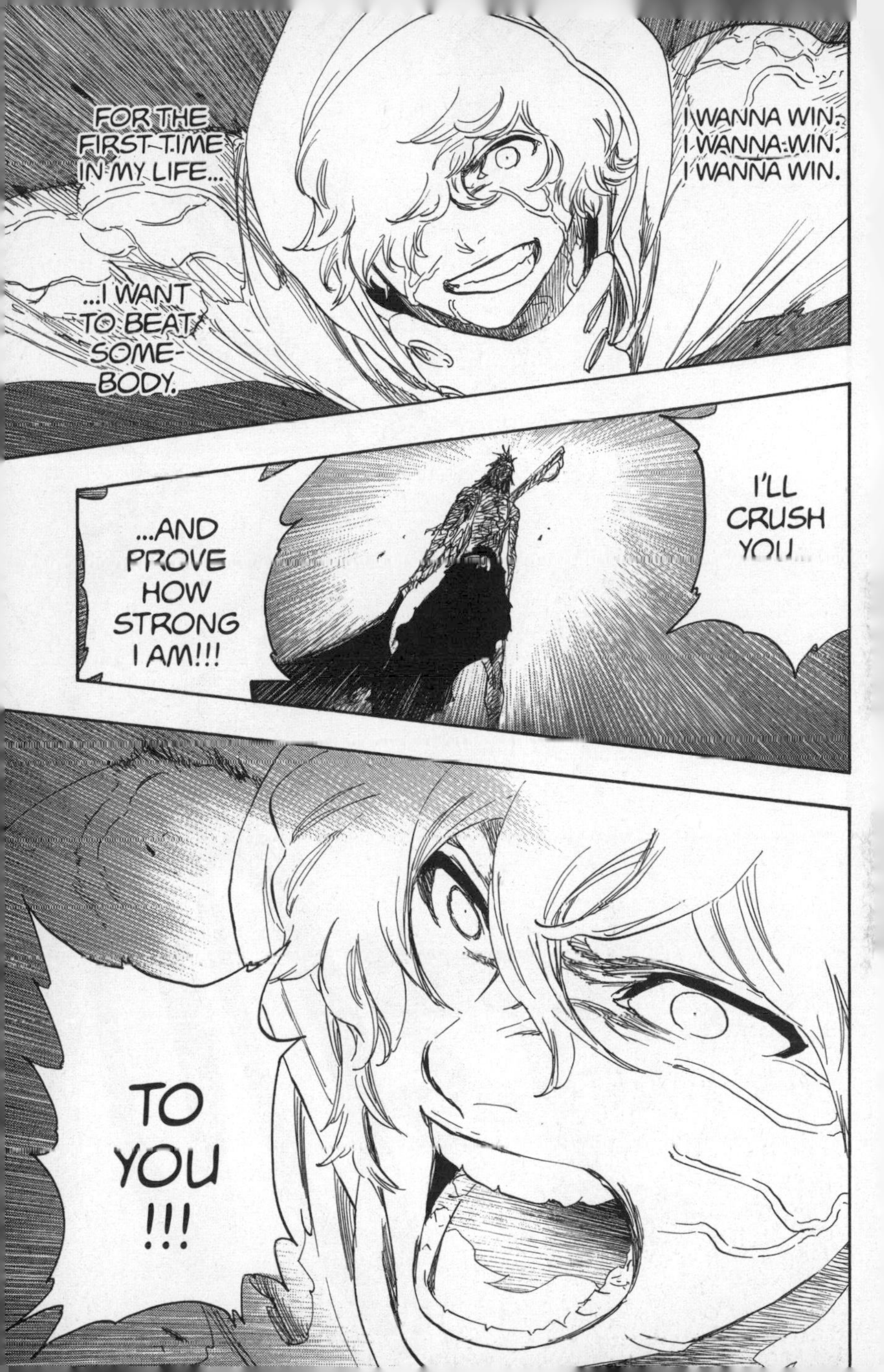
I WANNA WIN. I WANNA WIN. I WANNA WIN.
FOR THE FIRST TIME IN MY LIFE...
...I WANT TO BEAT SOME-BODY.
I'LL CRUSH YOU...
...AND PROVE HOW STRONG I AM!!!
TO YOU!!!

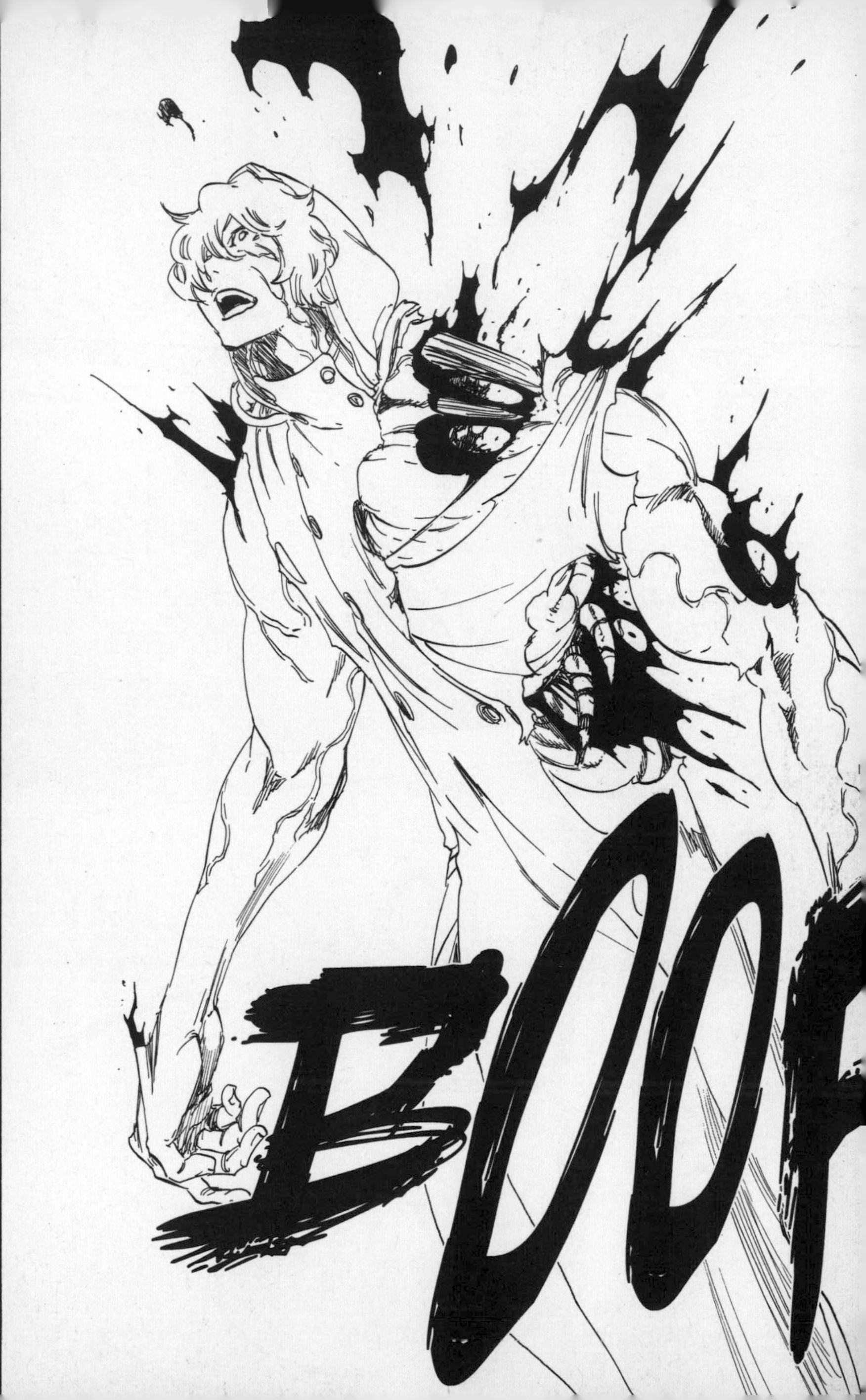
BOOF

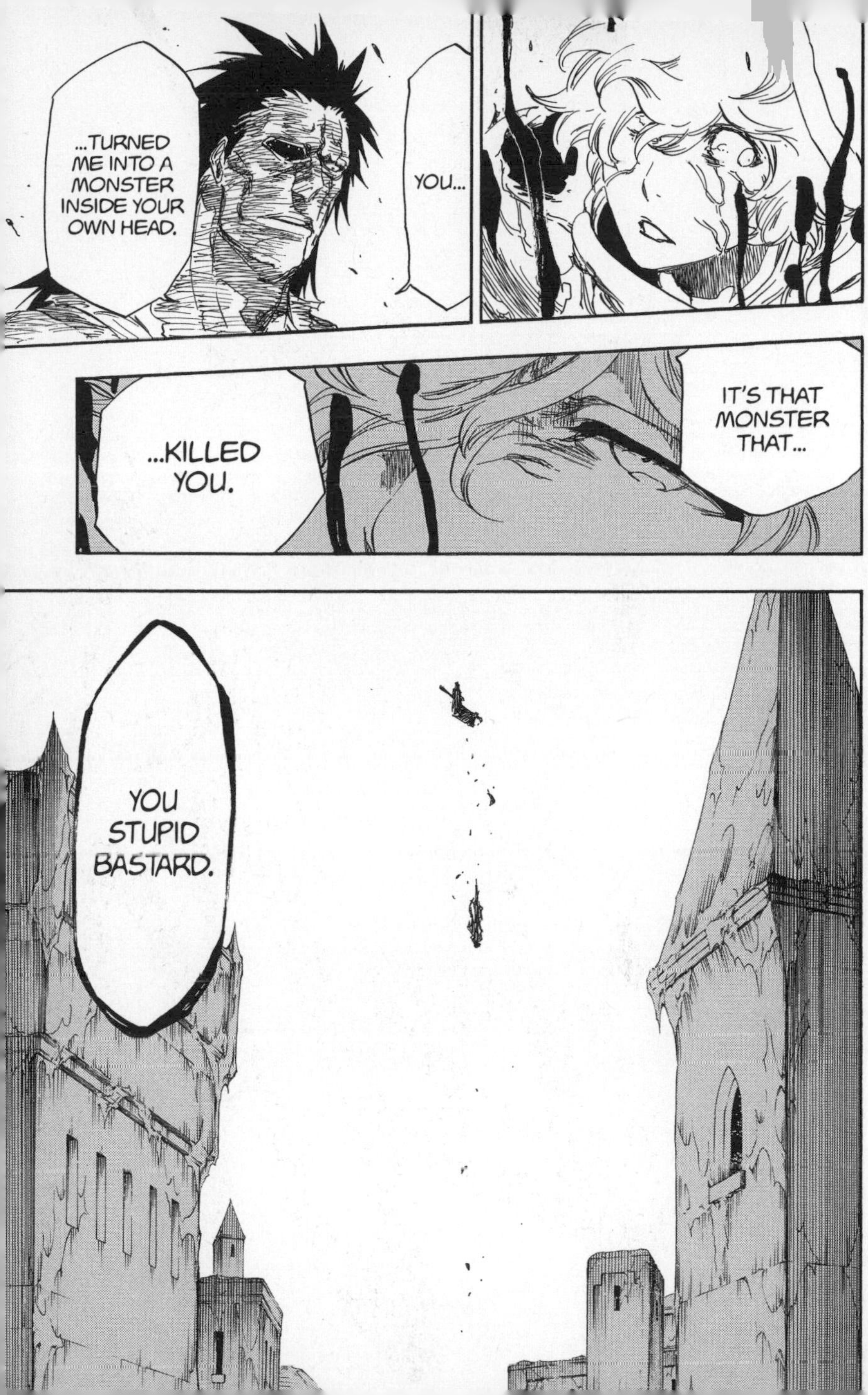
YOU...
...TURNED ME INTO A MONSTER INSIDE YOUR OWN HEAD.
IT'S THAT MONSTER THAT...
...KILLED YOU.
YOU STUPID BASTARD.

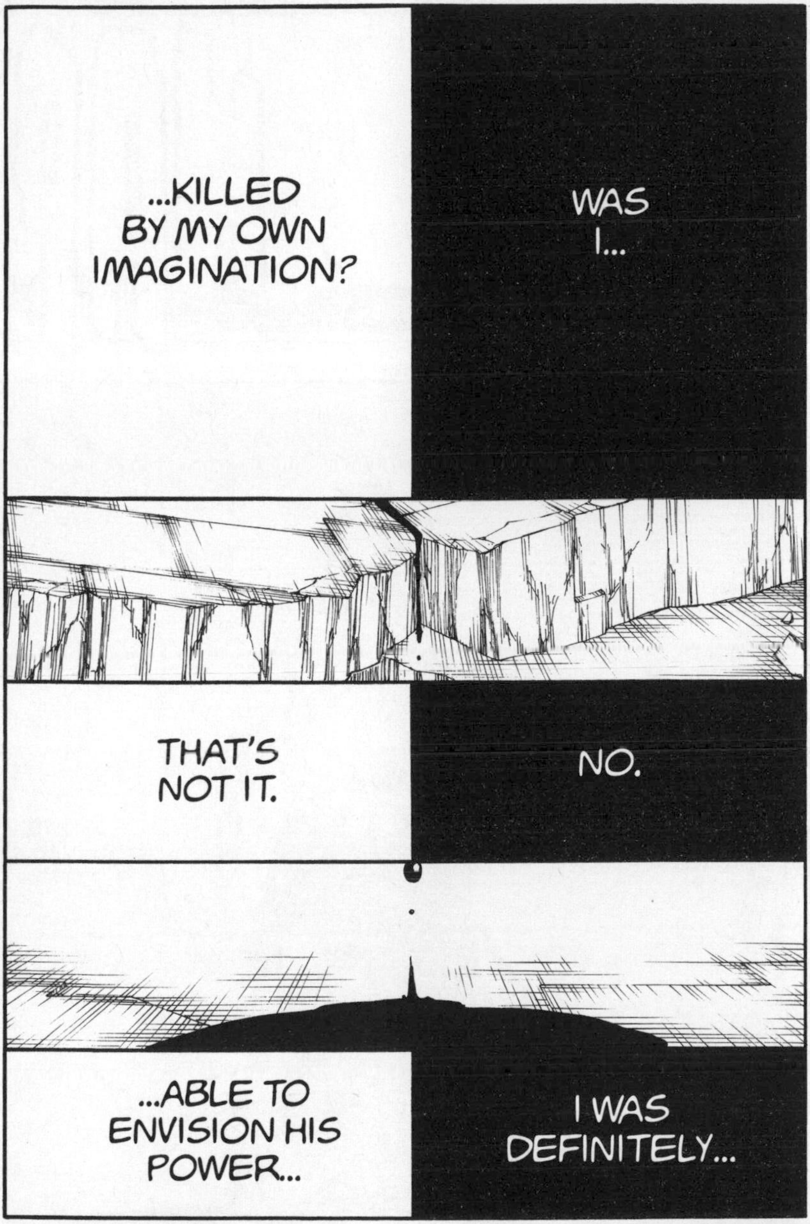
WAS I...
...KILLED BY MY OWN IMAGINATION?
NO.
THAT'S NOT IT.
I WAS DEFINITELY...
...ABLE TO ENVISION HIS POWER...

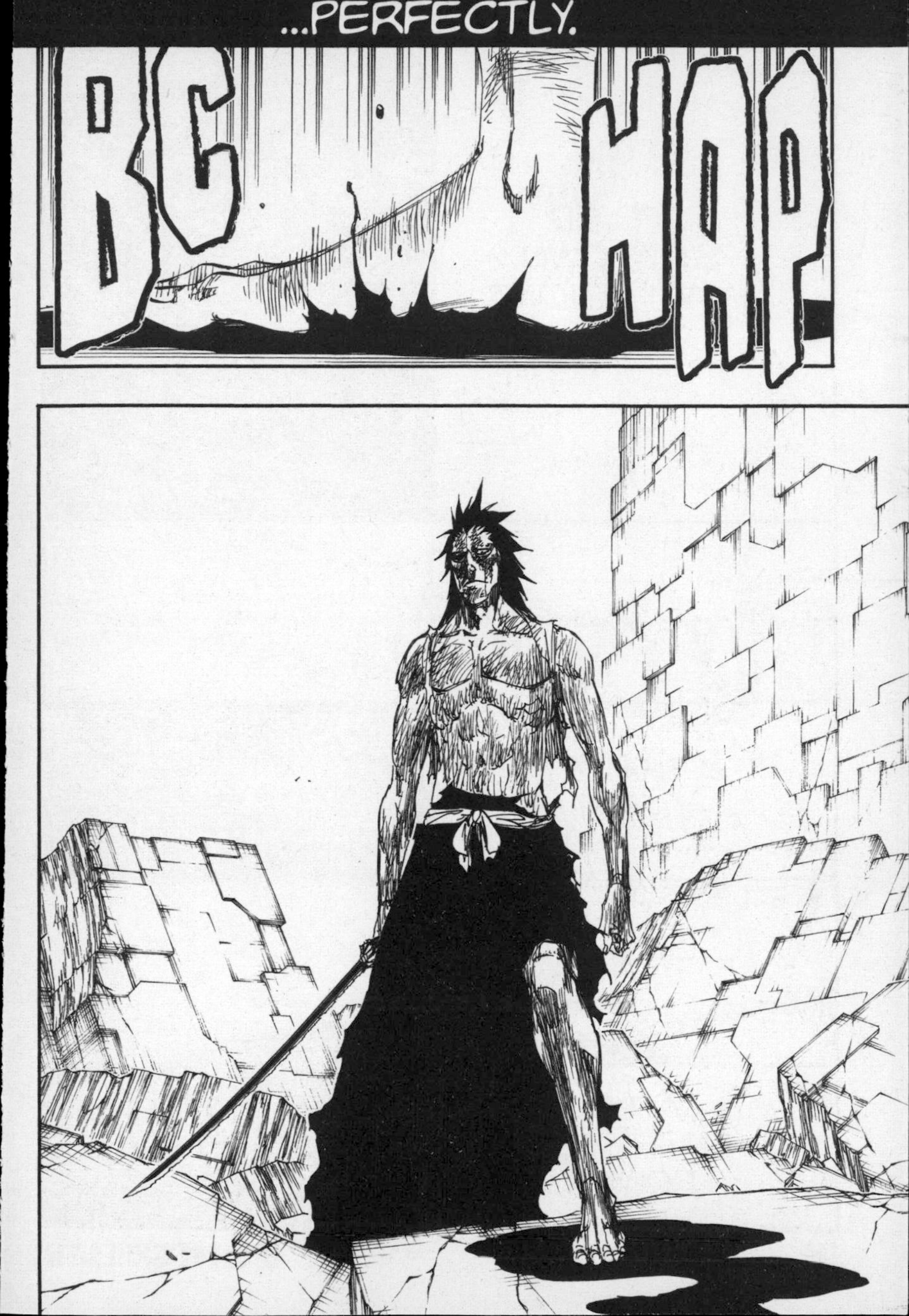
...PERFECTLY.
BCHAP

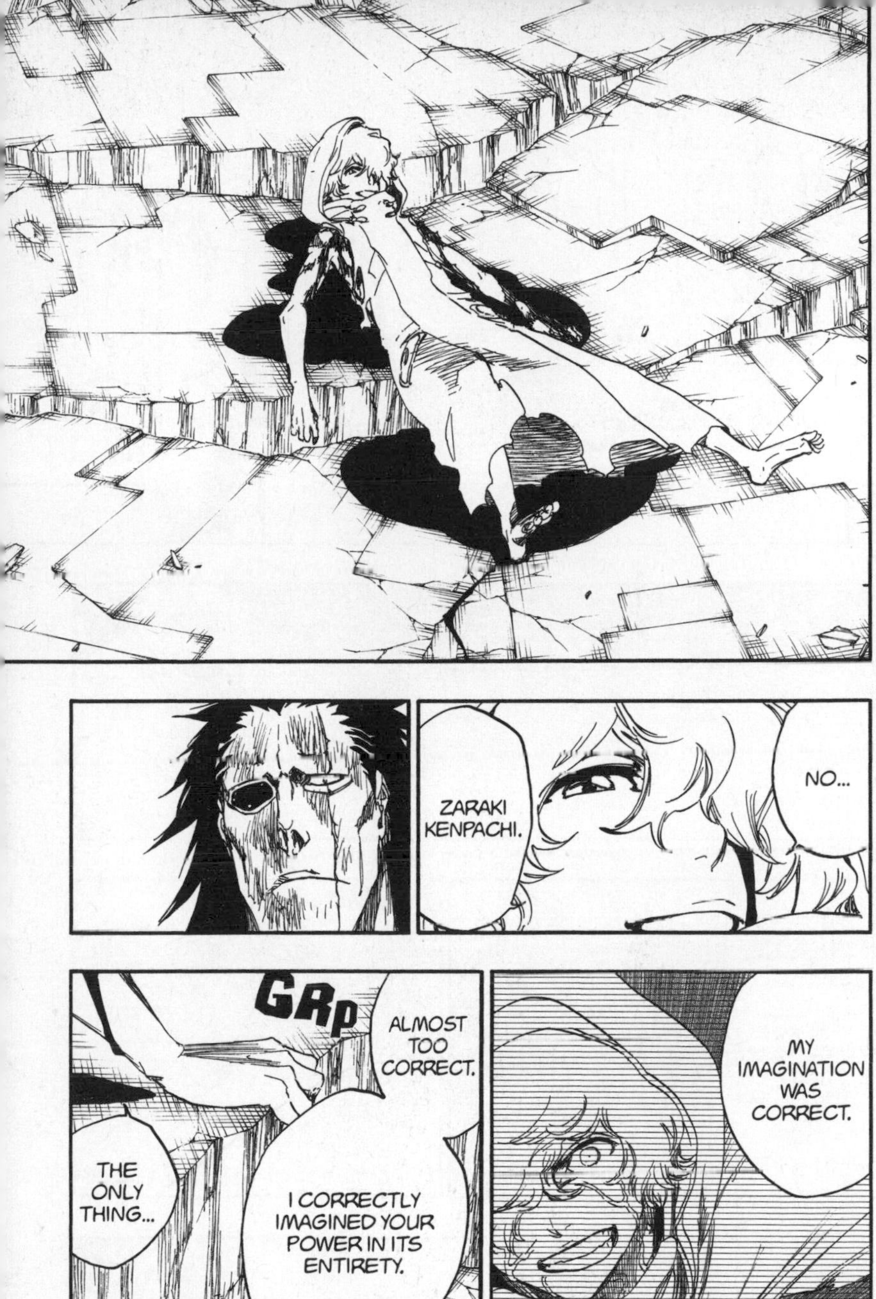
NO...
ZARAKI KENPACHI.
MY IMAGINATION WAS CORRECT.
ALMOST TOO CORRECT.
GRp
I CORRECTLY IMAGINED YOUR POWER IN ITS ENTIRETY.
THE ONLY THING...

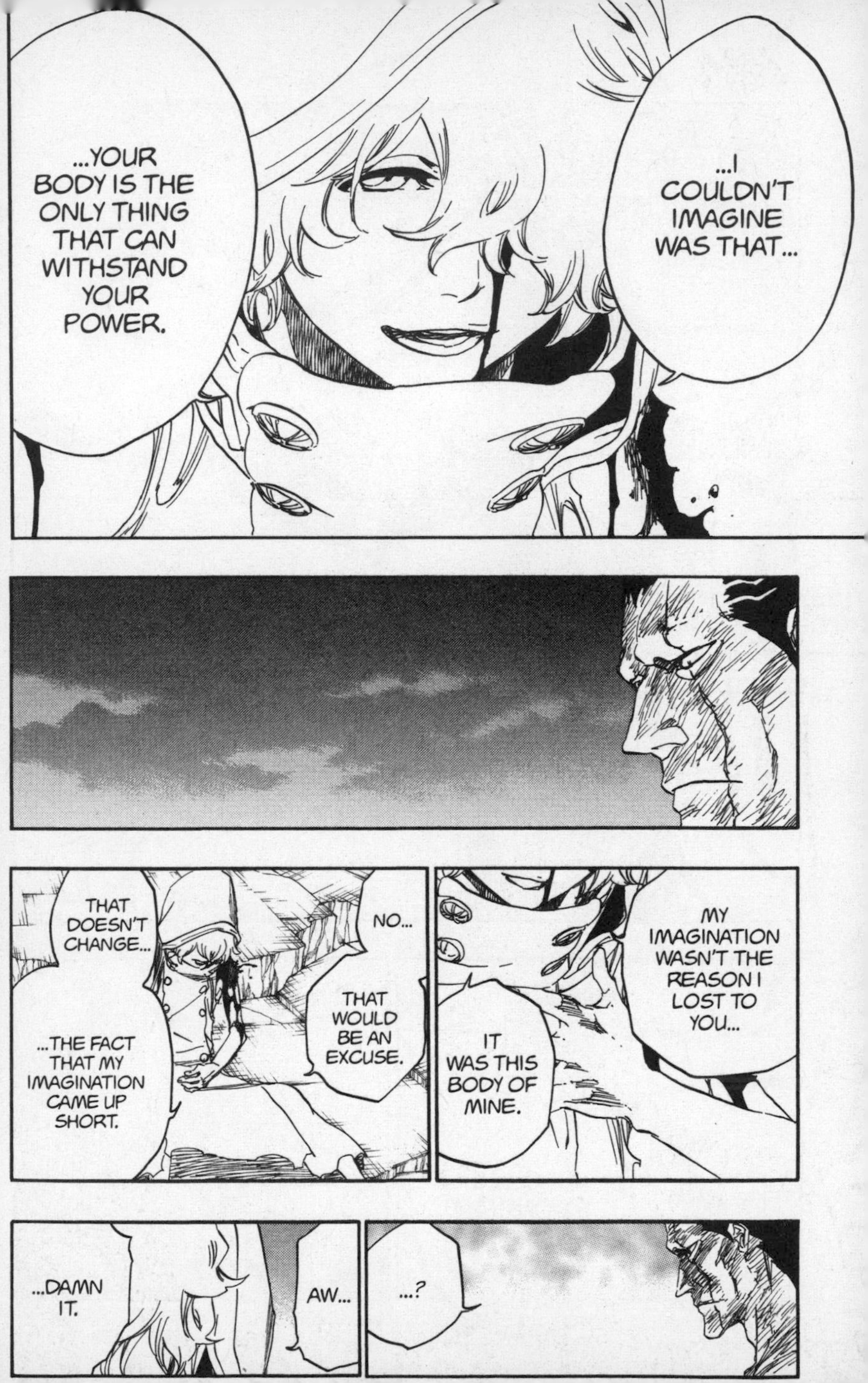
...I COULDN'T IMAGINE WAS THAT...
...YOUR BODY IS THE ONLY THING THAT CAN WITHSTAND YOUR POWER.
MY IMAGINATION WASN'T THE REASON I LOST TO YOU...
IT WAS THIS BODY OF MINE.
NO...
THAT WOULD BE AN EXCUSE.
THAT DOESN'T CHANGE...
...THE FACT THAT MY IMAGINATION CAME UP SHORT.
...?
AW...
...DAMN IT.

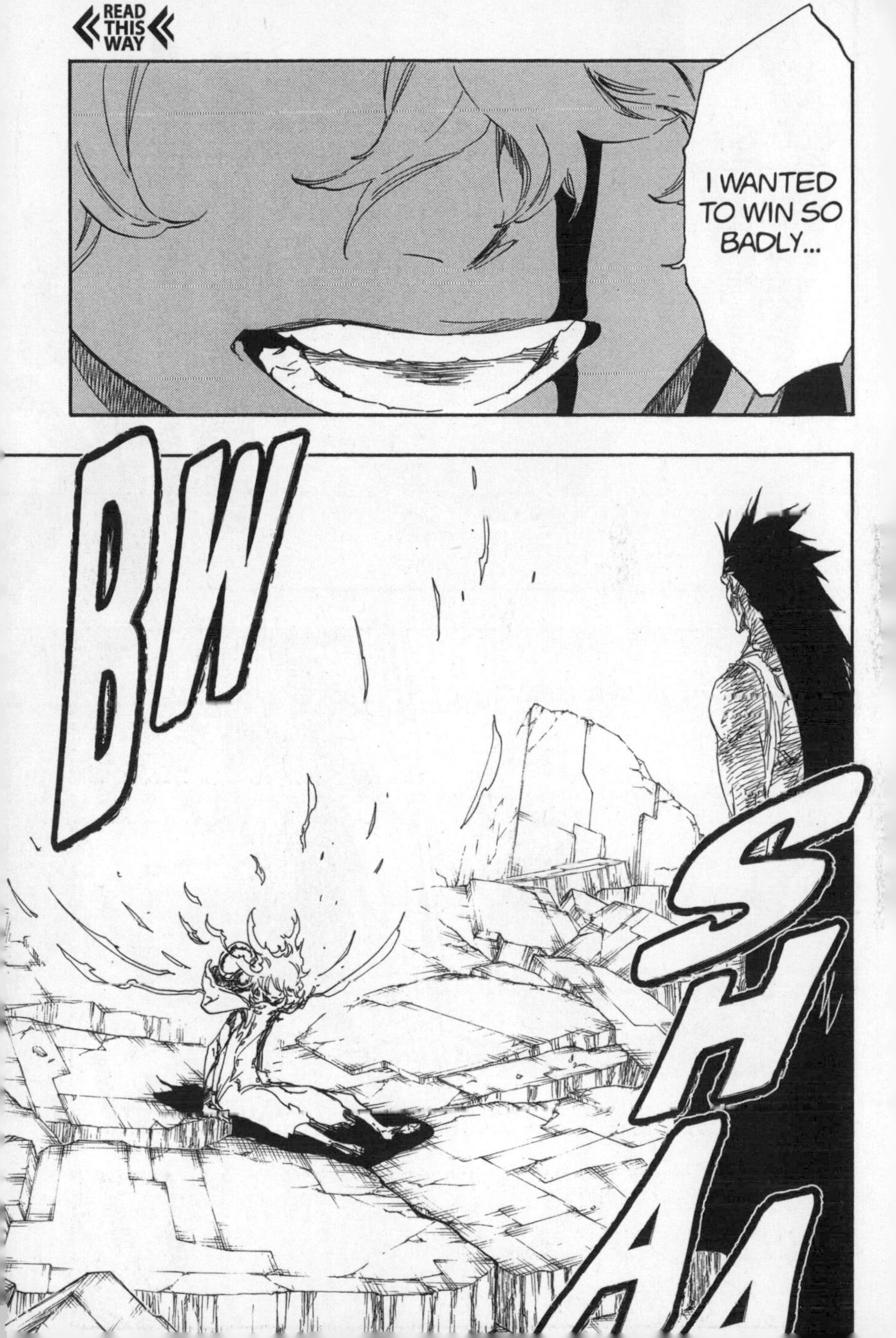
READ THIS WAY
I WANTED TO WIN SO BADLY...
SHAA
BW

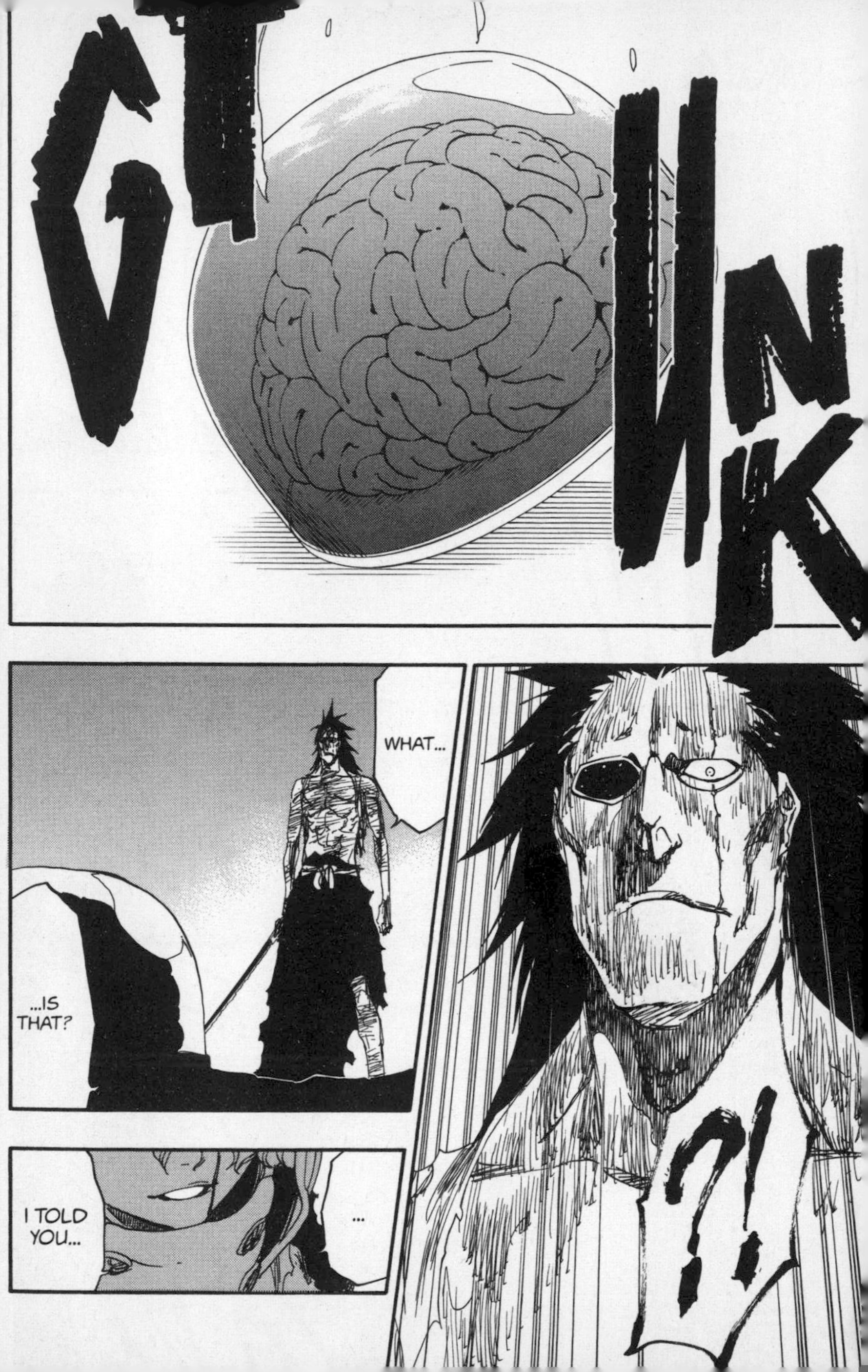
GLUNK
?!
WHAT...
...IS THAT?
...
I TOLD YOU...

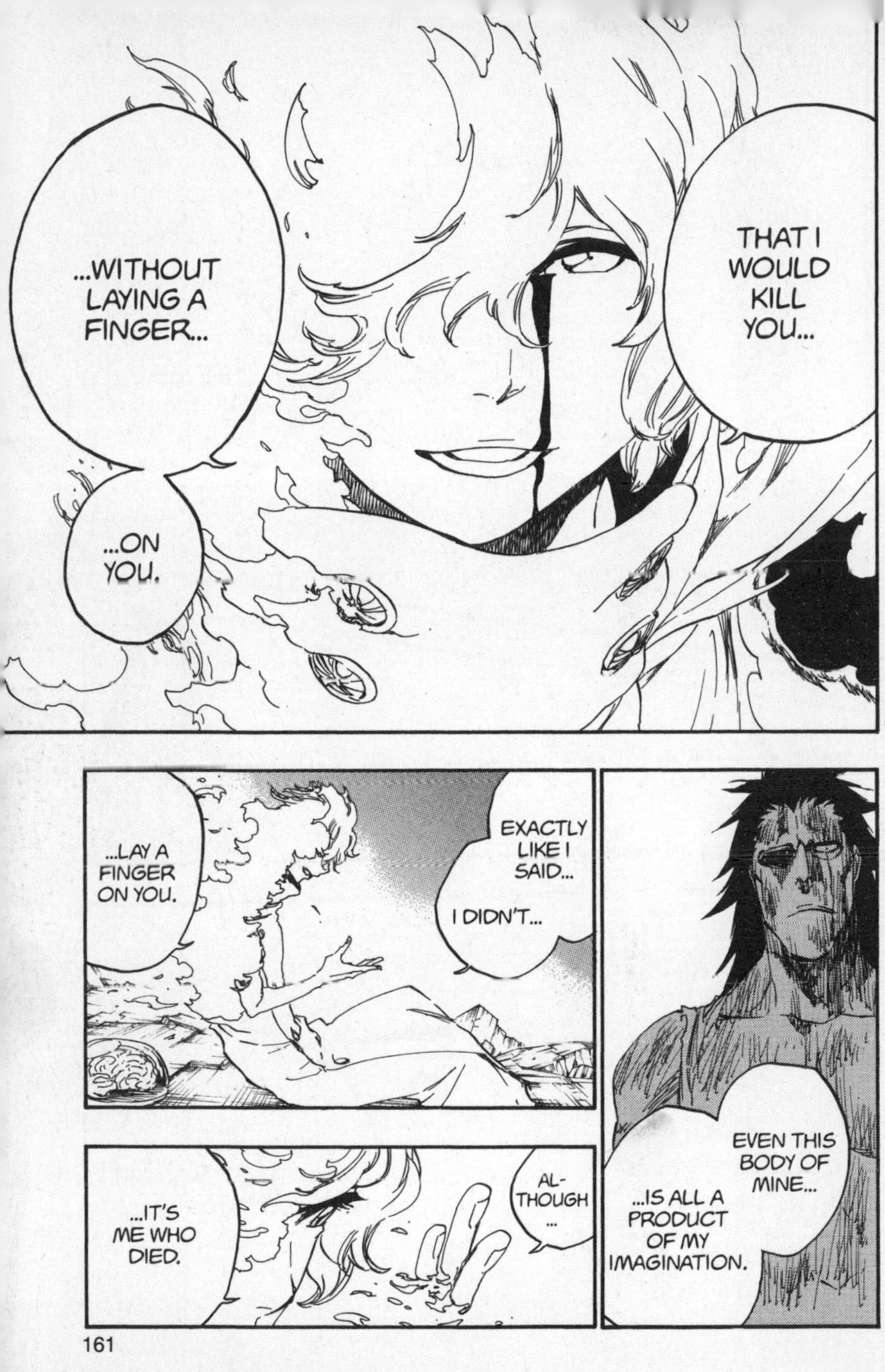
THAT I WOULD KILL YOU...
...WITHOUT LAYING A FINGER...
...ON YOU.
EVEN THIS BODY OF MINE...
...IS ALL A PRODUCT OF MY IMAGINATION.
EXACTLY LIKE I SAID...
I DIDN'T...
...LAY A FINGER ON YOU.
AL-THOUGH...
...IT'S ME WHO DIED.

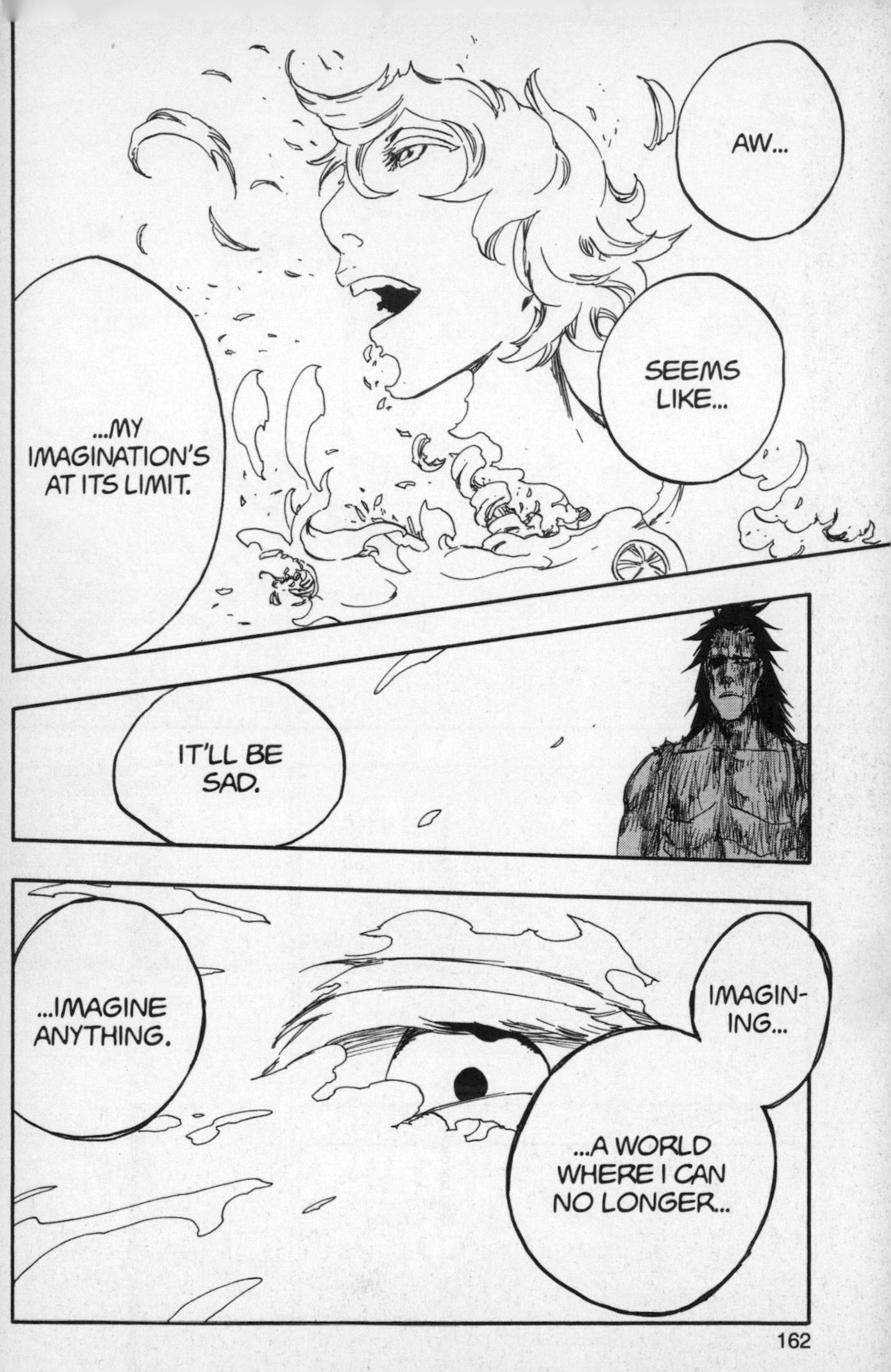
AW...
SEEMS LIKE...
...MY IMAGINATION'S AT ITS LIMIT.
IT'LL BE SAD.
IMAGIN-ING...
...A WORLD WHERE I CAN NO LONGER...
...IMAGINE ANYTHING.

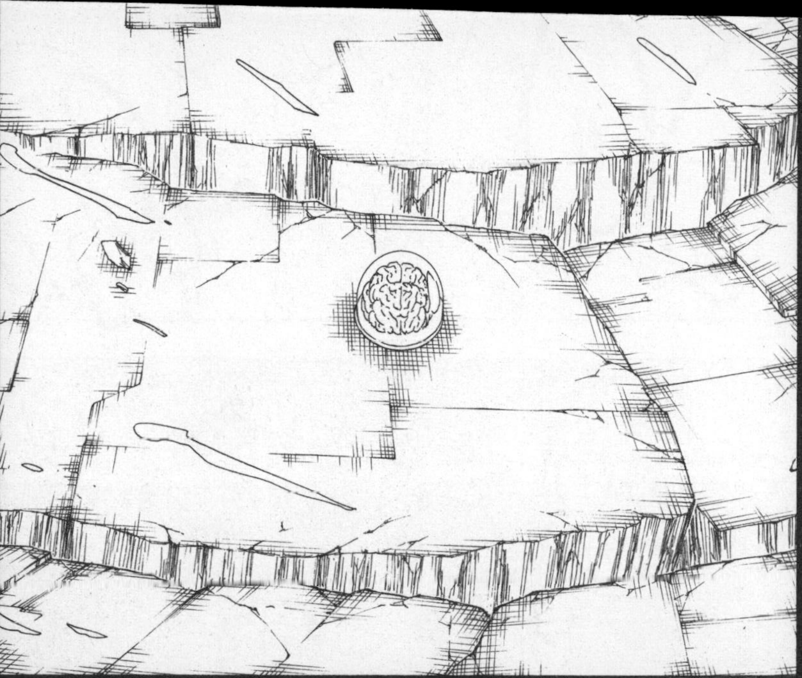

THE UNDEAD 6

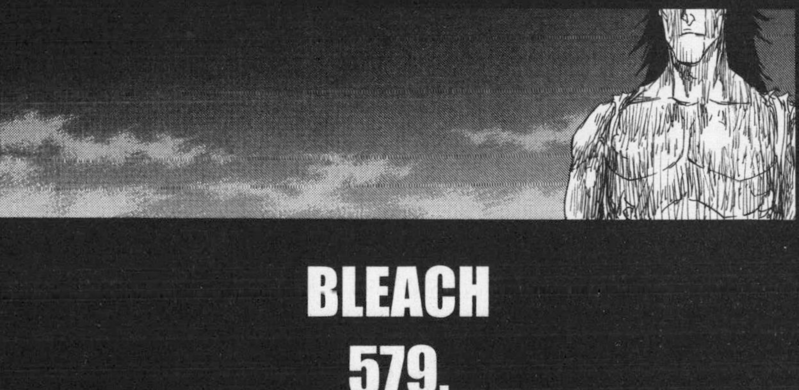

BLEACH
579.

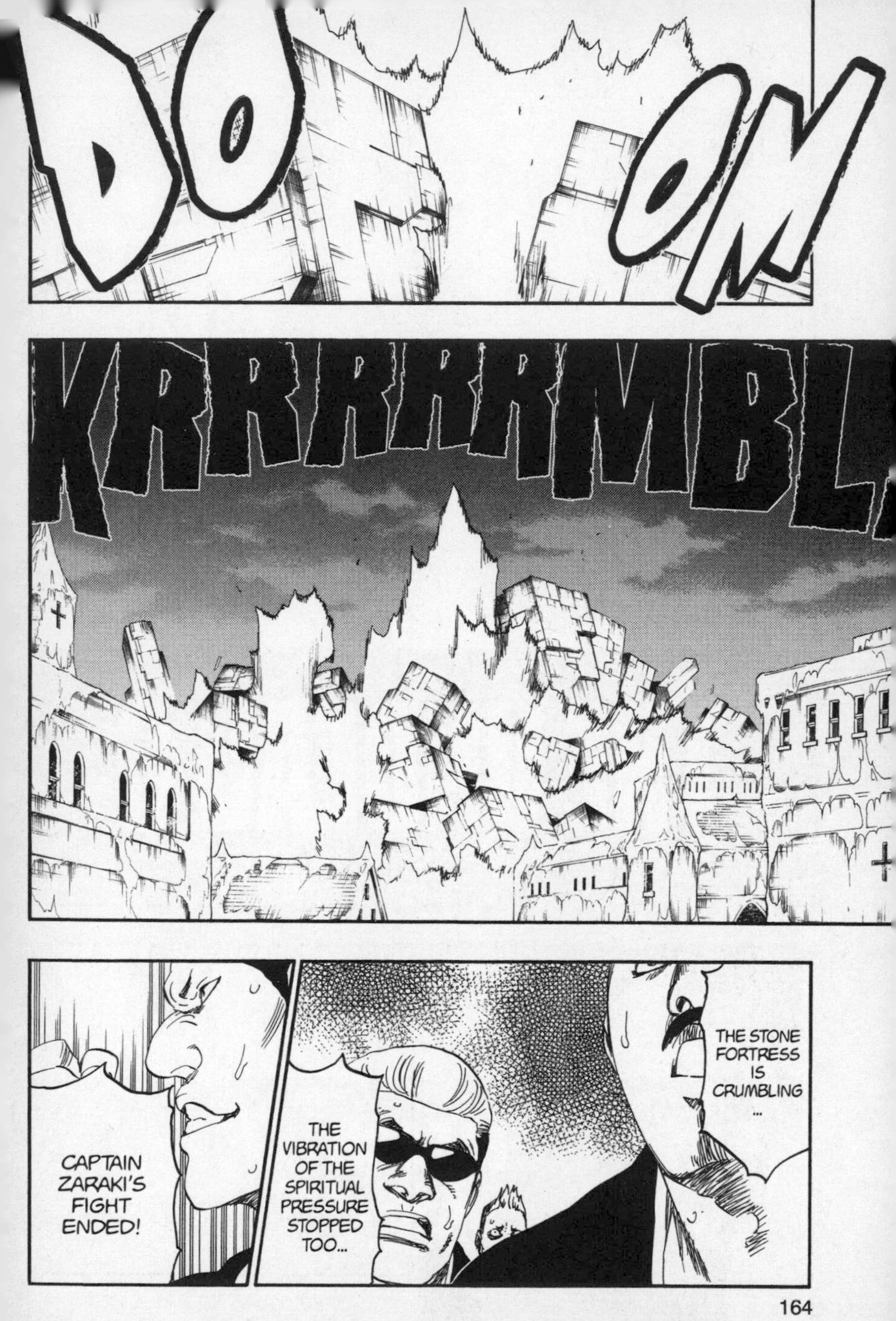
DO
OM
KRRRRRMBL
THE STONE FORTRESS IS CRUMBLING ...
THE VIBRATION OF THE SPIRITUAL PRESSURE STOPPED TOO...
CAPTAIN ZARAKI'S FIGHT ENDED!

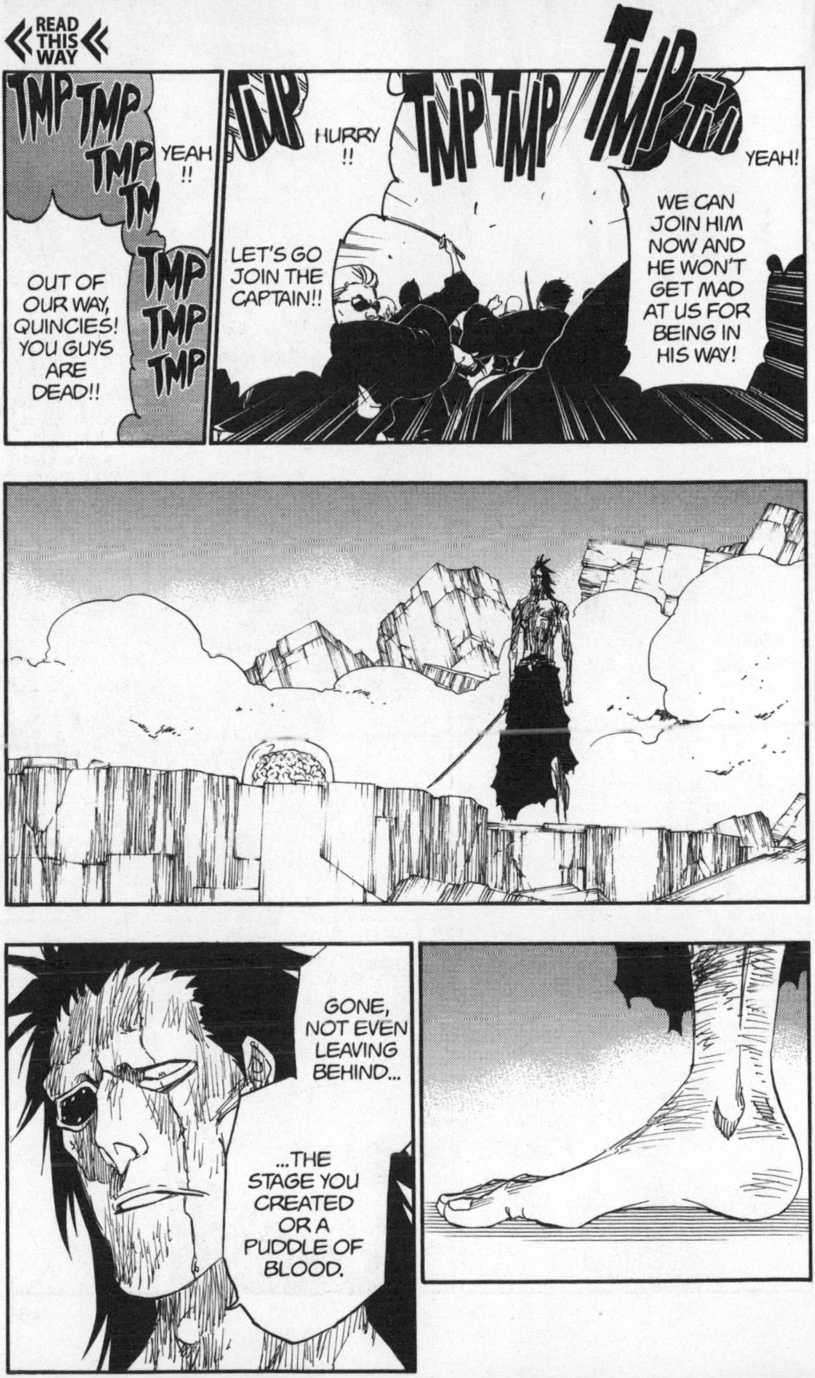
READ THIS WAY
TMP TMP TMP TMP TMP
YEAH!
WE CAN JOIN HIM NOW AND HE WON'T GET MAD AT US FOR BEING IN HIS WAY!
HURRY !!
LET'S GO JOIN THE CAPTAIN!!
TMP
TMP TMP TMP TM
YEAH !!
OUT OF OUR WAY, QUINCIES! YOU GUYS ARE DEAD!!
TMP TMP TMP
GONE, NOT EVEN LEAVING BEHIND...
...THE STAGE YOU CREATED OR A PUDDLE OF BLOOD.

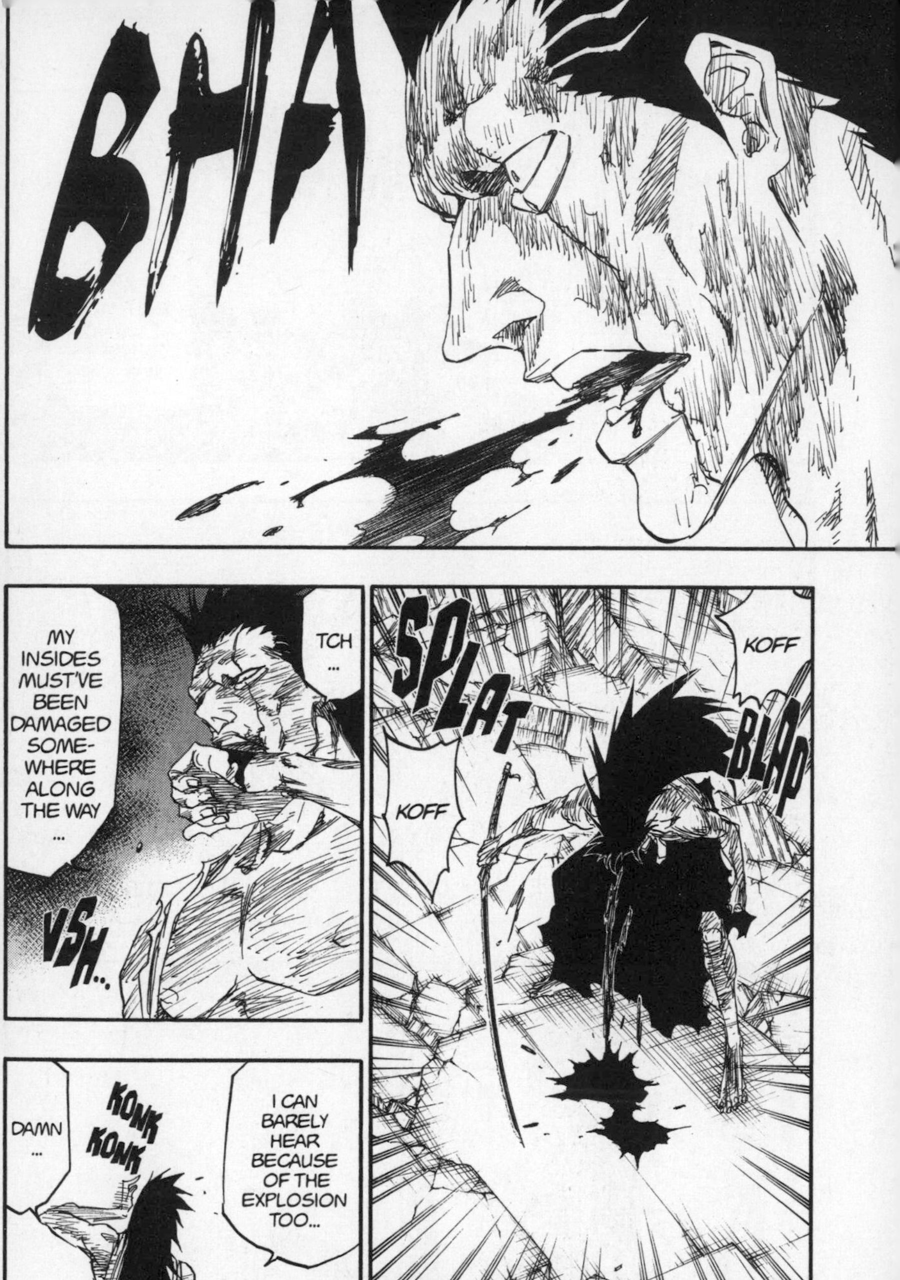
BHA
KOFF
SPLAT
BLAP
KOFF
TCH ...
MY INSIDES MUST'VE BEEN DAMAGED SOME- WHERE ALONG THE WAY ...
VSH...
I CAN BARELY HEAR BECAUSE OF THE EXPLOSION TOO...
KONK KONK
DAMN ...

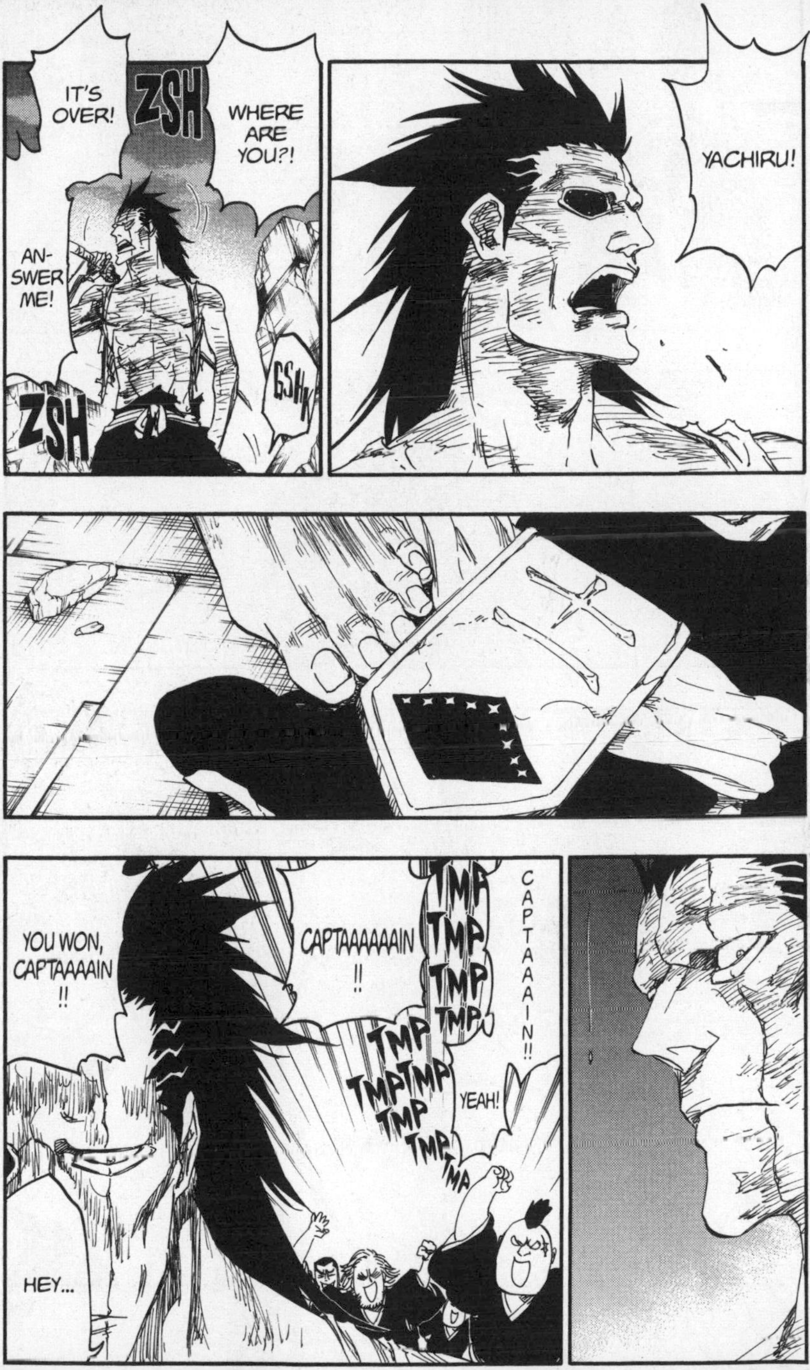
YACHIRU!
WHERE ARE YOU?!
ZSH
IT'S OVER!
GSHK
ANSWER ME!
ZSH
CAPTAAAAIN!!
TMP TMP TMP TMP
CAPTAAAAAAIN!!
YOU WON, CAPTAAAAIN!!
TMP TMPTMP TMP TMP TMA
YEAH!
HEY...

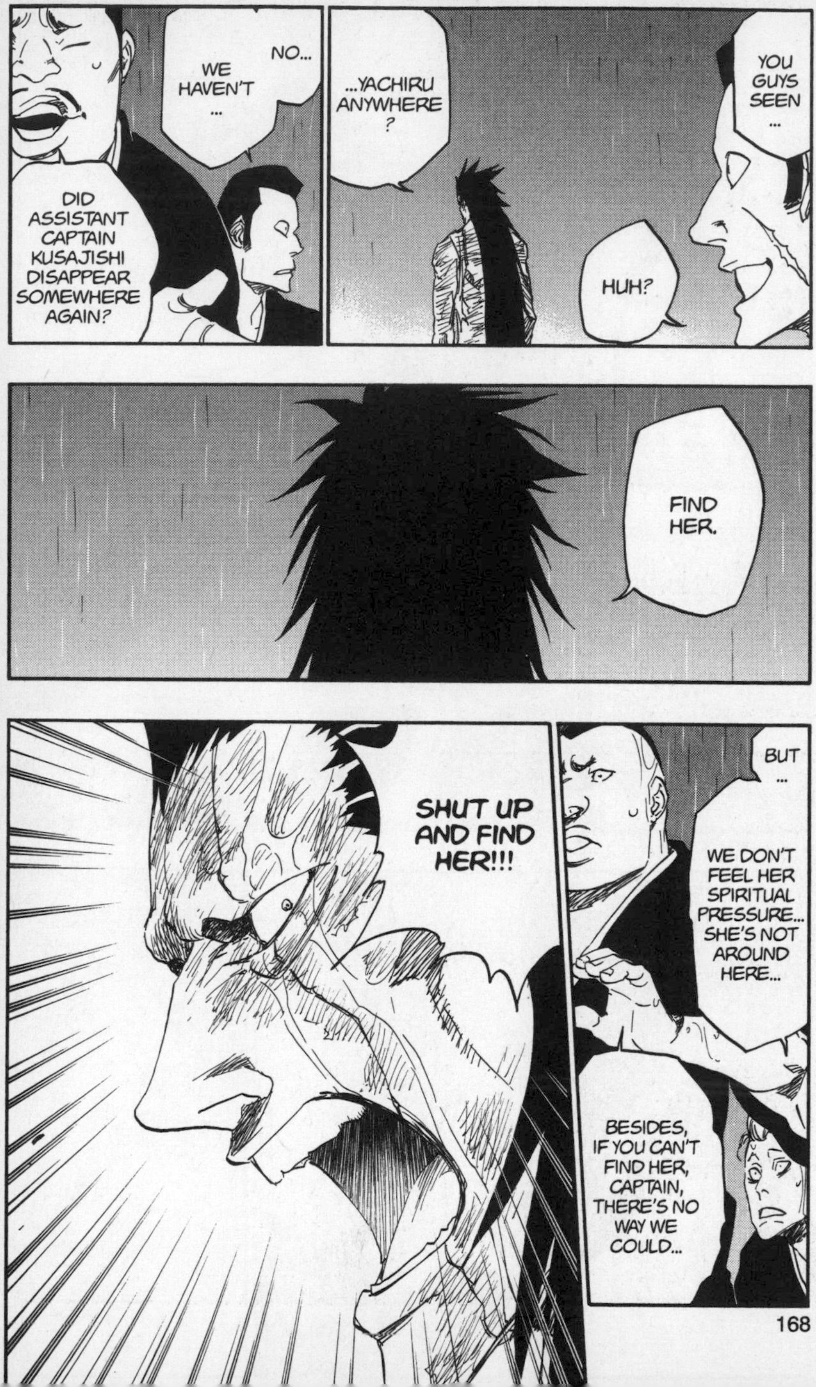
YOU GUYS SEEN ...
...YACHIRU ANYWHERE ?
HUH?
NO...
WE HAVEN'T ...
DID ASSISTANT CAPTAIN KUSAJISHI DISAPPEAR SOMEWHERE AGAIN?
FIND HER.
BUT ...
WE DON'T FEEL HER SPIRITUAL PRESSURE... SHE'S NOT AROUND HERE...
BESIDES, IF YOU CAN'T FIND HER, CAPTAIN, THERE'S NO WAY WE COULD...
SHUT UP AND FIND HER!!!

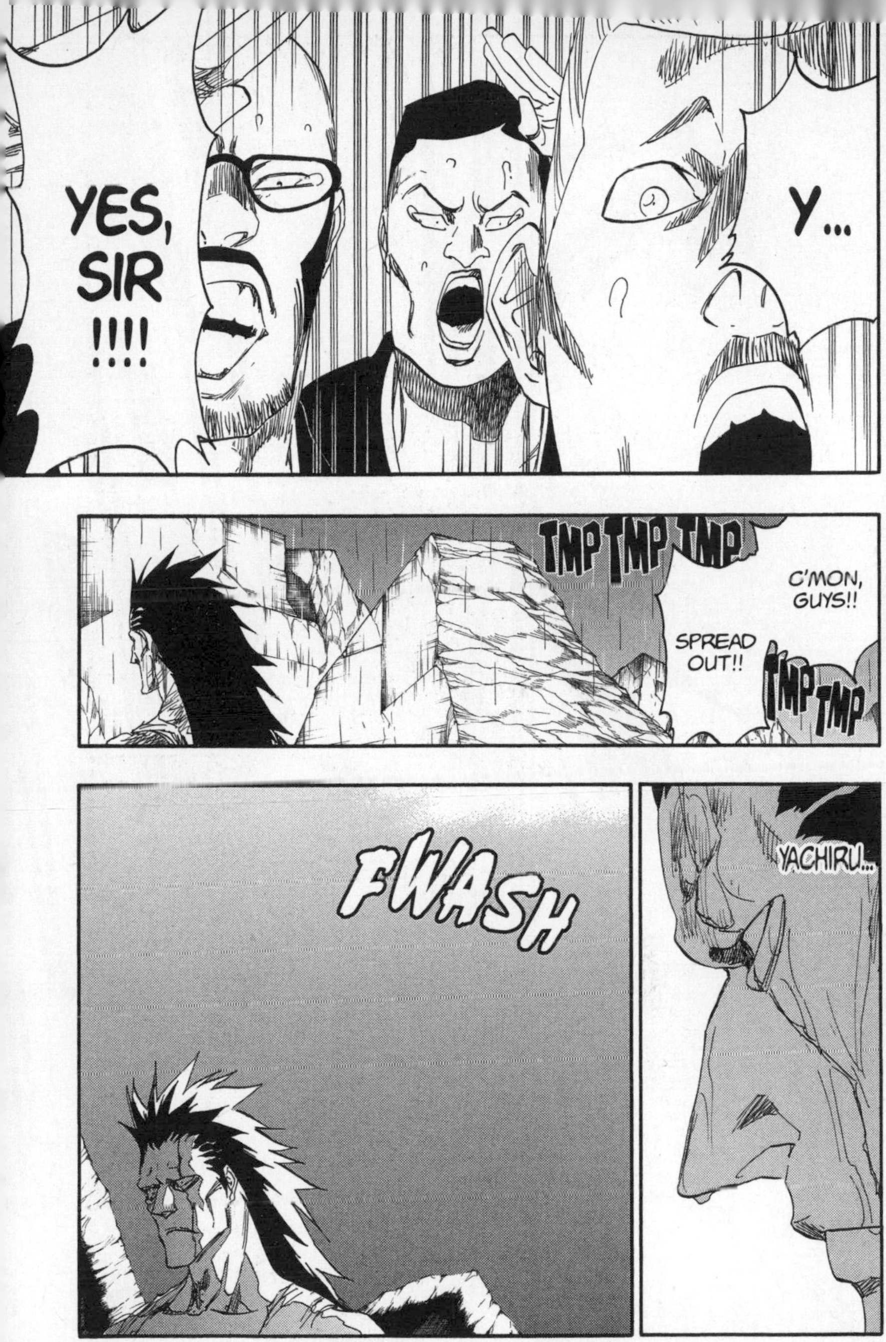
Y...
YES, SIR !!!!
C'MON, GUYS!!
TMP TMP TMP
SPREAD OUT!!
TMP TMP
YACHIRU...
FWASH

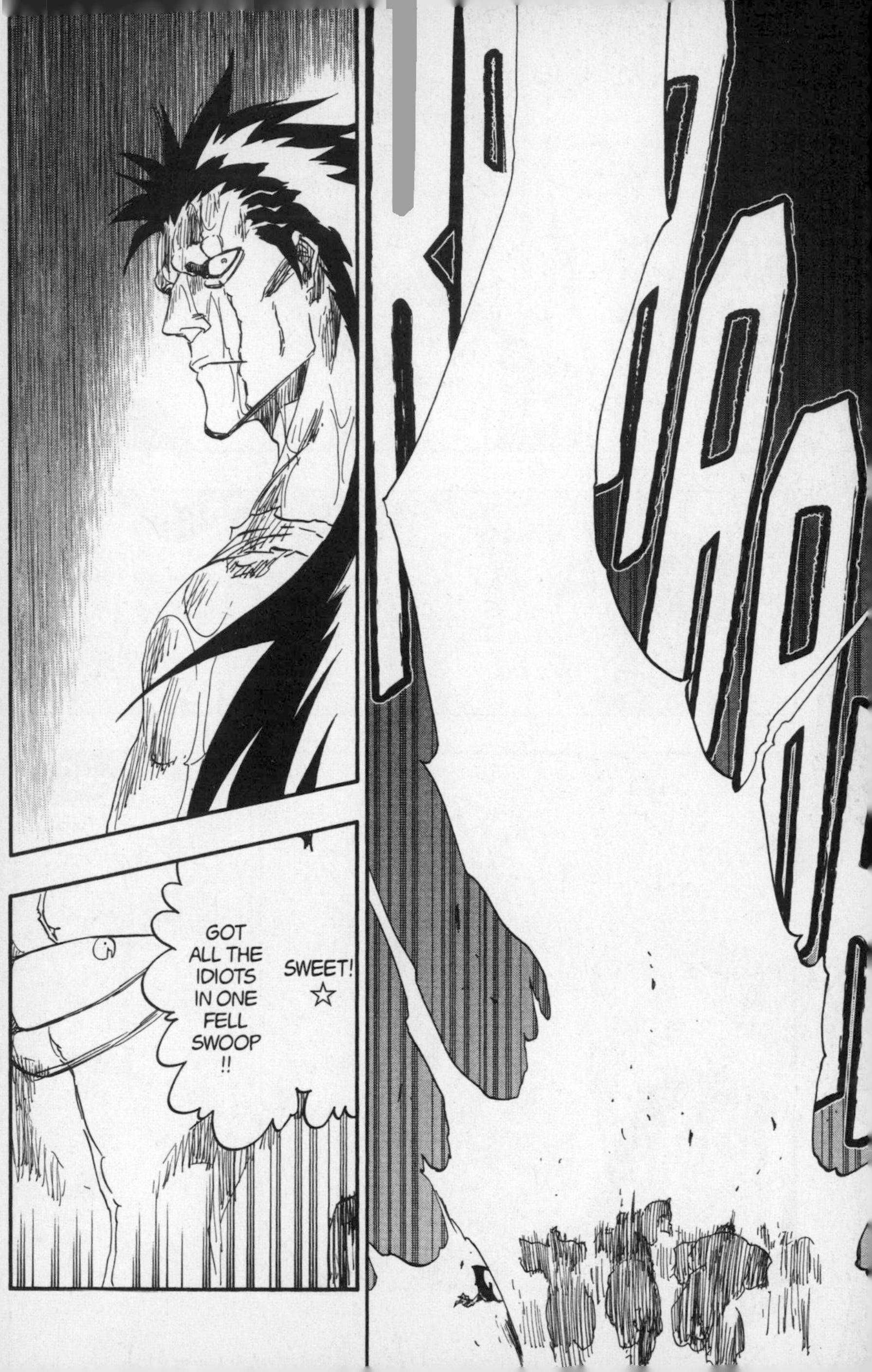
GOT ALL THE IDIOTS IN ONE FELL SWOOP !!
SWEET! ☆

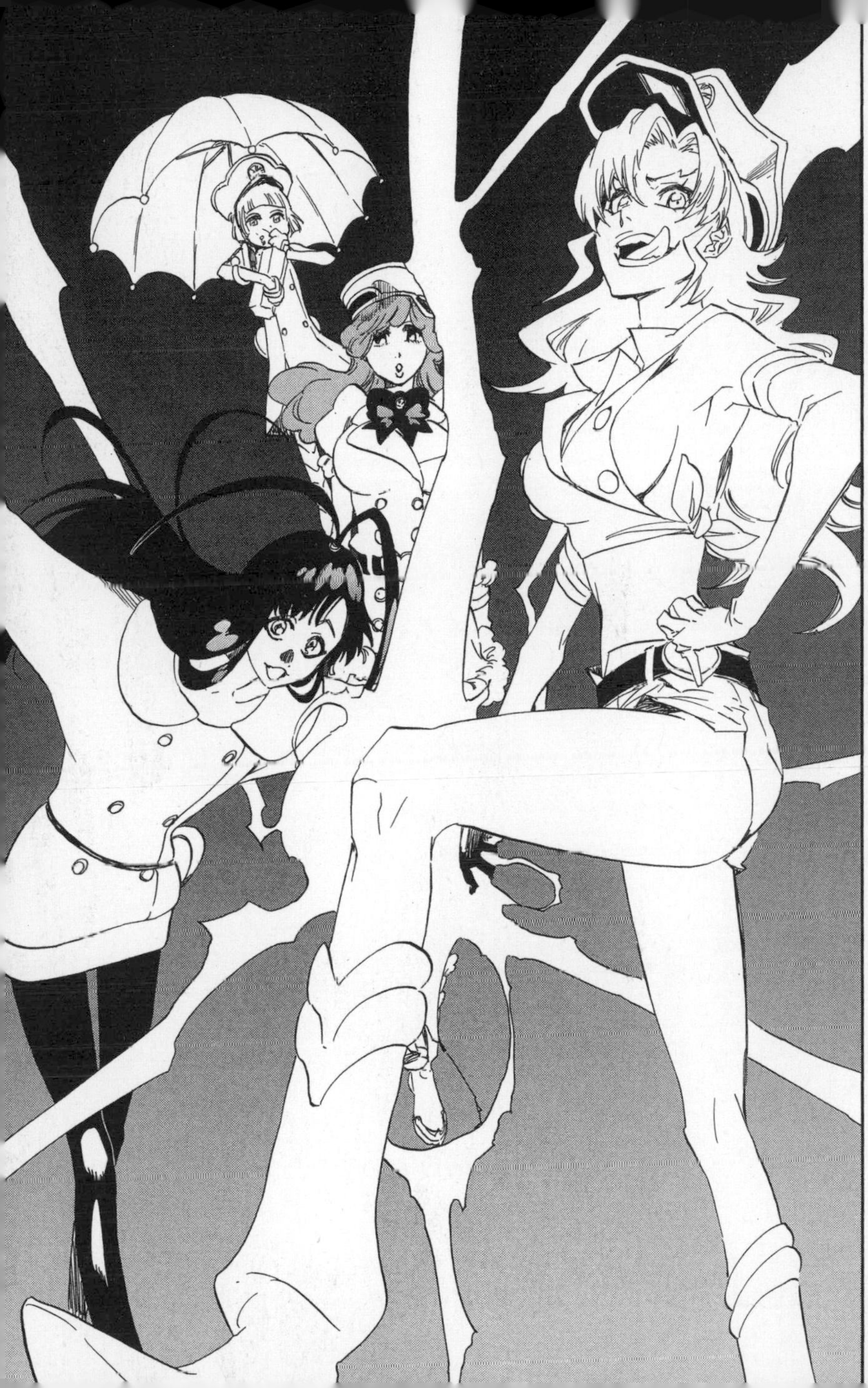

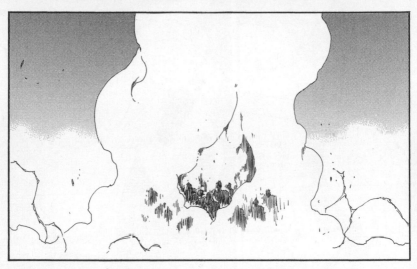

YASU!!

TETSU-ZO!!

DAMN IT!!

DZSH

DMP

C...

CAP...

...TAIN...

THE LIGHT

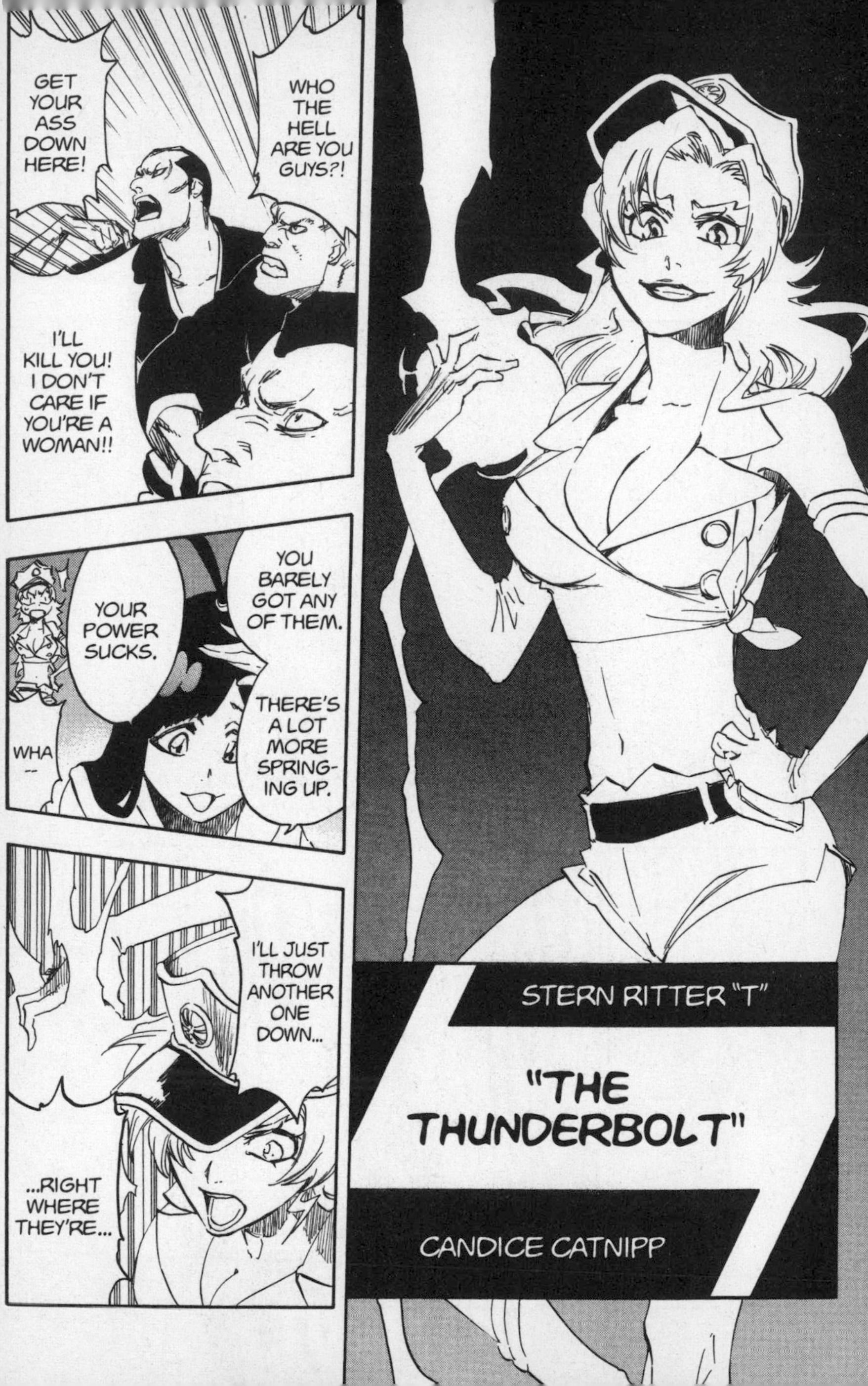
STERN RITTER "T"
"THE THUNDERBOLT"
CANDICE CATNIPP
WHO THE HELL ARE YOU GUYS?!
GET YOUR ASS DOWN HERE!
I'LL KILL YOU! I DON'T CARE IF YOU'RE A WOMAN!!
YOU BARELY GOT ANY OF THEM.
THERE'S A LOT MORE SPRING-ING UP.
YOUR POWER SUCKS.
WHA --
I'LL JUST THROW ANOTHER ONE DOWN...
...RIGHT WHERE THEY'RE...

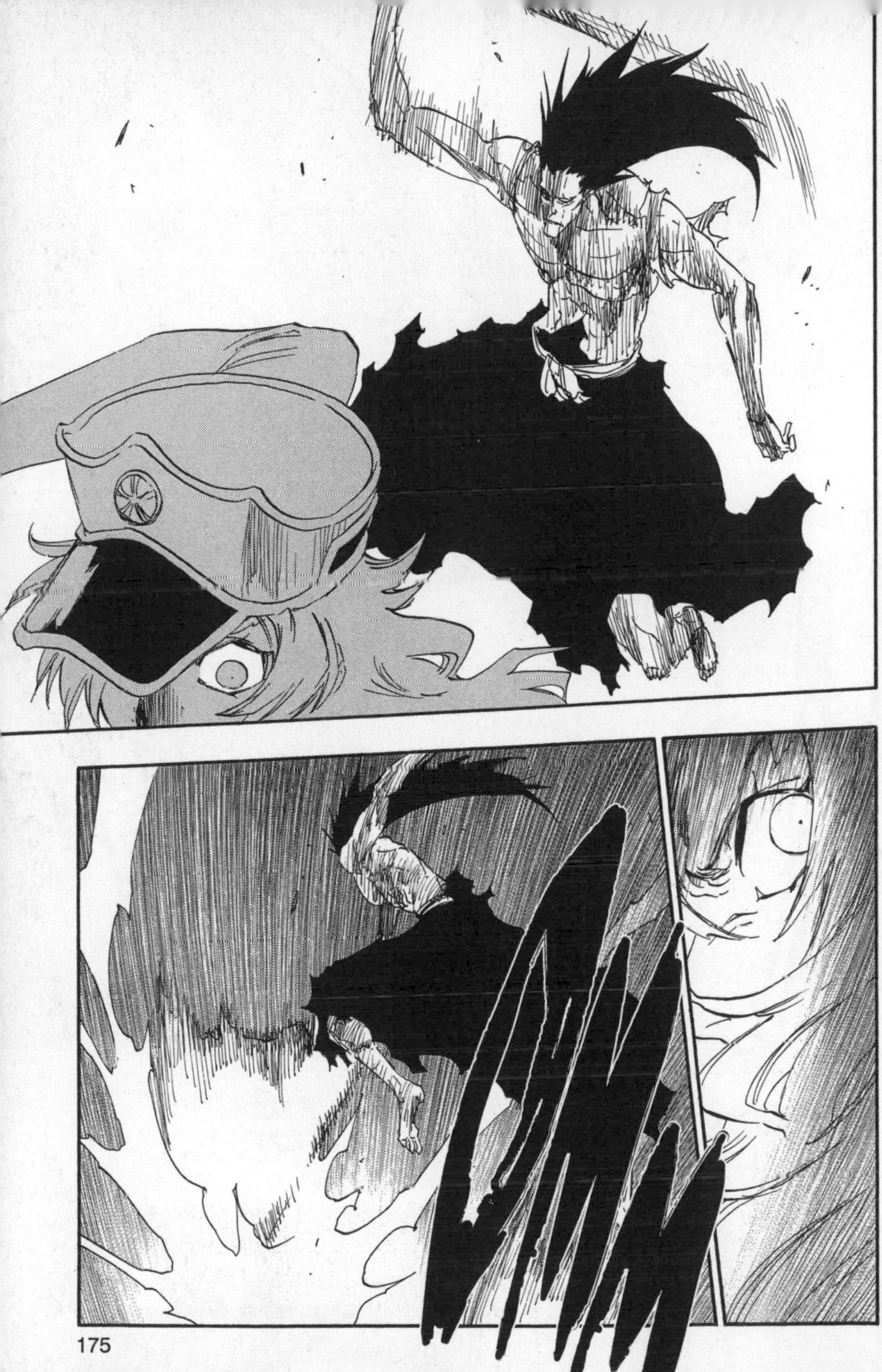

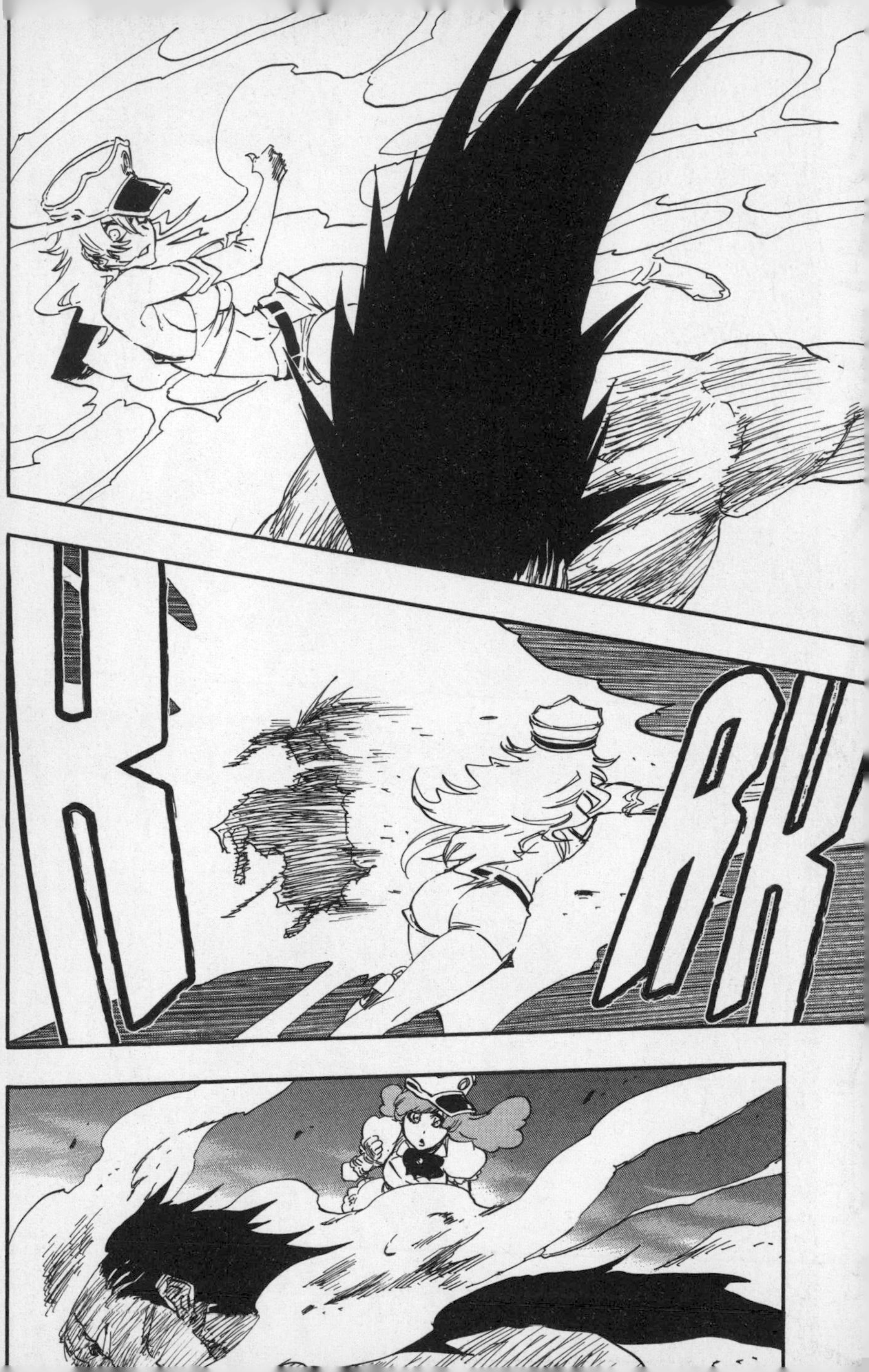
BRK

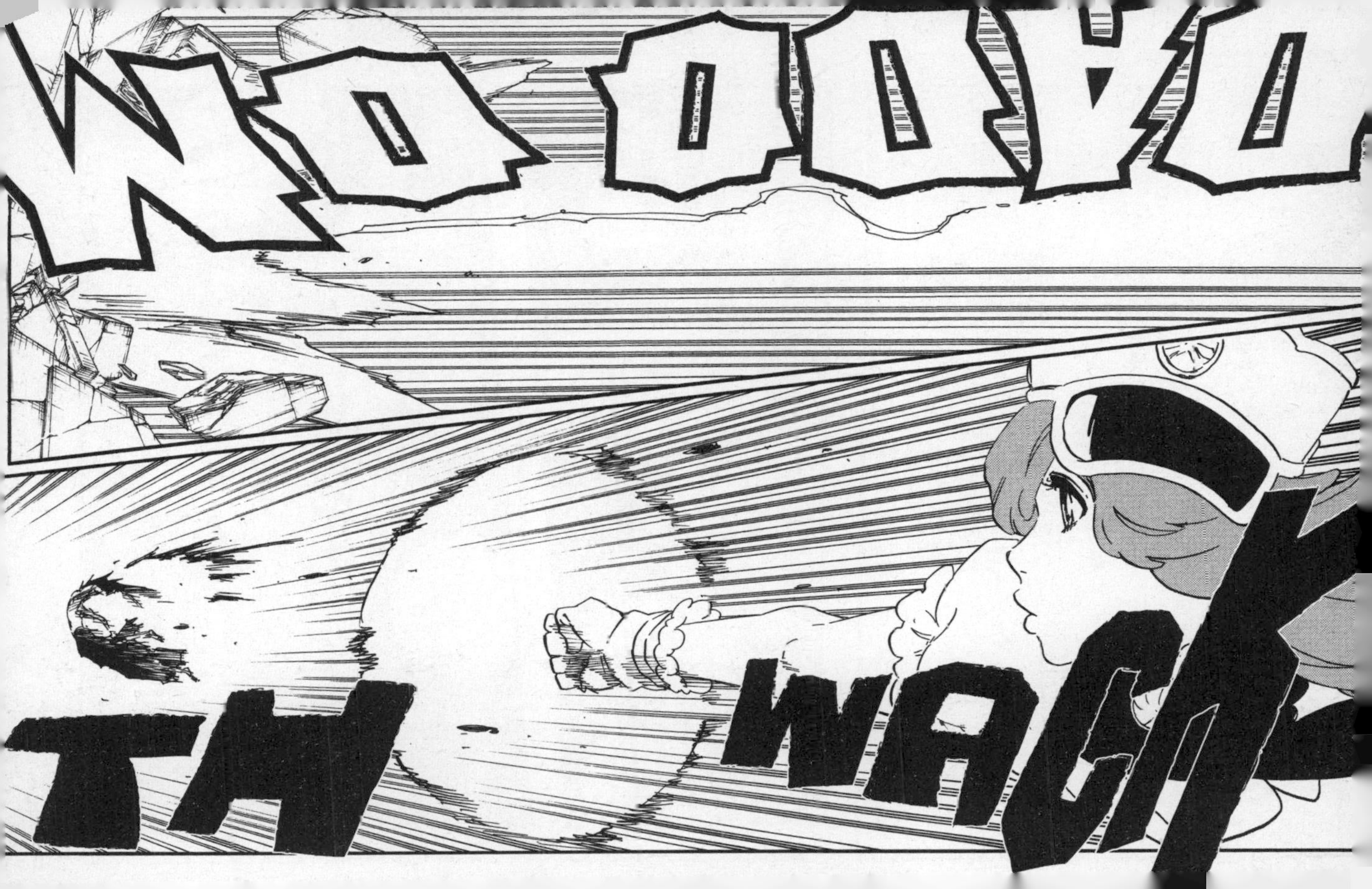
THWACK

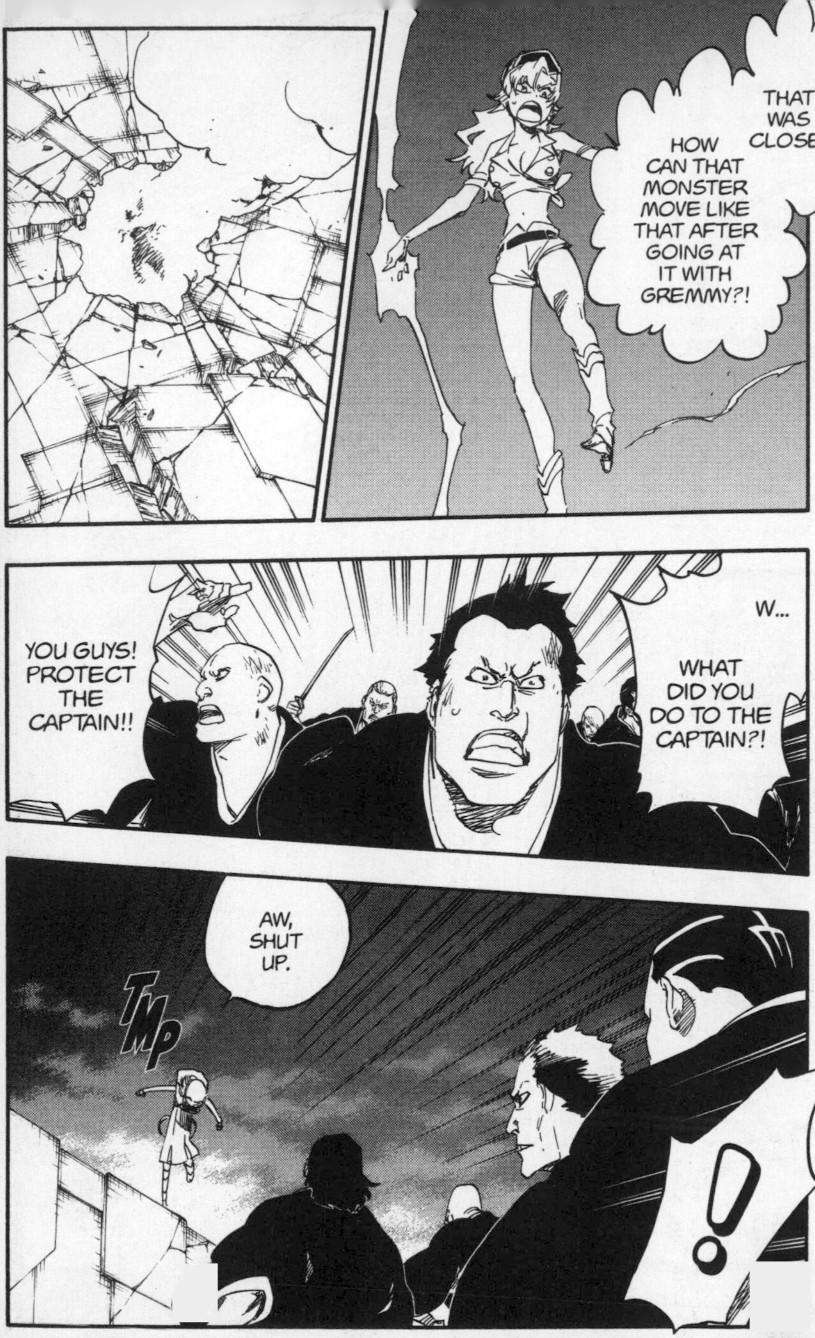
THAT WAS CLOSE!
HOW CAN THAT MONSTER MOVE LIKE THAT AFTER GOING AT IT WITH GREMMY?!
W...
WHAT DID YOU DO TO THE CAPTAIN?!
YOU GUYS! PROTECT THE CAPTAIN!!
AW, SHUT UP.
TMP
!

IT'S KENPACHI ZARAKI AFTER ALL.

IT'S WITHIN REASON.

THAT'S WHY WE DECIDED TO KILL HIM NOW WHILE HE'S BEAT UP.

OUT OF THE WAY, KID!!

GET IN OUR WAY AND WE'LL CRUSH YOU!!

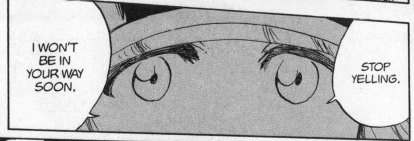

I WON'T BE IN YOUR WAY SOON.

STOP YELLING.

GRNCH

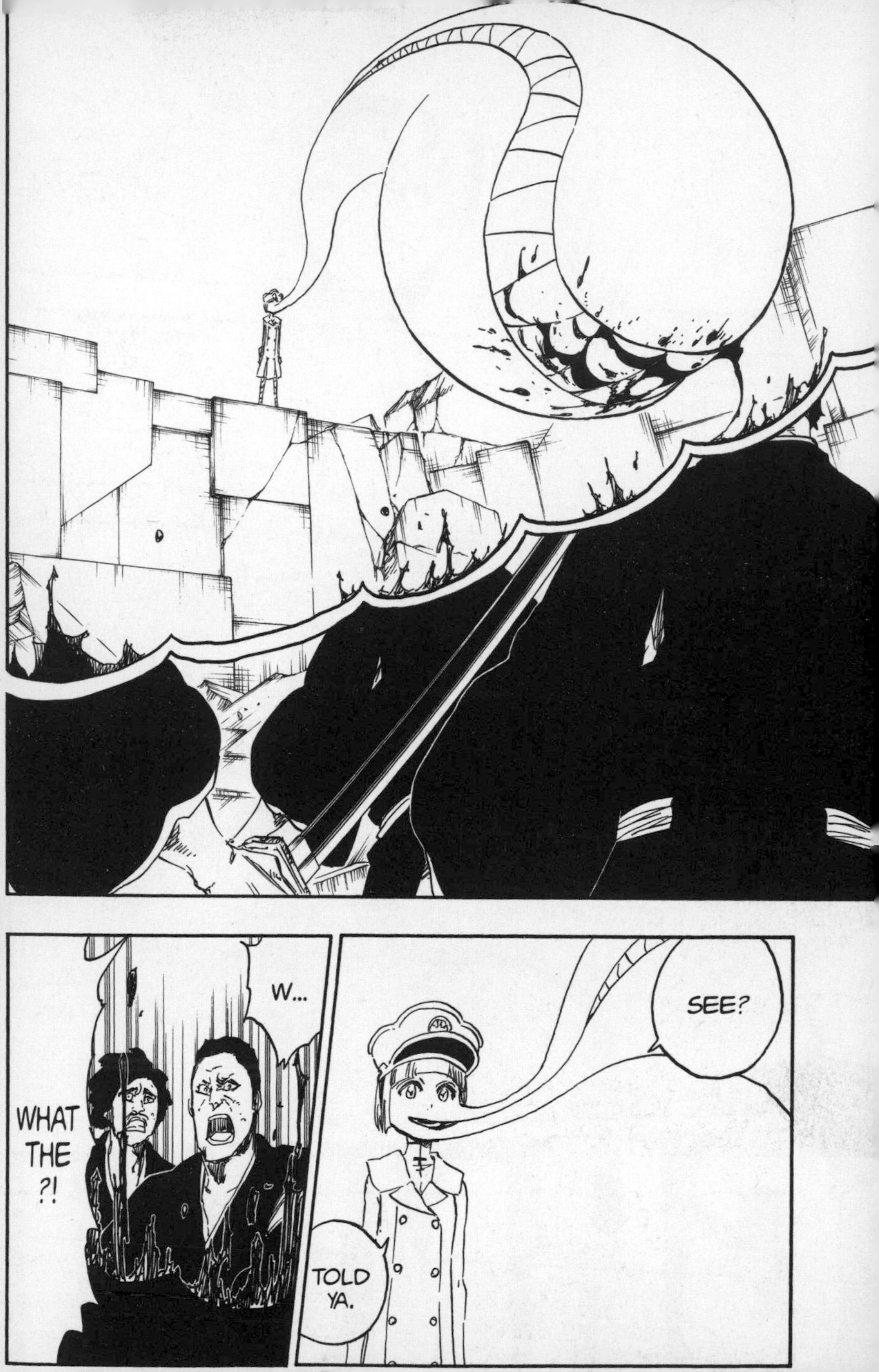
SEE?
TOLD YA.
W...
WHAT THE ?!

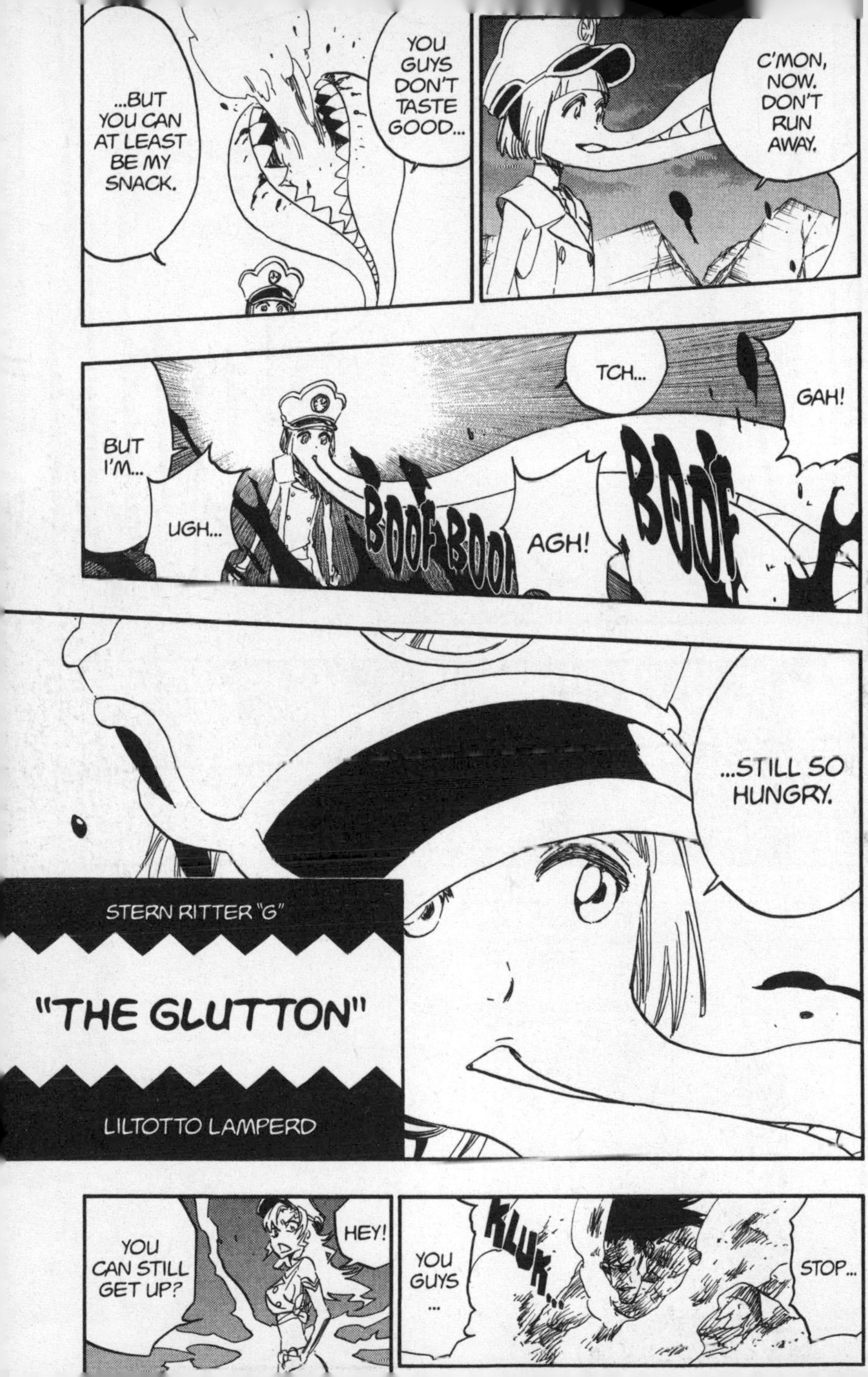
C'MON, NOW. DON'T RUN AWAY.
YOU GUYS DON'T TASTE GOOD...
...BUT YOU CAN AT LEAST BE MY SNACK.
GAH!
TCH...
BOOF
AGH!
BOOF BOOF
BUT I'M...
UGH...
...STILL SO HUNGRY.
STERN RITTER "G"
"THE GLUTTON"
LILTOTTO LAMPERD
STOP...
KLUK...
YOU GUYS
...
HEY!
YOU CAN STILL GET UP?

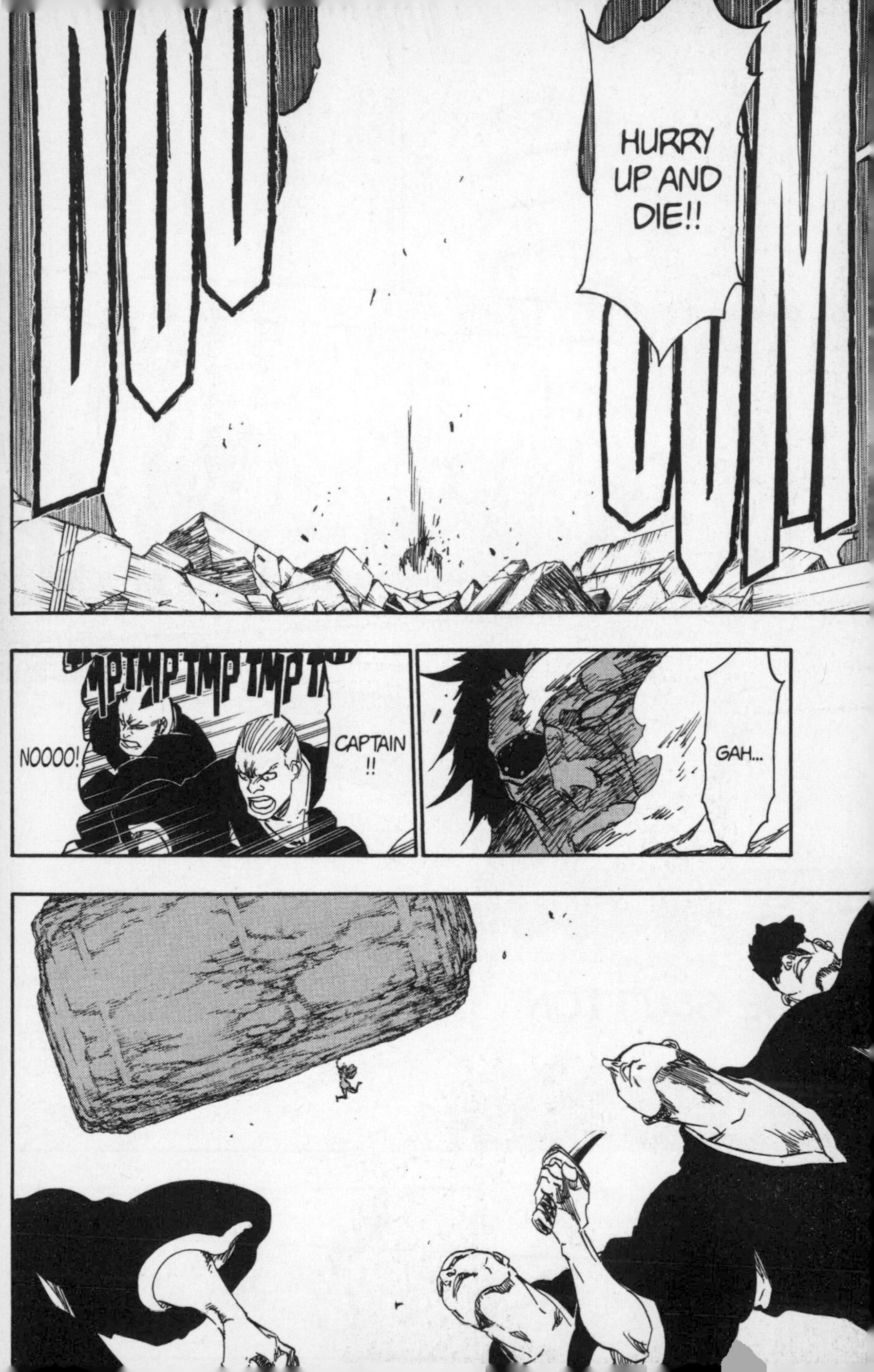
HURRY UP AND DIE!!
GAH...
TMP TMP TMP
CAPTAIN !!
NOOOO!

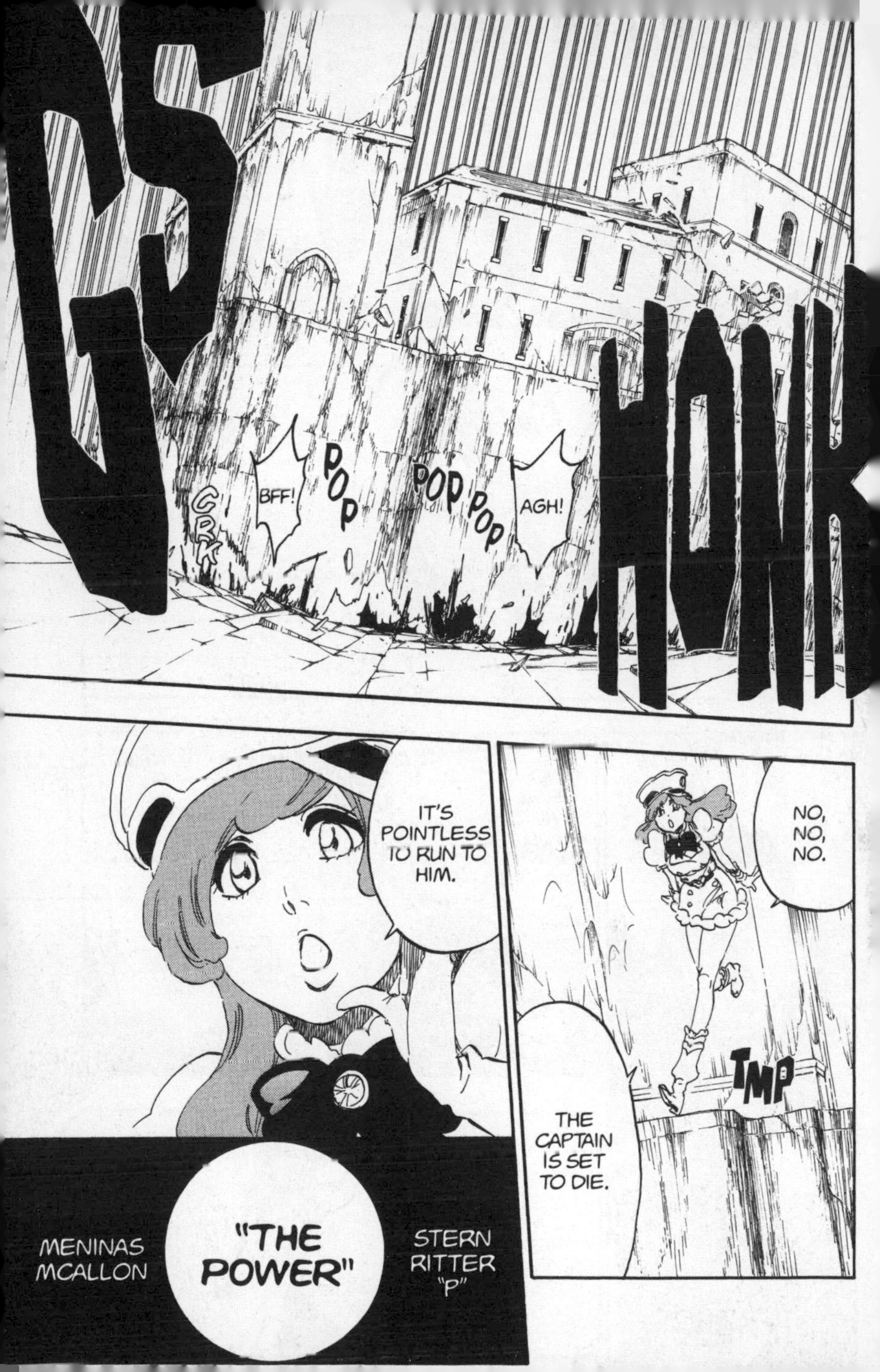
HONK
AGH!
POP POP
POP
BFF!
CRK
NO, NO, NO.
THE CAPTAIN IS SET TO DIE.
TMP
IT'S POINTLESS TO RUN TO HIM.
MENINAS MCALLON
"THE POWER"
STERN RITTER "P"

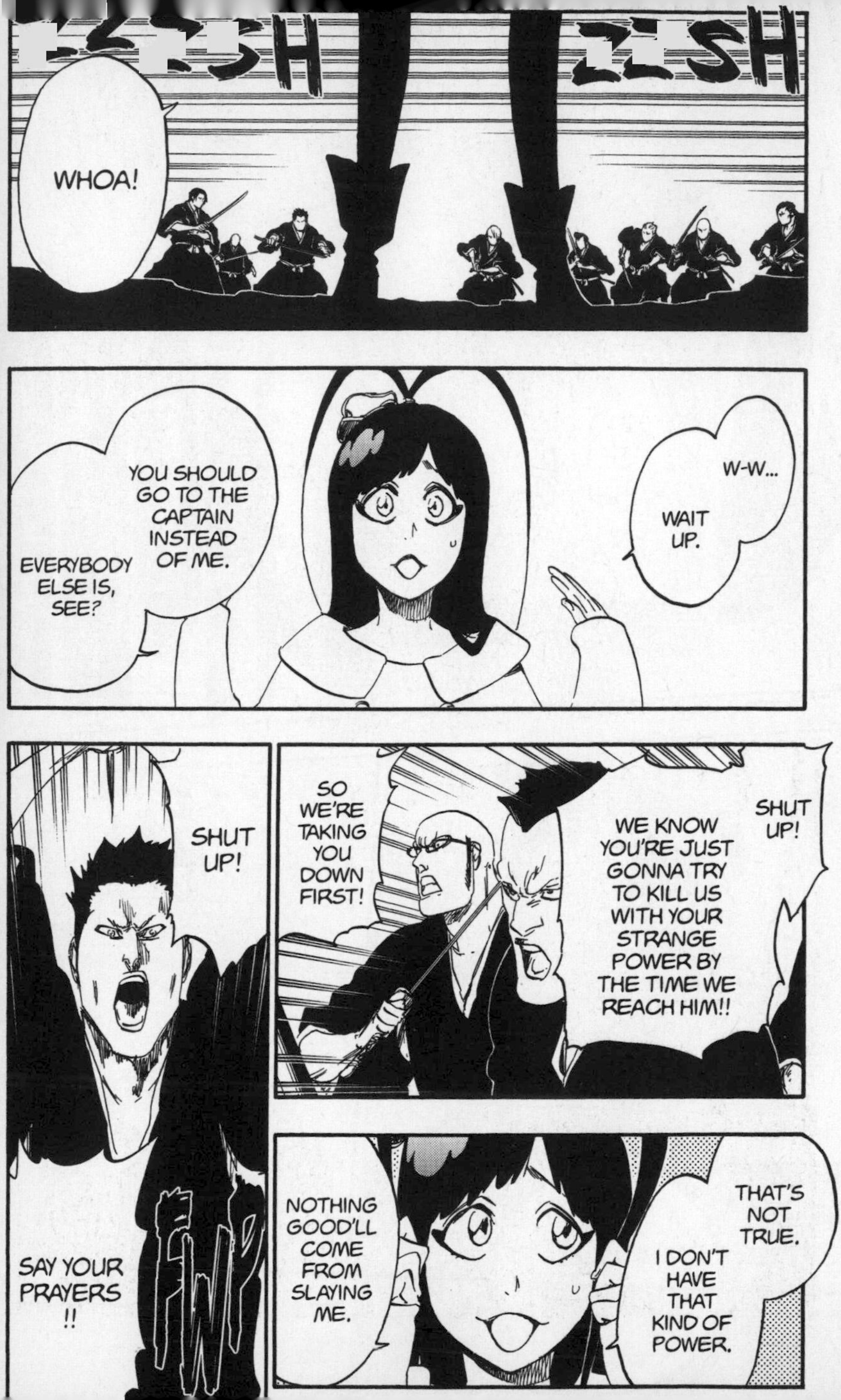
WHOA!
W-W...
WAIT UP.
YOU SHOULD GO TO THE CAPTAIN INSTEAD OF ME.
EVERYBODY ELSE IS, SEE?
SHUT UP!
WE KNOW YOU'RE JUST GONNA TRY TO KILL US WITH YOUR STRANGE POWER BY THE TIME WE REACH HIM!!
SO WE'RE TAKING YOU DOWN FIRST!
THAT'S NOT TRUE.
I DON'T HAVE THAT KIND OF POWER.
NOTHING GOOD'LL COME FROM SLAYING ME.
SHUT UP!
SAY YOUR PRAYERS !!

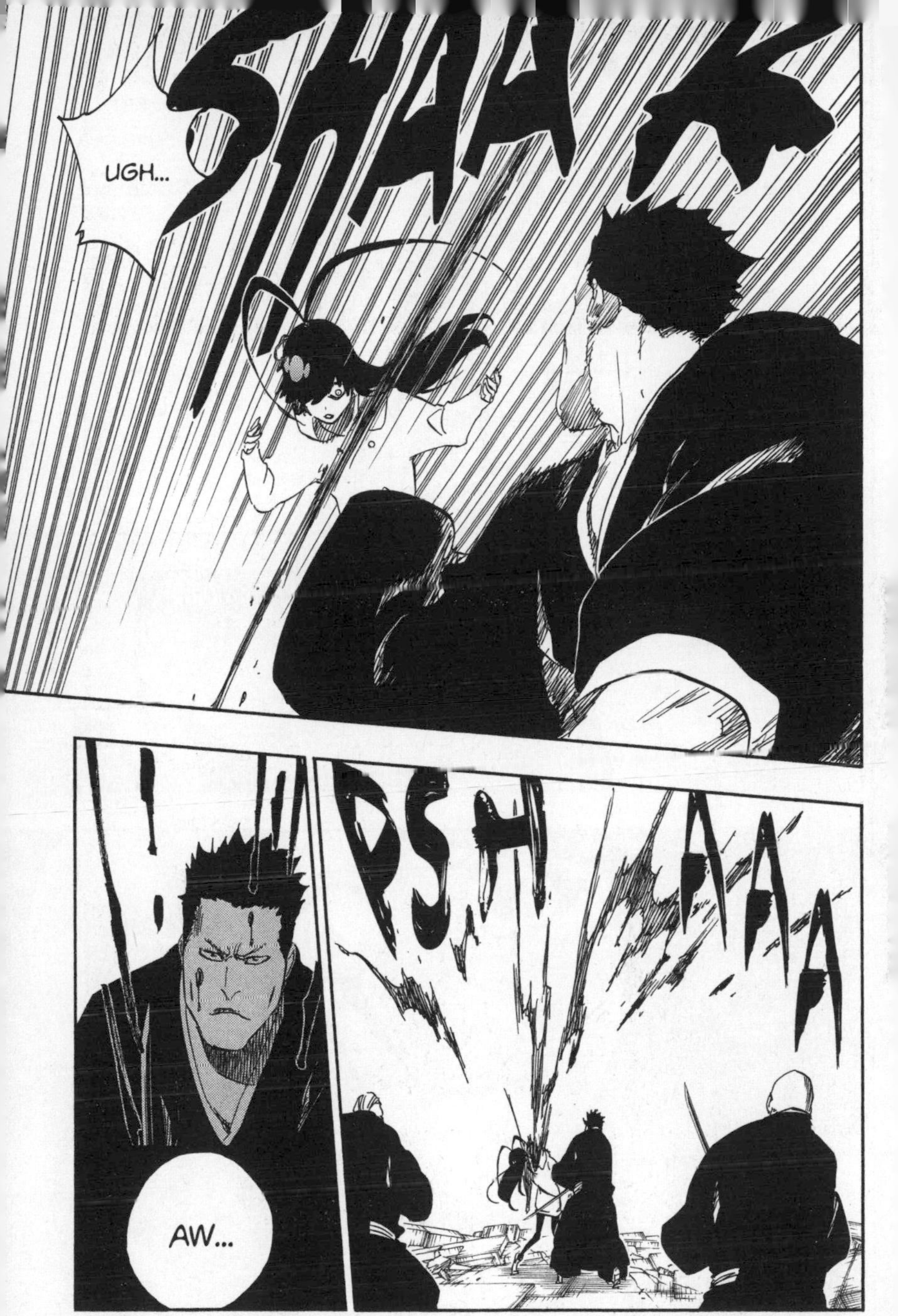
SHAAK
UGH...
DSHAAA
AW...

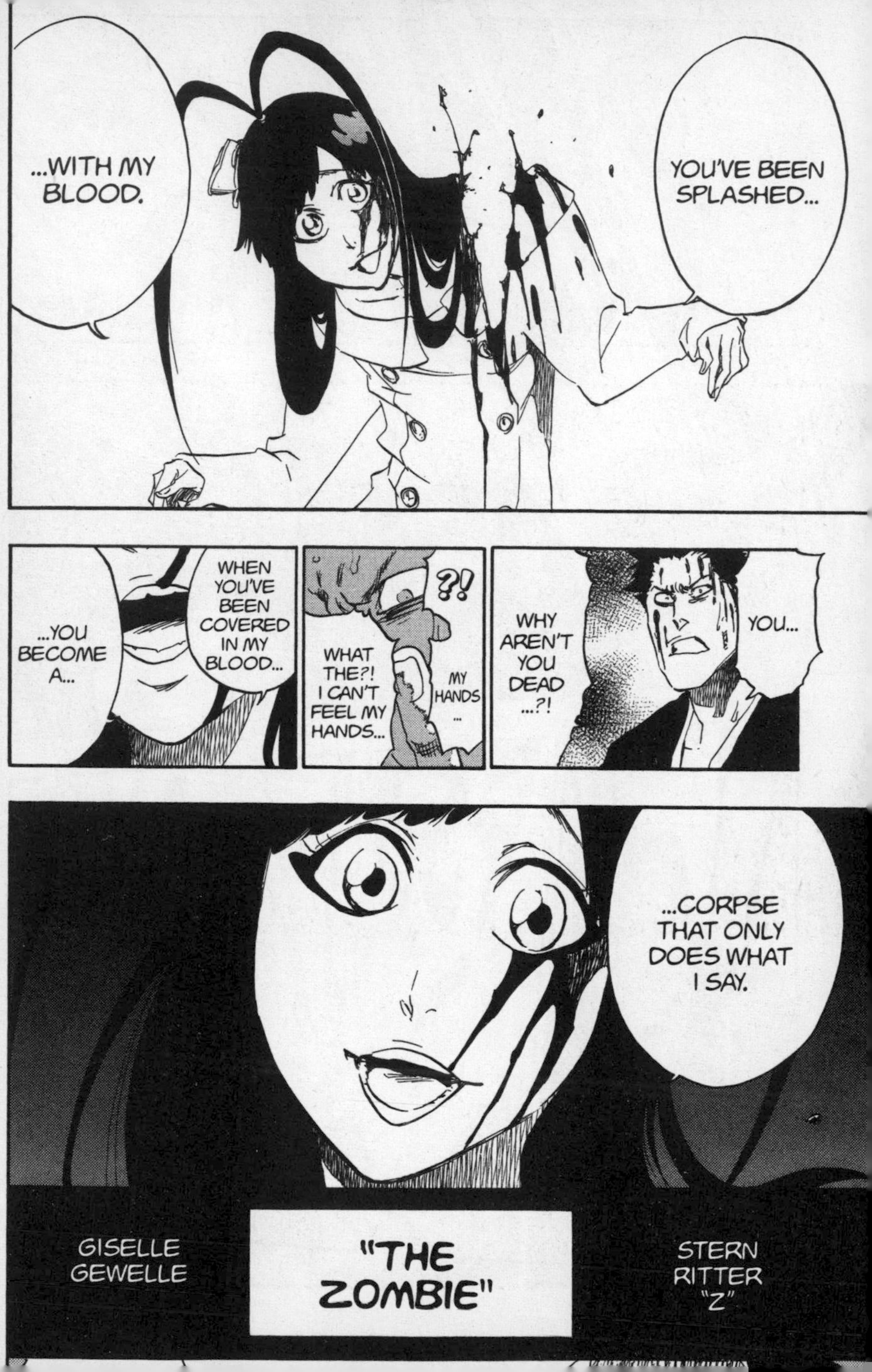
YOU'VE BEEN SPLASHED...
...WITH MY BLOOD.
YOU...
WHY AREN'T YOU DEAD ...?!
?!
MY HANDS ...
WHAT THE?! I CAN'T FEEL MY HANDS...
WHEN YOU'VE BEEN COVERED IN MY BLOOD...
...YOU BECOME A...
...CORPSE THAT ONLY DOES WHAT I SAY.
STERN RITTER "Z"
"THE ZOMBIE"
GISELLE GEWELLE

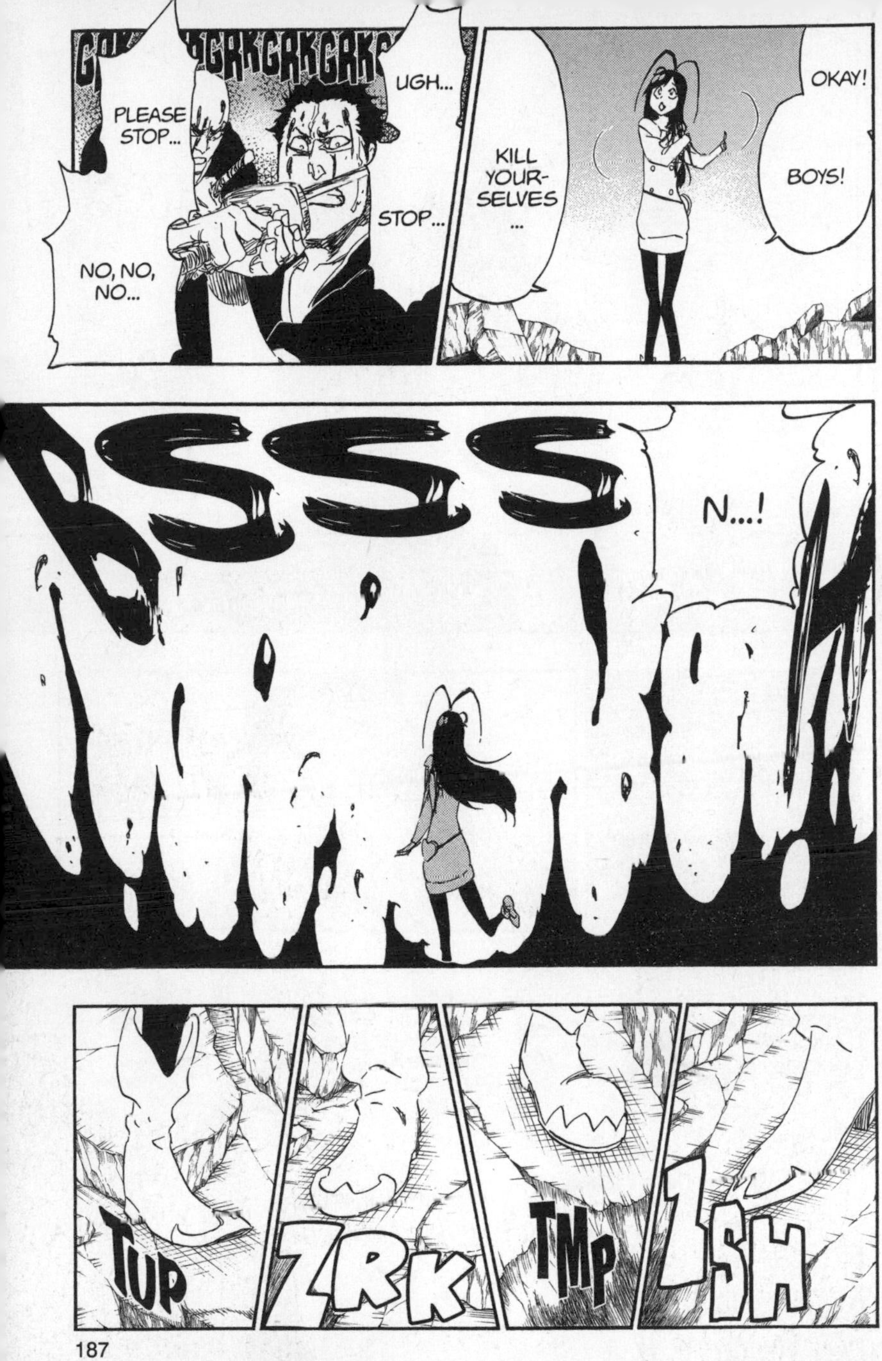
OKAY!
BOYS!
KILL YOUR-SELVES ...
UGH...
STOP...
PLEASE STOP...
NO, NO, NO...
N...!
TMP
ZRK
TUP

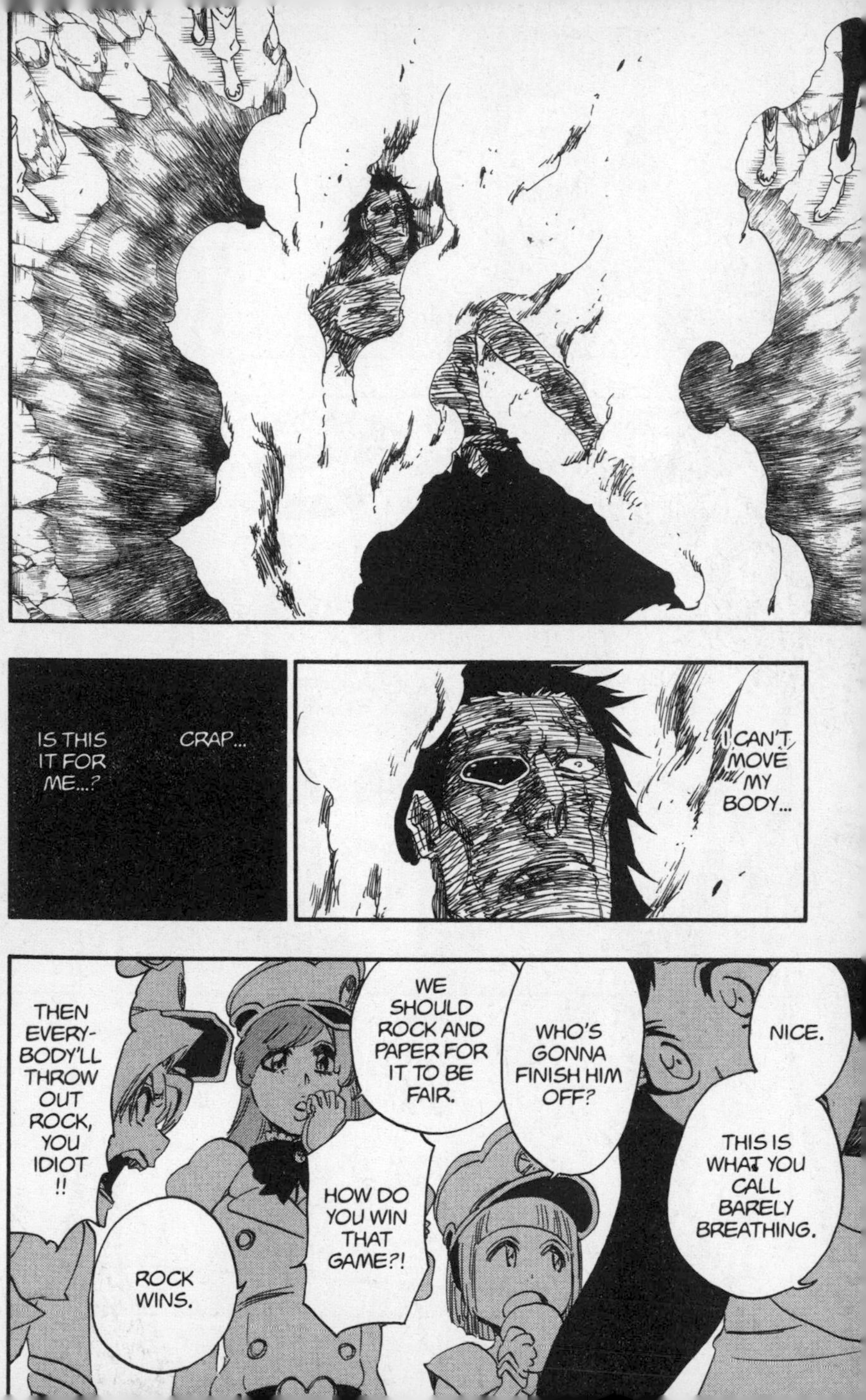
I CAN'T MOVE MY BODY...
CRAP...
IS THIS IT FOR ME...?
NICE.
THIS IS WHAT YOU CALL BARELY BREATHING.
WHO'S GONNA FINISH HIM OFF?
WE SHOULD ROCK AND PAPER FOR IT TO BE FAIR.
HOW DO YOU WIN THAT GAME?!
ROCK WINS.
THEN EVERYBODY'LL THROW OUT ROCK, YOU IDIOT!!

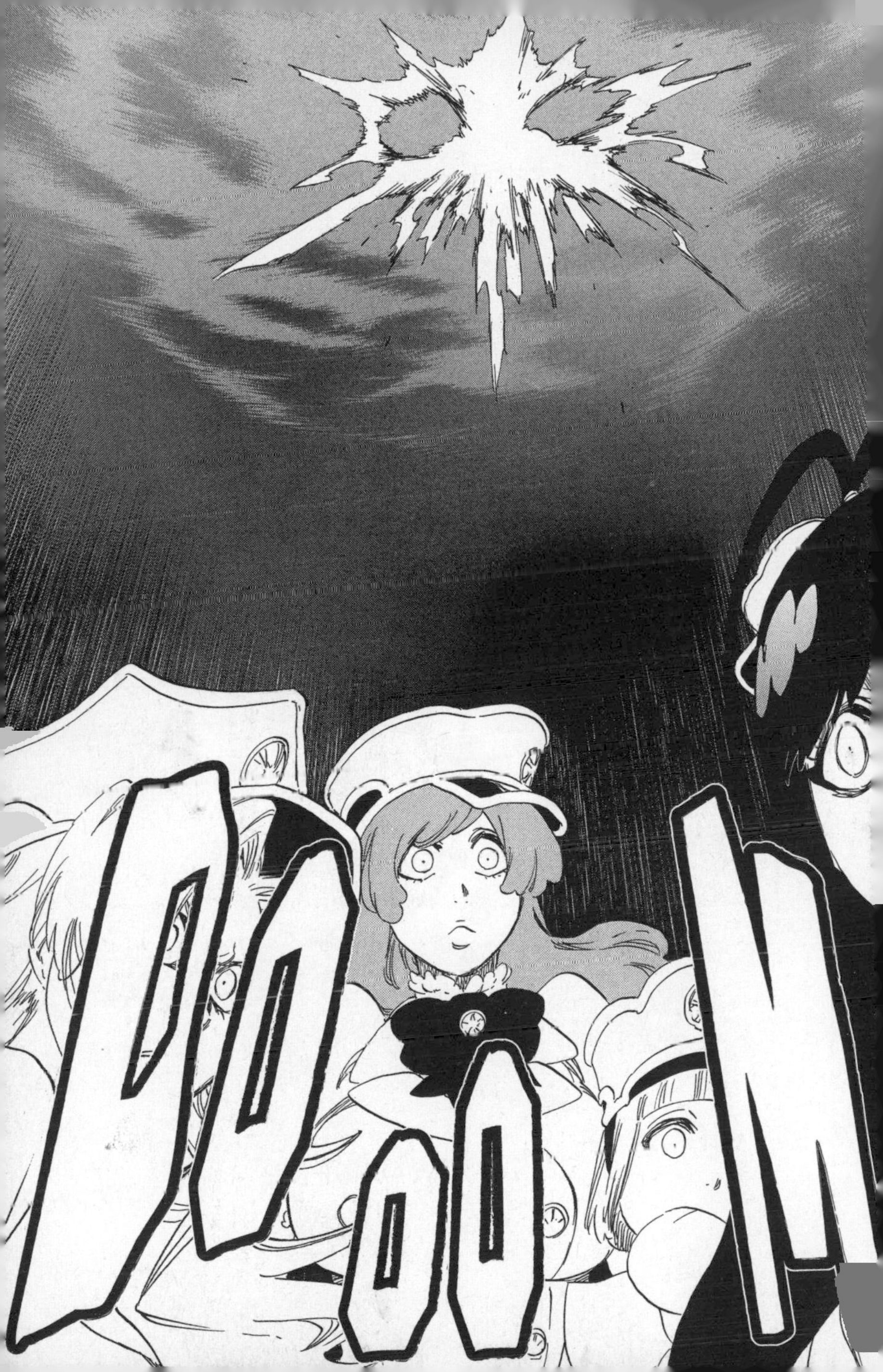
DOOOM

CONTINUED IN BLEACH 65

RELISH MASASHI KISHIMOTO'S ARTWORK IN ALL ITS COLORFUL GLORY

The Art of NARUTO

Complete your *NARUTO* collection with the hardcover art book, *The Art of NARUTO: Uzumaki*, featuring:

- Over 100 pages of full-color *NARUTO* manga images
- Step-by-step details on creating a *NARUTO* illustration
- Notes about each image
- An extensive interview with creator Masashi Kishimoto

Plus, a beautiful double-sided poster!

ART OF *SHONEN JUMP*

SHONEN JUMP
www.shonenjump.com

Available at your local bookstore or comic store

 RATED T FOR TEEN
ratings.viz.com

 VIZ media
www.viz.com

UZUMAKI -NARUTO ILLUSTRATION BOOK- © 2004 by Masashi Kishimoto/SHUEISHA Inc.

You're Reading in the Wrong Direction!!

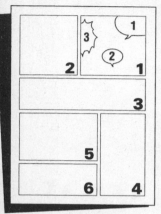

Whoops! Guess what? You're starting at the wrong end of the comic!

…It's true! In keeping with the original Japanese format, **Bleach** is meant to be read from right to left, starting in the upper-right corner.

Unlike English, which is read from left to right, Japanese is read from right to left, meaning that action, sound effects and word-balloon order are completely reversed… something which can make readers unfamiliar with Japanese feel pretty backwards themselves. For this reason, manga or Japanese comics published in the U.S. in English have sometimes been published "flopped"—that is, printed in exact reverse order, as though seen from the other side of a mirror.

By flopping pages, U.S. publishers can avoid confusing readers, but the compromise is not without its downside. For one thing, a character in a flopped manga series who once wore in the original Japanese version a T-shirt emblazoned with "M A Y" (as in "the merry month of") now wears one which reads "Y A M"! Additionally, many manga creators in Japan are themselves unhappy with the process, as some feel the mirror-imaging of their art skews their original intentions.

We are proud to bring you Tite Kubo's **Bleach** in the original unflopped format. For now, though, turn to the other side of the book and let the adventure begin…!

—Editor

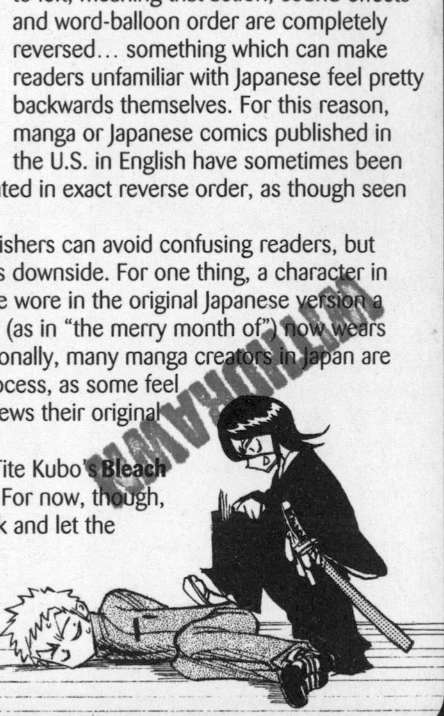